English Romantic Writers and the West Country

English Romantic Writers and the West Country

Edited by

Nicholas Roe

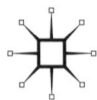

First published 2010 by
PALGRAVE MACMILLAN

Palgrave Macmillan in the UK is an imprint of Macmillan Publishers Limited, registered in England, company number 785998, of Houndmills, Basingstoke, Hampshire RG21 6XS.

Palgrave Macmillan in the US is a division of St Martin's Press LLC, 175 Fifth Avenue, New York, NY 10010.

Palgrave Macmillan is the global academic imprint of the above companies and has companies and representatives throughout the world.

Palgrave® and Macmillan® are registered trademarks in the United States, the United Kingdom, Europe and other countries.

ISBN 978–0–230–22374–5   hardback

This book is printed on paper suitable for recycling and made from fully managed and sustained forest sources. Logging, pulping and manufacturing processes are expected to conform to the environmental regulations of the country of origin.

A catalogue record for this book is available from the British Library.

Library of Congress Cataloging-in-Publication Data

English romantic writers and the West Country / edited by Nicholas Roe.
    p. cm.
    Summary: 'Long confounded with a monolithic British entity or misrepresented as Lakers and Cockneys, the diverse regional forms of English Romanticism are ripe for reassessment. Ranging west of a line between the Wye at Tintern and Jane Austen's Chawton, this book offers a first reconfiguration of Romantic culture in terms of English regional identity' – Provided by publisher.
    ISBN 978–0–230–22374–5   (hardback)
    1. English literature—19th century—History and criticism. 2. English literature—18th century—History and criticism. 3. Romanticism—England. 4. West Country (England)—In literature. I. Roe, Nicholas.
    PR457.E55 2010
    820.9'358423—dc22   2010002711

10 9 8 7 6 5 4 3 2 1
19 18 17 16 15 14 13 12 11 10

Printed and bound in Great Britain by
CPI Antony Rowe, Chippenham and Eastbourne

In memory of Jonathan Wordsworth
1932–2006

Contents

List of Illustrations

Foreword

Richard Holmes

It may surprise some readers to learn that Jonathan Wordsworth, despite his family name and ancestry (he was the direct descendant of William Wordsworth's younger brother Christopher), was a West Country man at heart. He was born and grew up in Dorset, where his father was a master at Bryanston, and always retained deep-rooted Wessex sympathies. Though he became most widely known as the Chairman of the Wordsworth Trust, Grasmere, Cumberland, he was always a passionate supporter of the Friends of Coleridge at Nether Stowey, Somerset. So the West Country theme of the present volume of essays is a shrewd and appropriate celebration. It is also a thought-provoking one, as you will see.

As a distinguished Romantic scholar and teacher at Oxford, Jonathan Wordsworth will always be remembered by students for his wonderful studies of his poet ancestor, *The Music of Humanity* (1969) and *Wordsworth: the Borders of Vision* (1982). But like many others, I feel especially indebted to him for his editorial work, such as his recovery of the manuscript readings of Wordsworth's early Dorset poem, *The Ruined Cottage* (1797–8) and the beautiful *Two-Part Prelude* (1799).

Above all I admired him for his superb *Woodstock Facsimile Series*, a library of some 180 early (often forgotten or neglected) Romantic texts, both poetry and prose, which he individually selected and edited with a series of crisp, succinct, highly original introductions. I think I have finally collected all of them. These were a vital part of what has been well described as his master-project of performing 'deep editorial archaeology' on Romanticism. For this reason, I am sure he would have been particularly delighted, as well as amused, by the intricate scholarship, vivid local colour, and splendid regional eccentricities displayed in so many of the contributions collected here.

The lively 'New Regionalism' in contemporary Romantic studies is in many ways the unifying dynamic behind these essays. This can be described essentially, if simplistically, as a back-to-the-roots movement. Partly inspired by the recently founded Centre for Regional Cultures at Nottingham University, it has refreshed and renewed the (now ageing) 'historicist' approach to Romantic criticism, as admirably explained in Nicholas Roe's Introduction.

As a result, it makes what is in effect a revolutionary claim: that the true roots of English Romanticism lay not so much in the Lake District and the Laker Poets of Cumberland, as is so often assumed, but in the early 'Bristol School' of the English West Country. Its four founding figures – Thomas Chatterton, and the young triumvirate of Coleridge, Wordsworth, and

Robert Southey – each receive fascinating and unusual reassessments to make good this claim. It is an extremely convincing one.

Backing them up, are a series of minutely detailed investigations of their cultural milieu, with great emphasis laid on the powerful 'nonconforming' and dissenting elements in the West Country tradition, both political and religious. These stretch from tragic memories of Monmouth's rebellion at Bridgwater, to the great anti-slave trade movement at Bristol, and Joshua Toulmin's anti-war sermons from the pulpit at Taunton.

There is also an experimental, provisional, exploratory – almost footloose – character to many of these essays, which is especially attractive. This is why I have referred to their regional 'eccentricity': meaning that in the best, geographical sense of the term. They aim to de-centre and disestablish; to pioneer and to provoke. The results can be both intellectually demanding, and even disorientating. Yet the haunting theme of 'stepping westwards' (from Wordsworth's later poem) runs through them almost like a tune: a tune played on a flute perhaps, like the one that Coleridge once heard teasing the moonlight in the Romantic ruins of Denbigh Castle.

Though properly academic, they succeed – sometimes despite themselves – in dancing us down the highways and evocative byways of Dorset, Somerset, Devon, Cornwall, and South Wales. They introduce the splendidly named 'megalith poets'. They re-examine the 'picturesque' of Gilpin. They wander along the banks of numerous rivers: the Wye, the Usk, the Avon, the Severn, the Parret, the Teme, the Otter. They bring us repeatedly, but by different routes and in very different moods, to the great, glooming Romantic monuments or ruins of the western borderlands – Stonehenge, Avebury, St Mary Redcliffe, Raglan Castle, Tintern Abbey, Dartmoor Tor.

Many figures arrive quite unexpectedly: Shelley launching bottles of poetry off Lynmouth beach, Hazlitt breakfasting in Alfoxden Park, Keats disembarking for a last brief visit to Lulworth Cove, Robert Bloomfield posing bookishly at Hay-on-Wye, and even Edward Thomas chasing springtime on a bicycle along the Mendip Hills. Perhaps most intriguing figure who emerges (through several notable essays) is the Dissenting bookseller Joseph Cottle, the original publisher of the *Lyrical Ballads*, the self-styled West Country Maecenas and poetry impresario, who spoke prophetically of 'the Augustan Age of Bristol', but wrote a crazily Romantic epic about King Alfred in twenty-four interminable books.

All these delights and provocations await you. Step westwards.

Acknowledgements

The idea for this book grew from conversations and papers at the Coleridge Summer Conference in 2002 and 2004. I thank the contributors for supporting this collection and Paula Kennedy and Steven Hall at Palgrave. The index was compiled by Dr Jim Stewart at the School of Humanities, University of Dundee.

About the Contributors

Paul Cheshire is author of a number of articles on Coleridge and his contemporaries. He has also written on the influence of seventeenth-century hermetic philosophy on Milton, and is currently engaged in researching the life and thought of William Gilbert within the context of the hermetic tradition. In addition to printed output he is editor of two websites: www.friendsofcoleridge.com and www.williamgilbert.com, and is a trustee of the Friends of Coleridge. He lives and works in Bath, England.

Richard Cronin is Professor of English Literature at the University of Glasgow. His last book was *Romantic Victorians: English Literature, 1824–1840*. His next will be *Paper Pellets: British Literary Culture after Waterloo*, forthcoming from Oxford University Press.

Graham Davidson is the editor of *The Coleridge Bulletin* and secretary to The Coleridge Summer Conference. In 1990 he published *Coleridge's Career*, and since then various papers, mostly on Coleridge. He is currently investigating Coleridge's early years, and this research has provided useful material for understanding Coleridge's troubled response to the West Country.

Tim Fulford is a Professor at Nottingham Trent University. The author of many monographs and articles on Romanticism, he is also the co-editor (with Lynda Pratt) of *The Collected Letters of Robert Bloomfield and his Circle* (online edition: *Romantic Circles*, 2009), and of *Robert Southey's Later Poems 1811–38* and *Collected Letters*.

Nick Groom is Chair in English at the University of Exeter (Cornwall Campus) and Director of ECLIPSE (Exeter Centre for Literatures of Identity, Place, and Sustainability). He has published widely on Romantic poetry and among his books are *The Making of Percy's Reliques* (1999), *Thomas Chatterton and Romantic Culture* (ed., 1999), and an edition of Chatterton's poems (2003). He is currently working on representations of the British environment and writing an introduction to the Gothic.

Anthony John Harding is Professor Emeritus, University of Saskatchewan. He works on nineteenth-century life-writing, literature of abolitionism, and ethics of reading. With the late Kathleen Coburn, he co-edited vol. 5 of the Bollingen edition of *The Notebooks of Samuel Taylor Coleridge* (2002). His other recent publications include 'Gendering the Poet-Philosopher: Victorian "Manliness" and Coleridgean "Androgyny"', in *Coleridge's Afterlives*, ed. James Vigus and Jane E. Wright (2008); 'An Ethics of Reading: a Conflicted

Romantic Heritage', *Keats-Shelley Journal* (2008); and *Coleridge's Responses*, volume 2: *Coleridge on the Bible* (2007).

Richard Holmes is the most distinguished Romantic biographer of our times. His *Shelley: the Pursuit* (1974) won the Somerset Maugham Award and was described by Stephen Spender as 'surely the best biography of Shelley ever written'. *Footsteps: Adventures of a Romantic Biographer* (1985) was hailed as 'a modern masterpiece'. *Coleridge: Early Visions* (1989) won the Whitbread Book of the Year Prize and was followed by *Coleridge: Darker Reflections* (1998) which covers the later part of Coleridge's life. *Sidetracks: Explorations of a Romantic Biographer* (2000) is a collection assembled from decades of 'wandering from the straight and narrow' of his major biographies and held together by a subtle autobiographical thread. His most recent book, *The Age of Wonder*, was published in 2008 to excellent reviews. Richard Holmes is a Fellow of the Royal Society of Literature and the British Academy and was awarded the OBE in 1992.

Peter J. Kitson is Professor of English at the University of Dundee. He is the author of *Romantic Literature, Race and Colonial Encounter* (2007) and (with T. Fulford and D. Lee) *Literature, Science and Explorations: Bodies of Knowledge* (2004); he is also the editor (with T. Fulford) of *Travels, Explorations and Empires* (8 vols, 2001–2) and (with D. Lee) of *Slavery Abolition and Emancipation* (8 vols, 1999). Kitson is President of the English Association (2007–10) and President of the British Association for Romantic Studies (2007–10).

Tom Mayberry is the County Heritage Officer for Somerset and Chairman of the Friends of Coleridge charitable trust. He is the author of *Coleridge and Wordsworth in the West Country* (1992) and *The Vale of Taunton Past* (1998), and he co-edited *The Archaeology of Somerset* (2007).

Michael O'Neill is Professor of English at Durham University. His most recent books include *The All-Sustaining Air: Romantic Legacies and Renewals in British, American, and Irish Poetry since 1900* (2007) and *Wheel* (2008), a collection of poems.

Joanne Parker is Lecturer in Victorian Literature at the University of Exeter's Cornwall Campus. She has published widely on the uses of history and prehistory in the literature of the long nineteenth century. She lives on Dartmoor and writes regularly for a popular walking magazine.

Lynda Pratt is Reader in Romanticism at the University of Nottingham. She has published widely on Southey and his circle. She was general editor of *Robert Southey: Poetical Works, 1793–1810* and is co-general editor of *The Collected Letters of Robert Southey* (2009–) and *Robert Southey: Later Poetical Works, 1811–1838* (2011).

Nicholas Roe is Professor of English at St Andrews University. He is the author of *Wordsworth and Coleridge: the Radical Years* (1988), *John Keats and the Culture of Dissent* (1997), *The Politics of Nature: William Wordsworth and Some Contemporaries* (2002), and *Fiery Heart: the First Life of Leigh Hunt* (2005).

Damian Walford Davies is Reader in Romantic and Victorian Literature in the Department of English and Creative Writing at Aberystwyth University. He is the author of *Presences that Disturb: Models of Romantic Identity in the Literature and Culture of the 1790s* (2002), editor of *Romanticism, History, Historicism: Essays on an Orthodoxy* (2009), and co-editor of *Wales and the Romantic Imagination* (2006) and of *The Monstrous Debt: Modalities of Romantic Influence in Twentieth-Century Literature* (2006). He is General Editor of the forthcoming *Oxford Literary History of Wales*.

Carol Kyros Walker is Professor Emerita, Department of English, City Colleges of Chicago. She received her PhD from the University of Illinois, where she studied with Professor Jack Stillinger. Until recently, in a parallel life, she taught classical ballet at the School of the Art Institute of Chicago in the Performance Department. She is the author, editor, and photographer of three books about Romantic travellers, all published by Yale University Press: *Walking North with Keats* (1992), Dorothy Wordsworth's *Recollections of a Tour Made in Scotland* (1997), and *Breaking Away: Coleridge in Scotland* (2002).

Timothy Whelan is Professor of English at Georgia Southern University, Statesboro, GA, where he teaches Early American Literature. His research interests are primarily British, especially the intersection of British Romantic writers and Nonconformity. Besides articles in various journals in Romanticism and the history of Nonconformity, Professor Whelan has published *Politics, Religion, and Romance: the Letters of Benjamin Flower and Eliza Gould Flower, 1794–1808* (2008), and is currently preparing for publication an eight-volume edition of *Nonconformist Women Writers, 1720–1840* (2010–11).

Saeko Yoshikawa is Associate Professor at Kobe City University for Foreign Studies. Her publications include 'The Abounding Honeysuckle: Edward Thomas, S. T. Coleridge, and the Quantock Hills', *The Coleridge Bulletin*, NS 32 (2008); 'Dwelling, Dreaming, Dying on the Earth: Wordsworth, Hardy, and the Land/Soil', *Voyages of Conception*, Japan Association of English Romanticism (2005); 'Traveller and Dweller: Wordsworth in Grasmere', *Poetica*, 54 (2001); and 'Topography as Epitaph or Epitaph as Topography: Wordsworth's *Excursion*', *The English Literary Society of Japan Studies in English Literature* (1998).

List of Abbreviations

CL   *Collected Letters of Samuel Taylor Coleridge*, ed. E.L. Griggs (6 vols, Oxford: Clarendon Press, 1956–71).

CN   S.T. Coleridge, *The Notebooks of Samuel Taylor Coleridge*, ed. Kathleen Coburn, Merton Christensen, and Anthony Harding, Bollingen Series 50 (5 vols: vol. i, New York: Pantheon Books, 1957; vols. ii–v, Princeton, NJ: Princeton University Press, 1962–2002).

PW   S.T. Coleridge, *Poetical Works*, ed. J.C.C. Mays, *The Collected Works of Samuel Taylor Coleridge*, Bollingen Series 75, 16 (6 vols, Princeton NJ: Princeton University Press, 2001).

Introduction

Nicholas Roe

March 1913. Edward Thomas sets off from London on a bicycle tour to Somerset, an act of energy and purpose that establishes the critical bearings of *English Romantic Writers and the West Country*. 'I had a wish', he tells us, 'that Spring would be arriving among the Quantocks at the same time as myself.' His route would lead

> under the North Downs to Guildford, along the Hog's Back to Farnham, down the Itchen towards Winchester, over the high lands of the Test to Salisbury; across the Plain to Bradford, over the Mendips to Shepton Mallet, and then under the Mendips to Wells and Glastonbury, along the ridge of the Polden Hills to Bridgwater, and so up to the Quantocks and down to the sea.[1]

Thomas's trajectory westwards became a voyage through imagined landscapes: William Cobbett's Farnham; George Wither's Alresford; and William Hazlitt's Winterslow. Salisbury Plain wakened thoughts of W. H. Hudson, John Aubrey, Samuel Drayton, and Sir Philip Sidney writing *Arcadia* at Wilton. Further west, Thomas's reflections turned to Stephen Duck the thresher-poet, to William Barnes – 'the man was Dorset' – and Thomas Hardy, 'a countryman of a somewhat lonely heart'.[2]

The pursuit of spring followed, roughly speaking, the path Wordsworth had taken in 1793 from London, via the Isle of Wight, Salisbury and the Plain, to Bath and Bristol. If we trace Wordsworth's wider poetic migrations between 1793 and 1798 we might say that, consciously or not, Thomas was tracking a topography of the imagination that led from the desolate vistas of an early poem like *Salisbury Plain* to the human landscapes of *Lyrical Ballads*. In this book Carol Kyros Walker brings to life the actual experience of Wordsworth's 1793 walk, and shows how his encounter with the West Country formed the remarkably self-sufficient, capable, independent, and psychologically rich poet whose landmark publication appeared at Bristol.

1

Thomas's westward trek proved similarly fruitful. His eyes were set on the Quantocks as 'the boundary between the south-west and the west' beyond which extended the 'rocky and wilder land' of Exmoor and, still further west, the granite tors of Dartmoor and, westermost, the undulating tracts of Bodmin Moor.[3] For Thomas, as earlier for William Hazlitt, the Quantocks meant English Romanticism and the places where Wordsworth and Coleridge collaborated on *Lyrical Ballads*. An expansive consciousness of landscape, space, and creative excitement suffuses the poets' writings from this time as it does Dorothy Wordsworth's 'Alfoxden Journal'. In 1798 Britain and France had been at war for five years, and both poets were turning away from London and metropolitan politics in quest of somewhere to start over. The Quantock Hills, two days from London by the fastest coach, offered the geographical and psychological remove that encouraged the poets' experiments with alternative insights and renewals. Here, as Richard Holmes's great biography showed us, were the provincial landscape and culture that inspired Coleridge's early visions.[4]

But why the Quantocks? Wouldn't another region of England, Wales, or Scotland have served as a visionary retreat? At a period of political and social unrest the Quantocks might be thought to have offered shelter from political persecution, and the shaded coombs and windswept uplands both nurtured and disciplined composition. This is the landscape Coleridge celebrates in *Fears in Solitude* and, as Peter Kitson's chapter reminds us, rather than retreating from revolution both poets had settled in the historical heartland of rebellion – as Coleridge, a Devonshire man, certainly knew. A dozen miles from Nether Stowey was Taunton, a parliamentary stronghold during the Civil War and an important centre for Nonconformity with an academy (c. 1670–1759) linked to the network of dissent that criss-crossed the country. The Duke of Monmouth's challenge for the throne in 1685 had gathered momentum in Dorset, only to meet defeat at 'sad Sedge-Moor' – Thomas Hardy's phrase.[5] Hundreds were executed in Judge Jeffreys's 'bloody assizes' that followed. When the French planned an invasion attempt in 1797, they targeted a remote area of the Somerset coast close to Coleridge's home at Nether Stowey. Was this fortuitous? A matter of wind and tide? Or did they anticipate a welcome from locals whose forebears had experienced murderous retribution? Certainly Coleridge and Wordsworth found a like-minded friend in Thomas Poole, the tanner of Nether Stowey who had founded a poor man's club in the village (Poole's enemies thought of the club as his 'private army'). For the poets, moving to Somerset was less an escape from the dangers of London than a homecoming in a provincial landscape long associated with disaffection. The geopolitical history of the West Country was unquestionably a factor in the Home Office decision to dispatch the spy – Coleridge's 'Spy Nosy' – to report on the 'nest of democrats' at Alfoxden, and we can see those associations continued in the next generation. Ten years later, in 1808, Leigh Hunt's friend J. P. Marriott founded the *Taunton Courier* – a liberal newspaper, modelled on Hunt's London *Examiner*, that circulated throughout the West Country. Hunt's brother John, publisher of the *Examiner*, actually made his home in 1819 a few miles from Taunton at Cheddon Fitzpaine: it was a settlement long postponed, for the Hunt brothers were descendants of an ancient family from South Molton, Devon. The assertive political-cultural independence of *The Examiner* in which Shelley and Keats found their first readers was a West Country inheritance.

Wending slowly westward, Thomas thought himself bound for enchanted ground: 'I would see Nether Stowey, the native soil of "Kubla Khan", "Christabel" and "The Ancient Mariner", where Coleridge fed on honey-dew and drank the milk of Paradise.' At the Quantocks, he entered a landscape of poetry where the 'warm red fields, the gorse smouldering with bloom, the soft delicious greenery of the banks . . . the dark, bleak ridges of heather or pine, [and] the deep-carved coombs' were imbued with the presence of Coleridge.[6] This would all sound impossibly belletristic but for the phrase 'native soil' in which Thomas's more exuberant language is rooted.

Thomas was not the first to locate Coleridge in this sun-warmed, water-threaded, deep-carved landscape nor (as Thomas knew) was he the first to attempt a topographical criticism of Coleridge's poetry. More than a century had passed since the twenty-year-old William Hazlitt visited Nether Stowey and Alfoxden and read some of the poems destined for *Lyrical Ballads*. Recalling that moment in later years, Hazlitt says that 'the sense of a new style and a new spirit in poetry came over me . . . It had to me something of the effect that arises from the turning up of the fresh soil, or of the first welcome breath of Spring . . . Coleridge and myself walked back to Stowey that evening, and his voice sounded . . . as we passed through echoing grove, by fairy stream or waterfall, gleaming in the summer moonlight.'[7] Moonlit in hindsight, Hazlitt's 'First Acquaintance with Poets' was grounded in substantial stuff – the 'turning up of fresh soil' in a landscape associated since King Alfred with an assertive, independent spirit typified by Bristol's commercial rivalry with London. Aware of the poets' later lives, Hazlitt was also writing with the 'embittered nostalgia' evoked by Michael O'Neill in an essay that interweaves Hazlitt's 1798 intuition of 'the *ur* principles of the Romantic revolutionary imagination' with Shelley's reignition of that spirit in *Queen Mab*, written in summer 1812 at Lynmouth, Devon; in his lyrical invocation of the west wind to 'quicken a new birth'; and in the *Triumph of Life*, where 'Shelley might almost be writing his poetic gloss on Hazlitt's prose elegy for revolutionary ideals.' And like both Hazlitt and Shelley, Thomas's encounter with the West Country mingles retrospection with latent fire.

The Wordsworths, Coleridge and Hazlitt at the Quantocks are just four in a prodigious list of West Country writers that includes William Barnes, Thomas Beddoes, Thomas Lovell Beddoes, William Lisle Bowles, Anna Eliza Bray, Thomas Chatterton, Joseph Cottle, William Crowe, Humphry Davy, William

Gifford, William Gilbert, Thomas Hardy, Benjamin Haydon, John Hunt (who settled at the Quantocks and later Exeter), Leigh Hunt, John Keats, Charles Lloyd, Robert Lovell, Hannah More, Richard Polwhele, Thomas Poole, John Hamilton Reynolds, Percy Shelley, Joanna Southcott, Robert Southey, John Thelwall, and Ann Yearsley. Many of these individuals were born and lived in the West Country. Others, like Keats and the Hunt brothers, had family associations with the region, travelled, and wrote there. Add to these the outspoken presence of the West Country dissenters heard throughout this book, and one can appreciate how the region's intellectual and cultural vitality stirred poetic creativity. That there was a distinct, West Country appeal to the Romantic imagination is underlined by Tim Fulford's shrewdly angled chapter on Robert Bloomfield. While Bloomfield's untypically western poem *The Banks of the Wye* (1811) responded to the sublime and picturesque scenery that enabled Wordsworth (and others) to come into poetic selfhood, Bloomfield discovered his own lyrical presence by dwelling on a largely unpoetic East England not previously identified by travellers, tourists, and poets as hallowed ground.

Following J. G. A. Pocock's revisionist historiography in the 1970s and 1980s, Scottish, Welsh, and Irish Romanticisms have emerged in contemporary studies with unprecedented clarity and complexity.[8] Meanwhile, the provincial diversity of English Romantic writing continues largely to be absorbed into the Anglo-British monoculture that obscured those archipelagic identities. While this book is alert to a wider horizon of 'many western islands' it calls attention to one of the intra-national, regional manifestations of English Romantic culture. In so doing it contributes to and furthers current reassessments of individual voices. Thanks to John Goodridge and Simon Kovesi the Northamptonshire poet John Clare is now in the mainstream of English Romantic culture; so is a contemporary writer from England's Midlands, Anna Laetitia Barbauld, born Anna Laetitia Aikin of Kibworth Harcourt, Leicestershire. Tim Fulford has restored Robert Bloomfield, Suffolk author of *The Farmer's Boy* (1800) and the best-selling pastoral poet of the age. Lynda Pratt has returned Robert Southey's poems and letters to print and won him new admirers. Interest in the Dorset poet William Barnes is gathering momentum, and north of the border Robert Burns, that 'obscure, nameless Bard' of Scotland's south west, is reconnecting with global fame.[9]

By accompanying inclusive anthologies and encyclopaedias of Romantic writing in the classroom, the concurrent revival of regional voices has given us a sharper awareness of the decentred energies of Romantic culture. These might be Scottish, Welsh, and English – or regional subdivisions of those as Gaelic, Highland and Lowland Scots, North East England, Birmingham, and the West Country. Other regional divisions are available, such as Orcadian and Cornish. In this endeavour geographical distance from the metropolis becomes one measure of cultural vitality, although suburban writing – for long a cultural/critical no-go area – presents some of the most compelling linguistic and formal challenges of English Romantic literature.

Regionalism, then, is a key critical dynamic of Romantic studies now – in the devolved nations of Scotland and Wales and, this book argues, in relation to England's regions. Lost voices have been recovered and alternative cultural geographies mapped.[10] Within this diverse cultural landscape there are, as one would expect, varying degrees of what used to be called 'marginality'. Unlike those exiles from the 'Visionary Company' Clare, Barbauld, Bloomfield, Southey, and the Welsh poet Iolo Morganwg, Burns has never been out of print or wanted readers and students. Each decade brings new biographies of the bard, and new editions of his work to supplement James Kinsley's three-volume edition of 1968. Burns clubs are active around the globe; in Scotland Burns has his own national day; and at Dumfries there is an impressive Robert Burns centre beside the Nith. Inventing Burns's canonical exclusion is a way of continuing to make a case for him – a strategy many times tried already and originally by the bard himself, who had a canny sense of how his poetry might play to prevailing tastes for the 'native' and 'remote' and so turn a penny in the marketplace. With the poets of the English regions, however, we can justifiably point to long-term neglect and unavailability. Canonical marginality and regional cultures are in fact most urgently in need of reassessment within England.

English Romantic Writers and the West Country shifts the focus to the English regions, and builds upon Tom Mayberry's and Berta Lawrence's pioneering studies to explore Romantic writing and the landscape and cultures of England's West Country.[11] The book's regional terrain extends south west of a line between the Wye Valley at Tintern, Jane Austen's Chawton, and John Keats's Chichester. Edward Thomas saw the Quantocks as 'the boundary between the south-west and the west'; beyond lay the 'rocky and wilder land' of stone circles, dolmens, and cromlechs that attracted antiquarians and proto-archaeologists like John Aubrey and William Stukeley. In the first chapter, Joanne Parker shows how in the period 1785–1835 literary texts of all kinds on English prehistory flourished – and that this proliferation of publications was particularly marked in the case of the south west's ancient monuments. Wordsworth's eerie encounter with Stonehenge in *Salisbury Plain* and *The Prelude* was just one instance of a fascination that stretches as far back as Henry of Huntingdon and Geoffrey of Monmouth, and draws in the literature of Arthur and Merlin with the poets Spenser, Daniel, and Drayton. Among Romantic-period megalith poets are Coleridge's college friend C. V. Le Grice, Joseph Cottle, Robert Lovell, and John Keats, plus a host that many readers will encounter in this book for the first time, including Frederick Paas, George Woodley, Nicholas Carrington, and Anna Eliza Bray. As Parker argues, these writers should not only be of interest as minor figures drawn to subjects that attracted Chatterton, Wordsworth, and Blake, or as mere popularisers of an outdated antiquarianism. Drawing inspiration, subjects, and rhythms from a stony landscape battered by the stormy Atlantic, they were in touch with the groundswell of English Romanticism.

Thomas Chatterton is reassessed here by Nick Groom as a distinctive and highly flavoured poet of West Country fauna and topography. While Chatterton's imagination was nourished by the local landscapes of Clifton Gorge and the Avon, Washford, Cleeve Abbey, Stanton Drew and the River Trym, Groom also shows him ranging across the tidal straits of the 'Severn Sea' that in Damian Walford Davies's ingenious essay in critical hydrography flow inland to influence both the composition and the cadences of Wordsworth's 'Tintern Abbey'. Drawing on the full tradition of English landscape poetry including Chaucer, Spenser, Shakespeare, and the Milton of 'Lycidas', Chatterton mingles these literary inheritances with the 'voice of the people' to create a vernacular English poetry that helped the later generations of Burns, Wordsworth, Bloomfield, and Clare. When Wordsworth's epigraph for *The Ruined Cottage* summoned Burns's 'Epistle to J. L *****k' to demand,

> Give me a spark o' nature's fire,
> 'Tis the best learning I desire[12]

he also invoked the promethean 'glemeing' and 'shimmering sense of newness and wonder' in Chatterton's poetry. Coleridge, who admired *The Ruined Cottage*, was well aware of Wordsworth's scotophile admiration for Burns; and it was Joseph Cottle, encouraged by Coleridge, who planned to publish Wordsworth's poem in Chatterton's Bristol.

Joseph Cottle, who figures throughout this book, was born on 9 March 1770 to a Cornish family then resident in Bristol. All too easily dismissed as a minor poet whose autobiographical *Early Recollections* was garrulous, egotistical, and unreliable, Cottle demands reappraisal as the Maecenas of West Country Romanticism. Brought up and educated in Baptist dissenting circles, by April 1791 Cottle had opened his shop at the corner of Bristol's High Street and Corn Street and started business as a printseller, stationer, binder, and bookseller. Six months later, across country in Cambridge, Coleridge's arrival at Jesus College marked the latest in a series of exilings usually held to have disconnected him from his 'sweet birth-place' at Ottery St. Mary. In a thoroughgoing reappraisal of the evidence, Graham Davidson traces the troubled continuities and divided allegiances that emerge in Coleridge's flirtatious and satirical verses about his native place. Summer 1794 saw Coleridge and Southey meet at Oxford, where they planned the Pantisocracy community 'O'er the ocean swell' in Pennsylvania, and later that year a friend and fellow-poet, Robert Lovell, introduced Southey to Cottle. At this moment Cottle had not commenced as a publisher, but he nevertheless offered Southey fifty guineas and fifty copies for his epic *Joan of Arc* – a poem that controversially sided with the French against Britain's war effort. When Coleridge arrived at Bristol early in 1795, Cottle advanced both poets thirty guineas for their poems. Having secured Southey and Coleridge, and with news of a young poet called Wordsworth in Dorset, Cottle's publishing ambitions were growing. In Paul Cheshire's vivid summary, 'Cottle's bookshop became the equivalent for Bristol poets of what City Lights in San Francisco was for the 1950s Beat Generation: a meeting place for the impoverished young writers and political radicals who converged on the city.'

So Cottle became the impresario of Bristolian culture, lending Coleridge money and selling lecture tickets, helping with wedding arrangements, and accommodating Southey's wife when her husband went abroad. He published and circulated Coleridge's *Watchman* magazine in 1796, and to present his poets to the public he commissioned portraits of them. Proposals followed for an edition of Coleridge's and Wordsworth's plays, *Osorio* and *The Borderers*, and a volume comprising 'Wordsworths Salisbury Plain & Tale of a Woman' (i.e. *The Ruined Cottage*; *CL*, i. 400). Cottle was the sponsor and printer of *Lyrical Ballads*; he published Southey's *Poems* (1799) and *Thalaba the Destroyer* (1801); and his own twenty-four book epic *Alfred* (1801) set the seal on this remarkable outpouring of verse.

Energised by Cottle's ambitions, Coleridge almost certainly had visions of his projected *Works* as Cottle publications:

[*a*] Imitations of the Modern Latin Poets with an Essay Biog. & Crit. On the Rest. Of Lit. – 2 Vol. Octavo.

[*b*] Answer to the System of Nature – 1 ~~Vol.~~ Oct

[*c*] The Origin of Evil, an Epic Poem.

[*d*] Essay on Bowles

[*e*] Strictures on Godwin, Paley &c &c –

[*f*] Pantisocracy, or a practical Essay on the abolition of Indiv[id]ual Property.

[*g*] Carthon an Opera

[*h*] Poems

[*i*] Edition of Collins & Gray with a preliminary Dissertation.

[*j*] A Liturgy On the different Sects of Religion & Infidelity – philosophical analysis of their Effects on mind & manners – .

[*k*] A Tragedy[13]

As originally envisaged by Coleridge, Wordsworth's philosophic poem *The Recluse* would have been another blockbuster from Cottle's Bristol School.

Coleridge's ambition to establish a provincial base for poetry, politics, classical culture, music, philosophy, and religion is one measure of the impetus that Cottle gave to English Romanticism. The sense that all of this was possible for Coleridge was not an opium-fuelled fantasy – Cottle had seemed to place it all within his grasp, and days later Coleridge listed twenty-seven more works he planned to write. Only John Murray in London's Albemarle

Street can rival the achievement and long-term influence of Cottle's publications. His bookshop still survives, and ought to be celebrated as a proud monument to Bristol's literary heritage.

Richard Cronin's chapter confronts Cottle's personality, and presents a compelling and far-reaching reassessment of his 'grand project' to establish a Bristol School of poets united in their opposition to the war, in their defiant provincialism and vocal distrust of the centralised state, and in their attachment to dissenting ideas. Cottle's decision in 1796 to publish Southey's *Joan of Arc* in quarto and to make it 'the handsomest book that Bristol had ever yet sent forth',[14] indicates that this radical, provincial epic was to be the flagship volume of the new Bristol School. Cottle established Southey's reputation as a notably prolific and controversial West Country poet and, Cronin shows us, did much to initiate the generic experiments of 'English Eclogues', conversation poems, and lyrical ballads. Lynda Pratt's authoritative remapping of Southey's career shows that while the Bristol identity that Cottle nurtured in the mid-1790s was obscured by the 'Lake School', Southey's West Country connections survived to link his career early and late. Likewise, Wordsworth's most impressive poem for the Victorians, *The Excursion*, grew from an earlier work that Cottle had hoped to publish: *The Ruined Cottage*. A poem of 'familiar power' and 'quiet, confident, provincial authority', *The Ruined Cottage* emerges in Cronin's essay as 'the masterpiece of West Country Romanticism'.

As a record of the Bristol School he had shaped and published, Cottle compiled an album of poems and letters of Southey, Coleridge, and Wordsworth. Spanning half a century, 1795–1844, Cottle's album also finds space for a local prodigy – the Bristol poet, barrister, journalist, traveller, and astrologer William Gilbert who is brought to gamey prominence for the first time in Paul Cheshire's chapter. The author of a visionary, millenarian poem *The Hurricane* (1796), Gilbert was legendary in Bristol circles yet has for two centuries remained isolated and misunderstood. Cheshire restores Gilbert to his proper milieu, an astonishing amalgam of poetry, magic, journalism, and astrology – and also places him within the Methodist network in Bristol's culture of dissent.

At the centre of this book are three chapters that offer fresh assessments of dissenting circles in Bristol, Taunton, and the West Country. Tim Whelan gazes north-eastwards to trace the longstanding links between Cambridge and Bristol dissent, links that enabled Coleridge to extricate himself from the wreckage of his student years and reinvent himself as a Bristol lecturer, journalist, and poet. Coleridge's Bristol lectures, *The Watchman* and his poem 'Religious Musings' were demonstrably influenced by these two dissenting communities, and most notably by George Dyer, William Frend, Benjamin Flower, and the Baptist circles represented by Robert Hall, John Ryland, Joseph Hughes, and James Harwood. Peter Kitson's chapter places Cottle's Coleridge of 1794–8 securely in the long tradition of West Country dissent, and directs our attention westward to the influential Taunton

Unitarian Joshua Toulmin by way of emphasising that Coleridge's removal to Nether Stowey cannot be regarded as a 'simple act of retirement from politics with Taunton and Toulmin's congregation a mere ten miles or so away'. As a poet, abolitionist, and reformer, as well as a generous bookseller and publisher, Cottle and his bookshop embodied the creative interchange between West Country dissent and the rising generation of poets. Through a detailed analysis of Nonconformist textual culture Anthony Harding reveals how dissenters' readings of the Bible – close, critical, rational, independent – were intrinsic to radical opposition in the 1790s. This eighteenth-century tradition shaped the responses of Priestley, Frend, and others to the crises of the 1790s, and aligned Coleridge's earnest, courageous, often original contributions with those of West Country Unitarians such as Estlin and Toulmin. If we attend to the experimental voices and forms of Coleridge's prose and poetry in the mid-1790s with 'Unitarian ears', Harding contends, we catch the tones of an uncompromising, lifelong 'inquiring spirit'. We also attune ourselves to the millenarian passion that impelled 'Religious Musings' and persuaded Wordsworth that a philosophic epic to be titled *The Recluse* might capture the spirit of the age.

Twenty years after the spring of *Lyrical Ballads* and *The Recluse*, March 1818 saw John Keats step down from the mail coach at Exeter having travelled for three days on an outside seat through one of the worst storms in living memory. Bound for Teignmouth, where he would spend two months caring for his consumptive brother Tom, Keats had also entered the West Country that family tradition told him was the home of his paternal ancestors. My chapter '"Over the Dartmoor Black"' explores that tradition and how in successive accounts of Keats's 'Bright Star' sonnet hearsay and myth solidified into 'fact'. When taken together Keats's migrations from London 1817–20 show a westward tendency, to the Isle of Wight (April 1817; June–August 1819); to Teignmouth (March–May 1818 and, wishfully, May 1819[15]); to the Chichester–Bedhampton area (January 1819); and to Winchester (August–October 1819). Furthermore each of these visits coincided with major phases of composition: *Endymion* (Isle of Wight, April 1817); *Isabella* and the verse epistle 'Dear Reynolds' (Teignmouth, March–May 1818); *The Eve of St Agnes* (Chichester–Bedhampton, January 1819); *Lamia* and *Otho the Great* (Isle of Wight, June–August 1819); *Lamia*, *Otho the Great*, *The Fall of Hyperion* and 'To Autumn' (Winchester, August–October 1819). Although it proved mistaken, the old supposition that Keats's last Dorset sojourn in October 1820 had stirred a 'poetical effort' in 'Bright Star' fitted an established pattern of composition in Keats – a pattern, moreover, that apparently responded to local Keats associations. When Keats bade adieu to Porphyro and Madeline at the end of *The Eve of St Agnes*, his first thought as he drafted his poem was that they were bound 'over the Dartmoor black' to his father's native place in the west.

In the final chapter Saeko Yoshikawa focuses on the motif of 'stepping westward' that structures the whole book, and moves from the Romantic period through to the nineteenth and twentieth centuries. Developing the association between 'stepping westward' and the 'poetic beginnings' of *Lyrical Ballads*, she draws attention to the later spring associated with Wordsworth's only return to the West Country in 1841, when he revisited Tintern and the Wye, Alfoxden, Nether Stowey, and the Quantock Hills. The revival of scenes and associated memories prompted him to retrace the composition of his poems and recount the biographical stories behind them – a late flowering that led to the autobiographical 'Fenwick Notes'. This Wordsworthian interplay of memory and creativity is developed in Yoshikawa's readings of two early twentieth-century poets, Thomas Hardy and Edward Thomas. Hardy's elegiac lyrics of 1912–13 and Thomas's *In Pursuit of Spring* confront crisis, and discover in the process of writing the intimations of renewal that make 'stepping westward' both a physical act and a symbol of creative renewal.

The chapters of this book are arranged in a broadly chronological sequence, beginning in the eighteenth century and extending into the twentieth. Its critical moment, however, is the start of the twenty-first century, as we approach the centenary of Edward Thomas's pursuit of spring and poetry. Appearing at a moment when devolution has energised creativity and criticism in Scotland and Wales, *English Romantic Writers and the West Country* seeks to encourage further critical-creative engagements with the regional identities of English Romantic writing, and with what it meant to be an English writer at a period when Keats traced the 'native music' of the English language to Thomas Chatterton.

English Romantic Writers and the West Country is dedicated to the memory of Jonathan Wordsworth, himself a West Countryman, and a scholar-editor whose insights did so much to illuminate William Wordsworth and West Country Romanticism. A native of Dorset, he was born a few miles from Racedown Lodge where Wordsworth began *The Ruined Cottage* – a poem that discovers tragic power at the heart of a provincial landscape of elm trees and crackling gorse. *The Ruined Cottage* was first published in Jonathan Wordsworth's *The Music of Humanity* (1969), a book that continues to inform and inspire scholars and students of English Romanticism. In 1973 he printed for the first time the two-part 1798–9 version of *The Prelude*. In his 'Revolution and Romanticism' facsimiles for Woodstock Books his prefaces to Chatterton, Coleridge, Wordsworth, Gilbert, Southey, More, and Yearsley capture the essence of West Country Romanticism. *William Wordsworth: the Borders of Vision* (1982) endures as a brilliant account of the West Country origins and subsequent evolution of Wordsworth's projected masterwork *The Recluse*. Jonathan Wordsworth taught English Literature at Exeter College and St Catherine's, Oxford, and between 1959 and 2006 was a trustee, Chairman and President of the Wordsworth Trust at Grasmere. He was Director of the

Wordsworth Conference for thirteen years from 1993, and a Scholar of the Friends of Coleridge at Nether Stowey, Somerset.

Notes

1. *In Pursuit of Spring* (London, Edinburgh, Dublin, and New York, 1914), 29–30.
2. *In Pursuit of Spring*, 186, 192.
3. *In Pursuit of Spring*, 30.
4. Richard Holmes, *Coleridge: Early Visions* (London: Hodder & Stoughton, 1989).
5. See 'A Trampwoman's Tragedy', line 8.
6. *In Pursuit of Spring*, 272–3, 275.
7. William Hazlitt, 'My First Acquaintance with Poets', in *The Complete Works of William Hazlitt*, ed. P. P. Howe (21 vols, London: J. M. Dent, 1930–4), xvii. 117.
8. J. G. A. Pocock, 'British History: a Plea for a New Subject 1973/1974', repr. *The Discovery of Islands: Essays in British History* (Cambridge: Cambridge University Press, 2005), 24–43; David Duff and Catherine Jones (eds), *Scotland, Ireland and the Romantic Aesthetic* (Lewisburg: Bucknell University Press, 2007); Murray Pittock, *Scottish and Irish Romanticism* (Oxford: Oxford University Press, 2008); John Kerrigan, *Archipelagic English: Literature, History and Politics 1603–1707* (Oxford: Oxford University Press, 2008).
9. *Poems, Chiefly in the Scottish Dialect, by Robert Burns* (Kilmarnock: John Wilson, 1786), iv.
10. See note 7, and Damian Walford Davies, *Presences that Disturb: Models of Romantic Identity in the Literature and Culture of the 1790s* (Cardiff: University of Wales Press, 2002); Damian Walford Davies and Lynda Pratt (eds), *Wales and the Romantic Imagination* (Cardiff: University of Wales Press, 2007); and Leith Davis, Ian Duncan, and Janet Sorenson (eds), *Scotland and the Borders of Romanticism* (Cambridge: Cambridge University Press, 2004). Jenny Uglow's *The Lunar Men: the Friends Who Made the Future* (London: Faber and Faber, 2003) established Birmingham as a crucible for Romantic science, a counterpart to the burgeoning industrial scene of Cornwall during the nineteenth century. Urban and suburban groups of writers, painters, and critics feature in Jeffrey Cox's study *Poetry and Politics in the Cockney School: Keats, Shelley, Hunt, and their Circle* (Cambridge: Cambridge University Press, 1998).
11. Tom Mayberry, *Coleridge and Wordsworth in the West Country* (Stroud: Alan Sutton, 1992); Berta Lawrence, *Coleridge and Wordsworth in Somerset* (Newton Abbot: David & Charles, 1970).
12. *The Ruined Cottage and the Pedlar*, ed. James Butler, Cornell Wordsworth Series (Ithaca, NY: Cornell University Press, 1979), 42.
13. *CN*, I. i. entry 161 G. 156.
14. Southey's own judgement. See the Preface to *Joan of Arc* in *The Poetical Works of Robert Southey* (London: Longman, Green and Co, 1876), 2.
15. *The Letters of John Keats*, ed. Hyder Rollins (2 vols, Cambridge, MA: Harvard University Press, 1958; 1972), ii. 112–13.

Part I
Landscapes and Legends

1

'More wondrous far than Egypt's boasted pyramids': the South West's Megaliths in the Romantic Period

Joanne Parker

On 30 October 1806, the wool-merchant turned antiquary William Cunnington rode out from his home at Heytesbury over the adjoining Salisbury Plain. As he recalled in a letter to his patron Sir Richard Colt Hoare, he had ridden for thirteen miles in thick fog when suddenly 'the sun burst out all at once and disclosed such a scene that few excepting poets could enjoy. Stonehenge never looked more grand.'[1] Cunnington and Colt Hoare spent thirteen years excavating and scrupulously recording finds from what they termed 'those British pyramids' – the barrows, or burial mounds, around Stonehenge – and have in consequence been hailed as 'the fathers of archaeological excavation in England'.[2] The first words of the introduction to their study *Ancient Wiltshire* support this image, presenting the two men as sober investigators: 'We speak from facts, not theory' it insists.

However, Cunnington also possessed a keen awareness of the sublime possibilities of ancient monuments. The man who claimed to eschew the imagination in his professional work at the same time introduced a tradition to his family and associates of approaching Stonehenge in a coach with the blinds pulled down in order to avoid disappointment for 'on this extended Plain at such a distance it appears nothing, and by the time you are at it all astonishment ceases'.[3] His allusion to a 'poet's' heightened response to the sudden sight of Stonehenge further suggests an awareness of the non-scientific, emotive responses to prehistory that were possible, and indeed he and Colt Hoare made a habit of celebrating their finds on Salisbury Plain with informal soirées at which a poet would be present 'to immortalize, and raise in living verse, the ashes of the Britons'.[4]

It is, therefore, far too simplistic to view Cunnington (as modern archaeologists typically have) as marking the demise of the sentimental and fanciful engagements with prehistory that had characterised earlier antiquarianism, and the emergence of the disciplined enquiry and rigorous empiricism that would eventually develop into the modern discipline of archaeology. Moreover, while the late eighteenth century may have witnessed the general eschewal of emotive responses to prehistory among antiquaries, which writers such as Stuart Piggott have noted, it also saw those responses broadly popularised in other genres of writing: such as poetry, travel narratives, and popular tourist guides.[5] Piggott's study of the cultural reception of ancient monuments in Britain concludes with a chapter on the early nineteenth century dismally entitled 'Relapse, Romantics, and Stagnation', and the historian Richard Hayman has dismissed texts from that period as merely 'the dregs of the Stukleyite genre'.[6] However, the period from 1785 until 1835 was in fact one in which literary texts on British prehistory flourished – and that proliferation of publications was particularly marked in the case of the south west's monuments. Those works should not be disregarded as merely popularising the ideas of earlier antiquaries. They played an active role in the development of tourism to the south west. They were influential in preserving the megaliths that still inspire wonder now, whether on Dartmoor, Bodmin, or at Avebury. And they developed ways of viewing and relating to prehistoric remains that are still influential in British culture today.

The south west of England has in excess of 7,000 prehistoric monuments spread across the counties of Cornwall, Devon, Somerset, Avon, Dorset, and Wiltshire. These include barrows, hill forts and other earthworks; hut circles, boundary markers and cairns; as well as the 'megalithic' remains – the stone circles, stone rows, cromlechs, and quoits named collectively for the awe-inspiringly huge slabs from which they are constructed. Romantic period writers in the south west therefore had ready access to a rich vein of prehistoric inspiration. They also inherited a long and varied tradition of interpreting the megaliths, whose original purposes still remain to varying degrees shrouded in mystery, though they are now generally agreed to have been constructed between 3,500 BC and 1,500 BC (so around 700 years before the period of the Iron Age 'Celts').

In the case of the south west's best-known megalithic monument, its reception history had started in the twelfth century, when Stonehenge was remarked upon by both Henry of Huntingdon and Geoffrey of Monmouth. Geoffrey had claimed in his 1136 *History of the Kings of Britain* that the stones were brought by the wizard Merlin from Ireland to mark the triumph of the British king Aurelius Ambrosius over the Saxon invader Hengist – a claim which was subsequently incorporated not only into the work of other medieval chroniclers, but also into several Merlin plays of the late sixteenth and early seventeenth century, as well as Spenser's *Faerie Queene*. Although most elements of this story had long since become redundant by the late eighteenth century, the association of the stones with the 'Britons' – and more specifically with the invasion of the Saxons – persisted, so that in a work like Joseph Cottle's long 1826 poem 'Dartmoor', it is the desolate and menacing moor with its stone rows and stone circles that checks the progress of the invaders as they pursue the 'Britons' westwards.[7]

Written just six years earlier than Geoffrey's work, Henry of Huntingdon's 1130 *History of England* was rather more cautious in its theorising about

Stonehenge, musing only that 'no one can conceive how such great stones have been so raised aloft, or why they were built there'.[8] In so speculating, however, it instituted a tradition which was to endure for centuries – that of musing hopelessly on the monument's origin, construction, and meaning. This had become a poetic convention by at least the late sixteenth century when Samuel Daniel described Stonehenge, in his 1599 work *Musophilus*, as a:

> Huge dumb heape, that cannot tell us how,
> Nor what, nor whence it is.[9]

Daniel was also one of the earliest writers to ponder on decay and impermanence before the stones, professing himself 'angry with time that nothing should remaine/Our greatest wonders wonder to expresse'.[10] It was a sentiment that would be developed by Romantic West Country writers such as Charles Valentine Le Grice, curate of St Mary's, Penzance. In early life, Le Grice had been a friend of Coleridge at Christ's Hospital and Cambridge.[11] Later, his 'Inscription for Lanyon Cromlech in its fallen state' – a prehistoric stone burial close to the town of Liskeard – contemplated how:

> [...] as the heart
> Aching with thoughts of human littleness
> Asks, without hope of knowing, whose the strength
> That poised thee here; so ages yet unborn
> (O! humbling, humbling thought!) may vainly seek,
> What were the race of men that saw thee fall.[12]

The publication of Daniel's poem coincided with the period during which the remainder of the south west's prehistoric remains were first being brought to public attention in the work of topographical writers. These early, patriotic recorders of British folklore, ruins, customs, family histories, and natural curiosities included several minor figures from the West Country, such as the Cornishman Richard Carew whose *Survey of Cornwall*, published in the 1580s, included, for instance, the story of a Fowey man digging for treasure beneath the menhir known as the Tristan Stone.[13] Carew also relayed information about Cornish remains to a fellow antiquary, William Camden, whose *Britannia*, first published in 1586, was to be the most influential of the topographical works from this period on later interest in megaliths.[14] Camden documented the sites of many prehistoric remains besides Stonehenge. So in his chapter on Cornwall, for instance, he recorded:

> [...] in a place called Biscaw-woune, are nineteen stones set in a circle, about 12 foot distant one from another; and in the centre, there stands

one much larger than any of the rest. One may probably conjecture this to have been some trophy of the Romans under the later Emperors; or of Athelstane the Saxon, after he had subdued Cornwall.[15]

Britannia's influence was so enduring that it was still being used as a reference work over two hundred years later. In his 1823 topographical guide to East and West Looe, the Cornishman Thomas Bond related following Camden's directions to find a local geological feature, the 'Cheese Wring', and the megalithic monuments in its vicinity:

> On the 6th August 1802, I went with a party of friends to see these natural and artificial curiosities, mentioned by Camden. [...] I made enquiry at the house at Redgate after this monument, but could get no account of it for some time though I questioned in a variety of ways; at last, however, we got information where it was situated.[16]

Camden's descriptions of the Cheese Wring and the monuments in its vicinity are quoted at length. However, where Camden, like most sixteenth-century topographical writers, offered no definite theories about the Cheese Wring itself, and merely recorded that the neighbouring stone circle, the Hurlers, was believed to be 'a trophie in memory of a battle' or a boundary marker, Bond was convinced that the former had 'druidical basons formed in it' and that the latter had been 'erected by the Druids for some purpose or other, probably a court of Justice'.[17]

The origin of Bond's theories lies in the work of the seventeenth-century antiquary John Aubrey. Aubrey lived in a period during which theories about Stonehenge's origin proliferated. For John Webb and Inigo Jones it was a Roman monument, Walter Charleton believed it to be Danish, Aylett Sammes insisted that it was Phoenician, while for Edmund Bolton it was certainly a memorial to Boadicea.[18] While this intellectual mêlée surrounded Stonehenge, however, the great stone circles at Avebury were almost entirely disregarded. The great innovation of Aubrey, who grew up in Wiltshire and thus knew the county well, was to 'discover' Avebury and determine that the two stone circles were structures of the same class. Furthermore, after discussing these megalithic remains with Scottish members of the newly formed Royal Society, he concluded that both should also be understood in relation to the complex of stone circles scattered across Britain.[19] The logical corollary of this insight was that the monuments could only be prehistoric. Aubrey also therefore moved away from previous attempts to connect each monument to a documented historical period and instead adopted the approach of comparative fieldwork. 'These antiquities are so exceeding old that no books doe reach them', he averred, 'there is no way to retrive [sic] them but by comparative antiquitie, which I have writ upon the spott [sic], from the monuments themselves.'[20]

After surveying several stone circles, Aubrey concluded 'by comparative arguments' that these were temples of the ancient British and that 'the Druids being the most eminent priests (or order of priests) among the Britaines [sic]: 'tis odds, but that these ancient monuments [...] were temples of the priests of the most eminent order, viz, Druids'.[21] Aubrey's great planned work, *Monumenta Britannica*, was never completed. However, many of his observations on megalithic monuments were included as notes and additions in Edmund Gibson's 1695 English-language edition of Camden's *Britannia*. In the addition to Wiltshire, for instance, seven competing theories about Stonehenge's origin are cited, but among them is the notion that 'it was a temple of the Druids [...] which Mr John Aubrey [...] endeavours to prove in his manuscript treatise'.[22]

The manuscript of Aubrey's work was also read in 1718 by the young Lincolnshire doctor William Stukeley. Inspired by Aubrey to carry out his own extensive fieldwork, Stukeley went on to publish two monumental studies of stone circles – *Stonehenge*, published in 1740, and *Abury*, published in 1743.[23] In the first of these he followed Aubrey's comparative approach to claim that all of the stone circles in 'our isle' were Druidical and 'analogous to our chapels, churches or cathedrals, according to their different magnitude', thereby firmly associating all stone circles with Druids in the British imagination.[24] Both volumes also painted in detail the Druidic ceremonies that Stukeley imagined had been performed there. At Avebury, he imagined:

> [...] sacrifices were offered and administered by the lesser orders of priests around the amber or central pyramid. The highest part of religion was to be performed by the archdruid and the upper order of priests before the magnificent cove of the northern temple, together with hymns, incense, musick, and the like.[25]

This populist approach was certainly self-conscious: in the first chapter of *Abury*, Stukeley wrote:

> The writers on antiquities generally find more difficulty in so handling the matter, as to make it agreeable to the reader [...] antiquities must be drawn out with such strong lines of verisimilitude, and represented in so lively colours, that the reader in effect sees them, as in their first ages.[26]

Although some 'megalith poetry' (like Samuel Daniel's verses on Stonehenge) had already been written, the life that Stukeley breathed into mute stones was crucial in transforming prehistoric remains into prospective literary subject-matter. His influence on William Wordsworth and William Blake's respective responses to Stonehenge has been discussed at length elsewhere.[27] However, Stukeley's influence was far broader than this. His Druidic readings of Stonehenge and Avebury (as well as his passing references to

Somerset's Stanton Drew and to the Hurlers) also affected many more monuments and other writers – particularly in the south west. The Bristol publisher and poet Joseph Cottle, for one, was certainly familiar with them, as he mentions Stukeley in the notes to his 1823 poem 'Dartmoor'.

The effect of Stukeley's work was also almost immediate. By 1754, the clergyman William Borlase could publish the first county study of prehistoric monuments: *Antiquities Historical and Monumental of the County of Cornwall*, which he asserted was 'greatly obliged' to Stukeley's two volumes.[28] Borlase's volume – the fruit of years of tramping across Cornwall amassing information – attributed a Druidical origin to each of the county's megalithic monuments, and many of its natural geological features. His view of the Druids, however, was rather different from Stukeley's. For Stukeley, the Druids were admirable in almost every way: their religious beliefs had been communicated to them by the Phoenician trader Hercules of Tyre, a student of the patriarch Abraham, and the symbolism of their temples indicated that they had believed in the trinity and foreseen the coming of Christ.[29] Although they *had* occasionally practised human sacrifice, as the writings of Caesar, Strabo, and Diodorus Siculus made inescapable, he argued that this was only because they had misunderstood 'Abraham's example'.[30] For Borlase, however, the Druids were more emphatically pagan. They worshipped Mercury and Apollo, revered stones as idols, and believed in fairies.[31] There is detailed description of their sacrifices: women and children were offered as well as criminals and conquered enemies (this was an innovation unimagined by earlier writers), and at those Cornish sites where there were multiple circles of stones, Borlase imagined that individual rings were used to 'prepare, kill, examine and burn the victim'.[32] During the sacrifices, he suggested, drums and trumpets were used to drown the cries of victims, and 'intemperance in drinking generally closed the sacrificing'.[33]

British antiquarianism made few real advances on Stukeley and Borlase's Druidic readings of megaliths for almost a hundred years – until the Three Ages system was introduced to Britain, radically altering understandings of prehistory.[34] That intervening century, 1750–1850, however, was by no means uninterested in prehistoric remains. On the one hand, excavation techniques and the careful cataloguing of finds were being developed in the work of Cunnington and Colt Hoare. On the other, this was also the period during which the association of Druids and megaliths was most enthusiastically and inventively disseminated and popularised – and this was particularly the case in the south west of England, where figures like the Dartmoor poet Frederick Paas brought to life for less scholarly audiences the past terrors that antiquaries had imagined at local sites:

> Upon the rough hewn altar's floor
> In thought I beheld the clotted gore
> The hair and brains all scattered round

The hard, and firmly trodden ground
Often the scene of deadly struggle
E'er the spirit left in the fatal gurgle.[35]

Alternative readings of prehistoric monuments were attempted by a few south-western authors. In 1823, in his visitors' guide to Dartmoor, the Reverend J. P. Jones of North Bovey in Devon attributed Cranbrook Castle near Drewsteignton (an earthwork now known to be from the Iron Age) to the Danes. One senses, however, that Jones was fighting against the tide and that the 'numerous visitors [...] continually exploring the vicinity of Moreton-Hampstead' at whom his pamphlet was aimed were in most cases led by an inclination to view Druidical remains. Describing a collection of rocks near Blackstone Tor he grumbled that they were 'generally supposed to have been a seat of druidical worship' but insists there is 'nothing, however, to sanction such an idea'.[36] Of a logan (or rocking) stone near Drewsteignton he protests 'there is not the least reason to suppose the spot was ever visited by Druids' (see Figure 1).[37] And he dismisses the geological formation known as Bowerman's nose as 'evidently formed by nature', although it is 'generally supposed to have been a rock idol'.[38]

While Jones worked hard to disillusion and enlighten Druid-obsessed visitors to his area, far more south-western writers were drawing on local

Figure 1 B. Cooke, after S. Prout, 'Logan Stone Near Drew Steignton, Devonshire' (London: W. Clarke and J. Carpenter, 1806).

Druidic remains as a valuable resource which might attract tourists and add to the cultural prestige of their region. Borlase had clearly had these two aims in mind in the 1750s. The 'Letter to the Reader' which prefaces his guide to the antiquities of Cornwall complained:

> English travellers are too little acquainted with their own country [...] Englishmen (otherwise well qualified to appear in the world) go abroad in quest of the rarities of other countries, before they know sufficiently what their own contains.[39]

In his second work, on the natural history of the region, he grumbled more specifically that Cornwall's remote location made it 'less distinctly seen and regarded by the polite, learned, and busy world'.[40] His work, he hoped, might 'awake attention to the real and publick interest of the County'.[41] Borlase, then, explicitly presented his home county's prehistoric remains as a lure to tourists, and later writers were quick to follow his lead.

One of the first to do so was William Chapple, steward to the Courtenay family's estates around Exeter. During his retirement from this post in the late 1770s, Chapple published a guidebook entitled *Description and Exegesis of the Drew's Teignton Cromlech*, as part of a more ambitious project to produce an enlarged, updated, and corrected edition of Tristram Risdon's seventeenth-century *Survey of Devon*.[42] The Drewsteignton monument (known to residents of the small West Devon village as Spinster's Rock) had been 'hitherto little regarded' Chapple observed, but it clearly conformed with Borlase's description of Cornwall's Druidical cromlechs.[43] Chapple was convinced that it had been 'an astronomical laboratory' used by the Druids for observation of the heavens and 'gnomical purposes', which meant that Devon might well have as Druidical a past as Borlase had claimed for Cornwall.[44]

Chapple's interest in the Drewsteignton cromlech seems to have been responsible for drawing that monument, and its neighbouring stone row and stone circle, to the attention of Richard Polwhele.[45] The first volume of Polwhele's seven-volume *History of Devonshire*, published in 1793, was subsequently to become the first concerted and developed endeavour to assert for Devon a Druidical inheritance to rival not only Borlase's Cornwall, but even Stukeley's Wiltshire. 'If the hills or the vallies which have been long consecrated to the genius of the Druids of Cornwall deserve so high an honour, I have little doubt but the same distinction is due to those romantic scenes in Devonshire, which we have hitherto been led to view with an incurious eye', he asserted.[46] Moreover, the history aimed to convey this reading of Dartmoor to a popular audience, eschewing 'deep scientifical disquisition' in favour of 'popular information and amusement'.[47]

Polwhele was a Cornishman by birth, who moved to Devon for his first living as a curate, and it is tempting to read his *History of Devonshire* as at times an exercise in convincing himself and others of the wisdom of this move. Seizing on Chapple's account of a cromlech less than twenty miles from his own parish, he asserted that Drewsteignton had been the 'arch-druidical seat' of the ancient British kingdom of Damnonia, which had encompassed both Cornwall and Devon.[48] Ignoring earlier topographers who had correctly derived the village's name from the local landowner Drewe, Polwhele translated the place-name as 'town of the Druids upon the river Teign', declaring:

> That this was the favourite resort of the Druids, is evident from a great variety of druidical remains which the most incurious spectator must necessarily observe [...] The only cromlech in Devonshire marks this spot as more peculiarly the seat of the druids: and the archdruid, perhaps, could not have chosen a more convenient place for his annual assembly.[49]

The Drewsteignton monuments shared, Polwhele asserted, 'the same style of wild magnificence' as Stonehenge (see Figure 2). And though he admitted 'in Danmonium, it appears that we can boast no structures like the temple

Figure 2 By and after T. H. Williams, 'Cromlech, Drewsteignton. With Druids' (Plymouth: T. H. Williams, 1804).

of Stonehenge', nonetheless he believed 'nothing is more probable than that such a temple once existed at Drewsteignton'.[50]

Polwhele dismissed Chapple's notion that the Drewsteignton cromlech was an observatory, instead following Borlase's more colourful theories to designate it 'the sepulchre of a chief druid or of some prince, the favourite of the druid order' at which site 'sacrifices were performed'.[51] Throughout his volume, Borlase is a point of reference for Polwhele. His descriptions of the processions and ministrations of the Dartmoor druids in their stone rows and circles are clearly indebted to accounts in *Antiquities Historical and Monumental of the County of Cornwall*. The Cornish antiquary's claims that worship of Saturn, Mars, and Mercury could be discerned in Cornish place-names is quickly countered with the suggestion that Belstone was 'the town of Belus' (an ancient Babylonian god), Mistor 'the rock of Misor' (a Phoenician deity), and Hessary Tor 'the rock of Hesus' (a Gaulish divinity).[52] Borlase's description of rock basins is cited – and numerous examples of these are located on Dartmoor.[53] And noting that 'in Cornwall, Borlase has noticed a great number of [...] stone deities', Polwhele counters, 'in Devonshire we have an ample field for such investigation'.[54]

Borlase's extension of the category of 'Druidic monuments' to include striking geological features which (he imagined) had been worshipped as rock idols caused Polwhele some problems in conceptualising Dartmoor as a Druidic landscape. 'The misfortune', he mused, 'is that nature has exhibited her wild scenery in so many places, that we know not whither to direct our first attention.'[55] Contemplating the scores of rocky tors on the moor he worried:

> We are afraid to fix on a Druid-idol, lest the neighbouring mass should have the same pretensions to adoration; and all the stones upon the hills and in the vallies should start up into divinities. If Bowerman's Nose, for instance, in the vicinity of Dartmoor, be considered as a rock-idol of the druids, there is scarcely a torr on the forest, or its environs, but may claim the same distinction. [...] we shall meet divinities at every step [...] Thus Dartmoor would be one wide Druid temple; and its dark waste, now consecrated ground, would breathe a browner horror.[56]

The last sentence – taken entirely out of context – was quoted and held up for ridicule in J. P. Jones's anti-Druidical guide to Ashburton.[57] In the passage as a whole, however, it is difficult not to sense growing doubt on Polwhele's part about the viability of Borlase's claims. Ultimately, however, Polwhele withdrew from scepticism and instead proceeded to turn Dartmoor into 'one wide Druid temple'. The notion worked too well in his favour, allowing him to transform areas of Devon with no megalithic remains into Druidic sites. Exmoor, for instance, though it possessed 'no tradition of the Druids' could be 'examined with an eye to druidical antiquities' simply because of its unusual geology, while the 'Valley of the Stones' near Lynton, was 'so awfully magnificent, that we need not hesitate in pronouncing it to have been the favourite residence of Druidism'.[58] At Drewsteignton, too, the presence of 'an awful precipice' and 'gloomy chasms' was claimed to further verify the village's Druidic past, for 'than this spot, none could be more adapted to religious worship'.[59] Underlying these claims was the presupposition that the ancient British had shared the aesthetic sensibilities of the late eighteenth century, and that their priests, in particular, had effectively anticipated Edmund Burke's understanding of the sublime – and exploited its effects as efficiently as the poets and novelists of the Gothic genre, to inspire in their audiences 'a sort of religious terror'.[60]

The aesthetic theories of Edmund Burke were of central importance to the development of interest in megalithic remains in the south west during the Romantic period. By suggesting that 'grand and terrible scenes' could produce sublime and positively cathartic effects in the observer, Burke provided a framework for the appreciation of areas such as the Scottish highlands and Welsh mountains which had hitherto been briefly dismissed by writers like Defoe as 'productive of nothing'.[61] Once these ideas had been disseminated to the south west, writers living in areas like Dartmoor and Bodmin which had been similarly classified as 'sterile' and 'barren wastes' were quick to appeal to the sublime in accounts of their local landscapes, in hopes of attracting just a few of the growing numbers of tourists keenly seeking out violent emotion from the landscape.[62] In his 1819 epic poem *Cornubia*, for instance, the Truro author George Woodley proclaimed:

> What though the gen'ral aspect, bleak and drear
> Repel and mock the superficial eye; [...]
> If rocks and hills, in grand succession piled
> If aught sublime and terrible, though rude,
> By nature framed can solace Nature's child
> Let him turn hither.[63]

Woodley made much of his home county's 'cliffs sublime'.[64] Inland Cornwall caused him more difficulty, however. Carn Brea, the modest hill above Redruth, is described in by-then antiquated terminology as an 'aged mountain', but devoid of any real mountains or raging cataracts, he was forced to apologise for the general 'dreariness of the interior scenery' where 'scarcely aught awaits th'offended sight'.[65] One feature did rescue these areas from total vacuity, however: their 'hoary monuments'. In Woodley's verse, therefore, rock megaliths fulfil the aesthetic function of rocky mountains. They are 'wild, misshapen things', 'reared [...] when rugged nature swayed alone the earth', and like Snowdon or Mont Blanc they inspire 'visions' and 'holy terror'.[66] The seeds of this imaginative displacement may lie partly in the Renaissance use of 'mountain' for an artificial tumulus or similar monument. The Bristol poet Thomas Chatterton, in composing his 1768 medieval forgery 'The Battle of Hastings', deliberately drew on this archaic sense in describing the stones of Stanton Drew as 'a wondrous pyle of rugged mountaynes'.[67] But the aesthetic substitution practised by Woodley and others may also have been inspired by Stukeley, who in *Abury* had described that monument as 'so many mountains'.[68]

Megaliths were not only considered sublime because of the rude physical qualities they shared with mountains. Among the defining properties of the sublime in Burke's formulation were silence, darkness, and obscurity. These attributes further encouraged the evaluation of megalithic remains as sublime, as it meant that the very uncertainty and lack of knowledge surrounding the structures' origin and meaning (previously conceived of in purely negative terms) could now provide a basis for aesthetic appreciation of them. The possibility that their mysterious past had involved the death, burial, and ritual sacrifice outlined by Stukeley, Borlase, John Toland, and others also enhanced the frisson of terror necessary to the sublime. And the evident difficulty involved in the stones' erection also contributed to this effect. Burke observed:

> When any work seems to have required immense force and labour to effect it, the idea is grand. Stonehenge, neither for its position nor ornament, has anything admirable; but those huge rude masses of stone, set on end, and piled on each other, turn the mind on the immense force necessary for such a work.[69]

Wordsworth's Salisbury Plain poems, although the best remembered, were by no means the only works to follow Burke in evoking the sublimity of Stonehenge. The Gothic novelist and Bath resident Ann Radcliffe composed a long poem about the monument in 1826, which opens by asking:

> Whose were the hands that upheaved these stones?
> Standing like spectres under the moon, [...]
> And whose was the mind that willed them reign,
> The wonder of ages, simply sublime?
> The purpose is lost in the midnight of time;
> And shadowy guessings alone remain.[70]

The remainder of the poem thrilled and terrorised readers by sharing Radcliffe's own 'shadowy guessings', which – tipping the poem from sublimity into Gothic horror – associated the stones with sorcerers, spectres, and croaking ravens. A few years earlier, in 1823, Oxford University had offered the Newdigate Poetry Prize for verses on the subject of Stonehenge. The winning entry, by Thomas Stokes Salmon, suggests that (although Wordsworth's verses on Stonehenge as yet remained unpublished) the judges were hoping that the sublime terrors of the monument might be evoked. The prize poem opens by evoking the silent, the dark and the obscure:

> Wrap't in the veil of time's unbroken gloom,
> Obscure as death, and silent as the tomb,
> Where cold oblivion holds her dusky reign
> Frowns the dark pile on Sarum's lonely plain.[71]

It then proceeds to invoke the 'dread genius of the clime' who conjures up visions of the monument's Druidic past before proceeding triumphally through time to the dawn of Christianity. That this formula was by then becoming somewhat stereotypical is suggested by a rather less serious entry, submitted anonymously into the same competition:

> Can I not fancy all these stones upright;
> Thy surpliced priests, with mistletoe bedight
> With open mouths to catch the morning air,
> And crowds on crowds with open mouths too, stare!
> List, where the anthems semiquavered rise
> From G to G, and echo to the skies![72]

It is possible that Salmon's poem – if not the choice of subject for the Newdigate competition itself – was inspired by another poetry contest which had focused on the south west. In 1820, the Royal Society of Literature announced its first competition, with a prize of fifty guineas – for a poem on the subject 'Dartmoor'.[73] The winning entry, by Felicia Hemans, bore as its epigraph Thomas Campbell's lines 'Come, Bright Improvement'. As there is nothing to suggest that Hemans had ever visited Dartmoor (and she explicitly mentions the moor only once in her long poem), the fame of the region's prehistoric remains and their Druidic associations had clearly travelled as far as her North Wales home by 1820.[74] The poem envisages in grisly detail a druidic ritual at one of the moor's megalithic sites, in which a human victim is 'bound on the shrine of sacrifice' at 'dread midnight' to the sound of 'druid harps'.[75] This scene of past inhumanity is then juxtaposed with description of the dreary fate of Napoleonic prisoners held on the moor, to suggest a continuing history of gloom associated with (or somehow arising from) Dartmoor's uncultivated landscape, before the poem progresses (as its motto might lead one to expect) to visions of a future in which the region will be 'by busy culture drest / And the rich harvest wave upon [its] brest'.[76] As far as Hemans was concerned, Dartmoor was to England 'a dark cloud on summer's clear blue sky', or a 'mourner, circled with festivity'.[77] The moor suffered from 'a curse of barrenness' and its prehistoric remains were simply testament to a long history of backwardness from which modern agriculture would soon rescue it.[78]

Hemans's 'Dartmoor' is interesting as a point of reference when reading other Dartmoor poems from the same period and a little later which were composed within the south west. The first is Joseph Cottle's 'Dartmoor' – an unsuccessful entry in the Royal Society's competition (and prefaced rather pointedly in his 1823 collection of verse by the letter of rejection). Like Hemans, Cottle traces the moor's history from past Druidic sacrifice to the possibility of land reclamation – the day when the moor will yield 'her blasted heaths to labour, fruits and fields'.[79] Unlike Hemans, however, the Bristol publisher had visited the moor and its monuments at least twice.[80] This is reflected not only in the framing narrative of the poem – a detailed account of a long walk across the moor – but also in his attitude to Dartmoor. Although he looks conventionally towards the eventual improvement of the land (a project that he, like Hemans, must have known was being mooted in the 1820s), he views the moor not as simply 'barren', but rather as a 'sepulchral wilderness' which can 'commingle joy with dread'.[81] On Cottle's Dartmoor, 'rock idols' 'awe' the visitor, and visions arise of Druids in 'reeking vestments', sacrificing their victims where now stands only 'dismantled stone'.[82] Cottle's poem seems poised between Polwhele's desire to advertise Dartmoor's sublimity and Hemans's commitment to progress, but it is difficult not to sense that the poem's conclusion was simply a gesture intended to impress the judging committee at the Royal Society of Literature which was, after all, committed to the advancement of culture. The notes to the poem cite Borlase, quote Polwhele at length on the subject of Drewsteignton, and refer to a recent excursion to admire the Stanton Drew stone circle.

Nicholas Carrington's poem 'Dartmoor' was not entered into the Royal Society's competition. In his introduction to the edition of Carrington's poems published posthumously in 1834, his son claimed that Carrington had intended to become a competitor but that 'the premium was awarded several months before he became aware that the time for presenting it had gone by'.[83] Whether or not Carrington missed the deadline, his interest in Dartmoor was not simply motivated by the prospect of a prize: as a resident of Plymouth Dock, by 1820 he had already compiled and published a whole collection of poetry inspired by the countryside of Devon.[84] Like Polwhele, Carrington was inspired to remedy the prejudice that existed against his home region. 'The region to be illustrated has been too long stigmatised as another Nazareth, whence [...] no good thing can proceed [...] it has become a kind of fashion to traduce Dartmoor', he lamented in the preface to his poem, blaming this ultimately on Camden's mistaken derivation of the name Dartmoor from dirt.[85]

The poem sets out to rectify this. It contains a short, conventional vision of how Dartmoor might be developed in its early pages, but like Cottle's poem it spends more time in proclaiming the aesthetic value of the moor's wild state and by half way through proclaims:

> Detested be the hand
> The sacrilegious hand, that would destroy
> These mouldering walls, which time has kindly spar'd
> [...] from human grasp
> Rapacious, be each sacred pile preserv'd.[86]

Like Cottle's poem, too, it is framed by a walk across the moor, during which Carrington – in Wordsworthian mode – reminisces about a childhood growing up within the shadow of Dartmoor:

> Dartmoor! Thou wert to me, in childhood's hour,
> A wild and wondrous region. Day by day
> Arose upon my youthful eye thy belt
> Of hills mysterious [...]
> I gazed on thee. How often on the speech
> Of the half-savage peasant have I hung
> To hear of rock-crowned heights on which the cloud
> For ever rests; and wilds stupendous, swept
> By mightiest storms.[87]

The influence of Wordsworth is evident elsewhere. A note to Carrington's description of Wistman's Wood in the poem contains lines from 'Hart-Leap Well', and the epigraph to 'Dartmoor' is a pair of lines from 'Tintern Abbey'.[88] It is difficult not to conclude that its author self-consciously aimed to do for Dartmoor what Wordsworth had done for the Wye Valley and Lake District.

The moor's prehistoric remains and 'rock idols' were part of this project. The passage above continues by remembering inspiring tales of 'forms / That rose amid the desert, rudely shaped / By superstition's hands when time was young' and the poet then walks to visit these sites.[89] At Drewsteignton he stops to view the 'venerable pile' of the cromlech, demanding:

> Who that stops to gaze
> Upon the hoary Cromlech, rudely rais'd
> Above the nameless dead, can look unmov'd?[90]

Carrington mentions both Polwhele and Jones in his notes to 'Dartmoor' but disregarded the latter's warnings about delusory Druids in favour of the former's more colourful theories. At the striking geological feature known as Bowerman's Nose – 'a Granite God!' – he indulges in visions of 'the frantic seer' who 'here built his sacred circle' and 'with bloodiest rites [...] awed the prostrate isle'.[91]

'Dartmoor', when it was finally published in 1826, was well received by both the press and public: a second edition was printed just six weeks after the first, and George IV awarded Carrington a prize of fifty guineas for the poem.[92] The success seems to have inspired the poet to indulge his Druid fantasies further, for that same year he went on to compose 'The Druids: Written on the Borders of Dartmoor' which promises:

> The unhallowed hymn arose e'en from this very spot
> [...] And Time has not yet flung to earth the rude
> Romantic altar [...]
> Still the awful circle stands
> Majestic – venerable – time-worn.[93]

The poem proceeds to a lengthy vision, in which Borlase's images of sacrificial women and children, and sounding trumpets and cymbals are dominant:

> [...] O here the fair,
> The brave – the mother and her spotless babe –
> [...] In one vile holocaust, to fancied gods
> Poured out their souls in fire; amid the blast
> Which the loud trumpet flung – the deafening clash
> Of cymbal – and the frantic, frenzied yell
> Of an infuriate priesthood.[94]

It seems likely that Carrington may have continued to further success and more lasting renown had he not contracted tuberculosis just a year later. After his death in 1830, however, his promotion of Dartmoor and its antiquities was taken up by another Devon resident, the prolific Tavistock novelist Anna Eliza Bray, who quotes Carrington's verses approvingly throughout her three-volume 1836 work *The Borders of the Tamar and the Tavy*.

Bray's text began life as a series of forty-two letters about Dartmoor's geography, wildlife, folklore, and history, which were written between 1832 and 1835 to the poet laureate Robert Southey, with a view to future publication, and published in 1838. She is careful to conventionally assert in these letters that the project was begun at Southey's instigation. However, Bray also clearly viewed herself as working within a nascent tradition of Dartmoor writing. The work has as its epigraph lines from Carrington's 'Dartmoor' which assert: 'I own the power / Of local sympathy'.[95] This privilege is used to justify Bray's project of asserting the aesthetic appeal of the moor's geography, in order to educate those who 'choose to see the faults and deficiencies' of an unfamiliar area.[96] Like Woodley before her, Bray defended her home county's weather and landscape by stressing its sublime qualities which 'raise in [the mind ...] deep and impressive reflections'.[97] Her principal aim, however, seems to have been to publicise the moor's wealth of prehistoric remains.

Bray had been a friend of Polwhele and like him drew on Dartmoor's actual megalithic monuments to transform the entirety of the moor into a Druidic landscape. Around a third of *The Borders of the Tamar and the Tavy* is concerned with the Druids and the evidence of their presence on Dartmoor. Every stone circle, stone row, and standing stone on the moor is ascribed a Druidic purpose, but Bray also discerns among scattered boulders the remains of an archdruid's chair, and among the declivities of the land a 'cursus' (an oval earthwork like the one which Stukeley had identified at Stonehenge) which she imagines must have been used for 'the sacred processions of the priests'.[98] Like Polwhele, any 'curious rock' is taken as proof that a place was 'not unknown to the druids' and she concludes that 'where we find so many vestiges of Druidical antiquity, it is most natural to conclude that even [...] springs were held in veneration at a very remote period'.[99]

Clearly, by Bray's time, J. P. Jones did not stand alone in having expressed doubts about such totalising Druidic readings of the moor. Bray refers darkly to 'some, who have never even investigated these remains upon the Moor – who have never even seen them' but who have 'notwithstanding, taken upon themselves to assert that there are none to be found'.[100] Her response was to follow in the footsteps of both Stukeley and Borlase who had stressed the importance of fieldwork and observation, and to go to what seems to have been considerable trouble for an early nineteenth-century woman, in investigating them at first hand. She recounts countless horseback excursions across the moor; describes three-foot trenches which she and her husband dug beneath cromlechs; and relates climbing (with great trepidation, and to the amusement of local shepherds) to the top of tors in search of the Druidic rock basins described by Borlase in his study of Cornwall's antiquities.[101]

Borlase's interpretations of monuments are frequently cited with approval in *The Borders of the Tamar and the Tavy*.[102] Like Polwhele before her, though, Bray sought to prove that Dartmoor's Druidic inheritance was superior to Cornwall's. Pew Tor, she claimed, was 'in every respect more perfect than the judgement seat at Karnbre, in Cornwall, described by Borlase'.[103] Indeed, she asserted that 'no part of this kingdom had [...] a more celebrated station of Druidism than Dartmoor'. Of Stonehenge's greater magnitude than the Dartmoor monuments she was dismissive:

> On the plains of Salisbury, Nature had done nothing for the grandeur of Druidism, and art did all. [...] On Dartmoor, the priests appropriated the tors themselves as temples [...] their circles were only memorials of their consecration [...] In such scenes a Stonehenge would have dwindled in comparison with the granite tors into perfect insignificance; it would have been as a pyramid at the foot of Snowdon.[104]

Like Woodley, and Carrington, Bray is significant as one of the first authors to have realised the cultural value of the south west's megaliths to local economies. It is easy to dismiss the work of these writers as simply reiterating earlier antiquarian theories. However, each is of interest in having combined that eighteenth-century antiquarian research with the period's aesthetic theories and applied it in the service of a local area and for a popular readership. Out of the writings of such Romantic period authors developed the nineteenth century's lucrative industry of producing sketches and engravings of megalithic remains, and the antiquarian tourism to the south west that continues to this day, aided by countless websites, and by latter-day popular guides such as Julian Cope's 2003 *Modern Antiquarian*.[105] And while Bodmin and Dartmoor's tors are no longer viewed as 'rock idols', and its megaliths are now known to predate the Druids by hundreds of years, the association of Druids with the south west prevails in the popular imagination.[106]

Bray's impulse in publishing *The Borders of the Tamar and the Tavy* was not just to increase the public's estimation of and interest in her local area, however. In a letter to the book's publisher, she expressed her concern that among the prehistoric remains on the moor 'many of the originals no longer exist, from the destruction which for the last few years has unfortunately been allowed on Dartmoor' and in the book itself she relates that 'Dartmoor has, indeed, been a field to the spoiler; and many of its most interesting memorials have been destroyed within the last twenty or thirty years.'[107] There seems, therefore, to be present in her work an impulse to preserve the moor's monuments by raising public consciousness about their plight. Similar concerns can also be seen in Carrington's work. In the notes to 'Dartmoor', he records the destruction of several prehistoric monuments, including one used to make the step of a chapel at Ivybridge.[108]

The desire to preserve megalithic remains underpinned the earliest detailed studies of them. Stukeley 'thought it proper' to preface his 1743 *Abury* by deploring the destruction of the monument that was taking place because of 'the wretched ignorance and avarice of a little village unluckily plac'd within it'.[109] That a weighty antiquarian volume was not the best means of directly effecting a popular shift in attitude towards megaliths is suggested, however, by the publication in pamphlet form in 1795 of Charles Lucas's poem 'The Old Serpentine Temple of the Druids at Avebury'. The poem describes recent damage to the Avebury stones, in spite of Stukeley's calls for this to cease:

> [... One] huge stone falls, and forms a cot,
> Surrounds the little garden with a wall,
> Or as a boundary lays across the fields.
> [... Another] extended lies within the humble cot,
> And forms the floor.[110]

Dedicated to Adam Williamson, who had inherited the prehistoric monument along with Avebury Manor in 1789, Lucas's poem aimed to ensure that 'the gigantic ruins will escape that persecution they have so grievously and wantonly suffered within the present century'.[111] Its method for effecting this was to present Stukeley's theories about the stone circles, but 'in fewer words and far less learned lore'.[112]

Lucas, who was the curate at Avebury, has attracted no comment in discussions of Stukeley's contribution to the preservation of the megaliths there. It seems likely, however, that he may have been central to the survival of the Avebury monument. In the same way, Woodley, Carrington, Bray, and the other popular writers who celebrated the south west's megaliths in the Romantic period should not only be of interest as minor literary figures, interested in some of the subjects that attracted Wordsworth and Blake – or as simply popularisers of outdated antiquarian theories and approaches. They should also, and more importantly, be viewed as having been of vital and practical importance to the survival of the south west's monuments in the nineteenth century – and up to the present day.

Notes

1. William Cunnington, copy of letter to Richard Colt Hoare, 30 October 1806, in 'The Cunnington Papers', book 13, fol. 3, Wiltshire Archaeological and Natural History Society, Devizes Museum.
2. Cunnington, letter to Thomas Leman, 17 October 1801, Wiltshire Archaeological and Natural History Society, Devizes Museum; Christopher Chippindale, *Stonehenge Complete* (London: Thames & Hudson, 1994), 125.
3. This tradition was recorded by Richard Fenton in *A Tour in Quest of Genealogy, Through Several Parts of Wales, Somersetshire and Wiltshire* (London, 1811), 268.
4. Philip Crocker, letter (no. 35) to Cunnington, 1806, Wiltshire Archaeological and Natural History Society, Devizes Museum.
5. See Stuart Piggott, *Ancient Britons and the Antiquarian Imagination* (London: Thames & Hudson, 1989), 150–9.
6. Richard Hayman, *Riddles in Stone* (London: Hambledon, 1997), 274.
7. Joseph Cottle, 'Dartmoor', in *Dartmoor and Other Poems* (London, 1823), 23–6.
8. Chippindale, *Stonehenge Complete*, 20–6.
9. In Chippindale, *Stonehenge Complete*, 42.
10. Samuel Daniel, 'Musophilus', in *The Complete Works of Samuel Daniel*, ed. Alexander B. Grosart (5 vols, Aylesbury and London, 1885), i. 237.
11. W. P. Courtney, 'Charles Valentine Le Grice (1773–1858)', *Oxford Dictionary of National Biography* (Oxford: Oxford University Press, 2004).
12. Charles Le Grice, 'Inscription for Lanyon Cromlech in its Fallen State', in *The Petition of an Old Uninhabited House in Penzance* (Penzance, 1823), 2.
13. Hayman, *Riddles in Stone*, p. 42.
14. Hayman, *Riddles in Stone*, p. 42.
15. *Camden's Britannia, Newly Translated into English*, ed. Edmund Gibson (London, 1695), 6.
16. Thomas Bond, *Topographical and Historical Sketches of the Boroughs of East and West Looe, in the County of Cornwall* (London, 1823), 196.
17. Gibson, *Camden's Britannia*, 10; Bond, *Topographical and Historical Sketches*, 204, 202.

18. See Rosemary Hill, *Stonehenge* (London: Profile, 2008) for more on this subject.
19. Ronald Hutton, *The Druids* (London: Hambledon Continuum, 2007), 52.
20. Quoted in Chippindale, *Stonehenge Complete*, 68.
21. Chippindale, *Stonehenge Complete*, 70.
22. Gibson, *Camden's Britannia*, 108.
23. Hutton, *The Druids*, 54.
24. William Stukeley, *Stonehenge: a Temple Restor'd to the British Druids* (London, 1740), 40.
25. William Stukeley, *Abury: a Temple of the British Druids* (London, 1743), 51.
26. Stukeley, *Abury*, 1–2.
27. See, for instance, A. L. Owen, *The Famous Druids* (Oxford: Oxford University Press, 1962), 163–6, 225–32; Tom Duggett, 'Celtic Night and Gothic Grandeur: Politics and Antiquarianism in Wordsworth's *Salisbury Plain*', *Romanticism*, 13.2 (2007), 164–76; Jason Whittaker, *William Blake and the Myths of Britain* (Basingstoke: Macmillan, 1999).
28. William Borlase, *Antiquities Historical and Monumental of the County of Cornwall* (London, 1769 [1754]), vii.
29. Stukeley, *Stonehenge*, 2, 40, 56.
30. Stukeley, *Stonehenge*, 54.
31. Borlase, *Antiquities Historical and Monumental*, 53–157.
32. Borlase, *Antiquities Historical and Monumental*, 199.
33. Borlase, *Antiquities Historical and Monumental*, 127.
34. I.e. the division of prehistory into Stone, Bronze and Iron Ages.
35. Frederick Paas, *The Arch-Druid: an Historical Poem* (Sidmouth, 1830), 4.
36. J. P. Jones, *Observations on the Scenery and Antiquities in the Neighbourhood of Moreton-Hampstead* (Plymouth, 1823), 5.
37. Jones, *Observations*, 16.
38. Jones, *Observations*, 37.
39. Borlase *Antiquities Historical and Monumental*, v.
40. William Borlase, *The Natural History of Cornwall* (Oxford, 1758), v.
41. Borlase, *The Natural History of Cornwall*, v.
42. Elizabeth Baigent, 'William Chapple (1718–1781)', *Oxford Dictionary of National Biography* (Oxford: Oxford University Press, 2004). See also Patricia Milton, *The Discovery of Dartmoor: a Wild and Wondrous Region* (Chichester: Phillimore, 2006), 60.
43. William Chapple, *Description and Exegesis of the Drew's Teignton Cromlech* (Exeter, 1779), 1.
44. Chapple, *Description and Exegesis of the Drew's Teignton Cromlech*, 138.
45. See the discussion of Chapple in Richard Polwhele, *The History of Devonshire* (3 vols, Exeter, 1793–1806), i. 151, 153.
46. Polwhele, *The History of Devonshire*, i. 147.
47. Milton, *The Discovery of Dartmoor*, 62.
48. Polwhele, *The History of Devonshire*, i. 140.
49. Polwhele, *The History of Devonshire*, i. 140.
50. Polwhele, *The History of Devonshire*, i. 154.
51. Polwhele, *The History of Devonshire*, i. 154.
52. Polwhele, *The History of Devonshire*, i. 147.
53. Polwhele, *The History of Devonshire*, i. 149.
54. Polwhele, *The History of Devonshire*, i. 146.
55. Polwhele, *The History of Devonshire*, i. 146.

56. Polwhele, *The History of Devonshire*, i. 146.
57. Jones, *Observations*, 5.
58. Polwhele, *The History of Devonshire*, i. 147.
59. Polwhele, *The History of Devonshire*, i. 146.
60. Polwhele, *The History of Devonshire*, i. 148.
61. Daniel Defoe, *A Tour Thro' the Whole Island of Great Britain*, 4th edition (London, 1748), 360.
62. Defoe, *A Tour*, 360, 361.
63. George Woodley, *Cornubia: A Poem in Five Cantos, Descriptive of the Most Interesting Scenery, Natural and Artificial in the County of Cornwall* (London, 1819), 6.
64. Woodley, *Cornubia*, 135.
65. Woodley, *Cornubia*, 104, 92, 93.
66. Woodley, *Cornubia*, 96, 95, 106.
67. Thomas Chatterton, 'The Battle of Hastings', in *Poems, Supposed to have been Written at Bristol, by Thomas Rowley, and Others, in the Fifteenth Century* (London, 1777 [1768]), 264. For more on Chatterton's view of Stanton Drew see Nick Groom's essay in this collection.
68. Stukeley, *Abury*, 21.
69. Edmund Burke, *A Philosophical Enquiry into the Origin of our Ideas of the Sublime and Beautiful* (Oxford World's Classics Series, Oxford: Oxford University Press, 1998), 77.
70. Ann Ward Radcliffe, 'Salisbury Plains: Stonehenge', in *Gaston de Blondville and St Alban's Abbey* (London, 1826), 109.
71. Thomas Stokes Salmon, 'Stonehenge: a Prize Poem' (Oxford, 1823), quoted in Chippindale, *Stonehenge Complete*, 150.
72. Anon, 'Stonehenge: a Poem' (Oxford, 1823), quoted in Chippindale, *Stonehenge Complete*, 152.
73. Walter Thornbury, *Old and New London* (6 vols, London, Paris, and New York: Cassell, Petter and Galpin, 1878), iii. 149.
74. See Milton, *The Discovery of Dartmoor*, 81.
75. Felicia Hemans, 'Dartmoor: a Prize Poem', in *The Works of Mrs Hemans* (Edinburgh, 1839), 207.
76. Hemans, 'Dartmoor: a Prize Poem', 214.
77. Hemans, 'Dartmoor: a Prize Poem', 205.
78. Hemans, 'Dartmoor: a Prize Poem', 205.
79. Cottle, 'Dartmoor', 29.
80. Milton, *The Discovery of Dartmoor*, 81.
81. Cottle, 'Dartmoor', 13, 23, 14. See Milton, *The Discovery of Dartmoor*, 69–80, on plans to improve Dartmoor in the early nineteenth century.
82. Cottle, 'Dartmoor', 4, 22, 20.
83. N. T. Carrington, *The Collected Poems of the Late N. T. Carrington*, ed. H. E. Carrington (London, 1834), 16. Carrington himself does not mention this in his own introduction to the first edition of the poem, however, claiming that the poem had no relation to the competition but was written at the suggestion of the secretary of the Plymouth Chamber of Commerce. For this explanation see N. T. Carrington, 'Dartmoor: a Descriptive Poem' (London, 1826), cviii.
84. N. T. Carrington, *The Banks of the Tamar* (Plymouth, 1820).
85. Carrington, 'Dartmoor: a Descriptive Poem', v, vi.
86. Carrington, 'Dartmoor', in *The Collected Poems of the Late N. T. Carrington*, 52.
87. Carrington, 'Dartmoor', 7.

88. Carrington, 'Dartmoor', ix, 163.
89. Carrington, 'Dartmoor', 8.
90 Carrington, 'Dartmoor', 64.
91. Carrington, 'Dartmoor', 86.
92. Carrington, 'Dartmoor', 17.
93. Carrington, 'Dartmoor', 70.
94. Carrington, 'Dartmoor', 71, 72.
95. Anna Eliza Bray, *The Borders of the Tamar and the Tavy* (2 vols, London, 1879 [1838]).
96. Bray, *The Borders of the Tamar and the Tavy*, i. 4.
97. Bray, *The Borders of the Tamar and the Tavy*, i. 18.
98. Bray, *The Borders of the Tamar and the Tavy*, i. 127, 154.
99. Bray, *The Borders of the Tamar and the Tavy*, i. 156, 142.
100. Bray, *The Borders of the Tamar and the Tavy*, i. 39.
101. Bray, *The Borders of the Tamar and the Tavy*, i. 223.
102. See, for instance, Bray, *The Borders of the Tamar and the Tavy*, i. 153.
103. Bray, *The Borders of the Tamar and the Tavy*, i. 210.
104. Bray, *The Borders of the Tamar and the Tavy*, i. 60–1.
105. Julian Cope, *The Modern Antiquarian* (London: Thorsons, 1998).
106. See Hutton, *The Druids*, 121, 123.
107. Bray, *The Borders of the Tamar and the Tavy*, i. 6, 52.
108. Carrington, 'Dartmoor', 210.
109. Stukeley, *Abury*, 16.
110. Charles Lucas 'The Old Serpentine Temple of the Druids at Avebury' (Marlborough, 1795), 21.
111. Lucas, 'The Old Serpentine Temple of the Druids at Avebury', 3.
112. Lucas, 'The Old Serpentine Temple of the Druids at Avebury', 8.

2

'Al under the wyllowe tree': Chatterton and the Ecology of the West Country

Nick Groom

In considering English Romantic poets and their relationship with the West Country, the place of Thomas Chatterton appears at first sight to be straightforward and uncomplicated. Chatterton is the Bristol poet. He was so in the eighteenth century; he remains so today. Eighteenth-century commemorations such as *The Ode, Songs, Chorusses, &c. for the Concert in Commemoration of Chatterton … performed at the Assembly-Room, in Princes Street, Bristol* characterised him as Bristolian, 'the Celebrated Bristol Poet'.[1] Recent work continues to site Chatterton in the city; indeed, the subtitle of an edited collection published in 2005 is *Thomas Chatterton's Bristol*.[2] He made the city and the city made him – and in a sense, Chatterton quite literally made its history: William Barrett's *History and Antiquities of the City of Bristol* (1789) includes medieval material 'forged' by Chatterton.

This is somewhat ironic. Chatterton himself despised Bristol. He was, rather, a Redcliffe man – Redcliffe being by the eighteenth century a district of Bristol gathered around the mighty Gothic church of St Mary Redcliffe.[3] Indeed St Mary Redcliffe, which lies at the heart of the pseudo-medieval world of Thomas Rowley Chatterton created, was a church built to challenge Bristol Cathedral. St Mary Redcliffe dwarfs its competitor, and its most decorated façade actually stares challengingly out towards the Cathedral. Moreover, Chatterton famously fled Bristol, making the fateful trip eastwards to London and spending what were to be the final four months of his life in Shoreditch and Holborn. There, he penned the occasional diatribe against his former home city, bequeathing to Bristol in his mock 'Will', 'all my Spirit and Disinterestedness'.[4] And Bristol has since reciprocated Chatterton's disdain by resisting all but the most concerted attempts to celebrate the poet: a statue erected around 1840 was twice moved before being dismantled in 1967; today there is merely a mediocre bronze figure of Chatterton placed on the waterfront, a small plaque in St Mary Redcliffe, and a modest display in the church muniment room. What remains of his birthplace is dilapidated and under threat from developers.

The late eighteenth-century cultural scene in Bristol was, however, saturated by the life and works of Chatterton. After his death Chatterton was remembered as a maverick antiquarian laureate of Bristol's medieval culture, and as a fierce satirical commentator on local political affairs and contemporary social life. The generation of Romantic poets who worshipped Chatterton 'this side of idolatry' certainly imagined him as a Bristolian. This was one of the reasons for their deep devotion: he was a local lad to Robert Southey and Joseph Cottle, and also effectively so for the Devonian Samuel Taylor Coleridge. Coleridge was even haunted by Chatterton at the altar of St Mary Redcliffe as he made his marriage vows: 'poor Chatterton's Church –/ The thought gave me a tinge of melancholy to the solemn Joy, which I felt'.[5] Chatterton was a tutelary spirit, a daemon of inspiration who visited his brood in dreams and visions and who was made manifest in their verses as an enigmatic and elusive figure.[6]

Considered as a Bristol poet, Chatterton was also therefore considered to be a city poet. At the time, Bristol was a commercial centre and major slaving port, and after London and Norwich was one of the biggest cities in the country; it was also, in the words of Horace Walpole, 'the dirtiest great shop I ever saw'.[7] So Chatterton's move to London can be seen as cementing his urbanity. This was not only evident in his meteoric career as a popular political satirist and journalist: even his medievalism seems to mark Chatterton as a metropolitan writer. The world of Thomas Rowley is primarily a built environment of churches and towers; a material culture of manuscripts and coins; a civic scene of heraldry and pageants, letter writing, and antiquarian acquisition. 'Stay curyous Traveller and pass not bye' (a verse inserted into 'A Discorse on Brystowe') specifically describes medieval monuments as a vernacular architecture built to defy the winds and storms and by this human mastery of the elements paving the way to Heaven. Moreover, 'Stay curyous Traveller ...' is also a reworking of Edmund Spenser's verse, 'June' – thus the church and the weather are themselves interpreted by means of an archaic English literary model reworked by the poet.[8] So in writing about the church in the guise of Thomas Rowley, Chatterton adopts the images and conceits, the language, metre, and form of earlier poets: Chaucer, Spenser, Shakespeare, Milton – the emerging English canon. And realising that Chatterton's urban imagination was highly textualised, later critics occupied themselves in tracing Chatterton's sources, revealing that his medieval texts were in part patchworks of earlier writers ingeniously woven together by the poet, before being translated into 'Rowleyese'. As such, they were 'forged'.

But there are other ways of reading Chatterton, less implicated in the authenticity debates of the Rowley Controversy, and consequently little explored by critics for over two hundred years. For all his urbanity, Thomas Rowley was supposedly born in the rural parish of Norton Malreward, and the Rowleyan writings are littered with allusions to the natural environment. Indeed, before he died Chatterton was developing a characteristic representation of local landscape and its flora and fauna in his contemporary, non-Rowleyan verse: an imaginative topography at times highly specific to the West Country. This environmental approach therefore resists the division of Chatterton's work into the traditional categories of 'forged' Rowleyana and ephemeral topical writings by reading his Rowley texts and his contemporary texts together, and contrasting his 'country' pieces with his 'city' productions. From this, a small body of Chattertonian nature poetry emerges. Chatterton's nature poetry has a distinctive, highly flavoured character, but would become instrumental in the imaginings and reinventions of certain landscape features for the English Romantic poets. Although as so often in Chatterton any potential remains desperately unrealised, his development of environmental writing gives us a glimpse of a poetic style that blends the intricate textuality of Rowley with the vivacious topicality of his contemporary work, while ultimately remaining rooted in the immediate context of the ecology and culture of the West Country.

In Chatterton's earliest verse, the landscape is textualised much as the city is – through familiar and derivative poetic shorthand and canonical allusion. The 'Bristowe Tragedie' opens with the standard medievalism of a crowing cockerel (Chaunticleer), a croaking raven, and a predictably foreboding red sky. 'The Tournament' ('Unknown Knyght' version) also features a morning call from a cockerel and describes the violence of the tourney with a stock Chatterton image of an oak struck by lightning. Similarly, the images of battle in 'Hastings II' rely on thunder, or on images such as of arrows flying like a flight of cranes; these extended metaphors seem to be derived from translations of classical epics (contemporaries noted that similar images appear in Alexander Pope's translation of *The Iliad*). Even the more accomplished 'Ælla' opens with a nod towards the diurnal passage of the sun.

These flights of cranes then are not any more real than the myrtle groves and saffron dreams that characterise Chatterton's hackwork for John Baker – verses he ghostwrote for his friend to speed his courtship of Miss Eleanor Hoyland.[9] A more elegant rendering of such familiar conceits is perhaps found in 'A Song. Addressed to Miss C----am of Bristol', but thankfully, Chatterton was soon parodying such arch and bloodless sophistication in his elegies: the first 'Elegy', for example, presents a landscape that shifts from sweet melancholy into a knowing apocalyptic cliché before swiftly collapsing at the absurd lament, 'lady Betty's tabby cat is dead' (40).

Likewise, Chatterton's handling of place is often unremarkable. An early working of Chatterton's St Werburgh of Redcliffe legend, 'Ynn Auntient Dayes', displays a lamentable confusion of natural imagery. The poem describes the Washford River in Somerset ('Waskar' in the poem) surrounded by dank fields; mist rises from the scene – and yet at the same time fishes glitter in the early morning sunlight, elm trees are swayed by the wind, and clouds scud across the skies. It is not the Washford River that flows through the grassland area of Cleeve Hill in Somerset, but an estuary of the imagination. Chatterton doubtless selected the spot because of the nearby remains of Cleeve Abbey – probably the best preserved Cistercian abbey in England, which by Chatterton's time had been converted into a farmhouse.

'The Storie of Wyllyam Canynge', in contrast, is far more successful. This piece begins with a description of a river, probably the Trym running into the Avon, and then the Avon into the Severn. As the water flows, it gradually becomes an allegorical figure, as if emerging from the pages of Michael Drayton's *Poly-Olbion* (1612–13):

> Anent a brooklette as I laie reclynd,
> Listeynge to heare the water glyde alonge,
> Myndeynge how thorowe the grene mees yt twynd,
> Awhilst the cavys respons'd yts mottring songe,
> At dystaunt rysying Avonne to he sped,
> Amenged wyth rysyng hylles dyd shewe yts head.

> Engarlanded wyth Crownes of osyer weedes
> And wraytes of Alders of a bercie scent,
> And stickeynge out wyth clowde agested reedes,
> The hoarie Avonne show'd dyre semblamente,
> Whylest blataunt Severne, from Sabryna clepde,
> Rores flemie o'er the sandes that she [hath] hepde.[10]

'The Storie' is possibly based on the popular song 'Midsummer Wish' (wrongly attributed to Chatterton as 'Where woodbines hang their dewy Heads'), as well as drawing upon such early poets as Chaucer and Spenser and of course Drayton. Chatterton is therefore blending material from popular songs with the early English tradition. This may be why he was so entranced by Percy's *Reliques of Ancient English Poetry* (1765), in which popular songs and ballads were anthologised alongside forgotten older poets – which would prove highly suggestive for Burns's first collection, *Poems Chiefly in the Scottish Dialect* (1786), and Wordsworth and Coleridge's work towards *Lyrical Ballads* (1798). Chatterton made a direct connection between traditions of English poetry tied to the land, contemporary popular verse forms, and the voice of the people – the 'real language of men'.[11] Indeed, in a very real sense Chatterton *was* that connection.

Like 'The Storie', 'Heccar and Gaira' also begins with a river. The passage of the African Caigra is sublime:

> Where the rough Caigra rolls the surgy wave,
> Urging his thunders thro the echoing/distant cave;

Where the sharp rocks, in distant horror seen,
Drive the white currents thro' the spreading green.[12]

Likewise 'The Death of Nicou', another 'African Eclogue', also begins with a protracted description of a river:

> On Tiber's banks, Tiber, whose waters glide
> In slow meanders down to Gaigra's side;
> And circling all the horrid mountain round,
> Rushes impetuous to the deep profound;
> Rolls o'er the ragged rocks with hideous yell;
> Collects its waves beneath the earth's vast shell:
> There for a while in loud confusion hurl'd,
> It crumbles mountains down and shakes the world.
> Till borne upon the pinions of the air,
> Through the rent earth the bursting waves appear;
> Fiercely propell'd the whiten'd billows rise,
> Break from the cavern, and ascend the skies:
> Then lost and conquer'd by superior force,
> Thro' hot Arabia holds its rapid course.[13]

Wylie Sypher argued long ago that Chatterton's source here was Alexander Catcott's hydro-geological theory *Treatise on the Deluge* (1768 edition).[14] Catcott, whose theories are attacked by Chatterton in his 'Epistle. To the Revd. Mr. Catcott' and then adopted for the 'African Eclogues', proposed that the waters of the world flow through subterranean channels, occasionally bursting to the surface.[15] But while the influence of Catcott is indisputable, the lines should also be read alongside the immediate experience of the Clifton Gorge, which coloured Chatterton's tumultuous descriptions. The cliffs in the 'African Eclogues' could, for instance, be modelled directly on St Vincent's Rocks in Clifton Gorge, about which *The Bristol and Hotwell Guide* boasted in 1793:

> in some places the rocks rise venerably majestic, perpendicular, or over-hanging, craggy, and bare; in others clothed with the most luxuriant shrubs and stately trees, all rising one after the other in their wildest state, displaying the greatest variety of verdure, accompanied with every hue, and elegance of colour, that Nature could bestow on her most favourite productions, to gratify the eye or charm the sense; the ground also on which we tread abounds with a variety of rare flowers, aromatic plants, and other herbaceous productions, not to be met with in any other part of *England*, here grow spontaneously, and the air being perfumed with their refreshing fragrance, the valetudinarian seems to breathe new life, and to enjoy again the blessings that await returning health and cheerfulness.[16]

But there are other environmental sources. The Bristol Channel – the 'Severn Sea' as Chatterton would have known it – was itself a particularly treacherous stretch of water. John Dolman, local preacher, described its capricious extremes:

> Sometimes it seemed as if GOD had closed his Hand and bound up the Wind in his Fist; so that the Whole Breadth (I think about seven Miles) appeared as smooth as a Bowling Green ...
>
> AT other Times I've been there when the Almighty seem'd to throw abroad his Fingers, and loose the Winds out of his Fist, so that the Waters held in the Hollow of his Hand seem'd troubled. O how did one Wave lift itself up against another! with what a Surge did they frequently meet, and dash each other in Pieces, as if their Rage knew no Bounds; tho' GOD has set a Boundery [*sic*] unto it. One of these boisterous Times whilst at an Anchor in a large Trow, half deck'd, I saw Part of the Top-Sail of another that was overset driving down, and some or all of her Men rowing in the Small-Boat to reach the Shore. A Sloop I likewise saw the same Time that seemingly weathered it very well, but as she was turning into the River *Avon* to go up to *Bristol*, down she sunk to the Bottom. When the Tide came we weighed Anchor, loosed our Sails, and proceeded on our Passage; we had not far gone before GOD seem'd to be angry with us, and I believe one and all on board (upwards of Forty Persons) thought we should have had a watery Grave; the Heavens gathered Blackness, the falling Hail pursued us, and GOD brought the Winds out of his Treasure much stronger than before ...[17]

The Severn estuary has the second largest tidal range in the world, and this gives rise to the phenomenon of the Bore: a funnelling effect in which water is forced upstream against the current of the river. Daniel Defoe, in his *Tour Thro' the Whole Island of Great Britain*, described the Severn Sea as

> indeed a most raging and furious kind of Sea. This is occasioned by those violent Tides called the *Bore*, which flow here sometimes 6 or 7 Feet at once, rolling forward like a mighty Wave, so that the Stern of a Vessel shall on a sudden be lifted up 6 or 7 Feet upwards on the Water, when the head of it is fast aground.[18]

This stunning effect informs the tumultuous movements of water in 'The Death of Nicou'. In other words, then, that poem, written from Chatterton's garret in London's Holborn, is a poem of nostalgia for the Severn Sea – and so despite its Orientalism, it is a peculiarly West Country poem. Likewise 'Narva and Mored', written a month previously in Shoreditch, mixes a yearning for old rural England with the fantastical fauna of elks and macaws. The African 'sons of war and blood' race through a thunderstorm to a sacred oak. The storm passes and the sun sets in the West, reflected in the water:

> Furious they twist around the gloomy trees,
> Like leaves in autumn, twirling with the breeze.
> So when the splendor of the dying day
> Darts the red lustre of the wat'ry way.[19]

The image of the autumn leaves on the breeze is quintessentially English. And it transpires that the lovers Narva and Mored have, in a way, gone to Britain – in the sense that they have been taken by slavers for British colonies in America:

> Far from the burning sands of Calabar;
> Far from the lustre of the morning star;
> Far from the pleasure of the holy morn;
> Far from the blessedness of Chalma's horn:
> Now rest the souls of Narva and Mored,
> Laid in the dust, and number'd with the dead.[20]

By describing the African landscape with English imagery and infusing the poem with the overwhelming menace of the slave trade, Chatterton seems preternaturally aware of what we now describe as a 'post-colonial' imagination.[21]

In contrast to these disguised views of the West Country from afar, 'Clifton' is a topographical study in the tradition of the landscape poem, and so promises local specificity.[22] But it comes from an unexpected quarter. The position of the poet seems to be conventional enough:

> Here as I musing take my pensive stand,
> Whilst evening shadows lengthen o'er the land,
> O'er the wide landscape cast the circling eye,
> How ardent mem'ry prompts the fervid sigh;
> O'er the historic page my fancy runs,
> Of Britain's fortunes – of her valiant sons.[23]

Yet having set this scene, Chatterton literally changes. His imagination runs to Saxons and Danes and civil war, and then makes an abrupt, personal shift to performances of Shakespeare's plays in Bristol by the late actor William Powell (also celebrated in 'To Mr. Powell'). The prospect poem becomes an elegy. This unexpected movement is suggested by the invocation of the 'historic page': it is as if the textuality of the 'historic page' image itself summons literature in the shape of Shakespeare's two plays that knit together British history and the supernatural – *Macbeth* and *Richard III*. So Chatterton is not merely echoing lines and images of earlier poets, rather the memory of Powell's Shakespearian roles – both being roles of usurpers – usurps the poem itself, and simultaneously reminds us of supernatural elements within national history. Chatterton is not in complete control of the magic he is weaving: he becomes instead its medium.

Such a loss of control over the idea of place occurs most strikingly in 'Elegy, Written at Stanton Drew'. Stanton Drew is a vast henge monument and the second largest stone circle complex in Britain; it lies just over seven miles south of Redcliffe, just beyond Rowley's birthplace at Norton Malreward.[24] The Stanton Drew stones were known as 'The Wedding' and had associations of thwarted love: 'a tradition which passes among the common people, *That as a Bride was going to be married, she and the rest of the company were chang'd into these stones.*'[25] By adding to this grim association the Gothick paraphernalia of (yet another) blasted oak, a Druid priest with a golden knife, and smoking blood (a favourite image), Chatterton imbues the stony-faced megaliths with a strange spirit of place.

It is perhaps tempting to see in 'Written at Stanton Drew' a forerunner of William Wordsworth's vision of Stonehenge on Salisbury Plain, but Chatterton's poem did not appear until the Southey–Cottle edition of Chatterton's *Works* in 1803, and Wordsworth, like other eighteenth-century laureates of the stones, only imagines he can see the Druids and hear them sing. Chatterton, however, discerns something else: mediating between his unrequited passion for Maria and the remote folk memory of the Ancient British rituals of human sacrifice, there is a 'troubled Spirit near' that 'Hovers in the steamy Air' – something uncontained by the conventions of this graveyard meditation.[26] This unnerving 'troubled Spirit' is unique to Chatterton's megalithic muse. The poet at Stanton Drew is not merely a visionary dreamer; he is fey. Again, for a moment, the poet cannot control his imagination: he has succeeded in summoning something supernatural, something that will continue to haunt later Romantic poems. Consequently, 'Written at Stanton Drew' offers a way of engaging with the historical resonances of particular places without lapsing into the tired tropes of eighteenth-century topographical verse. It disturbs the figure of the poet with eerie presences, unaccounted for elsewhere in the poem – and the poet's imagination is faced with recognising a manifestation of something within itself that lies beyond its own capacity to imagine.

The 'troubled Spirit' hovering 'in the steamy Air', like the weird calm following the thunderstorm in 'Narva and Mored', also indicates Chatterton's growing awareness of weather effects. The excessive piling up of meteorological conditions in 'Ynn Auntient Dayes' is calmed in 'Elinoure and Juga', which uses the same palette of riverscape and micro-climate in a far more controlled way. The 'daise-ey'd banke' is 'wette wythe mornynge dewe and evene danke', and like the Waskar (Washford River) the softly flowing river

Rudborne is strangely 'limed [glassy]' – this is a scene suspended in dreadful expectation, chilled by dankness. Clouds lour: 'mokie cloudis do hange upon the leme'. And although the place is overly dressed with 'levynde [blasted] okes' and 'lethale [deadly, or deathboding] ravens bark, and owlets wake the nyghte', these melodramatic intrusions are now entangled with the anxieties of Elinour and Juga themselves, who are fearful that their husbands have been slain in battle. At the muted climax of the eclogue, the two characters become at one with the dismal place through a process of (English) metamorphosis,

> lyke twa levyn blasted-trees,
> Or twayne of cloudes that holdeth stormie rayne;
> Theie moved gentle oere the dewie mees,

before sinking themselves in the river to drown.[27]

Chatterton is in fact particularly interested in the effects of bad weather – rain, characteristically English rain – rather than with the sunshine. 'February', for instance, is a sodden elegy:

> Ye channels, wand'ring thro' the spacious street,
> In hollow murmurs roll the dirt along,
> With inundations wet the sabled feet,
> Whilst gouts responsive, join th'elegiac song.[28]

This is typical everyday verse of the period, a witty embroidery of traditional weatherlore, urban drainage, and the fashionable incapacity of the gout. But Chatterton's poem is not simply a modish rewrite of 'A Description of a City Shower': 'February' is less gruesomely satirical and more deliberately mundane than Swift's apocalyptic sewer, and moreover Chatterton's attention is unusually fixed on the tiny detail of raindrops – 'The bounding hail, or drilling rain descend'. The progress of the storm is a physical reality:

> Now dropping particles of water fall;
> Now vapours riding on the north wind's wing,
> With transitory darkness shadow all.[29]

If 'February' is Chatterton's contemporary verse of inclement weather, 'Narva and Mored' is his African rain song. The swift clouds are depicted as 'distilling rain' (28), as if the Africans' understanding of weather phenomena is actually more enlightened than that of their pursuers and eventual captors, whose more conventional European cultural images of the weather follow hard on their heels:

> Upon whose top the black'ning tempest lours,
> Whilst down its side the gushing torrent pours.[30]

In England, the rainy climate was held to contribute to the national temper of the people: English phlegmatism. But Chatterton is not simply advocating that a racial difference is meteorologically determined; his point is more subtle: racial and cultural differences create different relationships with the weather, different ways of reading the rain. And so similarly, if 'Narva and Mored' is Chatterton's African rain song, then 'An Excelente Balade of Charitie' is his medieval parable of an unseasonal downpour.

'An Excelente Balade of Charitie' begins with the ripening sun as a prelude to the storm:

> In Virgyne the sweltrie sun gan sheene,
> And hotte upon the mees [meads] did caste his raie.

Local detail is added in apples and pears, traditional West Country fruit, and the pied goldfinch, a resident British songbird:

> The apple rodded [reddened, ripened] from its palie greene,
> And the mole [soft] peare did bende the leafy spraie;
> The peede chelandri sunge the livelong daie.[31]

These pears are significant: they recall the figure of Autumn in 'Ælla', garbed in a very similar dress:

> Whann the fayre apple, rudde as even skie,
> Do bende the tree unto the fructyle grounde;
> When joicie peres, and berries of blacke die,
> Doe daunce yn ayre, and call the eyne arounde.[32]

Moreover, fruiterers crying 'juicy Pears' mark the arrival of the autumn season in John Gay's *Trivia* (1716), as they do in James Thomson's 'Autumn' (1730; l. 625).[33] It is worth noting in passing therefore that although there is much apple poetry in, for example, John Philips's Georgic poem *Cyder* (1708), the only texts of the period to mention 'soft pears' are horticultural treatises.

Against this backdrop of seasonal local fruit, Chatterton is fascinated by the onset of the late summer rain shower – as his interest in dew, dank mists, and storms would suggest:

> The sun was glemeing in the midde of daie,
> Deadde still the aire, and eke the welken [the sky, the atmosphere] blue,
> When from the sea arist in drear arraie
> A hepe of cloudes of sable sullen hue,

The which full fast unto the woodlande drewe,
Hiltring [hiding, shrouding] attenes [at once] the sunnis fetive
[beauteous] face,
And the blacke tempeste swolne and gatherd up apace.[34]

Over a third of this poem, based on the parable of the Good Samaritan, is meteorological description. In 'Elinour and Juga' local fauna is mentioned fleetingly in the domestic agricultural detail of the hunt and the impact of Game Laws on the countryside:

No moe the amblynge palfrie and the horne
Shall from the lessel rouze the foxe awaie ['lessel' is glossed, 'in a confined sense, a bush or hedge, though sometimes used as a forest'].[35]

In contrast, 'An Excelente Balade' reveals that Chatterton's attention to such detail is far from incidental. Drawing on 'February', he again scrutinises the raindrops and their effect on the dry meadows and the grazing livestock:

The gatherd storme is rype; the bigge drops falle;
The forswat [sun-burnt] meadowes smethe [smoke], and drenche
[drink] the raine;
The comyng ghastness do the cattle pall [fright],
And the full flockes are drivynge ore the plaine.[36]

The shower becomes a storm. Lightning strikes and the inevitable thunder roars and rattles:

Dashde from the cloudes the waters flott [fly] againe;
The welkin opes; the yellow levynne [lightning] flies ...

Liste! now the thunder's rattling clymmynge [noisy] sound
Cheves [moves] slowlie on, and then embollen [swelled,
strengthened] clangs,
Shakes the hie spyre, and losst, dispended, drown'd,
Still on the gallard [frighted] eare of terroure hanges;
The windes are up; the lofty elmen swanges;
Again the levynne and the thunder poures,
And the full cloudes are braste [burst] attenes in stonen showers.[37]

Chatterton's meteorological imagination is thus characterised by high winds that threaten spires and sway trees, blasts of thunder and lightning, and rain – from misty precipitation to torrential downpours. Getting soaked in a shower of rain is a repeated image in Chatterton's poetry. One is reminded of the story about Coleridge, racing out into a storm and removing his hat so he could feel the rain on his head. Likewise, such weather forms the substance of Wordsworth's 'Thorn':

> 'Twas mist and rain, and storm and rain ...
> Head-foremost, through the driving rain (188–94),

and his lines,

> A whirl-blast from behind the hill
> Rush'd o'er the wood with startling sound:
> Then all at once the air was still,
> And showers of hail-stones patter'd round. (1–4)

These are not picturesque English pastoral showers, but a confrontation with nature wet in face and foot.

Rain is also of course crucial for the flora of England, and indeed Chatterton makes abundant use flower imagery. Again, he follows earlier, textual models before developing his own botanical aesthetic. 'Englysh Metamorphosis' for instance, which tells of the creation of Snowdon from the ashes of a giant, is taken from Spenser's *Faerie Queene* (II x 5–19). What is significant here, however, is Chatterton's relish for the detail of flowers, 'The mornynge tynge, the rose, the lillie floure', and place, 'Eft wandringe yn the coppyce, delle, and grove'.[38] This, too, is Spenserian and clearly Chatterton is still ramping like a young horse let loose in the fields of fancy – but his writing gradually draws closer to the flowers themselves, and to their habitats.

The first 'Mynstrelles Songe' in 'Ælla' is typical: the

> Bryghte sonne has ne droncke the dewe
> From the floures of yellowe hue;[39]

and while this too is ultimately Spenserian, the immediate source here is probably Swift's 'Panegyric on the Dean'.[40] But then Chatterton draws the scene into focus by describing with much sharper clarity:

> harke,
> How the ouzle [the blackbird] chauntes hys noate,
> The chelandree [gold-finch], greie morn larke,
> Chauntynge from theyre lyttel throate ...
>
> > See along the mees so grene
> > Pied daisies, kynge-coppes swote ...
> >
> > See! the crokynge brionie
> > Rounde the popler twyste hys spraie;

Rounde the oake the greene ivie
Florryschethe and lyveth aie.[41]

While Jeremiah Milles suggests the influence of Theocritus (*Idyll* xxvii, which Chatterton could have read in Dryden's translation), this level of natural history detail and specificity is unusual in the verse of the period.[42] And Chatterton rapidly seems to recognise that he has struck a rich seam here. He immediately moves into a second 'Mynstrelles Songe', which begins:

The boddynge flourettes bloshes atte the lyghte;
The mees be sprenged wyth the yellowe hue;
Ynn daiseyd mantels ys the mountayne dyghte;
The nesh [tender] yonge coweslepe bendeth wyth the dewe …[43]

and so on.[44] The specificity remains literary: there is nothing unusual about Chatterton invoking the 'nesh yonge coweslepe' (he also does so in 'February') – cowslips were mentioned in scores of songs after Ariel's song from *The Tempest*, and dozens of poems after 'Lycidas':

Bring the rathe primrose that forsaken dies,
The tufted crow-toe, and pale jessamine,
The white pink, and the pansy freaked with jet,
The glowing violet
The musk-rose and, the well-attired woodbine,
With cowslips wan that hang the pensive head,
And every flower that sad embroidery wears:
Bid amaranthus all his beauty shed,
And daffadillies fill their cups with tears … (142–50)

But other Chattertonian flora is less common.[45] In 'Eclogue the First', Roberte laments the loss of his small estate:

Oh! I coulde wayle mie kynge-coppe-decked mees [meadows],
Mie spreedynge flockes of shepe of lillie white;
Mie tendre applynges [grafted trees]; and embodyde [thick, stout] trees;
Mie Parker's Grange [liberty of pasture given to the Parker], far spreedynge to the syghte;
Mie cuyen [tender] kyne [cows] mie bullockes stringe [strong] yn fyghte:
Mie gorne [garden] emblaunched [whitened] with the comfreie plante [comfrey, a favourite dish at that time]:
Mie floure [marygold] Seyncte Marie shotteyng wythe the lyghte.[46]

The only works of English poetry that included reference to comfrey in the period 1760–1800 were a new edition of Drayton[47] and (on account of its medicinal properties) Gilbert West's translation of Pindar's 'The Triumphs of the Gout'.[48] The primrose was more popular, appearing in songs and fashionable poetry such as Mark Akenside's *Pleasures of the Imagination* as well as in Wordsworth's later 'Lines written in Early Spring'. The marigold ('floure Seyncte Marie'; marygold), however, was again scarce. It only merits inclusion in Erasmus Darwin's *The Botanic Garden* in two footnotes and appears just a handful of times in contemporary verse, mainly in the 1790s.[49] Coleridge, however, mentions the marigold in a footnote to 'Ode to Sara', in order to explain its supernatural radiance.[50] And yet it was popular a century before in work that was reviving in the later eighteenth century: the plays of Beaumont and Fletcher, the poems of Thomas Carew, William Browne's *Britannia's Pastorals*, Abraham Cowley's *History of Plants*, and of course Perdita's speech in *The Winter's Tale* and in Shakespeare's Sonnet XXV. Chatterton is reintroducing an earlier floral sensibility through his descriptions of local West Country habitats.

Similarly, after describing the deluge of the Tiber in 'The Death of Nicou', Chatterton again turns to flowers:

> On Tiber's banks, where scarlet jass'mines bloom,
> And purple aloes shed a rich perfume:
> Where, when the sun is melting in his heat,
> The reeking tygers find a cool retreat;
> Bask in the sedges, lose the sultry beam,
> And wanton with their shadows in the stream.[51]

This is not just poetic reaffirmation. There is a shimmering sense of newness and wonder at the natural world in this passage. 'Scarlet jasmines' are mentioned nowhere else in verse of the period, likewise 'purple aloes' – and so the botanical particularity lends a thrilling originality and immediate topicality to the verse. Even the 'reeking tyger' is wholly original. Chatterton is also the first poet to use root ginger in poetry (he was himself excessively fond of gingerbread): 'Narva and Mored' describes

> Where Gingers aromatic, matted root,
> Creep through the mead, and up the mountains shoot.[52]

These exotic sights, sounds, smells, and tastes would later influence the sensuousness of later poetry: Kubla Khan's 'honey dew', for instance, or Porphyro's spread for Madeline in *The Eve of St Agnes*:

> ... a heap
> Of candied apple, quince, and plum, and gourd;
> With jellies soother than the creamy curd,

> And lucent syrops, tinct with cinnamon;
> Manna and dates, in argosy transferr'd
> From Fez; and spiced dainties, every one,
> From silken Samarcand to cedar'd Lebanon. (xxx)

And as for Keats, his favourite line in Chatterton was supposedly from 'O! synge untoe mie roundelaie':

> Comme, wythe acorne-coppe & thorne,
> Drayne mie hartys blodde awaie;
> Lyfe & all yttes goode I scorne,
> Daunce bie nete, or feaste by daie.[53]

'O! synge untoe mie roundelaie' (a 'Mynstrelles Songe') is perhaps the most telling example of the growing confidence of Chatterton's nature poetry. It reads as if Chatterton has left his books and desk and got out into the fields. Every stanza of this lament of a lady for her dead lover is spun from flora and fauna. Like much of his earlier nature poetry, 'O! synge untoe mie roundelaie' begins with an invocation of water, 'Lycke a reynynge ryver bee', before figuring the memory of the lover through a succession of restrained allusions – 'morneynge lyghte', 'throstles note', 'evenynge cloude', 'baren fleurs', 'brieres'.[54]

The most striking lines, however, occur in the refrain,

> Mie love ys dedde,
> Gon to hys death-bedde,
> Al under the wyllowe tree.

This refrain recalls both Desdemona's song of 'willow' and Ophelia's lament.[55] Donald Taylor also notes the parallels in Percy's *Reliques*: the hero in 'Gil Morrice', roundelays and tabours in 'The Fairies' Farewell', and 'Lucy and Colin' for the raven and the death of the maiden. These are telling allusions. If the *Reliques* offered an alternative canon of popular indigenous verse – the language really spoken by men – the influence of Percy's collection on later work becomes all the more acute when one perceives it being reworked by Chatterton. 'O! synge untoe mie roundelaie' does not just demonstrate the possibilities of ballads and songs as raw poetic material: it is significant that it was Chatterton who made that innovation, a poet of the West Country. And he did so by amplifying the shared natural imagery of place and text. This also in part explains Chatterton's extraordinarily prolific output: he was composing within the frames of popular songs and ballads, and for his Rowley works then translating these lines into his medieval. English A quarter of a century later, Wordsworth and Coleridge took the

Reliques as a point of departure for rethinking poetic traditions: *Lyrical Ballads* was, in one sense, forged in the tradition of Chattertonian composition. This influence can be seen in the image of the willow tree. Until Chatterton, the best-known contemporary reference to willow was in John Philips's Miltonic poem, *The Splendid Shilling*, in which the poet is beset with dismal thoughts of a

> desperate Lady near a purling Stream,
> Or Lover pendent on a Willow-Tree.[56]

There are, however, surprisingly few mentions of the willow tree in other eighteenth-century poems, and over half of these occur in verse of the 1790s.[57] And while Chatterton's own lines are significantly quoted by Coleridge's friend Jospeh Hucks in his 'Ode to Pity', nearly all are merely passing references.[58] Typical of late eighteenth-century willow poetry is Joseph Holden Pott's 'Ode on a Favourite Seat' – the seat in question being under a willow tree – and none have Chatterton's shadows of melancholy and menace, echoing from Shakespeare's songs of Ophelia and Desdemona.[59] So Chatterton decants Shakespearian drama into the everyday landscape – much as he does in 'Clifton'. Interestingly, the willow song occurs at least once again in Chatterton's poetry in the fragment 'Heraudyn', first published in 1803. This appears to be a reworking of the motifs of 'O! synge untoe mie roundelaie', as if the verse had made as much an impression on Chatterton himself as it would do on later poets. The Shakespearian resonance is even stronger here, haunting the flora of Chatterton's landscapes:

> Ynge Heraudyn al bie the grene Wode sate,
> Hereynge the swote Chelandrie ande the Oue [ouzel],
> Seeinge the kenspecked amaylde flourettes nete,
> Envyngynge to the Birds hys Love songe true.
> Syrre Preeste camme bie ande forthe hys bede-rolle drewe,
> Fyve Aves and on Pater moste be sedde;
> Twayne songe: the on hys Songe of Willowe Rue
> The odher one —— [60]

Despite the prevalence of the willow, perhaps the most typical flower in Chatterton is the king-cup: 'Lyche kynge-cuppes brastynge wythe the morning due' ('Songe to Aella').[61] Reading Chatterton for his 'Natural History' project, John Clare noted that 'Chatterton seemd fond of taking his similes from nature his favourite flower seems to be the "kingge coppe"', and this was his favourite line.[62] As John Goodridge has pointed out, Clare used it in 'Summer Images': 'And slender king cup burnished with the dew / Of morning's early hours'.[63]

The king-cup is a crowsfoot, also called the butter-flower, butter-cup, gold-cup, and gold-knop.[64] The name is technically precise, and consequently unlike many other flowers the king-cup does not feature in botanical or horticultural treatises – it is a literary term. King-cups are mentioned by Spenser in his *Shepherd's Calendar*: 'Strow me the ground with daffadowndillies / And cowslips, and kingcups, and loved lilies', a passage considered in Chatterton's time to be the source of Milton's flower passage in 'Lycidas', mentioned above.[65] King-cups are also mentioned by Drayton and Jonson, and by Richard Savage in 'The Wanderer'.[66] Pope, however, specifically cited the plant in his criticism of Philips, who 'by a poetical Creation, hath raised up finer beds of flowers than the most indus-trious gardener; his roses, endives, lillies, king-cups, and daffidils blow all in the same season'.[67]

The king-cup was most often associated with spring (Spenser specified April), but also appears as part of the garland of June, popularly 'represented in a mantle of dark grass green; upon his head a coronet of bents, king-cups, and maiden-hair; holding in his left hand an angle, in his right Cancer, and upon his arm a basket of summer fruits'.[68] But perhaps because of Pope's censure, king-cups were subsequently little used by poets of the period – only a dozen or so times to the end of the century (including William Cowper's 1785 poem *The Task*), and again half of these appearances are in poetry of the 1790s.[69]

Among those poems of the 1790s that do recognise the king-cup is Coleridge's conversational poem 'The Nightingale', a poem that seems to bask in the strange radiance of Chattertonian nature. 'The Nightingale' begins with daylight fading and a stream running silently by. The nightin-gale begins to sing and the poet thinks of Milton before his thoughts turn to those 'youths and maidens' who do not hear the song of the nightingale in their 'ball-rooms and hot theatres'. Then Coleridge's memory is stirred and he remembers a grove filled with nightingales:

> And I know a grove
> Of large extent, hard by a castle huge
> Which the great lord inhabits not: and so
> This grove is wild with tangling underwood,
> And the trim walks are broken up, and grass,
> Thin grass and king-cups grow within the paths.
> But never elsewhere in one place I knew
> So many Nightingales ... [70]

So many features here speak of Chatterton: the waters of inspiration, the canonical textuality, the medieval backdrop, the rusticating neglect, and especially the king-cups. There are a host of Chattertons here, like the night-ingales: 'Their bright, bright eyes, their eyes both bright and full'.

Nightingales did hold a Chattertonian association for Coleridge: he had earlier described Milles's antiquarian edition of Chatterton's Rowley poems (1782) as 'An owl mangling a poor dead nightingale!'[71] And he was very familiar with the poet and his work, as his early and frequently reworked 'Monody on the Death of Chatterton' testifies. Like 'The Nightingale', the 'Monody' (first published in 1794[72]) reveals an engagement with the qualities of nature writing that were emerging in Chatterton's writing: its vivid specificity of flora and fauna, the muse-like qualities of water invoked, and in the uncanniness of place. Coleridge seems to have read the Rowley works deeply alongside other material, especially the 'African Eclogues', and in doing so catches Chatterton's ecological voice.

In the 1797 version of the 'Monody on the Death of Chatterton', Coleridge specifically asks of Bristol and its environs:

> Is this the land of song-ennobled Line?
> Is this the land, where Genius ne'er in vain
> Pour'd forth his lofty strain?[73]

In other words, 'Is this the land of Chatterton?' Just as he ponders Milton when hearing the nightingale, Coleridge straightaway recognises that Spenser has in part made the land through Chatterton, and he then locates Chatterton not simply in Bristol, but in the 'vales where Avon winds'. Chatterton is therefore figured not as a medievalist (Coleridge dismisses medieval romance in 'The Silver Thimble' as 'speaking Birds and Steeds with wings, / Giants and Dwarfs, and Fiends and Kings' (3–4)), still less a literary forger, but as a fleet-footed poet of nature, out and about in the countryside:

> Light-hearted youth! he hastes along,
>   And meditates the future song,
> How dauntless Ælla fray'd the Dacyan foes;
>   See, as floating high in air
>   Glitter the sunny visions fair,
> His eyes dance rapture, and his bosom glows![74]

He has become the spirit of the place, 'Clad in Nature's rich array ... thou loveliest child of Spring'.[75] Coleridge describes the early blooms and dewy blossoms, the wind and the lightning as evidence that Chatterton inhabits the region. Inspiration drives the figure of Chatterton from the woods 'that wave o'er Avon's rocky steep' to the coast:

> These wilds, these caverns roaming o'er,
>   Round which the screaming sea-gulls soar,
> With wild unequal steps he pass'd along

Oft pouring on the winds a broken song:
Anon, upon some rough rock's fearful brow
Would pause abrupt – and gaze upon the waves below.[76]

Here, Coleridge invokes the watery tumult of the 'African Eclogues', as if
the spirit of Chatterton is now gazing upon his exotic works and what they
have done in reimagining the seething waters of the Severn below. And then
recalling the 'Mynstrelles Songes' of 'Ælla', Chatterton's verse is described
as a 'moon-light roundelay' at which Coleridge's passions dance and 'weave
an holy spell!'[77]

Coleridge identifies two poetic ecologies working within Chatterton's verse:
one is in the precise detailing of flowers and birds, initially inspired by earlier
poets. Chatterton was often imagined as a flower himself, and Coleridge's 'On
Observing a Blossom on the First of February 1796' makes this association
explicit. The amaranthus that has blossomed in February, a 'teeth-chattering
month', is destined to perish; the untimely flower is compared 'to Bristowa's
bard, the wondrous boy', indicating that the cultural symbolism of flowers
can receive renewed associations.[78] But elsewhere, Coleridge eschews such
sentimentality and develops an increasingly precise floral sensibility in which
flowers remain as flowers. Flowers were the very stuff of his home life at
Clevedon and the garden of climbing roses, the murmuring sea, blossoming
myrtles, and twining jasmines frame Coleridge's conversational meditations
in 'Reflections on having left a place of retirement':

> the little landscape round
> Was green and woody, and refresh'd the eye.
> It was a spot which you might aptly call
> The Valley of Seclusion! (6–9)

Although by the time he wrote this poem Coleridge had already left his
idyll, the image of the country garden as a place of inspiration – as a place
to cultivate Chattertonian 'herbiage' – would remain.[79]

Similarly, 'This Lime-tree Bower my Prison' is a garden poem, set in his
garden at Nether Stowey – a garden of elms and bean flowers. The poet
imagines the walk he has been forced to miss – a walk across fields and
meadows to the sea, past a waterfall he has described to his guests. This
is the second of Chatterton's poetic ecologies: the imagined landscape as
an environment that supersedes the capacity of the imagination, whether
through the weather or through other, inexplicable elements:

> The roaring dell, o'erwooded, narrow, deep,
> And only speckled by the mid-day sun;
> Where its slim trunk the ash from rock to rock
> Flings arching like a bridge; – that branchless ash,

> Unsunn'd and damp, whose few poor yellow leaves
> Ne'er tremble in the gale, yet tremble still,
> Fann'd by the water-fall! and there my friends
> Behold the dark green file of long dank weeds,
> That all at once (a most fantastic sight!)
> Still nod and drip beneath the dripping edge
> Of the blue clay-stone. (16–20)

Coleridge adds a footnote explaining that the 'long dank weeds' are Adder's Tongue, also known as Hart's Tongue. Their choreographed animation is unsettling, reminiscent of the 'mystic mazes of the dance' in 'Narva and Mored', 'Like leaves in autumn twirling with the breeze'. Sitting alone in his garden, the force of the imagination is able to transplant Coleridge. He hovers about the sublime scene from which he is physically absent as its sole poetic witness. This sense of crossing the Rubicon of the imagination is there too in 'Dejection: An Ode'.[80] The poem begins with an epigraph to 'Sir Patrick Spence', a version of which appears in Percy's *Reliques*:

> Late, late yestereen I saw the new Moon,
> With the old Moon in her arms;
> And I fear, I fear, My Master dear!
> We shall have a deadly storm. (1–4)

Coleridge notes that a storm is forecast by this weather-wise bard, but the tranquillity of the night is unsettled by the 'green light that lingers in the west' (44), which Coleridge fears he could 'gaze on for ever' (43). Like Chatterton's acknowledgement of the 'troubled Spirit near' it is at the edge of perception and beyond explanation.

It is tempting too to find 'Kubla Khan' here: the poem begins by a river, 'the sacred river' and the waters, like those of the 'African Eclogues', are in 'ceaseless turmoil'. It is a poem about a secluded garden and a roaring cataract, the holy and the enchanted, imagination and inspiration – all features characteristic of Coleridge's writing when he feels Chatterton's presence. It could also be read as a poem about the Severn Sea, the Bore, and Clifton Gorge, and about Coleridge's garden at Clevedon and a walk from his cottage at Nether Stowey. Chatterton's strange alchemy of textuality and cultural meteorology, flora and fauna, place and environment exercised a powerful force on Coleridge's imagination. Coleridge could read the landscape around him through Chatterton. Chatterton was in memory, he was in flowers, he was in the West Country, and he was also, like those weird nightingales with 'bright, bright eyes, … eyes both bright and full', the mystery behind the place – an uncanny presence glimmering within those flashing eyes.

Notes

In this essay, Chatterton's poetry is either cited by page from the earliest printed editions, or, where appropriate, from the standard edition: Thomas Chatterton, *Complete Works*, ed. Donald S. Taylor, with Benjamin B. Hoover (2 vols, continuously paginated, Oxford: Clarendon Press, 1971). Editions are abbreviated by date of publication: *1777*, *1778*, *1784*, *1789*, *1798*, *1803*, and *1971*.

1. Mr Jenkins, *The Ode, Songs, Chorusses, &c. for the Concert in Commemoration of Chatterton, the Celebrated Bristol Poet* (London [1784?]); see Robert Jones, '"We Proclaim Our Darling Son": the Politics of Chatterton's Memory and the War for America', *Review of English Studies*, 53.211 (2002), 73–95.
2. Jonathan Barry, 'The History and Antiquities of the City of Bristol: Chatterton in Bristol', in *Angelaki*, 1.2, 'Narratives of Forgery', ed. Nick Groom (Winter 1993–4), 55–81; Jonathan Barry, 'Chatterton, More and Bristol's Cultural Life in the 1760s', in *From Gothic to Romantic: Thomas Chatterton's Bristol*, ed. Alistair Heys (Bristol: Redcliffe Press, 2005), 20–35; Timothy Mowl, 'A Rococo Poet for a Rococo City', in *From Gothic to Romantic: Thomas Chatterton's Bristol*, 36–52.
3. See Michael Liversidge, 'Romantic Redcliffe: Image and Imagination', in *From Gothic to Romantic: Thomas Chatterton's Bristol*, 53–63.
4. *1971*, 504.
5. *CL* (2000 repr.), i. 160, 7 October 1795.
6. For more on this Chatterton, see chapter 5 of my study, *The Forger's Shadow: How Forgery Changed the Course of Literature* (London: Picador, 2002).
7. In 1770 the country's population was some 6,448,000. Urban populations are estimated to have been London: 700,000; Norwich: 30,000; Bristol, Exeter, York, Newcastle, Colchester, Yarmouth: all over 10,000; remaining market towns: 1–2,000; see Roy Porter, *English Society in the Eighteenth Century* (2nd edition, Harmondsworth: Penguin, 2001), 39, 361. *The Yale Edition of Horace Walpole's Correspondence*, ed. W. S. Lewis (48 vols, New Haven and London: Yale University Press, 1937–83), i. 232, 22 October 1766.
8. E. H. W. Meyerstein, *A Life of Thomas Chatterton* (London: Ingpen and Grant, 1930), 188.
9. For this poetic tone see, for example, 'A Description of the Evening' by 'E.' in *The London Magazine, and Monthly Chronologer* (May 1740), 235; reprinted in *Colley Cibber's Jests; or, The Diverting Witty Companion* (Newcastle, 1761), 86–7: this may well have been Chatterton's source.
10. [Thomas Chatterton,] *Poems, Supposed to have been Written at Bristol, by Thomas Rowley, and Others, in the Fifteenth Century* (London, 1777), 278. Rowley's translation of Ecca's verse to Spring incorporated in 'Historie of Peyncters yn Englande' includes an allegorical figure of Spring:

> Whanne sprynge came dauncynge onne a flourette bedde,
> Dighte ynne greene raimente of a chaungynge kynde;
> The leaves of hawthorne boddeynge on hys hedde,
> Ande whyte prymrosen coureynge to the wynde;
> Thanne dyd the shepster hys longe albanne spredde
> Uponne the greenie bancke and daunced arounde,
> Whilest the soeft flowretts nodded onne his hedde,
> And hys fayre lambes besprenged onne the ground;
> Anethe hys fote the brooklette ranne alonge,
> Whyche strolled rounde the vale, to here hys joyous songe.

(William Barrett, *The History and Antiquities of the City of Bristol* (Bristol [1789]), 643). Similarly, the figure of Kenewalchae in 'Battle of Hastings [No. 2.]' (*1777*, 257–9) is inspired in form by Drayton's 'Dowsabell'.

11. William Wordsworth and Samuel Taylor Coleridge, *Lyrical Ballads*, ed. H. L. Brett and A. R. Jones (London and New York: Routledge, 1991), 245, 241 [254n].

12. Thomas Chatterton, *A Supplement to the Miscellanies of Thomas Chatterton* (London, 1784), 53.

13. Thomas Chatterton, *Miscellanies in Prose and Verse* (London, 1778), 61. 'Heccar and Gaira' was written on 3 January 1770, some months before Chatterton left for London, while 'The Death of Nicou' was composed on 12 June 1770 at Brooke Street, Holborn. 'To Miss B——sh, of Bristol' (c. June 1770) also begins with an exotic seashore, a reworking of the Orientalist sublime of the African Eclogues for a plea of unrequited love.

14. Wylie Sypher, 'Chatterton's African Eclogues and the Deluge', *PMLA*, 54 (1939), 246–60; see E. H. W. Meyerstein, 'Chatterton, Coleridge, and Bristol', *Times Literary Supplement* (21 August 1937), 606, and ensuing correspondence with Sypher (28 August 1937, 30 October 1937); see also *1971*, 1026.

15. Chatterton wrote to his mother on 14 May 1770, asking her to send his copy of 'Catcott's Hutchinsonian jargon on the Deluge' (*1971*, 571); 'Heccar and Gaira' is in Chatterton's hand on the rear endpapers of Alexander Catcott's *Remarks on the Second Part of the Lord Bishop of Clogher's* Vindication of the Histories of the Old and New Testament; *Chiefly, with respect to his Lordship's interpretation of the Mosaic account of the Creation and Deluge* (London, 1756) (Bodl., MS. Eng. poet. e. 6).

16. Edward Shiercliff, *The Bristol and Hotwell Guide* (Bristol, 1793), 66; quoted in part by Sypher, 'Chatterton's African Eclogues and the Deluge', 259. This passage also perhaps owes something to Samuel Johnson's *Rasselas*: 'The sides of the mountains were covered with trees, the banks of the brooks were diversified with flowers; every blast shook spices from the rocks, and every month dropped fruits on the ground' (*The Prince of Abissinia. A Tale* (2 vols, London, 1759), i. 4).

17. John Dolman, *Contemplations amongst Vincent's Rocks, near the city of Bristol* (Bristol, 1755), 77–9.

18. Daniel Defoe, *A Tour Thro' the Whole Island of Great Britain* (6th edition, 4 vols, London, 1761–2), ii. 310.

19. *1778*, 57.

20. *1778*, 58–9.

21. See Carolyn D. Williams, '"On Tiber's Banks": Chatterton and Post-Colonialism', in *Thomas Chatterton and Romantic Culture*, ed. Nick Groom (Basingstoke: Macmillan, 1999), 48–63: 58–60; and Kim Ian Michasiw, 'Chatterton, Ossian, Africa', in *Studies in English Literature*, 48.3 (Summer 2008), 633–52.

22. It was published in the *European Magazine* for 1792 and then in the 1803 edition edited by Robert Southey and Joseph Cottle. Chatterton was influenced by the bricklayer poet Henry Jones's *Clifton: A Poem, in Two Cantos* (Bristol, 1767): see Taylor's notes in *1971*, 987.

23. Edward Gardner, *Miscellanies, in Prose and Verse* (2 vols, Bristol, 1798), ii. 161.

24. It could be argued that 'Stanton Drew' is in fact a 'city' poem, as it is set in Druidic architecture. King's Circus in Bath was designed by John Wood on the model of Stanton Drew's stone circles.

25. William Camden, *Britannia: or, A Chorographical Description of Great Britain and Ireland* (3rd edition, 2 vols, London, 1753), i. col. 93. It was also believed that the three circles of stones represent 'the Sun, the Earth, and the Moon; and

some other Stones, representing the Planets *Venus, Jupiter,* and *Saturn'* (Daniel Defoe, *A Tour Thro' the Whole Island of Great Britain* (4th edition, 4 vols, London, 1761–2), ii. 304); see also John Wood, *The Origin of Building: or, The Plagiarism of the Heathens Detected* (Bath, 1741), 221. Chatterton's interest in planetary systems may have been piqued by this information: see his poem 'The Copernican System' (*Miscellanies*, 90–1).

26. Thomas Chatterton, *The Works of Thomas Chatterton*, ed. Robert Southey and Joseph Cottle (3 vols, London: Longman and Rees, 1803), i. 206.
27. *1777*, 20–2.
28. *1778*, 75.
29. *1778*, 73–4.
30. *1778*, 57. The intriguing phrase 'distilling rain' appears nowhere else in the poetry of the period.
31. *1777*, 203.
32. *1777*, 89.
33. John Gay, *Trivia: Or, The Art of Walking the Streets of London* (London [1716]), 41. 'Juicy pears' also appear again in autumn in Anne Williams's poem 'The Wish' in *Miscellanies in Prose and Verse* (London, 1766), 26; see also [Anon.,] *The Summer-Day. A Poem: In Four Cantos, Morning, Noon, Evening and Night* (London, 1769), 100. See further Thomas Creech's translation of Virgil's second eclogue in *Tonson's Miscellany* (5th edition, 6 vols, London, 1727), i. 313; Creech also mentions the 'juicy pear' in a translation of Theocritus (*The Idylliums of Theocritus with Rapin's Discourse upon Pastorals* (2nd edition, London, 1713), 43.
34. *1777*, 203–4.
35. *1777*, 20.
36. *1777*, 205.
37. *1777*, 205–6.
38. *1777*, 199.
39. *1777*, 82.
40. *The Works of Dr. Jonathan Swift, Dean of St. Patrick's, Dublin* (12 vols, London, 1766), vii. 161.
41. *1777*, 83–4.
42. Meyerstein (241n) suggests a pastoral based on this in *Boddeley's Bath Journal* ('Dick and Dolly', 14 May 1770); Taylor sees no parallel (*1971*, 793).
43. *1777*, 87.
44. Bronson sees an allusion to Surrey's sonnet on the Spring ('The soote season') in the final couplet of this verse: B. H. Bronson, 'Chattertoniana', *Modern Language Quarterly*, 11 (December 1950), 417–24 (see Taylor in *1971*, 930).
45. 'Anticipating' Shakespeare, Rowley has fairies hidden in 'Oslyppe Cuppes' (meaning oxlips or cowslips) in a verse in a footnote to 'The Parlyamente of Sprytres' (*1971*, 107n).
46. *1777*, 3.
47. Michael Drayton, *The Poetical Works* (Edinburgh, 1793), 388.
48. *The Works of the English Poets* (58 vols, London, 1779–80), lvi. 249.
49. Erasmus Darwin, *The Botanic Garden; A Poem* (London, 1791), 121, 156. The marigold appears, for example, in Samuel Bishop, *The Poetical Works* (2 vols, London, 1796), i. 28, 158, 168; the anonymous poem 'Flowers' in *The Bouquet* (2 vols, London, 1792), i. 11; Mary Chandler, *The Description of Bath. A Poem* (London, 1767), 25; Thomas May, of Henley, 'Pastoral I. In Imitation of Virgil's Eighth Eclogue', *Poems Descriptive and Moral; consisting of Imitations, Translations,*

Pastorals, Narrations, and various Reflections on the Beauties of Nature, &c. (Henley [1791?]), 17; and Christopher Smart, 'The Herald and Husband-Man. Fable XII', *The Poems, of the Late Christopher Smart* (Reading, 1791), 35. It also appears in Gay's 'Monday; or, The Squabble', *The Shepherd's Week* (London, 1714), 9n; and in Shenstone's Spenserian imitation 'The School-Mistress' (see *The Poetical Works of William Shenstone, Esq.* (Edinburgh, 1775), 304).

50. Samuel Taylor Coleridge, 'Lines Written at Shurton Bars, near Bridgewater, September 1795, in Answer to a Letter from Bristol', *Poems, by S. T. Coleridge. To which are now added Poems by Charles Lamb, and Charles Lloyd* (2nd edition, London and Bristol: Robinson and Cottle, 1797), 93–5n.

51. *1778*, 61.

52. *1778*, 57.

53. *1777*, 138.

54. *1777*, 136–8

55. *Hamlet*, IV. vi. 191–6.

56. John Philips, *The Splendid Shilling. A Poem, in Imitation of Milton* (London, 1705), 5.

57. While some mentions of the willow appear in popular songs (for example, 'Indian Song' in *The Banquet of Thalia, or The Fashionable Songsters Pocket Memorial* ([London?, 1788?]), 17) there appear to be passing references in less than twenty instances: Robert Anderson, *Poems on Various Subjects* (Carlisle, 1798), 53, 92, 212; Thomas Campbell, *The Pleasures of Hope* (Edinburgh, 1799), 20; William Cockin, *Occasional Attempts in Verse* ([Kendal] 1776), 103; William Dodd, *Poems* (London, 1767), 249; Anne Francis, *Miscellaneous Poems* ([Norwich] 1790), 218, 231, 254; [Chatterton's friend] Edward Gardner, *Miscellanies, in Prose and Verse* (2 vols, Bristol, 1798) [i.e. *1798*], ii. 42, 63; Salomon Gessner, *Rural Poems* (London, 1762), 17; Esther Lewis, *Poems Moral and Entertaining* (Bath, 1789), 116–17; John Lund, *A Collection of Oddities. In Prose and Verse, Serious and Comical* ([Doncaster, 1780?]), 56; John MacGilvray, *Poems* (London, 1787), 36; *Poems, chiefly by Gentlemen of Devonshire and Cornwall* (2 vols, Bath, 1792), i. 24 [by 'P.']; Joseph Holden Pott, *Poems* (London, 1779), 12–14; A. Williams, *Original Poems and Imitations* (London, 1773), 126; and William Woty, *The Blossoms of Helicon* (London, 1763), 138.

58. Joseph Hucks, *Poems* (Cambridge, 1798), 61n.

59. There is of course no comparison with Wordsworth's 'Lines left upon a Seat in a Yew-Tree' (*Lyrical Ballads*, 38). See also Anne Francis's 'The Invitation' (which also includes cowslips and a Druid), and her self-explanatory 'Elegy on a Favourite Cat and Dog, buried under a Weeping-Willow' (*Miscellaneous Poems*, above n.57).

60. *1803*, ii. 135.

61. *1777*, 24.

62. Margaret Grainger (ed.), *The Natural History Prose Writings of John Clare* (Oxford: Clarendon Press, 1983), 177–8. See John Goodridge, 'Identity, Authenticity, Class: John Clare and the Mask of Chatterton', *Angelaki*, 1.2, 'Narratives of Forgery', ed. Nick Groom (Winter 1993–4), 131–48, 137.

63. Goodridge, 'Identity, Authenticity, Class', 139. Chatterton claimed that Iscam's line 'Flowretts straughte wyth dewe' ('The Parlyamente of Sprytres') had been plagiarised from Rowley's 'Lyke Kynge Cuppes brasteynge wyth the Mornynge dew' (*1971*, 106n).

64. Thomas Martyn, *Flora Rustica: Exhibiting Accurate Figures of Such Plants as are either Useful or Injurious in Husbandry* (4 vols, London, 1792–4 [1791–5]), i. n.p. [117]. See also a translation of Jean-Jacques Rousseau's *Letters on the Elements of Botany*, trans. Thomas Martyn (2nd edition, London, 1787), 303.

65. John Milton, *Poems upon Several Occasions, English, Italian, and Latin*, ed. Thomas Warton (London, 1785), 26n.

66. Richard Savage, *The Works of Richard Savage, Esq.* (2 vols, London, 1777), ii. 59.

67. *Guardian* 40 (27 April 1713): *The Works of Mr. Alexander Pope, in Prose*, 2 vols (London, 1741), ii. 280.

68. John Barrow, *Dictionarium Polygraphicum: or, The Whole Body of Arts Regularly Digested* (2 vols, London, 1758), ii. 37.

69. [Anon.] *Miscellaneous Poems. By a Young Gentleman* (London, 1725), 4; Henry Boyd, *Poems, chiefly Dramatic and Lyric* (Dublin, 1793), 518; William Brimble, *Poems, attempted on Various Occasions* (Bath, 1765), 20; William Cowper, *The Task, A Poem, in Six Books* (London, 1785), 246; Eliza Day, *Poems and Fugitive Pieces* (London, 1796), 92; Edward Howard, Earl of Suffolk, *Miscellanies in Prose and Verse* (London, 1725), 179; James Hurdis, *The Village Curate, A Poem* (2nd edition, London, 1788), 38; Mary Leapor, *Poems upon Several Occasions* (London, 1748), 27; Hugh Mulligan, *Poems chiefly on Slavery and Oppression* (London, 1788), 48; Thomas Nicholls, *The Harp of Hermes* ([London?, 1797?]), 54; Richard Polwhele, *The Old English Gentleman, A Poem* (London, 1797), 49; Edmund Rack, *Poems on Several Subjects* (London, 1775), 67; Anna Seward, *Original Sonnets on Various Subjects; and Odes paraphrased from Horace*, 2nd edition (London, 1799), 45n [footnote only]; Isaac Thompson, *A Collection of Poems* (Newcastle upon Tyne, 1731), 5; and Jane West, *Poems and Plays* (4 vols, London, 1799), i. 198.

70. *Lyrical Ballads*, 42.

71. This was in a note written for but never printed in his 'Monody on the Death of Chatterton': BL, Ashley MS 408, fols. 36r–7v; reproduced in *Coleridge's Poems: A Facsimile Reproduction*, ed. J.D. Campbell and W. Hale White (Westminster: A. Constable, 1899), 67–8. See Paul Magnuson, 'Coleridge's Discursive "Monody on the Death of Chatterton"', *Romanticism on the Net*, 17 (2000); and Nick Groom, 'Love and Madness: Southey Editing Chatterton', in *Robert Southey and the Contexts of English Romanticism*, ed. Lynda Pratt (Aldershot: Ashgate, 2005), 19–25: 23n.

72. Thomas Chatterton, *Poems, Supposed to have been Written at Bristol, by Thomas Rowley, and Others, in the Fifteenth Century* (Cambridge, 1794), xxv–xxviii.

73. Coleridge, *Poems* (1797), 20.

74. Coleridge, *Poems*, 21.

75. Coleridge, *Poems*, 22.

76. Coleridge, *Poems*, 25.

77. Coleridge, *Poems*, 26.

78. Coleridge, *Poems*, 107–8. Coleridge provides a footnote to leave no room for ambiguity. His phrase 'wondrous boy' presumably influenced Wordsworth's more familiar appellation for Chatterton, the 'marvellous boy'. On Chatterton figured as a flower, see David Fairer, 'Chatterton's Poetic Afterlife 1770–1796: a Context for Coleridge's *Monody*', in *Thomas Chatterton and Romantic Culture*, 228–52.

79. That is, both 'verbiage' and 'herbage'. Other examples include 'The Eolian Harp' (dated to 20 August at Clevedon), which also recalls the 'white-flower'd Jasmin, and the broad-leav'd Myrtle' (4), the bean-flowers, and the murmur of the sea; and 'Lewti or the Circassian Love-Chaunt', which again begins by the water and describes jasmines (67).

80. Written 4 April 1802.

Part II
The Bristol School: Cottle, Coleridge, and their Circles

3
Joseph Cottle and West Country Romanticism

Richard Cronin

In October, 1799, Coleridge travelled from Bristol with his publisher, Joseph Cottle, to meet Wordsworth at Sockburn-on-Tees. The three men embarked on a tour of Wordsworth's beloved Lake Country, but on 30 October, at Greta Bridge, Cottle left the party and travelled south. 'It was a tactful departure', notes Mary Moorman, 'Wordsworth and Coleridge wanted to be by themselves.'[1] That leave-taking has a symbolic value: it marks the birth of the Lake School of Romantic poetry, and yet Joseph Cottle, the man so brusquely dismissed by Moorman, staked a claim to have originated that school himself, and not in the Lake District but some 250 miles to the south, in Bristol:

> Many might think it no small honour (without the slightest tincture of vanity) to have been the friend, in early life, of such men as *Southey*, *Coleridge*, *Wordsworth*, and *Lamb*: to have encouraged them in their first productions, and to have published, as it respects *each* of them, his *first* Volume of Poems.[2]

Typically, this is not quite accurate, but it was, as Cottle rightly insisted, 'a distinction that might never occur again to a Provincial bookseller'. It seemed to Cottle an 'extraordinary circumstance that Mr. Coleridge in his "Biographia Literaria" should have passed over in silence, all distinct reference to Bristol, the cradle of his literature, and for many years his favourite abode'. He was moved to publish his *Early Recollections* to correct Coleridge's omission, to celebrate a period in the life of his city when 'so many men of genius were there congregated', as to justify the designation, 'The Augustan Age of Bristol',[3] and, with pardonable egotism, to remind the reading public of his own status as the provincial West Country Maecenas.

But Cottle goes further than that. He demands recognition not just as the publisher of Southey, Coleridge, and Wordsworth, but as their fellow poet. He begins and ends his book with a list of his own publications, and he carefully records the rather guarded compliments that they earned him – Wordsworth's praise of 'Malvern Hills' and the 'Monody on Henderson', the poem addressed to him by Coleridge in which he is complimented for writing verse on which the eye may 'gaze undazzled' (i. 282–4), even Coleridge's admission that the preface to the second edition of Cottle's *Alfred* was 'well written'.[4] It may be that Cottle's friends were more sincere when they commented behind his back. When he published *Alfred*, an epic in twenty-four books, Southey wrote, 'I fear the Reviews will half induce him to hang himself',[5] which was particularly hard since Cottle had so clearly modelled his poem on Southey's own *Joan of Arc*, for which in 1796 Cottle had paid Southey fifty guineas and published in a handsome quarto.[6] As Lamb pointed out, Cottle 'imitates Southey, as Rowe did Shakespeare'.[7] In the event, Southey's fears were unfounded. Cottle's enormous poem was largely ignored. The one extensive notice, in the *Monthly Review*,[8] was dismissive but its tone is more regretful than savage – *Alfred* is an unfortunate instance of epic 'pretensions' indulged by one of only 'moderate talents'. It is not really an epic so much as 'a plain *tale*; not highly elevated above prose, either by imagery or versification', an instance of 'the bad consequences resulting from some hasty opinions lately promulgated respecting simplicity of diction'. Cottle, it seems, is a victim of Wordsworth's preface to the second edition of *Lyrical Ballads*. Cottle had published the first edition himself, but the reviewer seems unaware of this: 'With Mr. Cottle we are totally unacquainted.' Nevertheless, the reviewer confidently enrols him as a humble follower of the poetic school of which Cottle seems to have thought of himself as the founder. Coleridge, it might be felt, gave the conclusive riposte to any such claim in 1804 when he grouped Cottle with Campbell and Rogers as 'pseudo-poets' who contrive 'both by their writings and moral characters' 'to bring poetry into disgrace'. The name Cottle, Seamus Perry notes, 'has been written over, but is still discernible'.[9] This was ungenerous to a man who had so often lent Coleridge money. Cottle's moral character is, I grant, easier to defend than his writings,[10] and yet Cottle's poetry does, I think, serve to indicate that when he published Southey, Coleridge, and Wordsworth it was not only because he recognised their talent, or, in his own words, 'predicted for them that distinction which the Public at first rather tardily admitted': he was enrolling them in a project of his own, a single grand project that seems to underlie his activities as both publisher and poet. I will begin by sketching what I take that project to have been.

First, and most obviously, there is Cottle's local patriotism. *Alfred* is designed explicitly and proudly as an epic of the West Country.[11] When a timid counsellor suggests that Alfred delay battle until his army is reinforced by Mercians, the King responds witheringly. Mercia is not to be relied on. 'Now be our trust / Dependent on ourselves!' (ix. 272–3):

> Let others shrink,
> Inglorious from the conflict, to herself
> If Wessex be but true, altho' her ranks

> May not with Danes compare, yet shall her zeal
> Furnish new armies, troops invincible,
> And compensate for each deficiency,
> By her own courage. (ix. 236–42)

This aspect of the poem is the more evident if it is compared to *Alfred: A Poem* published by the Laureate, Henry James Pye, in 1801, the year after Cottle's *Alfred*. Pye's Alfred is very emphatically a British monarch, assisted in his defeat of the Danes by the Welsh, Irish, and Scottish Kings. At the end of the poem Pye invites us to see in Alfred's victory 'Cambria's, Caledonia's, Anglia's name / Blended and lost in Britain's prouder fame' (vi. 537–8). He then admits 'Erin's sons' to this united body, which will remain

> Link'd in eternal amity and peace,
> While Concord blesses, with celestial smiles,
> The favoured empire of the British Isles. (vi. 548–50)

Cottle's *Alfred* by contrast is an expression of his 'local fondness' (10, 80), but, then, so was the whole of his career. His poems, from *Malvern Hills* (1797) to *The Fall of Cambria* (1808) and *Dartmoor, and Other Poems* (1823), celebrate a West Country that includes Devon, Cornwall, and Wales, a nation within a nation of which the capital is Cottle's own city of Bristol. In this Cottle was no more than a typical citizen of Bristol of his time. It was a city in which civic pride ran deep. In his *New History* of the city, for example, the Rev. George Heath does not simply insist that Bristol is England's second city, he makes it London's rival: St Paul's and Westminster Abbey are matched by Bristol Cathedral and 'the Church of St Mary at Redcliff';[12] it is not outdone by London in its cultural facilities, its theatre, schools, and its five newspapers; it is London's equal, too, in the variety of goods on sale in its shops, and outdoes London in their cheapness and the civility of the shopkeepers; and its Exchange represents a concentration of wealth that, relative to its population, exceeds that of London itself. Heath divides England into two nations, a nation of the East, in which 'the two finest cities' are London and Oxford, matched by a nation of the West of which Bristol is 'the capital Key and great Mart' and the place of Oxford is taken by Bath 'the most elegant City in the Kingdom without exception'.[13] He draws the boundaries of the Western nation widely. Its capital, Bristol, 'stands so near the confluence of the River Avon with the Severn, that it enjoys the Navigation and Trade of that great river and adjacent Country: and of a vast extent of Sea Coasts down the British Channel: of Somerset, Devon, Cornwall and Wales'. This describes very precisely the nation within a nation of which Cottle appointed himself laureate. His brief career as a publisher should also be understood in this context. In publishing the four young poets he advanced a claim that his native Bristol might, just as well as London, be a centre from which an ambitious young writer might launch a literary career. He seems to have communicated his local patriotism to his young friends, not just Southey, who, as a native Bristolian like Cottle himself, might be expected to share it, but Coleridge too. 'I love Bristol & I do not love London', he wrote to Thomas Poole in July 1796.[14]

But it was not just local pride that in the years in which he met Southey and Coleridge induced Cottle to proclaim himself a citizen of West England. He identified East England, the nation governed from London, with Pitt's war machine. His Bristol acquaintances, he remembers in *Early Recollections*, were united in their 'detestation of the French war',[15] and it was the main purpose of one of the very first volumes that he published, his own *Poems* of 1795, to express that detestation. Cottle's Preface identifies 'War, A Fragment' as the volume's most important poem. He offers it to the public 'from a belief, that it is the duty of every man to raise his feeble voice in support of sinking humanity, and not to be content with thanking God, that he feels indignant at the enormities of war, without labouring to inspire the same abhorrence in the breast of others'.[16] He insists on the disconnection between the interests of those who instigate wars and those who fight them: 'the peasantry of a country are unacquainted with what is termed the political interests of different states, and from their occupations, necessarily imbibe sentiments of benevolence; and yet, these are the instruments in the hands of tyranny for propagating war, and all its horrid consequences' (Preface, viii). The poem itself enforces the point through the sentimental tale of Orlando who is seduced from his happy village life by a company of soldiers who 'Laugh'd at [his] garments, dwelt on [his] distress' ('War, A Fragment', 136), and dies in battle gazing forlornly on the picture of Catherine, the village girl that he loves. This figure, the peasant ripped from his village home and domestic attachments by war, recurs in a very large number of the poems written by Cottle's school of poets, from *Joan of Arc* to *The Ruined Cottage*. The only war that Cottle is prepared to countenance is a defensive war fought to repel an invading army or to overthrow a tyrannical ruler:

> Yet; if invaded rights the task demand,
> If men behold oppress'd their native land,
> By foreign despots, wand'ring far for prey,
> Who locust-like, with ruin mark their way;
> Or, see their Prince direct the Nation's helm,
> In ruin's surge, his people to o'erwhelm:
> Reward for foulest deeds a venal tribe,
> Nor shun to blacken whom he cannot bribe
> . . . .
> 'Twill then be right to grasp the blazing spear.
> ('War, A Fragment', 323–34)

This does more than justify the defensive war being fought by revolutionary France against the invading Allied armies; it comes close to proclaiming the justice of a civil war designed to overthrow the British state.

Cottle claims citizenship of a West England, then, as a signal of his opposition to the war, but he has other reasons too, and reasons that proved longer-lasting. By 1801, when he published *Alfred*, he had clearly, like Coleridge, Southey, and Wordsworth, come to the view that Napoleonic France represented a greater threat to peace than Britain under Pitt. *Alfred* defends our 'clift-bound isle in this tremendous hour' (ix. 321) against the assault of the Danes in a manner clearly designed to inspire Cottle's countrymen in their defence of Britain against Napoleon's invasion force.[17] But his Alfred is emphatically King of Wessex rather than of England, as a happy consequence of which Cottle succeeds in writing a national epic that contrives to avoid even a single reference to London, the nation's capital city. Cottle's insistence on identifying himself as a West Country poet is an expression of his hostility to the centralised state, and this too was a matter in which his young protégés agreed with him. In *The Prelude*, Wordsworth's pained bewilderment as he paces London's streets joins with the presentiment that he claims to have felt in Robespierre's Paris where

> Liberty, and Life, and Death would soon
> To the remotest corners of the land
> Lie in the arbitrement of those who ruled
> The capital City. (x. 108–11, 1805 text)

In this as in most other matters it is Southey who seems closest to Cottle. *Joan of Arc* ends with Joan crowning Charles at Rheims. Her later fortunes, her betrayal, imprisonment, and ignominious death, are admitted into the poem only as dim forebodings of her future fate that Joan must ignore if she is to fulfil her sacred mission. But Southey's decision to end his poem where he does has another effect. It allows him to write a French national epic that excludes Paris almost as effectively as *Alfred* excludes London. *Joan of Arc*, like *Alfred*, is at once a national and a provincial epic, in which Joan's journey takes her from her native Domrémy, to Chinon, Orléans, and at last to Rheims. The King's court has moved to Chinon, because Paris is in the hands of the English:

> Paris with her servile sons
> A headstrong mutable ferocious race,
> Bow'd to the invader's yoke, since that sad hour
> When Faction o'er her streets with giant stride
> Strode Terrible, and Murder and Revenge,
> As by the midnight torches' lurid light
> They mark'd their mangled victims writhe convuls'd,
> Listen'd the deep death groans. (iii. 62–9)[18]

A note refers to the massacre of the Armagnacs by the Burgundians in May and June 1418, but the poem goes on to observe that this is just one episode in the history of a city 'drench'd with human blood', and doomed centuries later to 'know the damning guilt / Of Brissot murder'd, and the blameless wife / Of Roland!'. This is recognisably the same Paris in which, Wordsworth was to claim, he foresaw the full horrors to which the centralised nation state was exposed.

Hostility towards centralisation was, for Cottle, an expression of his religious as much as his political values. As a Baptist he professed a proudly sectarian faith, that is, a faith that insisted on the full independence of local churches. On this he was in full agreement with the Unitarian Coleridge.[19] But his faith was also sectarian in the more informal sense in which the word may denote a broad and loose range of attitudes: amongst them, anti-Catholicism; the narrowness of mind that Hazlitt regretted in the Dissenting community as well as the attachment to civil liberties that impressed him;[20] a generous sympathy for the poor together with a conviction of the moral virtue of hard work; a contempt for self-indulgence, whether revealed in drinking, gambling, or sexual laxity; the high value set on domestic virtues and on female modesty; and a tendency to adopt a preacherly tone often underlined by the use of biblical rhythms. Once again, Cottle's *Alfred* is the best guide to this. Alfred is Cottle's hero in large part because his translation of the Bible into English gives Cottle ample opportunity for condemnation of the wicked Catholic preference for the Vulgate. Cottle frequently dwells on the evils of war, but almost as often on the evils of strong drink. His Alfred lodges for some time with an aged cottager, and imbibes from him the simple ethic that the cottager learned from his own father:

> 'Rise betimes,
> 'Let thy first thoughts ascend to heavenly things,
> 'Be frugal, fear not work, and never drink
> 'Aught but this brook'. (xiii. 319–22)

In such passages Cottle claims – and some readers will find the effect comical – an epic universality for his own provincial, Nonconformist values. It is more surprising that so many of those virtues are shared by Southey's Joan of Arc, who is also represented, somewhat oddly given Southey's Church of England upbringing, as a Nonconformist heroine. Southey is loud in his condemnation of Catholic superstition while still allowing Joan her paranormal powers, and the effect is to convert Joan's 'voices' into the inner voice of conscience that, for all Nonconformists, supersedes the authority of the priesthood. Southey is almost as emphatic as Cottle in his condemnation of strong drink, whether imbibed by bishops, politicians, country squires, university dons, or electors (ix. 511–60), and the prophecy that most nearly prompts Joan to despair is not that she will be burnt alive, but that she will be chained to the stake with her breasts exposed (ix. 266–83).

So, in Bristol in the 1790s, Cottle grouped together a school of poets united in their opposition to the war, in a defiant provincialism through which they expressed their distrust of the centralised state, and in their attachment to a set of values that might be described as sectarian, or more politely as Nonconformist. His decision in 1796 to publish Southey's *Joan of Arc* in quarto and to make it, in Southey's words, 'the handsomest book that Bristol had ever yet sent forth'[21] indicates that he had identified Southey's poem as the flagship volume of the new school. Surprisingly, its other members agreed. 'Why the poem is alone sufficient to redeem the character of the age we live in from the imputation of degenerating in Poetry', wrote Lamb in June,[22] and in November Coleridge assured Thelwall that the poem established Southey as the peer of Homer, Milton, and Tasso: 'The first and fourth books of the *Joan of Arc* are to me more interesting than the same number of Lines in any poem whatsoever.'[23] The reaction was almost as swift. Lamb qualified his verdict within days of announcing it: 'Perhaps I had estimated Southey's merits too much by number, weight and measure.'[24] By December Coleridge agreed with Thelwall that Southey was incapable of 'that *toil* of thinking, which is necessary in order to plan *a Whole*',[25] and by March the following year he had decided that Southey had utterly misconstrued the bent of his talents which were for dramatic rather than epic poetry.[26] Little wonder that when, some years later, it became known that Cottle himself was planning to publish *Alfred* in an attempt to match Southey's achievement even his own poets responded with derision.

Joan of Arc and *Alfred* are both of them poems deeply divided against themselves; epics on the horrors of war that nevertheless choose warriors as their heroes, republican epics that end one of them in a coronation and the other with Alfred reasserting his sovereignty through his defeat of the Danes. They are provincial epics, or a better term might be cottage epics.[27] They are poems that reveal Southey and Cottle as writers ill at ease with the genre they have chosen, and both pass on their discomfort to their heroes. Southey's Joan is a woman whose 'mission' diverts her from her proper life. She is a village girl who must involve herself with court affairs that she finds distasteful, a tender-hearted maiden who must lead her people into battle and cleave her way violently through the armed ranks of the English, a woman whose true ambition is to lead a life of quiet, loving domesticity with her Theodore but who is obliged instead to live a life of lonely celibacy. Cottle's Alfred seems equally uncomfortable in his role as king. He is a poet and a scholar forced to become a military leader, a king whose preferred life is one of rural retirement. Hence his decision, for which his motives remain obscure, to leave his army and spend so much of the poem living the life of a humble cottager. 'My little reign / Hath not disclosed my character', he complains (xi. 71–2). *Joan of Arc* and

Alfred are not so much poems that betray the inappropriateness of the epic enterprise in Bristol in the 1790s as poems that take that inappropriateness as their unacknowledged subject. The provincial epic is, after all, a blatant misnomer, at any rate for most eighteenth-century commentators on the genre who thought of the epic as the most powerful expression and agent of the unity of the culture that had produced it.[28] For such commentators national cultures centred on their epic poems in much the same way that nation states centred on their capital cities, so that the epic poem was a peculiarly inappropriate enterprise for a school of poets dedicated to the celebration of a decentralised state.

It was a point that Southey's and Cottle's colleagues quickly grasped. Lamb concluded that the true value of *Joan of Arc* was located in the 'anecdotes interspersed among the Battles',[29] and Coleridge agreed. Southey's true talent was for the 'soothing & sonnetlike description' in which Coleridge continued to think Southey 'unrivalled'.[30] The cumbersome epic framework of *Joan of Arc* was only a distraction. By 1801, when Cottle published *Alfred*, Lamb repeated his point with a good deal more asperity:

> Four-and-twenty Books to read in the dog-days! I got as far as the Mad monk the first day, & fainted. Mr. Cottle's genius strongly points him to the *Pastoral*, but his inclinations divert him perpetually from his calling.[31]

Cottle thought the epic poem the proper mark of the cultural importance of the school of poets that he published; the twelve books of *Joan of Arc*, the twenty-four books of *Alfred*, both poems issued in imposing quarto volumes. But it seemed to Lamb and Coleridge that the provincial epic was not so much a radical generic innovation as a contradiction in terms. That recognition, I suspect, does much to explain why it was that in the years following the publication of *Joan of Arc*, almost all of Cottle's poets, including Southey, involved themselves in a range of apparently erratic generic experiments: reviving established genres such as the sonnet, the tragedy, and various kinds of topographical poetry such as the retirement poem and the inscription poem; cultivating generic hybrids, the best remembered of which is the lyrical ballad; and devising genres which the poets thought of as quite new, the Coleridgean conversation poem, for example, or the poems that Southey titled 'English Eclogues' and described as bearing 'no resemblance to any poems in our language'.[32]

There is some evidence that Cottle himself came to agree that the true monument to the West Country school of poetry over which he presided was not *Alfred* or *Joan of Arc*, nor even *Lyrical Ballads*, the volume through which he has achieved his modest place in literary history. He agreed to publish *Lyrical Ballads* after Wordsworth had recited some poems that struck him as having 'a peculiar, but decided merit' and would, he thought, be 'well received'.[33] It meant declining Coleridge's suggestion that he publish 'Wordsworth's Salisbury Plain & Tale of a Woman which two poems with a few others which he would add & the notes will make a volume'.[34] When he looked back at that decision almost forty years later he seems to have had second thoughts. In a note to *Early Recollections* he wrote, 'This Poem of "Salisbury Plain" (except an extract in Vol. 1, Lyrical Ballads) has not yet been published. It was always with me a great favourite, and, with the exception of the "Excursion," the poem of all others, on which I thought Mr. Wordsworth might most advantageously rest his fame as a poet.'[35] In 1798 Cottle had passed up the opportunity to publish together in one volume 'Adventures on Salisbury Plain' and the poem that was to become the first book of *The Excursion*: he had missed his opportunity, he may by then have recognised, of bringing out the volume that would have best defined his whole project.

Cottle's school of poets was most easily defined geographically, by its connection with the West Country, and by its opposition to the war on revolutionary France. On both counts 'Adventures on Salisbury Plain' would have recommended itself to Cottle. But it is *The Ruined Cottage* that seems the poem more closely implicated in the project.[36] E. P. Thompson was the first to suggest that Wordsworth found the clue for Margaret's story in *Joan of Arc*:[37]

> Of unrecorded name
> Died the mean man; yet did he leave behind
> One who did never say her daily prayers
> Of him forgetful; who to every tale
> Of the distant war, lending an eager ear,
> Grew pale and trembled. At her cottage door,
> The wretched one shall sit, and with dim eye
> Gaze o'er the plain, where on his parting steps
> Her last look hung. Nor ever shall she know
> Her husband dead, but tortur'd with vain hope,
> Gaze on – then heart-sick turn to her poor babe,
> And weep it fatherless. (vii. 320–31)

But Southey, who knew Wordsworth's poem in manuscript, may have anticipated Thompson's discovery. At any rate, when he revised this passage for the 1798 edition of his poem, he brings his war widow still closer to Wordsworth's Margaret:

> Nor ever shall she know
> Her husband dead, but cherishing a hope,
> Whose falsehood inwardly she knows too well,
> Feel life itself with that false hope decay ...[38]

The poem fixed itself in Cottle's mind too. As he wanders through Wessex his Alfred is struck by the devastation wrought by the Danish invasion:

> How beat my heart,
> When as I pass'd some cottage, roofless, burnt,
> I saw the little garden, still adorn'd
> With many an humble plant, and bedded round,
> With the wild thyme, tho' half o'ergrown with weeds,
> That springing up, declared no master near
> To check them, or relieve the scatter'd flowers
> That from beneath peep'd out. (xi. 131–42)

Wordsworth had taken one of the 'Anecdotes interspersed among the battles' that Lamb admired in *Joan of Arc* and freed it from its incongruous context. In a crass, some might say characteristically crass, manoeuvre, Cottle undoes all that work. The 'Anecdote', the 'soothing & sonnetlike description', is welded back into the ponderous epic machinery from which Wordsworth had released it.

Southey and Cottle both write cottage epics. Southey takes as his hero a young woman obliged against her will to abandon her village home for the court and the camp, and Cottle chooses a poet and a scholar who, by an accident of birth, is also a king and hence disqualified from the life of rural retirement that he would prefer. The heroes are incongruous, because so is the project. Southey and Cottle write epics as a way of claiming authority for their own provincial, Nonconformist values, but the genre they choose contradicts the values that they espouse. As Wordsworth shows, the value of the provincial is better sustained by a 'tale of silent suffering, hardly clothed / In bodily form' (293–4). Jonathan Wordsworth remains, for me, the best reader of *The Ruined Cottage*, not just in his admiration of the poem but in his impatience with it, as when he finds it 'appallingly propagandist', deformed by 'overt moralizing' and by 'priggishness as grotesque as anything the later Wordsworth ever produced'.[39] His irritation reveals his sensitivity to the peculiarity of the poem's narrative voice, from noticing which many readers seem to have been distracted by Wordsworth's insistence to Isabella Fenwick that the Pedlar was 'chiefly an idea of what I fancied my own character might have become in his circumstances'.[40] This may be true but the Pedlar, unsurprisingly, is what he is, precisely because of those circumstances – the circumstances of his schooling, for example, which was quite unlike Wordsworth's. Instead of a classical education he 'learned to read / His bible' (54–5), and the rhythms of the Bible continue to inform his every utterance, so that the pious tags which intersperse his speech seem wholly unselfconscious, as when Margaret and Robert's children are described as 'their best hope next to the God in heaven' (184) or, however much it rankles with many modern critics, when the

Pedlar remarks that to the misery produced by two bad harvests 'It pleased heaven to add / A worse affliction in the plague of war' (187–8). The Pedlar's school is defined by its distance from any metropolitan centre, 'Far from the sight of city spire, or sound / Of Minster church' (57–8), and the Pedlar's profession seems chosen as a guarantee that his wandering life will remain at a distance from cities. His is a definitively provincial existence, and so are the values that he espouses. Southey and Cottle are strident in their approval of water-drinking: Wordsworth explains why. Through his focus on the well on which a spider's web encroaches, and the 'useless fragment of a wooden bowl' (145), he makes of the water that Margaret was in the habit of offering to wayfarers the proper mark of the community that joins human beings each to each. The broken bowl is 'useless', and the epithet signals the Pedlar's attachment to the central provincial values of industry and thrift. Robert's youthful virtues are all of them summed up in the description of him as 'an industrious man' (172), and the decline of both husband and wife is marked by phrases such as 'the idle loom' (470) and 'a sleepy hand of negligence' (440). Weeds represent an offence against ethical rather than aesthetic standards – 'worthless stone-crop' (368), 'unprofitable bind-weed' (372), and the toadstool with its 'lazy head' (488) – and the values against which they offend are definingly and defiantly provincial. Even the Pedlar's literary taste is marked by its distance from London: 'His eye / Flashing poetic fire, he would repeat / The songs of Burns' (70–2).

Unlikely as it may seem, the Pedlar seems to be modelled on Southey's Joan of Arc. She is the 'destined Maid': he is the 'chosen son' (76). She hears voices, and so does he, though the voices he hears are firmly naturalised:

> To him was given an ear which deeply felt
> The voice of Nature in the obscure wind,
> The sounding mountain and the running stream. (77–9)

The Pedlar is even, like Joan, suspected of 'madness' (93). But Southey, like Cottle after him, faced with the problem of how to confer dignity and authority on the provincial values that his character embodies, can think only of dressing her up as an epic hero. Wordsworth devises for his Pedlar a voice that can assume dignity and authority without any need for fancy dress. One of the chief functions of the young man to whom the Pedlar tells the story is to point out his success:

> He had rehearsed
> Her homely tale with such familiar power,
> With such a countenance of love, an eye
> So busy, that the things of which he spake
> Seemed present ... (266–70)

There is nothing quite like the voice that speaks *The Ruined Cottage* in Wordsworth's earlier poetry. It is distinguished by the almost oxymoronic quality that the young man calls 'familiar power', and located in a character, the Pedlar, whose authority is wholly unqualified by the quiet acceptance of his own social status that leads him to address his young auditor as 'sir'. His is the voice that Southey and Cottle were both straining after, the voice of quiet, confident, provincial authority, which is why *The Ruined Cottage*, as Joseph Cottle himself, it may be, came to recognise, is the masterpiece of what I have called West Country Romanticism. In this poem of Wordsworth's Cottle's project finally and fully justified itself, but it may also be the case that Wordsworth would not have written *The Ruined Cottage* in quite the way he did if it had not been for Cottle's project. He can seem a ridiculous figure, Joseph Cottle, garrulous, egotistical, imitative, muddled, his legs swaddled up against the rheumatism, memorable now only for the people with whose lives his own briefly made contact, but it may be that he had a greater influence on his more talented younger colleagues than they recognised at the time, or than we have recognised since.

Notes

1. Mary Moorman, *Wordsworth: a Biography* (2 vols, Oxford: Clarendon Press, 1957–65), i. 447.
2. Joseph Cottle, *Early Recollections; Chiefly Relating to the Late Samuel Taylor Coleridge, During His Long Residence in Bristol* (2 vols, London: Longman, Rees and Co, and Hamilton, Adama, and Co, 1837), i. 309. Strictly, Cottle could claim that he was the first publisher only of Charles Lamb.
3. Cottle, *Early Recollections*, Preface, i. viii–x.
4. Cottle, *Early Recollections*, i. 273–4, 282–4; ii. 149.
5. *New Letters of Robert Southey*, ed. Kenneth Curry (2 vols, New York: Columbia University Press, 1965), i. 228.
6. See *The Poetical Works of Robert Southey* (London: Longmans, Green and Co, 1876), 2.
7. *The Works of Charles and Mary Lamb*, ed. E. V. Lucas (7 vols, London: Methuen, 1905), vi. *Letters 1796–1820*, 185.
8. *Monthly Review*, 35 (May 1801), 1–9.
9. *Coleridge's Notebooks: a Selection*, ed. Seamus Perry (Oxford: Oxford University Press, 2002), 89 and 229.
10. The fullest and most sympathetic account of Cottle is by his namesake Basil Cottle, *Joseph Cottle and the Romantics: the Life of a Bristol Publisher* (Bristol: Redcliffe Press, 2008). This biography was published posthumously, and has been 'edited and where necessary elucidated' by Dr Myra Stokes.
11. For alternative accounts of Cottle's *Alfred* that do not stress its West Country character, see Stuart Curran, *Poetic Form and British Romanticism* (New York: Oxford University Press, 1986), 168–9; Lynda Pratt, 'Patriot Poetics and the Romantic National Epic: Placing and Displacing Southey's *Joan of Arc*', in *Placing and Displacing Romanticism*, ed. Peter Kitson (Aldershot: Ashgate, 2001), 88–105; and Lynda Pratt, 'Anglo-Saxon Attitudes? Alfred the Great and Romantic National Epic', in *Literary Appropriations of the Anglo-Saxons from the Thirteenth to the*

Twentieth Century (Cambridge: Cambridge University Press, 2000), 138–56. For an account of the 'cult of Alfred' that developed from the late sixteenth century, see Clare A. Simmons, *Reversing the Conquest: History and Myth in Nineteenth-Century British Literature* (New Brunswick and London: Rutgers University Press, 1990), 25–41.

12. The Rev. George Heath, *The New History Survey and Description of the City and Suburbs of Bristol* (Bristol: W. Matthews, 1794), 54.

13. Heath, *The New History Survey and Description of the City and Suburbs of Bristol*, 32.

14. *CL*, i. 227.

15. Cottle, *Early Recollections*, 28.

16. Joseph Cottle, *Poems, containing John the Baptist. Sir Malcolm Alla, a tale, shewing to all the world what women's love can do. War, a fragment. With a monody to John Henderson and a sketch of his character* (Bristol: Joseph Cottle, 1795), Preface, ii. The first edition was published anonymously, but Cottle acknowledged his authorship of the expanded second edition, which appeared in the following year.

17. In choosing Alfred as his hero Cottle was able to ease his progress from radical opposition to the war to nationalistic support for it, because, as Clare A. Simmons shows, Alfred might at the same time figure the ideal king for a Tory such as Pye, while still maintaining a special place in the affections of republicans. Catherine Macaulay lived in 'Alfredhouse' and placed a bust of Alfred over the door, and Major John Cartwright, the veteran parliamentary reformer, persisted throughout his career in the claim that his ambition was to revive the ideal Commonwealth that had been instituted by Alfred. See Simmons, *Reversing the Conquest*, 35–6.

18. Robert Southey, *Joan of Arc, an epic poem* (Bristol: Joseph Cottle, 1796). Quotations are from this, the first edition of the poem, unless otherwise stated.

19. On Cottle's religion, see Timothy Whelan, 'Joseph Cottle the Baptist', *Charles Lamb Bulletin*, 111 (July, 2000), 96–108.

20. See *The Complete Works of William Hazlitt*, ed. P. P. Howe (21 vols, London: J. M. Dent and Sons, 1930–4), iv. 47 and vii. 239–42.

21. Southey's own judgement. See the Preface to *Joan of Arc* in *The Poetical Works of Robert Southey*, 2.

22. *The Works of Charles and Mary Lamb*, vi. 13.

23. *CL*, i. 258.

24. *The Works of Charles and Mary Lamb*, vi. 27.

25. *CL*, i. 294.

26. *CL*, i. 313.

27. On the importance of the cottage in the 1790s for both sides in the great political debate, see John Barrell, 'Cottage Politics', in his *The Spirit of Despotism: Invasions of Privacy in the 1790s* (Oxford: Oxford University Press, 2006), 210–46.

28. The transition from a notion of epic as formally unified to the notion that the epic poem at once expressed and produced the unity of the culture within which it was written is most commonly associated with Vico and Herder, but it was very widely disseminated.

29. *The Works of Charles and Mary Lamb*, vi. 15.

30. *CL*, i. 293.

31. *The Works of Charles and Mary Lamb*, vi. 185.

32. See the Preface to *English Eclogues* in *The Poetical Works of Robert Southey*, 149.

33. Cottle, *Early Recollections*, i. 309.

34. *CL*, i. 400.

35. Cottle, *Early Recollections*, i. 314 (note).

36. All quotations from *The Ruined Cottage* are from the 'B' manuscript as given in *The Ruined Cottage and The Pedlar*, ed. James Butler (Ithaca, NY: Cornell University Press, 1979), this being the version of the poem closest to the version read by Cottle in 1798.

37. See E. P. Thompson, 'Disenchantment or Default? A Lay Sermon', in *Power and Consciousness*, ed. Conor Cruise O'Brien and William Dean Vanech (London: University of London Press, 1969), 151.

38. Robert Southey, *Joan of Arc*, 2nd edition (Bristol: N. Biggs for Longman, 1798), vii. 334–7.

39. Jonathan Wordsworth, *The Music of Humanity: a Critical Study of Wordsworth's* Ruined Cottage (London: Nelson, 1969), 17–18.

40. *The Fenwick Notes of William Wordsworth*, ed. Jared Curtis (London: Bristol Classical Press, 1993), 79.

4
William Gilbert and his Bristol Circle, 1788–98

Paul Cheshire

> It is necessary to inform the reader, of my having been a
> bookseller in Bristol, from the year 1791 to 1798; from the
> age of 21 to 28: and having imbibed from my tutor and
> friend, the late John Henderson, (one of the most extraor-
> dinary of men) some little taste for literature, I found
> myself, during that period, generally surrounded by men
> of cultivated minds.
>
> Joseph Cottle[1]

One of the 'men of cultivated minds' who figure in Cottle's *Early Recollections*
is William Gilbert, as 'a young Barrister' who had been born circa 1763 in
Antigua (Cottle, i. 162). They first met in 1788 when Gilbert was on an outing
from an asylum where he was under the care of John Henderson, the revered
'tutor and friend' referred to above. According to Cottle, Gilbert 'continued
in the Asylum about a year, when his mind being partially restored, his
friends removed him, and he wholly absented himself from Bristol, till the
year [1795], when he re-appeared in this city, but whence no one could tell,
and he never told' (Cottle, ii. 315).[2] During this second three-year stay in
Bristol, Cottle introduced Gilbert to Coleridge, Southey, and Wordsworth,
and Gilbert published his visionary millennialist poem *The Hurricane:
a Theosophical and Western Eclogue.*[3]

Intriguing descriptions by Cottle's Bristol circle have until the last ten
years been the sole source of information about this 'wreck of a once splendid genius' (Cottle, i. 62). Much more is now known about Gilbert's previous
life.[4] During part of his six-year absence from Bristol, for example, Gilbert
had been in London writing articles on 'macrocosmal astrology' whose
object was 'the enlightening of mankind'. He had also advertised for pupils
to whom he would teach astrology and 'the nature and use of talismans'[5] (see
Figure 3). No one who has read Gilbert's *Conjuror's Magazine* articles can rea-
sonably doubt that when he came to Bristol he was already an exponent of
ideas hitherto considered to have been acquired from Coleridge during the

JOHN HENDERSON, B.A. PEM.COL.

From a Portrait by Palmer. in the Possession of Mr. Cottle.

Figure 3   John Henderson 1757–1788. Tutor and friend to Joseph Cottle and William Gilbert; 'Celebrated for his wonderful acquirements in Alchymy, Judicial Astrology, and other abstruse and curious learning'. Frontispiece to Joseph Cottle, *Malvern Hills with Minor Poems and Essays* (London: Cadell, 1829).

period of their acquaintance.[6] Such complexities of influence and exchange show how advisable it is to be sceptical of 'the popular myth of the Romantic author as an isolated creative genius'.[7] This warning is particularly applic-able to Gilbert because he appears to be such an isolated and misunderstood figure that it takes an effort to place him, as I shall do here, within an interactive cultural group. It is tempting to leave him as he saw himself: 'one, who saw in a light different from ALL THE WORLD' (*Hurricane*, 103).

1788–9, Asylum at Hanham: John Henderson and Joseph Cottle

As one instance of the unsoundness of Gilbert's mind, he was a confirmed astrologer. (Cottle, i. 64)

Gilbert's one-year confinement in Richard Henderson's asylum at Hanham, a village four miles outside Bristol, is likely to have started towards the end of summer 1788.[8] The owner was a former Methodist preacher and John Wesley was a regular visitor, praising Henderson in his Journal as 'the best physician for lunatics in England'. The breakdown that led to William Gilbert's confinement was, according to Cottle, an episode of mania. Having lost a legal case, Gilbert set about following the gospel's injunction to 'Sell all that thou hast, and distribute to the poor', and threw the household goods out of the window of a Portsmouth lodging house (Cottle, ii. 325). Such breakdowns were common enough for 'Religion and Methodism' to be recognised as an admission category for Bedlam, and a successful cure was often effected by someone sympathetic to the condition. Gilbert's Methodist family had strong connections with John Wesley and this is his most likely route to Henderson's care.[9]

Richard Henderson had used the building as a school until 1780.[10] His son John taught at the school, which Joseph Cottle attended, forming the close bond with him as a tutor and mentor that continued long after the school had closed. John Henderson was said to have taught Latin at Kingswood School at the age of eight, and Greek at Treveca, an evangelical theological college, at the age of twelve. His brilliance and promise became widely known and an education at Pembroke College, Oxford was funded by evangelical well-wishers such as Dean Tucker and Hannah More. But Henderson would not dance to his sponsors' tune; he remained fiercely independent to the point of eccentricity, and after leaving Oxford spent his time at Hanham pursuing the metaphysical interests (astrology, Hermetic Christian occultism) that Gilbert subsequently professed, and helping his father with the care of the asylum's inmates.[11]

One example of the care he gave Gilbert during his stay at Hanham is on record. In 'Explanation of the Number 666', Gilbert wrote that 'Mr. John Henderson, whose cometary splendors not long since illuminated the sphere of learning, first called my attention to this number in the year 1788. I went up stairs, and in less than half an hour, returned with the answer I now publish' (*CM* (February 1792), 220). John Henderson was also important as the link between Gilbert and Cottle. Henderson occasionally walked into Bristol with Gilbert, during his stay at Hanham, and on one such afternoon he called on Cottle introducing Gilbert as the 'Young Counsellor' (Cottle, ii. 314; see Figure 3).

'As one instance of the unsoundness of Gilbert's mind, he was a confirmed astrologer', Cottle wrote, portraying Henderson alongside him as the man of common-sense (Cottle, i. 64). Cottle gives no inkling that his 'tutor and friend's' astrological studies were public knowledge, and sufficiently well known for Boswell to describe Dr Johnson taking tea with 'Mr. John Henderson, student of Pembroke College, celebrated for his wonderful acquirements in Alchymy, Judicial Astrology, and other abstruse and curious learning'. John Henderson died on 2 November 1788 aged 31: he is without doubt the West Country's major influence on William Gilbert. Like Thomas Chatterton, he was a legendary figure: Coleridge's notebook of the period has 'Life of John Henderson' listed as a projected work for which Gilbert would have been a rich source of information.[12]

Another regular visitor to the asylum was Hannah More, who was sponsoring the upkeep of an inmate. Over thirty years later she recalled how,

> on one of her visits to Hannam Madhouse [...] whilst waiting alone in a parlour, a tall wan looking man came into the room & shutting the door after him seated himself by her on the sofa to her very great dismay; he then pulled a small book out of his pocket printed in the black letter nearly 200 Years before & *showed her* in which it was foretold that about the time in which they then were 'the Kingly Power should be lost but not the Kingly life' – The King was *at that time* under coercion in a state of derangement.[13]

George III's first publicly known period of madness lasted three months from late November 1788. The place, date, and reading matter are right for William Gilbert. If this unnamed figure isn't Gilbert, Henderson's asylum was doing a remarkable job of turning deranged people into astrologers. Gilbert's movements after leaving the asylum are uncertain. The next fix on him is in London where his first contribution to *The Conjuror's Magazine* appeared in September 1791. His 'Remarkable Fulfilment of Events, Notified by the Solar Eclipse June 4, 1788' drew on black letter seventeenth-century sources:

> Having now ascertained according to rule, the governors of this eclipse, we will read the effects, not from any ex post facto law, but from aphorisms, the latest of which I shall quote from a book printed in 1665.
> RULE. An eclipse or comet in the 11th House causes death and destruction of grandees.
> OBS. The numerous deaths of peers in Great Britain, during the operation of this eclipse, has been remarked by persons without any reference to Astrology; and in France, where it fell in the same House, the effects on Aristocracy have been still more notorious. (*CM* (September 1791), 46–7; see Figure 4).

Writing over the initial 'B', William Gilbert's astrological prognostications on the epochal events surrounding the French Revolution were seized on enthusiastically by readers who wrote asking for contact. His success may have encouraged him to advertise 'Proposals for instructing Pupils in

REMARKABLE
FULFILMENT OF EVENTS,
NOTIFIED BY THE SOLAR ECLIPSE JUNE 4, 1788,

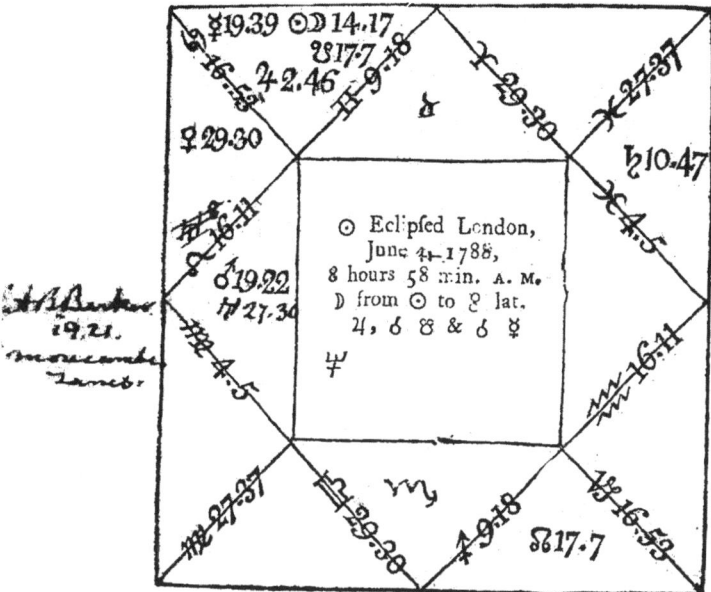

Figure 4 Astrological chart from William Gilbert, 'Remarkable Fulfilment', *The Conjuror's Magazine*, 1.2 (September 1791), 46–8.

Spiritual Knowledge' (*CM* (May 1792), 400), although in the same issue of the *Conjuror's Magazine* a rival astrologer mounted a strong attack on his grasp of astrology (ibid. 404–5). It is hard to know whether Gilbert's sudden and unexplained disappearance – 'What is become of Mr. B.? Has W. E. touched him too closely?' (editorial comment, *CM* (July 1792), 464) – signalled a tactical retreat, or Gilbert's preoccupation with newly recruited pupils. His final article in the magazine appeared in July 1793, and then follow two 'missing years' before his return to Bristol in 1795.

Bristolia's bards

> Arise, my Muse, attune thy trembling string,
> In lofty notes, of fam'd BRISTOLIA, sing.
>
> (R. J. Thorn[14])

In 1795 the young ex-student poets Coleridge and Southey and their fellow Pantisocrats plotted the formation of an idealistic commune in America.

However rural their dreams these were kindled in late night discussions over pipes of Oronoko tobacco in inns and shared lodgings in Oxford, London, and Bristol. Although Bristol's *Mathews Guide* of 1793 proudly claimed it was England's second city, this claim was forty years out of date.[15] The trade with Africa had dwindled, the tidal port was inaccessible for two-thirds of the year, and although Bristol had been in the vanguard of industrial development, by the 1790s the industrial revolution had flourished in the Midlands leaving Bristol behind but in the vanguard of the next phase – industrial pollution.

This discrepancy between Bristol and its self-image found expression in 1794 in a local poetic duel. *Bristolia: a Poem*, by R. J. Thorn, was dedicated 'To the numerous, and respectable inhabitants of this great, commercial city', and larded city and citizens with fulsome praise: 'Thou wear'st the form of old, Majestic ROME, / And (save great LONDON) second art to none' (33–4). Robert Lovell's riposte, *Bristol: a Satire*, took a different view of city and citizens: 'To the liberal and literary *inhabitants* of Bristol; this poem, descriptive of the illiberal and illiterate, is respectfully inscribed by the author' (see Figure 5).[16] His poem began:

> Low in a drear and gloomy Vale immur'd,
> By mud cemented, and by smoke obscur'd,
> A city stands, and BRISTOL is its name,
> By trade and dullness consecrate to fame. (1–4)

Lovell also mocked Thorn's poetic pretensions, 'BRISTOL no more a vulgar sound we hear, / But soft BRISTOLIA soothes the list'ning ear' (35–6), and Chatterton was canonised as the victim of an uncaring and ignorant public:

> To thee the posthumous applause they pour'd;
> When living starv'd thee, and when dead ador'd.
> Return oh! Muse to BRISTOL's matchless Sons,
> In avarice *Dutchmen* and in science *Huns*. (153–6)

Robert Lovell was to die in 1796, too early to develop as a poet, but he was in the forefront of Pantisocracy: it was he who introduced Southey and Coleridge to their future publisher Joseph Cottle, and he was first of the three to marry a Fricker sister. In praising Chatterton, and in all of these other ways, Lovell is one herald of the Bristol Romantic movement.[17]

The circle to which Lovell and others of his generation belonged was portrayed anonymously in a scurrilous local publication *The Observer, Part 1st: being a transient glance at about forty youths of Bristol*.[18] This pamphlet has attracted interest because it contains early thumbnail sketches of Robert South*y – 'really the man of virtue' (14) – and S. T. Coler**ge, who 'would […] do well to appear with cleaner stockings' (15). The 'Observer' gives Robert

DEDICATION.

TO THE

LIBERAL AND LITERARY

INHABITANTS

OF

B R I S T O L;

THIS POEM,

DESCRIPTIVE OF THE

ILLIBERAL AND ILLITERATE,

Is refpectfully infcribed by

THE AUTHOR.

Figure 5   Robert Lovell's Dedication, from *Bristol: a Satire* (1794).

Lov**l qualified approval: his *Bristol, a Satire*, 'is not illy written' but 'savours much of ill-nature' (16). R. J. Thor**e's vapid poeticisms are sent up: 'Fade ye writings of Shakespeare, of Milton, of Dryden, and of every other genius of eminent abilities, when placed in competition with the effulgent productions of this transcendant Poet!' (9).

The ideological affiliation of the 'Observer' is clear. Coleridge is praised for exposing war as 'human butchery and legalised murder', and the slave trade as 'infamous traffic' (14–15). Less historically serious, perhaps, but useful for getting a sense of the daily lives and temptations of young men is the moral map of Bristol that can be drawn from his comments. 'Can the frequenting Brothels, Theatres or Billiard-Tables enhance a young man in the estimation of the world?' (4). Even C.F. W*l***ms's 'frequent appearance at the Assembly Coffee-House' (8) is counted against him. The 'Observer' wants his fellows to be conventional and virtuous, and Southey is held up as the paragon. There is also some pithy criticism of poetry, as when an 'unsuccessful Poetaster' is advised to '*think* more, and write less' (42). All of this gives us a sense of passion, energy, ambition, and rivalry, as a new generation faces the Choice of Hercules, torn between billiard-tables, revolution, and respectability.

Joseph Cottle's 'Bristol Album 1795'

> As a nucleus, so many men of genius were there congregated as to justify the designation, 'The Augustan Age of Bristol'. (Cottle, i. ix–x)

One Bristol figure who doesn't appear in *The Observer* is Joseph Cottle. Social differences might explain this, but his family background was not unlike Robert Southey's. Both had draper fathers, and their various careers indicate the mobility of Bristol society at this time. Cottle's elder brother Amos secured enough financial backing for a good education, and took a degree at Cambridge University. Joseph, slower and by his own account less hard working, had his rather more unorthodox education under the guidance and tutorship of John Henderson – and it was Henderson who advised Cottle to become a bookseller. He opened his first bookshop in 1791, at the age of twenty-one.[19] Four years later Cottle's bookshop became the equivalent for Bristol poets of what City Lights in San Francisco was for the 1950s Beat Generation: a meeting place for the impoverished young writers and political radicals who converged on the city.

Cottle seems to have been aware at the time of the significance of what he was later to call 'The Augustan Age of Bristol'. One sign of this is an album, the first page of which is boldly headed 'Bristol Album 1795' (see Figure 6).[20] The sense of time and place in this album's title is clear. It is not 'Cottle's Album', not even 'Cottle's Bristol Album'. He had a sense of history in the making, as well as an aspiration to be part of it, and he tried to capture it for posterity.[21]

The first poem in the album is 'English Dactylics, to a Soldier's Wife', written and signed 'Robert Southey. May 25. 1795'. Overleaf, and dated the following day, is the beginning of William Gilbert's 'The Aurora of Human Happiness: An Ode' written in an elaborate copperplate hand that gradually

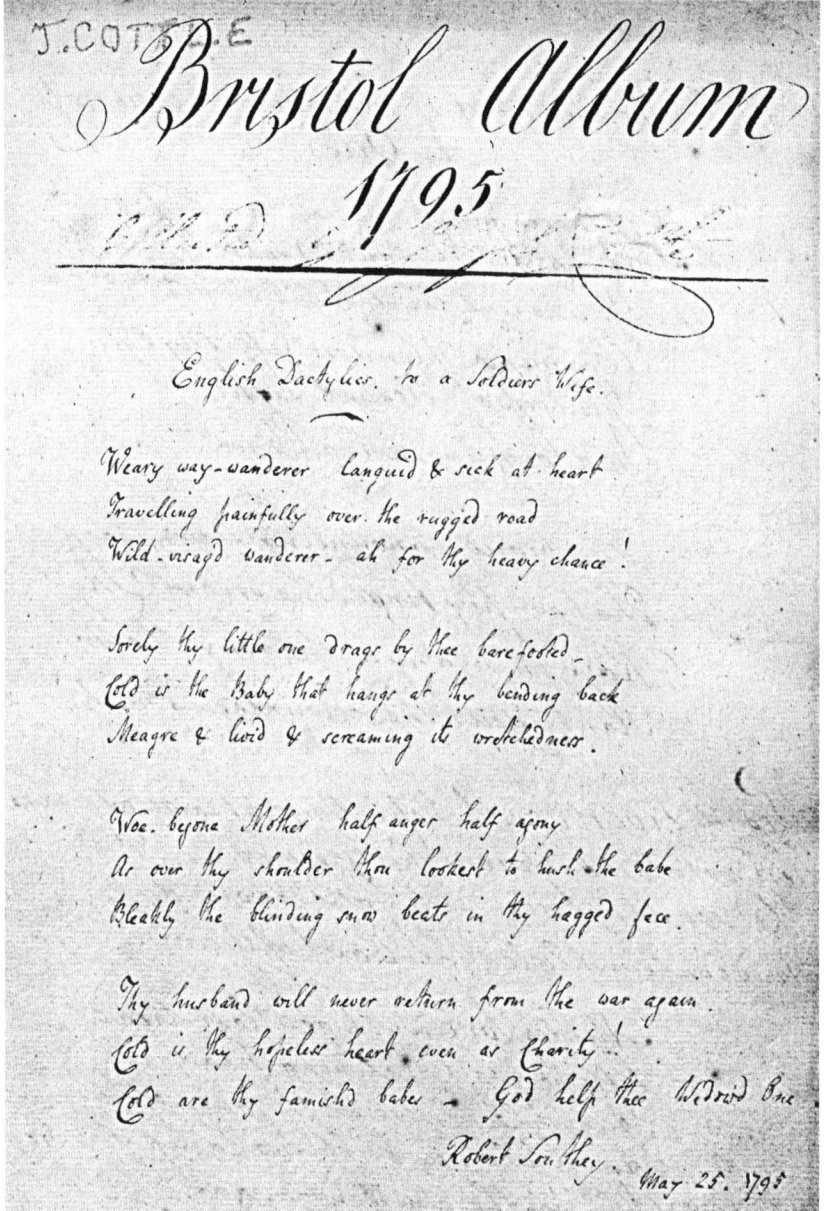

Figure 6 Title page of Joseph Cottle's 'Bristol Album 1795', with Robert Southey's autograph 'English Dactylics, to a Soldier's Wife' as the first entry.

becomes spidery towards the end, as if he was pressed for time (see Figure 7). These lines are the first sign of William Gilbert's reappearance at Bristol:

The Aurora of Human Happiness
An Ode

Shades away! The Day Star's high!
Down to Erebus and Night
Ye who love the dark Domain!
Beaming Splendors fill My Eye;
Splendors of Celestial Light,
In a long, unceasing Train!

The proud, announcing, Dawn is o'er
That amply tinged the orient Sky:
Rays, in many a streamy Show'r,
Slant adown the Mountains high!

Proud Liberty, with Step intense, at large appears:
Her Foot elastic spurns the Ground:
She sends a boundless Gaze around,
And contemplates the Vast of Years.

Milder Love with gentlest tread,
Lifts her soft declining head:
And while her eye with fondness swims,
And while her purpling Lamp she trims,
Paces o'er the ambient meads,
As Liberty, her Guardian, leads.

Peace above surveys the Scene,
Happy treads the silent Green;
Till a long and joyous Band,
From the distance sailing on,
All sincerely hand in hand,
Beat with measur'd steps the Lawn.

Love awaits their pleas'd Retreat—
Peace around the Spring Air mellows—
Liberty exults in Glory;
Mildly deigns to hear the Story
Told by Shepherds of their Fellows—
Of the Loves with Love that meet.

Wm Gilbert
Bristol. May. 26th-95—

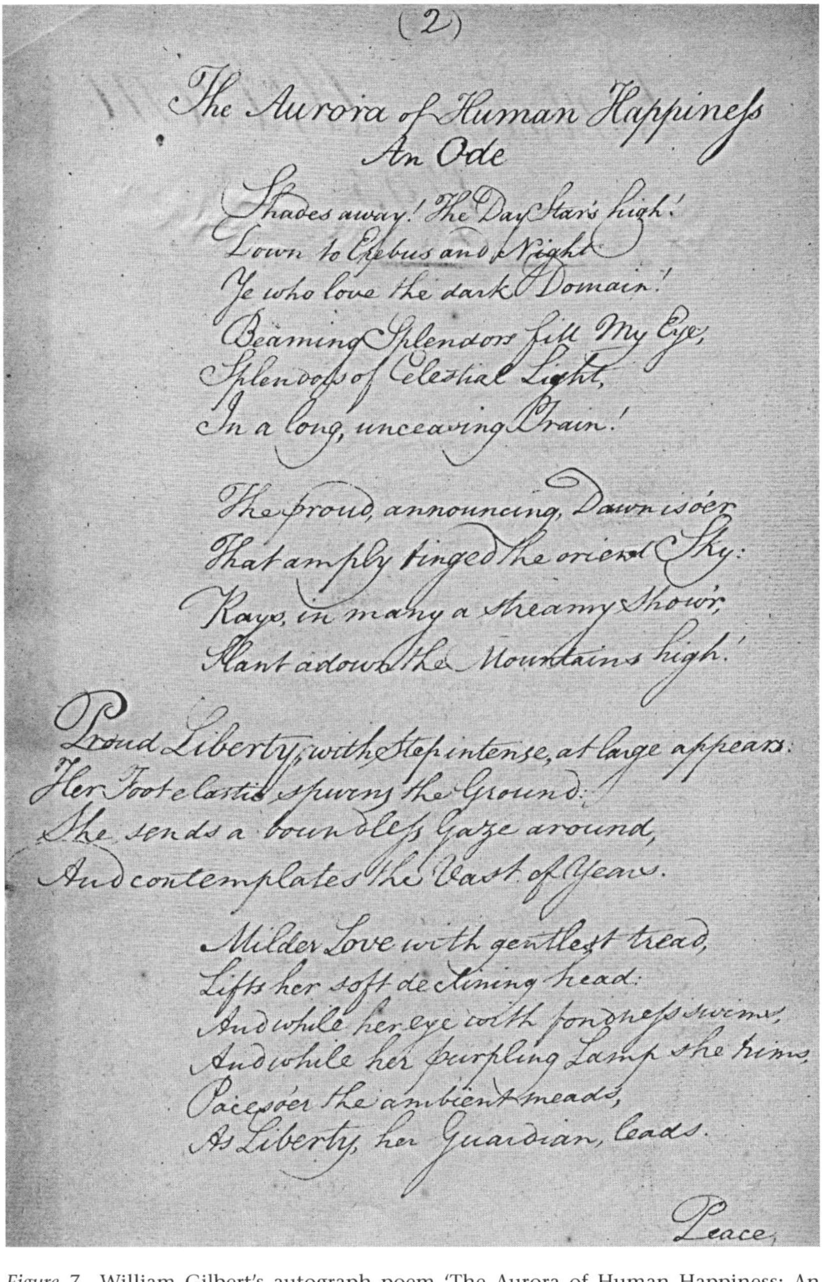

(2)

The Aurora of Human Happiness
An Ode

Shades away! The Day Star's high!
Down to Erebus and Night
Ye who love the dark Domain!
Beaming Splendors fill My Eye,
Splendors of Celestial Light,
In a long, unceasing Train!

The proud, announcing, Dawn is o'er
That amply tinged the orient Sky:
Rays, in many a streamy Show'r,
Slant adown the Mountains high.'

Proud Liberty, with Step intense, at large appears:
Her Foot elastic spurns the Ground:
She sends a boundless Gaze around,
And contemplates the Vast of Years.

Milder Love with gentlest tread,
Lifts her soft declining head:
And while her eye with fondness swims,
And while her purpling Lamp she trims,
Paces o'er the ambient meads,
As Liberty, her Guardian, leads.

Peace,

Figure 7 William Gilbert's autograph poem 'The Aurora of Human Happiness: An Ode', lines 1–20, from Joseph Cottle's 'Bristol Album 1795'.

In mood if not exactly in form or quality this ode is reminiscent of Milton's 'On the Morning of Christ's Nativity'. A joyful, epoch-making event is heralded in the heavens, and shepherds rejoice on the lawn. It has the feel of a millennial, revolutionary hymn. Milton's poem of cosmic renewal was striking a chord in spring 1795: Coleridge's 'Religious Musings', dated a few months earlier to Christmas Eve 1794, was initially titled 'The Nativity'. Gilbert's second and third stanzas have four lines apiece, creating a variation on the six-line stanza form and giving the poem an interesting structure. 'Proud Liberty' steps in with an alexandrine as if to represent the impact she makes on the world order. While the poem resumes its regular trochaic tetrameter at the fourth stanza, the rhyme scheme is varied creatively throughout. In choosing this poem to contribute to the Album, Gilbert was celebrating hopes for 'liberty' and 'peace' that were shared by Southey, Cottle, and other bards of Bristol.

Contributions to the Album between May 1795 and July 1796 include Robert Lovell's sonnet, 'Stonehenge' (3), later reprinted in *The Watchman*; Coleridge's 'Lines Written at the King's Arms, Ross' (5v–6); and poems by John Rose (a bookseller) and Thomas Beddoes (of the Pneumatic Institute), both of whom were also Bristol radicals. There was a poem by Amos, Joseph's brother. More remarkable than all of these, and worthy of separate study, the poem 'Evening', 'Written by an Insane Man at Dr Fox's', consists of 26 lines of blank verse written in the kind of poetic diction that Coleridge was to employ two months later when he started the 'Eolian Harp' with the words, 'My pensive Sara … '. The identity of the 'insane' poet/patient is not known, but Dr Edward Long Fox, another Bristol radical active in campaigning against the 'Gagging Acts', had recently taken over Richard Henderson's asylum after being in attendance there for several years, making for another link with William Gilbert.[22]

The Album later became a scrap-book for an assortment of pasted-in letters, poems and other holographs, but the early entries up to June 1796 are all poems written by members of Cottle's Bristol circle and leave a record, as he had intended, of Bristol's 'Augustan Age'. The next trace of Gilbert's Bristol writing is in a collective miscellany that is much more well known – *The Watchman*.

Gilbert vs. Coleridge, 1796

> Bless us! I was *most* intimate with poor Gilbert, who was as mad as a March hare, & who has written letters to me referring to & prolixly repeating conversations of mine which not only never had, but never *could* have, taken place! (Coleridge, *Marginalia*, iii. 990)[23]

Coleridge printed two Gilbert contributions in *The Watchman*. 'The Commercial Academic: No. I' by 'Mr. G—rt', printed 2 April 1796, was first attributed to Gilbert by Lewis Patton.[24] Macroeconomics may be a surprising departure from macrocosmal astrology, but Cottle writes that Gilbert 'seemed to delight in nothing so much as discussion, whether on the unconfirmed parallactic angle of Sirius, or the comparative weight of two straws' (Cottle, i. 63). The strutting barrister rhetoric has enough in common with Gilbert's prose style to give credibility to Patton's attribution. Coleridge's praise is qualified (Gilbert's 'reasonings are perhaps not unimpregnably solid') but he is hungry for contributions and a regular series has been promised: 'The Editor returns his grateful acknowledgements to Mr. G—rt for the following Essay, and will anxiously expect the remaining Numbers' (*Watchman*, 168). Coleridge waited in vain.

My hypothesis is that Gilbert was prompted to write 'The Commercial Academic' in response to Coleridge's 'On the Slave Trade', printed in *The Watchman* eight days previously (*Watchman*, 130–40). Coleridge's article argues that our vices (and the slave trade) arise from '*imaginary* Wants. [...] But if each among us confined his wishes to the actual necessaries and real comforts of Life, we should preclude all the causes of Complaint and all the motives to Iniquity' (*Watchman*, 130–1). Gilbert attacks this anti-luxury argument by saying, first, that the aspiration for happiness is natural, and commerce is the exchange of mutual needs to that end; secondly, 'Commerce is always opened for the attainment of luxuries, not necessaries'. Thirdly, 'Luxuries are *necessaries*. Luxuries I mean as a general term for everything beyond the rudest food and cloathing; [...] If we confine the wants of man to the wants of the mere animal, we unravel the web of society and brutalize our nature' (*Watchman*, 169). Having made his case for the intrinsic harmlessness of commerce *per se* and the naïvety of trying to separate luxuries as evils, he goes on to argue that it is unequal commerce such as importing goods in exchange for money that causes problems, and leads to war when one nation feels it has been harmed by the exchange.

The slave trade is not mentioned but Gilbert's argument is applicable to the importing of West Indian slave goods. Perhaps he was trying to advance a better anti-slave trade argument, perhaps he was delighting in discussion. Although passages in *The Hurricane* condemn the institution of slavery, the redress is left to cosmic forces and what appears to be the infusion of African spirits into European bodies: 'With every lump of Sugar, a certain portion of *Essence* of America and of Africa is swallowed' (*Hurricane*, 63). If Gilbert felt that continuing the consumption of sugar was helping the abolitionist cause on some kind of magical level, it is hard to see him participating fruitfully in the boycotting campaign.

'Fragment by a West-Indian', Coleridge's cento of 22 slightly modified lines from *The Hurricane* in the final number of *The Watchman* (see *Watchman*, 350–1) has had more critical attention. Patton calls these lines 'a charming bit of verse' which is not a description that has ever been applied to

The Hurricane as a whole (see *Watchman*, li). Jonathan Wordsworth saw it as Coleridge's attempt to 'form a brief Conversation Poem' out of Gilbert's then unpublished work.[25] Rightly so: this extract is equivalent to taking a detail of the sky from Turner's *The Slave Ship* and naming it *The Charming Sunset*. Judging from his Advertisement preceding the published poem (*Hurricane*, viii), Gilbert did not object to Coleridge's presentation of his poem; he expressed his gratitude to 'A Friend' who 'printed some lines of this Poem in a Miscellany'. But he also mentioned that this friend (i.e. Coleridge) 'passed [...] a very strong opinion against the Metre of some verses', and proceeded to lay down his side of the argument: 'What is Metre? It is the focus of Union between the Sense and the Sound; in the best English Poets, at least: It is a contrivance to throw the accent, *not where a common reader or speaker would throw it*, but where an IMPASSIONED ORATOR or JUDICIOUS ACTOR would throw it' (*Hurricane*, viii). There is little deference in the tirade that follows, and Paul Kaufman went so far as to think that Coleridge gave Gilbert's views some consideration.[26] Starting in October 1796 Coleridge borrowed twice from the Bristol Library for a period of well over three months John Foster's *An Essay on the different nature of Accent and Quantity* (Eton, 1763).[27] According to Kaufman 'It was this study of Foster which stimulated the experiment with accentual verse in *Christabel*' (115).

Gilbert mentions in his notes to *The Hurricane* a debate with a 'friend' over whether the terrestrial paradise was located in Judaea or Abyssinia (*Hurricane*, 88–9). The identification of Coleridge as this friend is problematic but the two men certainly had this interest in common; commentators on 'Kubla Khan', most notably John Livingstone Lowes, have researched Coleridge's interest in the Abyssinian paradise and his reading on the subject. John Beer has uncovered parallels between Coleridge's thought and passages in *The Hurricane*, and as a sign of their intimacy noted that Gilbert identified Coleridge as the author of a line from Southey's *Joan of Arc* (Beer, 99). But Beer was unaware of Gilbert's earlier *Conjuror's Magazine* writings and, having traced Coleridge's adoption of fountains of light from Boehme and others, inferred that when Gilbert wrote of fountains in a passage such as 'EUROPE is the *fountain* of *Slavery;* AMERICA the FIELD of FREEDOM: The *Fountain* of it is GOD in *Man*, and FIRE in NATURE' (*Hurricane*, 85), this indicated that he 'was reproducing, in however garbled a form, images and ideas that he had first heard on the lips of Coleridge himself' (Beer, 98–9). Six uses of 'fountain' in Gilbert's *Conjuror's Magazine* articles contradict this view. For example: 'The Hebrews were the fountain of all nations' (*CM* (November 1791), 110); 'the COURSE OF LIFE must accompany the Talisman, which proceeds from its fountain' (*CM* (February 1792), 224). Beer's work (needless to say) remains valuable for its identification of the common ground shared by Coleridge and Gilbert, and invaluable for its exposition of this rich subject matter. Beer has demonstrated conclusively how interested Coleridge was in 'Accounts of all the strange phantasms that ever possessed your philosophy-dreamers from Tauth [Thoth] the Egyptian to Taylor, the English Pagan' (*CL*, i. 260). I can only add that this is a syllabus on which Gilbert would have had plenty to offer him.

The Hurricane: a Theosophical and Western Eclogue

> I AM NOT UNDERSTOOD. 'Tis well.
> I UNDERSTAND MYSELF. It is better.
>
> (*Hurricane*, 92)

That the three Gilbert writings discussed above were disseminated by courtesy of Cottle and Coleridge is a clear sign of his indebtedness to the Bristol circle. Coleridge's selection and shaping of *The Hurricane*'s lines for his *Watchman* cento in particular could be seen as an act of grooming, of showing Gilbert he could write a poem that meets its public halfway. But *The Hurricane* in all its intractability was published by Gilbert himself towards the end of 1796.[28]

It is not hard to see why *The Hurricane* has been neglected, why it has not been included in anthologies of Romanticism. In summary, the poem sounds trivial. A lonely young man on an Antigua shore during the build-up to a hurricane longs for love, and gets his wish granted when Elmira, an angelic girl, the sole survivor of a shipwreck, takes shelter in his house during the storm. As poetry it does not survive direct comparison. In the *Conjuror's Magazine* Gilbert had referred to James Thomson as 'my favourite English poet' (*CM* (March 1792), 341) and when *The Hurricane*'s descriptive blank verse passages are set alongside *The Seasons*, Gilbert's indebtedness is plain.[29] The scenario cannot support the freight of symbolism imposed by the metaphysical notes, so the visionary energy of his warring continents seems weak alongside William Blake's *Continental Prophecies* written in 1793–5. Blake's *Prophecies* must be derived from the same esoteric traditions, although I can see no sign of direct borrowing, or conclusive evidence (pace Schuchard) that the two poets met.[30]

To make the case for *The Hurricane* one should perhaps invoke Robert Southey's backhanded compliment in praise of Landor's *Gebir*: 'the poem is such as Gilbert if he were only half as mad as he is, could have written'.[31] I would argue that the disinhibition resulting from Gilbert's madness, and the freedom that self-publishing permits – the accidents of its creation that have allowed its faults – are the very qualities that make *The Hurricane* special. This is the unfiltered documentary imperfection that Tom Waits admired in Bob Dylan and The Band's *Basement Tapes*, a sequence of experimental home recordings that were not intended for public release: 'I like my music with the rinds and the seeds and pulp left in – so the bootlegs I obtained in the Sixties and Seventies, where the noise and grit of the tapes became inseparable from the music, are essential to me.'[32] *The Hurricane*'s mix of verse and copious notes need to be treated as a whole. The notes are not subsidiary to the verse, they are essential to the full work's hybrid vitality. Like Dante's *Il Convivio*, *The Hurricane* is a prosemetric work.[33] When Gilbert reaches a rhapsodic state, his writing can suddenly lift off, his prose rising into majestic rhythms, before breaking up into dottiness a page or so later. It is this unedited precariousness that is peculiarly Gilbertian. He could be characterised as the Syd Barrett of Romanticism: an inseparable tangle of genius, eccentricity, and madness.[34]

However *The Hurricane* is regarded artistically, Gilbert certainly deserves a place within the history of ideas. The continuation of astrological practice and hermetic philosophy into the late 1790s seems, as Patrick Curry has shown, to be a part of a resurgence that accompanied the Age of Revolution.[35] The surveys of millennialism in the Romantic era by Morton Paley and Tim Fulford show how widely held the expectation of a coming divine intervention was.[36] In Ernest Lee Tuveson's definition this is the belief that 'history under divine guidance, will bring about the triumph of Christian principles, and that a holy utopia will come into being'.[37]

Turning back to Bristol, Robert Southey's *Joan of Arc* published at the end of 1795 reflected the contemporary millennialist outlook and has clear thematic connections with *The Hurricane*. Both poems showed spiritual agencies intervening in history at decisive epochs, and both were intended to reflect and comment on the momentous period their authors were living through. There is an interesting comparison to be made between Southey's divinely inspired warrior Joan and Gilbert's passive Elmira, who seems to figure a rebirth of the innocent after the divine retribution has passed. But such a comparison requires a detailed appraisal of Southey's *Joan* and an untangling of the complications of Coleridge's contribution to its second book that space does not allow here.[38]

Southey's part in Gilbert's Bristol life following his return from Portugal in May 1796 does him credit. The first reference to Gilbert in his letters is typical of his generous support. In January 1797, not long after its publication, he tried to get a review of *The Hurricane* published:

> I wish Bob would insert a review of my writing in the *British Critic*. It is upon a strange poem with still stranger notes, written by a man of brilliant genius and polished manners who is deranged. It is easy to imply this without doing it in such terms as would wound his feelings.[39]

Southey's deft handling of Gilbert's feelings would be interesting to read if they can be traced. But his review of 'a strange poem with still stranger notes' was a simple task in comparison with the problem caused by Gilbert's sudden disappearance in 1798, which necessitated what must surely be one of the strangest letters Southey was ever to write.

1798: A lonesome pilgrimage 'unknown where'

Joseph Cottle described how 'One morning information was brought to us that Wm. Gilbert at an early hour had departed precipitately from Bristol, unknown where, and that without speaking to any of his friends' (Cottle, ii. 316). When his friends compared notes all agreed that Gilbert had recently been talking of going to the 'Nation of Gibberti, who inhabit East and South of Abyssinia' as mentioned in his notes to *The Hurricane* (*Hurricane*, 77). These he believed to function as ambassadors for Abyssinia, which was the divine powerhouse of the coming millennial transformation. A letter from Southey to William Roscoe of Liverpool dated 26 July 1798 substantiates Cottle's account.[40] The fact that Liverpool was assumed to be Gilbert's port of departure bears out what has been said earlier concerning the decline of Bristol:

> Mr William Gilbert is now in Liverpool, from whence he intends to work his passage to Africa. he is a man of much information & much genius, but afflicted with that worst calamity, mental derangement; & should he leave England without money, & on the wild idea of being divinely called to Africa, the fatigues of such a voyage & the situation he would be in at its close would probably be fatal to him.[41]

Roscoe found no sign of Gilbert, and his Bristol friends never heard from him again. The first news of him came thirty years later. Cottle met Gilbert's niece and understood from her that Gilbert had 'sailed from England to Charleston in America, where he died, about the year 1825' (Cottle, ii. 317). But Gilbert has not been traced in Charleston SC archives, and two family documents place him in the West Indies in late 1798, and at Antigua in 1807, so his movements after 1798 still remain a mystery.[42]

This mystery is appropriate for the Gilbert whose whereabouts 'no one could tell, and he never told' after his first Bristol disappearance in 1788 (Cottle, ii. 315). Why did he never subsequently get in touch with friends he had been intimate with over a three-year period? Perhaps, as Gilbert felt, such 'a *lonesome pilgrimage* through the World [...] was unavoidable to one, who saw in a light different from ALL THE WORLD' (*Hurricane*, 103). Perhaps he was wrong, and the Romantic myth of the 'isolated creative genius' had him in thrall after all.

Notes

1. Joseph Cottle, *Early Recollections* (2 vols, London: Longman Rees & Co, 1837), i. 1. Hereafter Cottle.
2. I have amended Cottle's dates – see below.
3. *The Hurricane: a Theosophical and Western Eclogue. To which is subjoined a Solitary Effusion in a Summer's Evening* (Bristol: For the author, by R. Edwards, 1796).

4. For an outline biography see Paul Cheshire, 'An Introduction to William Gilbert (1763–1825?)', hereafter cited as *Introduction*, at www.williamgilbert.com. Hereafter cited as *Gilbert Website*.

5. *The Conjuror's Magazine, or Magical and Physiognomical Mirror* (2 vols, August 1791–July 1793, London: W. Locke and H. D. Symonds). February 1792, 204; May 1792, 400. Hereafter cited *CM*. All articles identified as Gilbert's are available on *Gilbert Website* with editorial notes. Marsha Keith Schuchard's 1999 conference paper 'Rediscovering William "Hurricane" Gilbert' (*Gilbert Website*) was the first to make this identification. I draw different conclusions, but I gratefully acknowledge my debt to her research.

6. *Pace* John Beer, *Coleridge's Poetic Intelligence* (Basingstoke: Macmillan, 1977), 99.

7. Lynda Pratt, 'Creation Myth', *TLS* (31 October 2008), 7–8, 8.

8. Cottle's date, 1787, is too early. Until 11 October 1787 Gilbert was a key witness in a court martial case at London, retained by the defendant. See *Trial of Major John Browne* (London: J. Bell, 1788), 126. Gilbert's pamphlet *An Opinion on the Power of Courts Martial [etc.]* (London: J. Bell 1788), 22 signs off 'W. Gilbert, London, February 13th 1788'. Note E4 to Gilbert's 'Remarkable fulfilment of events' (*CM* (September 1791), 46–8) shows he left London in June 1788 and did not return until February 1790. To have established a relationship with Henderson, who died 2 November 1788, Gilbert's Hanham year must have started mid/late 1788.

9. For Henderson and Wesley, see John Wesley *The Journal of the Rev. John Wesley*, ed. Nehemiah Curnock (8 vols, London: R Culley, 1909–16), viii. 14. For breakdowns, see Roy Porter, *Mind Forg'd Manacles* (Cambridge, MA: Harvard University Press, 1987), 33, and 67–8 for Whitefield effecting a cure of a 'Methodically mad' Bedlam inmate. See *Introduction*, 3, for an outline of Gilbert's family Methodist associations.

10. Bristol Record Office 39801/F/22; *Bonner and Middleton's Bristol Journal* (20 May 1780).

11. See *Oxford Dictionary of National Biography* (*DNB*) (Oxford: Oxford University Press, 2004) for an outline.

12. James Boswell, *Life of Johnson*, ed. R.W. Chapman (Oxford: Oxford University Press, 1980), 1295 (12 June 1784); *CN*, i. 174.

13. Hannah More, *Reminiscencies* (1827) in *Women Morality & Advice Literature: Manuscripts and Rare Printed Works of Hannah More (1745–1833) and her Circle from the Clark Library Los Angeles* (Marlborough: Adam Matthew, 2005), *Guide*, 74. Transcr. Janice Devereux. I have substituted 'Hannam' for 'Hammoon' after viewing the MS on microfilm.

14. Romaine Joseph Thorn, *Bristolia: a Poem* (Bristol: Owen Rees and J. N. Longman, 1794), 7.

15. Michael Manson, *Riot! The Bristol Bridge Massacre of 1793* (Bristol: Past & Present Press, 1997), 15–24. See also Madge Dresser, *Slavery Obscured: the Social History of the Slave Trade in an English Provincial Port* (London: Continuum, 2001), 7–37.

16. [Robert Lovell], *Bristol: a Satire* (London: printed for the Author, 1794).

17. Richard Garnett, 'Lovell, Robert (1771–1796)', rev. Rebecca Mills, *Oxford Dictionary of National Biography* (Oxford: Oxford University Press, 2004). http://www.oxforddnb.com/view/article/17063 (accessed 21 January 2009).

18. *The Observer, Part 1st: being a transient glance at about forty youths of Bristol* (Bristol: J. Reed, [1795]), published 'some time after [1] July 1795'. See Georges Lamoine, *Notes on Bristol Literary Circles, 1794–1798* (Toulouse: Institut de Recherches

Interdisciplinaires de l'Université de Toulouse – Le Mirail, 1973), 9. I refer to its author as the 'Observer' hereafter.

19. Basil Cottle, *Joseph Cottle and the Romantics: the Life of a Bristol Publisher* (Bristol: Redcliffe Press, 2008), 16. Quoting *Felix Farley's Journal* (9 April 1791).
20. Division of Rare and Manuscript Collections, Cornell University Library, Wordsworth Collection (#4622 Bd. Ms. 8 ++). Lamoine provides transcriptions of some of the album's poems. See also Cottle, *Joseph Cottle*, 35–6 for a general description. Lamoine's 1796 date for Southey's 'English Dactylics' is presumably a typing error.
21. The Rugby MS now at the Harry Ransom Centre, University of Texas at Austin, is a collection of the material submitted by Coleridge as copy for *Poems* (1796) and (1797). See *PW*, I. ii. 1175–1182.
22. William Llewellyn Parry Jones, *The Trade in Lunacy* (London: Routledge & Kegan Paul, 1972), 112.
23. S.T. Coleridge, *Marginalia*, ed. G. Whalley et al., *Collected Works of Samuel Taylor Coleridge*, Bollingen Series 75, 2 (5 vols, Princeton and London: Routledge, 1980–2001).
24. S.T. Coleridge, *The Watchman*, ed. Lewis Patton, *Collected Works of Samuel Taylor Coleridge*, Bollingen Series 75, 1 (Princeton and London: Routledge, 1970), 168–72.
25. William Gilbert, *The Hurricane 1796*, Intro. Jonathan Wordsworth (Oxford: Woodstock Books, 1990).
26. Paul Kaufman, '"The Hurricane" and The Romantic Poets', *English Miscellany*, 21 (1970), 99–115.
27. Disappointingly, I can find no trace of Gilbert in the Bristol Library borrowing records.
28. Published after September 1796 when *The Monthly Magazine* announced that it 'is in the Bristol press' (651) and before 17 December when Coleridge sent a copy to Thelwall (*CL*, i. 286).
29. James Thomson, *The Seasons and the Castle of Indolence*, ed. James Sambrook (Oxford: Oxford University Press 1972). Compare the storm description in *Summer*, 1103–1222, with *Hurricane*, 22–3.
30. See Schuchard for the undoubted connections.
31. Joseph Cottle, *Reminiscences of Samuel Taylor Coleridge and Robert Southey* (London: Houston and Stoneman, 1848), 219.
32. *The Observer* (Sunday, 20 March 2005).
33. Dante, *Il Convivio (the Banquet)*, trans. Richard Lansing (New York: Garland, 1990). Each book of Dante's work starts with a short poem, followed by a long philosophical commentary that completely outleaps it. Lansing (xv) describes this hybrid form as prosemetric. The term suits *The Hurricane* perfectly.
34. I have borrowed parts of this argument from *Introduction*.
35. Patrick Curry, *Prophecy and Power: Astrology in Early Modern England* (Cambridge: Polity Press, 1989).
36. Morton Paley, *Apocalypse and Millennium in English Romantic Poetry* (Oxford: Oxford University Press, 1999); Tim Fulford (ed.), *Romanticism and Millenarianism* (New York: Palgrave, 2002).
37. Paley, *Apocalypse and Millennium*, 3.
38. This is followed up in my 2008 paper 'Robert Southey and his "Crazy Astrologer"' presented at the Robert Southey and the Contexts of Romanticism Conference, Keswick, March 2008, which I hope to prepare for separate publication.
39. Robert Southey, *New Letters*, ed. Kenneth Curry (2 vols, New York: Columbia University Press, 1965), i. 120.

40. Ignoring Cottle's usual unreliable dating of 1796 (Cottle, i. 66).
41. Liverpool Central Library, MS. 920 ROS 4672. Transcr. Paul Jarman to whom my thanks.
42. Elizabeth Gilbert (sister) to Mary Fletcher, 19 November 1798, asks for prayers 'in the behalf of our family here & particularly for him who is in the W. Indias'. The only other male family member was in England at this time, and her wording suggests topical cause for concern. See John Rylands University Library Methodist Archive Research Centre Fl 3/1/9. Prob11/1472 Will of Nathaniel Gilbert (d. 1807), places William (his brother) in Antigua.

5

S. T. Coleridge, Joseph Cottle, and Some Bristol Baptists, 1794–96

Timothy Whelan

After Samuel Taylor Coleridge delivered one of his political lectures in Bristol in 1795, an observer noted that the speaker was to be praised for 'disseminating that knowledge which so nearly concerns us all, that is, political'. 'Undaunted by the storms of popular prejudice [and] unswayed by magisterial influence', the writer argued, Coleridge had spoken 'in public what none had the courage in this City to do before, – he told Men that they have Rights' (Cumberland, 1795, 14). Not exactly. Radical political discourse had been prominent in Bristol for some time before Coleridge's lectures. In fact, it is likely Coleridge's lectures that year were attended by several individuals – all Dissenters and friends of Joseph Cottle, the Bristol printer and bookseller – who were already sympathetic to Coleridge's politics. Even before his arrival in Bristol, Coleridge had been introduced to Baptist political radicalism during his time as a student at Jesus College in Cambridge. Thus, when Coleridge lectured in Bristol on the 'rights of man', the proper role of government, the evils of the slave trade, and the immorality of England's war with France, he was participating in a rich tradition of West Country Dissent that had been ongoing in Bristol and Cambridge since 1775.

Joseph Cottle (1770–1853), Coleridge's primary link with Dissenting politics in Bristol, Cambridge, and the Midlands in 1795–6, spent his youth attending the Baptist church in the Pithay in Bristol (his father was a deacon there); during the 1790s, however, he became a frequent attendant at the Baptist church in nearby Broadmead. After the death of his father in 1800, Cottle became a regular attendant at Broadmead, a mixed congregation (Baptist and Independent) pastored at that time by John Ryland, Jr., one of the more influential figures of his day among British Particular Baptists. By 1808, Cottle, along with his mother and three sisters, had all become members at Broadmead.[1] Cottle's childhood was spent in the shadow of two of Bristol's leading Baptist ministers and teachers, James Newton (1733–89) and Caleb Evans (1737–91). Newton served as assistant pastor at the Pithay church and classical tutor at Bristol Baptist College from 1758 to 1789; for nearly thirty years, he boarded in the Cottle home at the corner of St James, in the Barton (Cottle, 1847, 53). An even greater figure as a writer and Baptist leader was Caleb Evans. After serving many years as assistant pastor to his father, Hugh Evans (1712–81), the younger Evans became senior pastor at Broadmead and principal of the Baptist Academy in 1781, remaining in those positions until his death ten years later. Evans first gained notoriety as a political writer in 1775 with *A Letter to the Rev. Mr. John Wesley, occasioned by his Calm Address to the American Colonies*, a blistering attack on Wesley's claim (via Samuel Johnson) that 'taxation without representation is not tyranny' (34). In *British Constitutional Liberty*, a sermon preached at Broadmead on 5 November 1775, Evans declared, 'Let the vassals of despotism glory in the forging chains of slavery for all around them: but let the freeborn subjects of King George, glory in the preservation and spread of civil and religious liberty' (29–30).

The most celebrated of Evans's students at the Baptist Academy was Robert Hall (1764–1831).[2] Hall received his introduction to Dissenting politics as a student at John Collett Ryland's academy in Northampton. After completing his studies at Bristol Academy and Aberdeen, Hall returned to Bristol, becoming assistant pastor to Evans and classical tutor in the Academy in 1785. In 1791 he left Bristol for Cambridge, where he replaced the immensely popular but politically controversial Robert Robinson (1735–90) as pastor of the Baptist church in St Andrew's Street. Robinson, a founding member of the Constitutional Society in 1780 and staunch critic of the slave trade, became heterodox in his theology in his latter years. George Dyer, Robinson's biographer, attended frequently at St Andrew's Street during his years in Cambridge, first as a student at Emmanuel College in the late 1770s and later between 1786 and 1792, at which time he became a committed Unitarian. Another attendant when Hall arrived was William Frend of Jesus College, a radical reformer and Unitarian who exerted considerable influence upon Coleridge during his first two years in Cambridge.

Both Dyer and Frend would eventually sever their ties with St Andrew's Street over Hall's opposition to Socinianism, but they continued to support the political ideals found in his two anti-Burke pamphlets, *Christianity Consistent with a Love of Liberty* (1791) and *An Apology for the Freedom of the Press* (1793). While Hall was composing his *Apology*, Frend was completing his controversial pamphlet, *Peace and Union*, which appeared in February of 1793 and led to his trial and dismissal from the university. According to one of his classmates, Coleridge became an avid reader of political pamphlets that spring; the pamphlets by Hall and Frend would not have escaped his notice (C. Le Grice, 1834, 606). We know he attended Frend's trial and was vocal in his opposition to the actions taken by the university against him (Chambers, 1938, 20–1). Though he may have been largely apolitical when he arrived at Jesus College in November of 1791, by the spring of 1793 Coleridge had become an avowed liberal, both in matters of politics and religion, identifying with the anti-Pitt, anti-aristocratic, anti-orthodox elements of Cambridge (Watson, 1976, 54). His transformation was largely the result of his acquaintance with Frend and his exposure to a vocal community of politically radical Dissenters, led by Robert Hall and the congregation at St Andrew's Street.[3]

Shortly after Frend's trial, a group of reformers in Cambridge and nearby Hertfordshire founded the liberal Whig newspaper, the *Cambridge Intelligencer*, in July of 1793. Benjamin Flower was the paper's sole editor during its controversial ten-year existence. One of the earliest publishers of Coleridge and Southey, Flower was, like Frend and Dyer, a radical reformer and Unitarian and a regular attendant at St Andrew's Street between 1793 and 1798. Flower also attended Ryland's academy in Northampton, leaving six years before Hall arrived.[4] In *The French Constitution* (1792), Flower praised the principles of France's new constitution while at the same time criticising numerous inconsistencies in English politics, including parliament's failure to abolish the slave trade. Opponents of the slave trade, however, had been active in Cambridge prior to Flower's arrival. Robert Robinson had preached an important sermon against slavery at St Andrew's Street in 1788. In February 1792, after a vibrant debate in the local paper, the freeholders of Cambridge sent a petition to parliament requesting the immediate abolition of the slave trade (*Cambridge Chronicle*, 17 February 1792). Coleridge's decision to choose the slave trade as the subject of his prize-winning Greek Ode in the spring of 1792, a subject to which he would return in one of his lectures in Bristol in 1795, was almost certainly indebted to this public debate. In all of these ways the Baptist community at Cambridge provided the impetus for Coleridge's subsequent leap across country to Bristol.

The slave trade had been intensely debated in Bristol for some time prior to Coleridge's lecture. Thomas Clarkson's visit there in June of 1787 led to the formation of an auxiliary of the London Abolition Committee, with Caleb Evans and Robert Hall of Broadmead playing significant roles (Latimer, 1893, 472–3). On Monday, 28 January 1788, more than 800 Bristolians met at the city's Guildhall 'to take into consideration the most fit and wholesome measures for the total abolition of the Slave Trade' (*Bristol Gazette*, 24 January 1787). Hall described the meeting in a letter to his father on 10 February, noting the 'opposition' of the 'merchants and their dependents' and his fear that 'the abolition will not take place speedily, if at all. The trading and mercantile interest will make great outcry; the scheme will be thought chimerical, and after producing a few warm speeches, will, I fear, die away' (Gregory, 1853, 23). Hall contributed to the debate in the form of two letters that appeared in William Pine's *Bristol Gazette* on 7 and 14 February 1788 (Whelan, 2000c, 212–24). A few months later, Caleb Evans and a group of West Country Baptist ministers, including Hall, sent five guineas to Granville Sharp and the London Committee, publicly resolving 'to recommend earnestly to the members of all our churches ... to procure the abolition of a traffic so unjust, inhuman, and disgraceful; and the continuance of which tends to counteract and destroy the operation of the benevolent principles and spirit of our common Christianity' (*Bristol Gazette*, 12 June 1788).

The political and social activism of Cottle and his Bristol Baptist friends was remarkably similar to that encountered by Coleridge in Cambridge between 1792 and 1794. Coleridge's Bristol lectures of January–February 1795, his lecture on the slave trade delivered that June at the Assembly Coffee House in Bristol, his speech on the Pitt and Grenville Bills in November 1795, and the political discourse of *The Watchman* in the spring of 1796, all owe a debt to these two Dissenting communities. Both communities were closely linked through the person of Robert Hall, and merged into Coleridge's political conscience through his friendships with Cottle, Dyer, Frend, and Flower.

Parliament's failure in February 1795 to abolish the slave trade – that 'traffic in the Flesh and blood of our Fellow-creatures', as Flower put it in his editorial on 7 March in the *Cambridge Intelligencer* (a paper Coleridge recommended in his last *Watchman* to all his readers) – provoked Coleridge in his lecture that June to remind his Bristol audience of merchants, politicians, and plantation owners, many of whom profited from the commerce in sugar and rum generated by this 'Tartarean confederacy', that

> A part of that Food among most of you is sweetened with the Blood of the Murdered ... O blasphemy! Did God give Food mingled with Brothers blood! Will the Father of all men bless the Food of Cannibals ... ? (*Lectures 1795*, 248)

Coleridge argued that if the people of England would have 'simply left off the use of Sugar and Rum, it is demonstrable that the Slave-merchants and Planters must either have applied to Parliament for the abolition of the Slave Trade or have suffered the West India Trade altogether to perish – a consummation most devoutly to be wished'. To Coleridge, 'the first and constantly acting cause of the Slave Trade ... [is] the consumption of its Products!' Consequently, 'the Guilt' for all the horrors of human trafficking must 'rest on the Consumers' (*Lectures 1795*, 247).

Coleridge's opinion on the sugar and rum boycott was influenced not only by the writings of Benjamin Flower but also by two popular pamphlets: William Fox's *An Address to the People of Great Britain, on Abstaining from West India Sugar and Rum* (1791) and Samuel Bradburn's *An Address to the People called Methodists, Concerning the Wickedness of Encouraging Slavery* (1792). Fox, a Dissenting bookseller in Holborn Hill, London, accused every consumer of West Indian sugar of 'participat[ing] in the crime'. 'The slave-dealer, the slave-holder, and slave-driver', he contends, 'are virtually the agents of the consumer, and may be considered as employed and hired by him to procure the commodity.' The figurative cannibalism so graphically described by Coleridge is present in Fox's pamphlet as well, for 'every pound of sugar', that 'loathsome poison' 'steeped in the blood of our fellow-creatures', he argued, contained 'two ounces of human flesh' (Fox, 1791, 8–9, 3). Samuel Bradburn (1751–1816), a well-known Methodist minister and friend of John Wesley who often preached at Wesley's chapel in the Broadmead section of Bristol, energised England's 400,000 Methodists to join the sugar boycott with the publication of his *Address*.

By linking sugar consumption with cannibalism, Coleridge and his Dissenting colleagues made the consequences especially pertinent to the women of England. 'When they read the abstract of the evidence repeatedly laid before the public', Flower writes,

> when they attend to the conduct of some of the West India Ladies towards their slaves – With what horror and anguish must they behold a system which divests the sex of their peculiar glory; their amiableness, their sensibility, a system which transforms the loveliest part of God's creation into savages and brutes! (Flower, 1792, 452–3)

Bradburn also exposes the corruption of this feminine ideal of 'refined feelings, and exquisite sensibility' among the female advocates and practitioners of the slave trade. Not only do the slaves 'fear being eaten by the white people', but 'what is still more shocking', he writes, 'some women of fortune, are guilty of inflicting punishments not less horrid and indecent than those inflicted by the men, and that frequently *with their own hands*!' (Bradburn, 1792, 3, 4, 5). Coleridge could not resist making his own contribution to this image of perverted English femininity, embedded now within abolitionist rhetoric. 'Sensibility indeed we have to spare', he remarks in his lecture:

> what novel-reading Lady does not over flow with it to the great annoyance of her Friends and Family – Her own sorrows like the Princes of Hell in Milton's Pandemonium sit enthroned bulky and vast – while the miseries of our fellow creatures dwindle into pigmy forms, and are crowded, an unnumbered multitude, into some dark corner of the Heart where the eye of sensibility gleams faintly on them at long intervals. (*Lectures 1795*, 249)

The remedy was a genuine spirit of benevolence, a trait Coleridge was convinced had become rare among the English, despite Godwin's efforts in *Political Justice*. Cottle, also an abolitionist, would have agreed. In his Preface to *Poems* (1795), he asks, why do corrupt governments and tyrannical leaders not understand

> that all mankind are brethren? the offspring of one common Parent, who has placed his children in this world in order to prepare them for a better,

by cherishing universal benevolence? not by tyrannizing over, and like wolves, worrying each other, but by softening the incidental asperities of life, and by the interchange of kind and beneficent attentions. (Cottle, 1795, ii)

If Coleridge's disgust at the slave trade united the young poet-preacher to his Dissenting friends in Cambridge and Bristol, so did his opposition to the policies of the Pitt administration, especially the war with France. When Cottle first met Coleridge in 1794, Coleridge was still 'hot with the French Revolution' (Cottle, 1847, 24), not to mention the radical scheme of Pantisocracy and his recently acquired Unitarianism. At the time of the 1795 lectures, Cottle recalled that Coleridge and Southey 'both felt a detestation of the French war then raging, and a hearty sympathy with the efforts made in France to obtain political ameliorations'. 'Almost every young and unprejudiced mind participated in this feeling', Cottle says, albeit without mentioning his own involvement as a Foxite Whig and avid political reformer (Cottle, 1847, 14). Like Coleridge in the closing sentence of his February 1795 lecture on the war, Cottle was convinced he had a 'duty' to 'raise his feeble voice in support of sinking humanity', feeling 'indignant at the enormities of war' and hoping 'to inspire the same abhorrence in the breasts of others' (Cottle, 1795, ii). In the Preface to his *Poems* (1795), Cottle described war, including the current war with France, as the 'worst of scourges; which has too frequently desolated the world, converted the seats of comfort into the haunts of despair, and scattered wretchedness and murder over the fairest portions of the earth', forcing millions of his 'deluded fellow creatures' to obey the 'pleasure' of a 'tyrant' 'by killing those, whose only crime, like their own, is that of submitting, to be led like sheep to the slaughter' (Cottle, 1795, v, ix). When good people fight for the mere pleasure of rulers who wish 'to urge oppression's claim, / For the love of vengeance, or for thirst of fame', he argues in 'War, a Fragment', they will only extend 'War's tartarean brand' and 'Fall with the Murderer's dagger in their hand!' (Cottle, 1795, 93). Just as Coleridge would argue in his Bristol lectures, the ultimate solution to war and social injustice was a truly benevolent Christianity that, Cottle proposes, would 'reconcile the contentions of men, exterminate that selfish principle, which is the bane of public and private virtue, and transform the inhabitants of the world into beings of a nobler order' (Cottle, 1795, xv).

As a committed poet and generous bookseller and publisher, Cottle deserves much more credit than he has received for the extent of his influence upon Coleridge between 1795 and 1798. It was through Cottle that Coleridge first met Josiah Wade (1761–1842), who would eventually maintain a closer and longer friendship with Coleridge than Cottle himself. Wade entered the Baptist scene in Bristol as a pew-renter at Broadmead from 1787 to 1790. By the mid-1790s, however, he was regularly attending the Baptist church in the Pithay, where the Cottles had been members for many years. During the summer of 1794, shortly before Coleridge's initial visit to Bristol with Southey, both Cottle and Wade contributed monies to rebuild the Baptist meeting house in Salisbury.[5] Wade would spend more than forty years as an attendant at the Pithay church, mostly under the ministry of the Rev. Thomas Roberts (1780–1841), a former student at Bristol Academy and minister from 1807 to 1841. Wade introduced Coleridge to Roberts during the first year of his ministry, and Coleridge would often attend services at the Pithay church during his visits to Bristol, describing Roberts as 'the only extemporary preacher he had ever listened to with pleasure' (Fuller, 1842, 27–8).

The personal connections between Wade, Coleridge, and Roberts were deep and lasting. On a visit to the West Country in December 1813, Coleridge, at that time severely weakened by his opium addiction, requested that Wade and Roberts would 'Pray for my recovery [and] for my infirm wicked Heart, that Christ may mediate to the Father to lead me to Christ, & give me a living instead of a reasoning Faith!' (*CL*, i. 462). A few weeks later, shortly after Robert Hall had preached in the Pithay church, Coleridge, in a letter to Roberts, promised him that 'Should I recover I will – no – no may God grant me power to struggle to become *not another* but a *better man* – O that I had been a partaker with you of the discourse of Mr Robt Hall!' (*CL*, i. 463). In May 1842, shortly after Wade's death, John Foster (1770–1843), the Baptist essayist and close friend of both Cottle and Wade, provided a rare appraisal of the private life and religious character of a man who was second only to Thomas Poole among Coleridge's closest West Country friends. 'For years I had dined with [Wade] about once a month', he writes to Josiah Hill,

> usually in the company of Roberts, to whom he had been a faithful friend, and an attendant on his ministry ... He was not a literary nor properly speaking an intellectual man; it having been from mere generous good-will to a man floating loose on society, that he had, some forty years since, put his house and purse at the free service of Coleridge, and partly his associates. (Ryland, 1860, i. 275–6)

Besides Wade, Coleridge would soon meet three other men, all friends of Cottle and associated with the Baptist congregation in Broadmead, who would play varying roles during Coleridge's time in Bristol and, in some cases, in his later years as well. John Ryland Jr. (1753–1825; see Figure 8) was trained at his father's Northampton academy, where Benjamin Flower was his friend and classmate (Whelan, 2003, 101–3, 105, 113). In 1785 the younger Ryland succeeded his father as pastor of the Baptist church in Northampton, whereupon the elder Ryland moved his academy to Enfield and established the school that John Keats would attend in 1803. Like his father, the younger Ryland had opposed the war with America, supported Lord George Gordon's Protestant Association, worked to repeal the Test

Figure 8   John Ryland, D.D. (1753–1825), taken from the frontispiece to *Pastoral Memorials*, ed. J. E. Ryland (London, 1828).

Acts in the late 1780s, and welcomed the French Revolution and political reform in England. In December 1793 Ryland Jr. assumed the pastorate at Broadmead, replacing Caleb Evans, who had died in 1791. Shortly thereafter, he met Cottle, who was now serving on the Committee of the Bristol Education Society, the fundraising arm of the Baptist Academy.[6] In collaboration with Isaac James (Robert Hall's brother-in-law) and Nathaniel Biggs, Cottle printed and sold at least eight works by Ryland. It was Cottle who most likely introduced Coleridge to Ryland in early 1795, and it is conceivable that Ryland attended one or more of Coleridge's lectures that year.

Coleridge would later attend services at Broadmead with Cottle during his visits to Bristol, and on at least one occasion (in 1807) he corresponded with Ryland (Cottle, 1847, 360; *CL*, iii. 35–6).

Joseph Hughes (1769–1833), Ryland's assistant at Broadmead, was another Baptist minister who would become a friend and correspondent of Coleridge. Hughes had studied under Robert Hall in Bristol in the mid-1780s. While still a student, he became active in Dissenting politics, joining, along with Hall and Evans, the Bristol auxiliary of the Abolition Committee in 1787 (Clarkson, 1808, 366–7; Leifchild, 1835, 115). After completing an A.M. at Aberdeen University, Hughes returned to Bristol, replacing Hall as classical tutor in 1791. Like Hall, Ryland, and Cottle, Hughes was an ardent political reformer in the early 1790s. In a letter to a London friend near the close of 1793, Hughes writes, 'Politics have run high here [in Bristol] as elsewhere. Dissenters have exhibited loyal declarations in different parts. A meeting of a few was called at Bristol. I was present [Cottle probably attended as well] ... [and] though no decisive republican myself I would sign no memorial but what a republican might with full satisfaction subscribe.' Hughes would have been in full agreement with Coleridge's lecture on the slave trade, for like William Fox, Flower, Bradburn, Coleridge, and many other abolitionists, he had resolved in 1792 '*never to use sugar* whilst it is derived to us through the medium of the Slave Trade' (Leifchild, 1835, 125, 129).

Hughes left Bristol for London in 1796, where he would begin an illustrious career as pastor of the Baptist church in Battersea and as a founding secretary of the Religious Tract Society and the British and Foreign Bible Society. He may have attended Coleridge's lectures at the Royal Institution in 1808, but we know for certain that he attended at least one of Coleridge's lectures on drama presented at the Willis's Rooms in London during May and June of 1812 (Coburn and Harding, 1957–2002, 4159). Coleridge often attended meetings of the British and Foreign Bible Society. Foster, a close friend of Hughes, writes to his former landlady in Colchester on 22 August 1815, about a recent appearance by Coleridge at a Society meeting: 'Hughes tells me in mingled language of admiration and compassion, that he [Coleridge] made, a week or two since in Wiltshire, at a Bible Society meeting where Hughes was, a speech of profound intelligence; only, as was to be expected, too abstract for a popular occasion' (Ryland, 1860, i. 293–4). Coleridge and Hughes corresponded on several occasions, even critiquing each other's writings and activities, including their ideas about the formation of London University in the mid-1820s.[7]

During his first visit to Bristol in August 1794, Coleridge met another individual connected with Cottle and his Baptist friends. Referred to only as 'Mr. Harwood', he first appears in a letter from Coleridge to Southey on 1 September 1794, in which Coleridge sends his compliments to Shad (the servant of Southey's aunt, Miss Tyler) as well as Josiah Wade and a Mr and Mrs Harwood, 'for whom I retain high esteem & respect'. Apparently, the

Harwoods had been so impressed by Coleridge's presentation of Pantisocracy that they were seriously contemplating joining the group. On 18 September, just after his return to Cambridge, Coleridge writes again to Southey, full of enthusiasm and referring once again to Mr Harwood and the servant boy, Shad (*CL*, i. 100, 103). This 'Mr. Harwood' was James Harwood (b. 1771), who came to Bristol from Birmingham in late 1792 or early 1793, establishing himself as a linen-draper (the same profession as Josiah Wade) at 15 Maryport Street (Matthews, 1794, 41). His father, John Harwood (d. 1792), was a successful grocer and chandler in Birmingham, in partnership with Thomas King (1755–1831).[8] Both men served as deacons in the Baptist church at Cannon Street, Birmingham, where the outspoken reformer and political writer, Samuel Pearce (1766–99), pastored from 1789 to 1799. After Harwood's death in 1792, King succeeded him as proprietor of the business. The younger Harwood apparently received his legacy and removed to Bristol, where his fiancée, Maria Holden (1773–1841), resided. Initially the Harwoods probably worshipped with Cottle and Wade at the Pithay church; in November 1799, however, they joined the Baptist congregation at Broadmead. They would remain in Bristol until 1814, when they returned to Birmingham, where Harwood became a prosperous haberdasher, linen-draper, and tea dealer.[9]

Before Coleridge left Bristol for Cambridge in mid-September 1794, Harwood gave him a letter of introduction to Robert Hall. Harwood probably heard Hall preach on occasion at Cannon Street, and it may be that Hall stayed with the Harwoods on his visits to Birmingham. A week later Coleridge met with Hall over breakfast in the home of one of Hall's friends. Most likely this 'friend' was Benjamin Flower, who at that time was publishing *The Fall of Robespierre*, a collaboration between Coleridge and Southey, as well as serving as the song leader for Hall's congregation at St Andrew's Street, Cambridge. Hall includes a brief account of his meeting with Coleridge in a letter of 29 September 1794 to his brother-in-law, Isaac James, a writer, bookseller, member of the congregation at Broadmead, friend of Cottle, and classical tutor at the Baptist Academy, 1796–1825.[10] 'Pray how do politics go on with you at Bristol?' Hall asks:

> Mr. Harwood has just favoured me with a letter recommending to my acquaintance a Mr. Coleridge of Jesus College, and accordingly I breakfasted with him a few mornings since at a friend's. He is a very ingenious young man, but intoxicated with a political and philosophical enthusiasm, a sophic, a republican, and leveller. Much as I admire his abilities, I cannot say I feel disposed to cultivate his intimacy; it is difficult or rather perhaps impossible to come into contact with such licentious opinions without contracting a taint. (Warren, 1910, 60–1)

Hall's reaction to Coleridge was not uncommon at that time, for as Coleridge confessed to Southey in his letter of 18 September, many people 'have fled from me' because of 'sitting so near a madman of Genius!' (*CL*, i. 103). Cottle would later bring Hall and Coleridge together again in Bristol (Cottle, 1847, 97).

Besides assisting Coleridge with his introduction to Hall in Cambridge, Harwood also supported Coleridge's early career as a journalist. Along with Cottle and Wade, he provided Coleridge with contacts among the Baptists during his trip to the Midlands early in 1796 seeking subscribers to the *Watchman* (*CL*, i. 179–80). In *Biographia Literaria*, Coleridge mentions that during his visit to Birmingham he met with many Dissenters who were sympathetic to his political opinions. At one meeting he had an encounter with a Calvinist tallow-chandler who was 'one of the thorough-bred, a true lover of liberty', who 'had proved to the satisfaction of many, that Mr Pitt was one of the horns of the second beast in the Revelations, that spoke like a dragon' (Coleridge, 1817, i. 170). This Calvinist tallow-chandler was none other than the same Thomas King of the Baptist church in Cannon Street, the former business partner of John Harwood, James Harwood's father.

During his *Watchman* tour through the Midlands, Coleridge met two other influential Calvinists, one who would probably have been known to Cottle and his Baptist friends in Bristol. While visiting Worcester, Coleridge wrote to Wade on 10 January 1796, 'Tomorrow I shall go through the Manufactory with Mr Barr - and on Tuesday morning set off for Birmingham - Worcester is a beautiful Town ... I did not sleep at Mr Barr's - Mr Flight the partner having arrived from London that very evening' (*CL*, i. 175–6). Martin Barr (1756–1813) was a porcelain manufacturer. His business partner was Joseph Flight (1762–1838), who, along with his brother, John (1766–91), had amassed considerable wealth after the purchase of the Worcester China Factory in 1783 by their father, Thomas Flight (1726–1800), principally by selling French porcelain that John Flight had purchased for purposes of imitation during his frequent visits to France. The senior Flight had been the London agent for the factory since 1768. After John Flight's untimely death in 1791, Tom Flight found a new partner in Martin Barr, a devout Calvinist and member of the Independent congregation at Angel Street in Worcester (Sandon, 1996, 162–6).[11]

On the particular night that Coleridge visited in the home of the Barrs, the partner coming from London was probably Tom Flight, for Joseph Flight, though unmarried, had been living for some years in Worcester and would probably have had his own residence. The senior Flight, a deacon in the Baptist congregation at Maze Pond, Southwark, was well known among Particular Baptists throughout England, serving on many occasions as a messenger to the Particular Baptist Fund and the Body of Protestant Dissenting Deputies. Like Cottle and his Baptist friends in Bristol and Cambridge, Flight was also a radical reformer. In October 1790 he signed, along with his fellow deacons at Maze Pond, a letter to his pastor, James Dore, praising the 'wonderful Revolution' in France while complaining bitterly about the increasing religious persecution in England. The deacons thanked Dore for his 'repeated exertions to advance the cause of Humanity and Universal Freedom' and requested him to commence a series of lectures on the 'principles of nonconformity, and of civil and religious Liberty' (Anon., 1936–7, 16). Among Tom Flight's close acquaintances was Benjamin Flower, a lifelong friend of Flight's son, Bannister (Flower, 1808, xxi–xxii, xxxviii–lxvii).

Another Bristol Baptist who was known to Cottle, Harwood, and the other individuals discussed so far, and who may well have attended one of Coleridge's lectures in 1795, was Thomas Mullett (1745–1814), for many years a prosperous paper-maker and stationer in Bristol. In the mid-1780s he began serving as an American agent for a number of English and American business concerns, including that of his friend Henry Cruger, M.P. for Bristol in 1774 and 1784. Mullett's wife was Mary Evans (1743?–1800), sister to Caleb Evans (the Mulletts became members at Broadmead in the late 1760s[12]). By the early 1790s, Thomas Mullett had moved his business to London, now in partnership with his nephew, Joseph Jeffries Evans (1768–1812), who also became his son-in-law when he married Mullett's daughter, Mary Anne (1777–1857), in 1796. Despite his move to London, Mullett never relinquished his ties to Bristol, visiting frequently on matters of business and family. After his wife's death in 1800, Mullett and his son-in-law became Unitarians, worshipping with the General Baptist congregation at Worship Street, London, under the ministry of John Evans, a distant relation of J. J. Evans and a former student of Robert Hall at Bristol Academy.[13]

Like Cottle and the other Bristol Baptists discussed previously, Thomas Mullett was an advocate of political reform in the 1790s. As his obituary in the *Gentleman's Magazine* notes, 'Few understood better than did Mr. Mullett the rights of the subject; none advocated with more manly firmness the principles of civil and religious liberty, which he knew included in all their ramifications the prosperity of mankind' (Anon., 1815, 84). Writing to Horatio Gates, famed military commander for the American forces during the Revolutionary War, 24 November 1791, Mullett describes his attendance at the annual dinner of the London Revolution Society:

> You would have felt an elevation at the Revolution Society at the London Tavern on the 4th November ... Common Sense *Paine* was invited – his health was drank, with thanks to him for his able defence of the Rights of Man; on which he thankd the Society, & proposd as a toast – the Revolution of the World! ... [I] have never witnessd a popular Assembly of more decorum, or with so much of the 'feast of reason, and the flow of Soul'.[14]

During his years in London, Mullett, primarily through his son-in-law, developed friendships with Henry Crabb Robinson and Anthony Robinson, the latter having been a student of Robert Hall at Bristol

Academy before becoming a Unitarian lay minister and periodical writer and editor in London (Sadler, 1872, ii. 23). Both Robinsons were friends of Coleridge, as was J. J. Evans. In 1803 Evans and his wife visited the Lake District, calling at the Coleridge home at Greta Hall on 5 September. They visited with Sara Coleridge and 'two of the children, who were very well looking ones'. Unfortunately, as Evans wrote in his journal, 'the poet was from home', Coleridge being on a walking tour of Scotland at the time (Evans, 1870, 64). One final connection between Mullett and Coleridge involves another Bristolian, James Webbe Tobin (1767–1814), son of a West Indies planter and brother to the playwright John Tobin (1770–1804). Tobin became friends with Cottle, Coleridge, and Southey in the mid-1790s, and was sympathetic to the Pantisocratic scheme. On 8 September 1807, Tobin married Jane Mullett (d. 1837), Thomas Mullett's daughter and Caleb Evans's niece, thus joining Tobin to two of Bristol's prominent Dissenting families, both of which had long histories of involvement in the political reform movement as well as friendships with Coleridge (Evans, 1870, 64–5).

Accordingly, it is not hard to understand Cottle's surprise and disappointment when Coleridge, in his *Biographia Literaria*, 'passed over, in silence, all distinct reference to Bristol, the cradle of his literature, and for many years his favourite abode; the enlightened inhabitants of which city ever warmly patronized him' (Cottle, 1837, i. vii). Of course, Coleridge had his reasons, as did many other former radicals of the 1790s (such as Robert Hall), for not dwelling on his earlier political activities – but one unfortunate consequence was to obscure his links with the Bristol Baptist community explored in this essay. Coleridge's letters, speeches, and published writings between 1794 and 1796, demonstrate that he was 'disseminating' a brand of political 'knowledge' at the heart of which was the belief that human beings did indeed 'have Rights' (Cumberland, 1795, 14). His message found fertile ground among the Bristol Baptist Dissenters who were already committed to the ideals of political reform prior to his arrival in the city. By the mid-1790s, however, political reaction and government-sponsored repression had isolated those Dissenters who still supported the cause. Their isolation serves to enhance the significance of Coleridge's lectures that year, and helps explain why Cottle and his Baptist friends took so readily to the young, idealistic Unitarian poet-preacher-reformer. At a time when many were choosing to remain quiet, Coleridge publicly refused, at great risk to himself, to let those ideals 'die away', as Hall had prophesied in 1788 (Gregory, 1853, 23). In so doing, Coleridge served as a catalyst to a Dissenting community in need of a fresh voice, a true 'watchman' carrying the torch of freedom, justice, and human rights into a political arena fraught with fear, compromise, and apostasy. For that alone, Coleridge deserves a place – a place Cottle and his Baptist friends gladly gave him – in the history of radical politics in Bristol in the 1790s.

Notes

1. For more on Cottle's Baptist and Independent connections, see Whelan (2000b, 98–9).
2. For Cottle's tribute to Hall, see Cottle (1847, 56–63).
3. For more on Coleridge and the Cambridge Baptists, see Whelan (2000a, 38–47).
4. George Dyer served as an usher for Ryland in the early 1780s. See Whelan (2003, 101–3, 105, 113).
5. See Broadmead Subscription Book, no. 3, 1772–1813, Bd/A2/2, Bristol Record Office; for Cottle's and Wade's signatures in the collection book for the Baptist church in Salisbury, see Saffery-Whitaker Papers, acc. 180, B/4, Angus Library, Regent's Park College, Oxford.
6. For Cottle's friendship with Ryland and Hughes, see Cottle (1829, 366).
7. See *CL*, iv. 965; v. 300, 447, 455; vi. 1048–50, 1053–6.
8. For John Harwood, see *Universal British Directory* (1791–8), ii. 222; Langley (1939, 34, 129–30); Rippon (1790–1802, i. 495–6).
9. See Cannon Street Baptist Church Book, 1778–90, Birmingham Central Library; Broadmead Members List R1-4; Broadmead Church Records, 1779–1817, Bd/M1/3, f. 349, Bristol Record Office; Morgan, 1896, section VII (n.).
10. James (b. 1759), the son of a Baptist minister, came to Bristol in 1773 as a student at the Baptist Academy (Hayden, 1974, 2–3). He was a bookseller (and sometimes undertaker) first in North Street and then in Wine Street, near Josiah Wade's residence. He was known to both Coleridge and Southey.
11. I am indebted to Professor John Briggs for information on Barr's church affiliation.
12. See 'Alphabetical List of Members in 1802', compiled by John Ryland, Jr., Broadmead Records, Bd/R/1/4d, f. 31, Bristol Record Office.
13. For Mullett, see Anon. (1815, 83–5); Evans (1870, 60–3); Moon (1979, 137).
14. Thomas Mullett to Horatio Gates, 24 November 1791. Thomas Addis Emmet Collection, Manuscripts and Archives Division, New York Public Library, Astor, Lenox and Tilden Foundations.

Bibliography

Anon., 'A Diaconal Epistle, 1790', *Baptist Quarterly*, 8 (1936–7), 216.

—— 'Memoirs of Mr. Thomas Mullett', *Gentleman's Magazine*, 85 (1815), 83–5.

Baptist Annual Register, ed. J. Rippon (4 vols, London: Dilly, Button, and Thomas 1790–1802).

Bradburn, S., *An Address to the People called Methodists, concerning the Wickedness of Encouraging Slavery* (5th edn, London: M. Gurney, 1792).

Chambers, E. K., *Samuel Taylor Coleridge: a Biographical Study* (Oxford: Clarendon Press, 1938).

Clarkson, T., *History of the Rise, Progress, and Accomplishment of the Abolition of the African Slave-Trade by the British Parliament* (2 vols, London: Longman, 1808).

Coleridge, S. T., *Biographia Literaria* (2 vols, London: R. Fenner, 1817).

—— *Lectures 1795 on Politics and Religion*, ed. Lewis Patton and Peter Mann, *Collected Works of Samuel Taylor Coleridge*, Bollingen Series 75, 1 (London: Routledge & Kegan Paul, 1971).

—— *The Notebooks of Samuel Taylor Coleridge*, ed. Kathleen Coburn, Merton Christensen and Anthony Harding, Bollingen Series 50 (5 vols: vol. i, New York: Pantheon Books, 1957; vols. ii–v, Princeton, NJ: Princeton University Press, 1962–2002).

Cottle, J., *Early Recollections; Chiefly Relating to the late Samuel Taylor Coleridge, during his long residence in Bristol* (2 vols, London: Longman, 1837).

—— *Malvern Hills: With Minor Poems and Essays* (2 vols, London: T. Cadell, 1829).

—— *Poems, Containing John the Baptist, Sir Malcolm and Alla, ... [and] War a Fragment* (Bristol: J. Cottle, 1795).

—— *Reminiscences of Samuel Taylor Coleridge and Robert Southey* (London: Houlston and Stoneman, 1837).

Cumberland, R., *The Observer, Part 1st, being a transient glance at about forty youths of Bristol* (Bristol: J. Reed, 1795).

Evans, C., *British Constitutional Liberty* (Bristol and London: W. Pine and C. Dilly, 1775a).

—— *A Letter to the Rev. Mr. John Wesley, Occasioned by his Calm Address to the American Colonies* (London: E. and C. Dilly, 1775b).

Evans, J. M., *Family Chronicle of the Descendants of Thomas Evans, of Brecon, from 1673 to 1857* (Bristol: [privately printed], 1870).

Flower, B., *The French Constitution* (2nd edn, London: G. G. J. and J. Robinson, 1792).

—— *A Statement of the Facts, relative to the conduct of the Reverend John Clayton, Senior ...* (Harlow: B. Flower, 1808).

Fox, W., *An Address to the People of Great Britain, on the Propriety of Refraining from West India Sugar and Rum* (10th edn, London: M. Gurney, 1791).

Fuller, J. G., *Memoir of Thomas Roberts* (London: Houlston and Stoneman).

Gregory, O. (ed.), *The Works of Robert Hall* (6 vols, London: H. G. Bohn, 1842).

Hayden, R., *The Records of a Church of Christ in Bristol* (Bristol: Bristol Record Society, 1974).

Langley, A. S., *Birmingham Baptists, Past and Present* (London: Kingsgate Press, 1939).

Latimer, J., *The Annals of Bristol in the Eighteenth Century* (Frome and London: Butler and Tanner, 1893).

Le Grice, C., 'College Reminiscences of Mr. Coleridge', *The Gentleman's Magazine*, New Series, 2 (1834), 606.

Leifchild, J., *Memoir of the late Rev. Joseph Hughes, A.M.* (London: T. Ward, 1835).

Matthews, W., *Matthews's New Bristol Directory for the Year 1793–4* (Bristol: Matthews, 1794).

Moon, N., *Education for Ministry: Bristol Baptist College 1679–1979* (Bristol: Bristol Baptist College, 1979).

Morgan, A. F., *Kith and Kin: the History of the Morgan Family* (Birmingham: Charles Cooper, 1896).

Ryland, J. E., *Life and Correspondence of John Foster* (2 vols, Boston: Gould and Lincoln, 1860).

Sadler, T., *Diary, Reminiscences, and Correspondence of Henry Crabb Robinson* (3rd edn, 2 vols, London and New York: Macmillan, 1872).

Sandon, J., *The Dictionary of Worcester Porcelain. Volume 1: 1751–1851* (Woodbridge, Suffolk: Antique Collector's Club, 1996).

Universal British Directory of Trade, Commerce, and Manufacture (5 vols, London: Printed for the Patentees [Peter Barfoot and John Wilkes], 1791–8).

Warren, R. H., *The Hall Family* (London: J. W. Arrowsmith, 1910).

Watson, G., 'The Revolutionary Youth of Wordsworth and Coleridge', *Critical Quarterly*, 18.3 (1976), 49–66.

Whelan, T., 'Coleridge and Robert Hall of Cambridge', *Wordsworth Circle*, 31 (2000a), 38–47.

—— 'Joseph Cottle the Baptist', *Charles Lamb Bulletin*, NS, 110 (2000b), 96–108.
—— 'Robert Hall and the Bristol Slave-Trade Debate of 1787–88', *Baptist Quarterly*, 38 (2000c), 212–24.
—— 'John Ryland at School: Two Societies in Northampton Boarding Schools', *Baptist Quarterly*, 40 (2003), 90–116.

6
Coleridge's Bristol and West Country Radicalism

Peter J. Kitson

In the 1790s S. T. Coleridge was a Dissenter in both politics and religion. Numerous critics have discussed the nature of Coleridge's then Unitarian beliefs, but what has so far insufficiently been highlighted are the ways in which his dissent was fashioned, deepened, and reinforced by the poet's West Country background, specifically the political and religious milieu of the thriving commercial city of eighteenth-century Bristol and the surrounding area. It was the experience of Bristol and West Country opposition that turned Coleridge from an opponent of the government in politics and an anti-Trinitarian in religion into a Protestant Dissenter more fully immersed in the milieu and history of post-Reformation religious radicalism. Although he had abandoned much of this belief by 1805, his West Country experience had substantial implications for Coleridge's intellectual and literary career and the formation of what one might term early British Romanticism. The young Coleridge first became acquainted with Bristol, and subsequently its West Country environs, through his friendship with his fellow poet and radical, Robert Southey, who had spent his childhood there (Holmes, 1989, 89–106). Coleridge began his actual residence in the city in January 1795 after Southey had dutifully fetched him back from London to make him live up to his obligations to marry Sara Fricker, whose sister, Edith, Southey was also courting. It was here that Coleridge's most active and ardent Dissenting days were spent lecturing against the war with revolutionary France, established religion, and the transatlantic slave trade. His political and religious views and activities were thus indelibly marked and crucially shaped by the people that he met and encountered during this period of his life.

Coleridge's career as lecturer, journalist, and commentator on political and religious matters began when he arrived in this thriving commercial city. Bristol, with around 55,000 inhabitants, claimed to be the second city of the nation and its colonial possessions, and it boasted a vibrant public life with several newspapers, theatres, and a large lending library. It was the third biggest urban constituency after London and Westminster (Bradley, 1990,

196–223; Little, 1967, 204). The city had strong links with the American colonies, returning MPs who had opposed the war waged against them almost twenty years earlier, and it was second only to London as a port engaged in the transatlantic slave trade. After London the city also had the most varied Dissenting community composed of Independents, Baptists, Presbyterians, Quakers and Unitarians (Bradley, 1990, 199; Andrews, 2003, 130–3). Energetic, Nonconformist, and outward-looking, Bristol acted as a catalyst for Coleridge's developing political and religious opinions expressed in a series of lectures and pamphlets.

Coleridge acquired his Unitarian beliefs while at Jesus College, Cambridge though his contact with Unitarians such as William Frend, Benjamin Flower, editor of the *Cambridge Intelligencer*, and his friend, George Dyer. Yet the religious and political dissent Coleridge promoted in his Bristol Lectures was significantly different from that of many of his contemporary Unitarian friends, many of whom, like the Wedgwoods, were commercial, propertied, wealthy, and very well-connected (Bradley, 1990, 205; Ditchfield, 1991, 39–67). This unusual aspect of Coleridge's politics was noted, on more than one occasion, by his friend the political lecturer John Thelwall. In a letter of 1798 Thelwall commented regarding Coleridge, 'Mount him but upon his darling hobby horse "the republic of God's own making", & away he goes like hey go mad, splattering & splashing thro thick & thin & scattering more *levelling* sedition, & constructive treason, than poor *Gilly* or myself ever dreamt of' (quoted in Walford Davies, 2002, 301; White, 2006, 119). One of the reasons for this is that Coleridge's dissent was deepened by his wish to ground it on the historical basis that he discovered through his reading and discussions in the West Country radical milieu both past and present.

Bristol and Dissent

Bristol and the West Country had long traditions of political and religious Dissent stretching back to the English Civil War, and the area as a whole was at the centre of major historical political debates and divisions. As a major trading port Bristol was in competition with London's Royal monopolies. During the Civil War the city sided with the parliamentary cause, as did Taunton, and the city was twice besieged, once by Royalists (1643) and then by parliamentary forces (1645). The Mayor defied the King's order to hold the city and, as the south west succumbed to Royalist attack, Bristol was besieged by Prince Rupert, yet, when the tide of war turned Rupert himself was unable to hold the city and it fell to the armies of Cromwell and Fairfax in 1645 (Little, 1967, 123–4). Bristol and the south west emerged from the Civil War a deeply divided country. Within the city itself there was radical activity. In 1648 civilian and army radicals organised a Leveller petition against the Presbyterians' attempts to negotiate with a defeated Charles I

(Underdown, 1973, 52). Thomas Edwardes, the Presbyterian hammer of the sects and author of *Gangraena*, claimed that employment in Bristol was impossible for those who failed to follow 'the new Light and New Way' of radical Puritanism (Underdown, 1971, 42). Bristol also contained one of only two of the printing presses outside London and the Universities and many political pamphlets were printed there coinciding with the height of Leveller activity in 1648 (Brailsford, 1970, 508–9). Christopher Hill provides evidence of radical activity in the city and A. L. Morton argues for the presence of the radical antinomian sect, the Ranters (Hill, 1972, 75, 97, 245, 249–50; Morton, 1970, 111). From the seventeenth century onwards radical ideas gained a currency in the city and the division in its civic life would be reflected during the Restoration and beyond.

As James E. Bradley comments, 'by 1775, virtually every variety of English dissent could be found in Bristol' (Bradley, 1990, 206). It is not exactly clear why Bristol and the south west became a major centre of religious dissent; perhaps the answer lay in the urbanised nature of the city as dissent tended to be concentrated in such areas. The city, as a major port, also had access to the free press of Holland. Between 1715 and 1718, nearly 20 per cent or so of the city's population were Nonconformist and of that number, around 6 per cent were Quakers. Given the comparatively small number of dissenters nationally, this is a very substantial dissenting minority (Watts, 1978, 285–6). It was during Cromwell's Interregnum that the rise of Nonconformity began. The first fully Baptist congregation appeared at the close of 1652 (Little, 1967, 135). More significant for the future, however, was the arrival of the Quakers in 1654. George Fox, the Quaker leader, visited Bristol in 1560 and the Quakers established their first meeting house in 1654. It was at Bristol in October 1656 that the leading Quaker enthusiast James Nayler and his friends notoriously re-enacted the arrival of Christ in Jerusalem that is commemorated on Palm Sunday. Nayler rode into the city on horseback attended by followers who sang 'Holy, holy, holy' and strewed his muddy path with garments. On 16 December 1656 he was convicted of blasphemy in a highly publicised trial before the Second Protectorate Parliament. Narrowly escaping execution, Nayler was punished with two floggings, branding of the letter B on his forehead, piercing of his tongue with a hot iron, and two years' imprisonment with hard labour. The tale of Nayler's arrival into Bristol was well known and reprinted several times; for instance in Samuel Seyer's *Memoirs Historical and Topographical of Bristol and its Neighbourhood* (1823), Nayler is described as 'the most extraordinary fanatic who ever appeared in Bristol, or perhaps in the kingdom' (Seyer, 1823, ii. 513). In his annotations to a review by Southey in the *Quarterly Review* in 1813, Coleridge comments how 'poor Nayler' had 'declared himself God in the flesh' and that in any other period or country he 'would have been burnt alive' (Coleridge, 1853, 154–5). Incidents such as this would, no doubt, have featured prominently in the six lectures comparing the English Revolution of the mid-seventeenth century with the French Revolution that in 1795 Coleridge projected to deliver in the city. By Coleridge's time the Bristol Quakers had two meeting houses, one in the Friars and the other in Temple Street. They were noted for their wealth (Bradley, 1990, 206).

It was not until the close of the eighteenth century that Unitarianism as a denomination began to emerge in Bristol, largely from the substantial Presbyterian congregations which transformed themselves into Unitarian meetings. The Bristol Unitarians were never numerically impressive and never as strong as in Manchester or Birmingham, with a congregation of around 250 people, but they were noted for their wealth. They originated from the move towards Unitarianism among the Presbyterian congregation of the Lewins Mead Chapel (Bradley, 1990, 205). In 1770 this congregation invited John Prior Estlin to be an assistant to their minister, the Rev. William Richards. Estlin would become the major Unitarian presence in the city for almost fifty years, retiring in 1816 (Andrews, 2003, 131). He would also become a mentor and friend to Coleridge from 1795 until their falling out in 1814. It was Estlin who introduced Coleridge to prominent West Country dissenters such as Joshua Toulmin, the Unitarian minister of the Mary Street chapel in Taunton, and David Jardine, the minister of the Trim Street chapel at Bath, in both of whose meeting houses Coleridge would often preach. Presbyterians, Independents, Congregationalists, and Baptists were also strong in the city. The Baptists had three chapels of which Caleb Evans's at Broad Mead was the largest (Bradley, 1990, 206).

Bristol was also the focus of much anti-government opposition in the latter half of the eighteenth century (Bradley, 1990, 195–223). The city traded heavily with the American colonies and was somewhat out of sympathy with the anti-colonial policies of Lord North's government. In the election of 1774, Bristol's two sitting MPs were dismissed and replaced by Henry Cruger and Edmund Burke: the former was an American citizen and the latter, of course, a national politician. Burke was to represent the city from 1774 to 1780 (Little, 1967, 176–9). How the political ideas of the American Revolution affected Bristol is not easy to determine, but transatlantic links made it possible for those ideas to infiltrate the West Country. It is significant that Bristol was the location for the first American consulate in Britain (September 1792) and General Kosciusko, the Polish patriot and hero of the American Revolution, was warmly greeted when he visited Bristol on 13 June 1793. Many Loyalist émigrés settled in the city and Thomas Poole's introduction to politics seems to have been a much-treasured gift of a lock of George Washington's hair that he received from a member of an émigré Loyalist family (Sandford, 1996, 33). Certainly, Bristol as a city of dissent and opposition with historical traditions of Nonconformity would make it an attractive place for Coleridge to settle.

Coleridge among the Dissenters at Bristol and Taunton

Through his introduction to the dissenting life of Bristol and the south west, Coleridge encountered a number of important people who would make a key contribution to the development of his thought, and thus the development of British Romanticism. We know that among the audience at the political and religious lectures he gave at Bristol in 1795 were John Prior Estlin, the wine merchants the Morgans, and the Cottle brothers Robert, Amos, and Joseph. Because of the controversial nature of his lectures, Coleridge was prevented from preaching at Lewins Mead, although he preached at Rev. David Jardine's chapel in Trim Street, Bath, sometime in 1795, at Rev. John Howel's Bridgwater Chapel, and at Joshua Toulmin's chapel in Taunton (Stephenson, 1932, 174–5). It was Estlin who was the key figure in introducing Coleridge to the Dissenting milieu of the West Country. Estlin was the author of several standard Unitarian discourses and sermons, including his reply to Paine's *Age of Reason*, the *Evidences of Revealed Religion* (1796). His most significant work, *The Nature and the Causes of Atheism,* demonstrates the strong influence of Coleridge's earlier Bristol 'Lectures on Revealed Religion' of 1795 which he attended.

In January 1797 Coleridge wrote to Estlin requesting letters of introduction to John Howell and Joshua Toulmin, the Unitarian ministers at Bridgwater and Taunton respectively (*CL*, i. 301). More politically radical than Estlin, Toulmin understood and partially constructed the Protestant Dissenting history of the West Country. His first post had been as a Presbyterian minister at Colyton, Devon where his charismatic preaching led him to be offered the ministry of the Unitarian Baptists in their General Baptist Chapel in Mary Street, Taunton. Here he remained until moving to Birmingham in 1804 to become minister of the New Street chapel. The Presbyterians of Tancred Street Chapel had seceded from the Mary Street chapel earlier in the century. Toulmin, like Poole and Coleridge, encountered much political opposition at Taunton: an effigy of Thomas Paine was burnt in front of his house in Fore Street and, for a time, his home was regularly attacked at night with stones and fireworks. Toulmin wrote that hatred of Dissenters was felt everywhere: 'at Taunton it discovered itself, and I was the marked object of its spleen, tho' not of its violence; for it did there proceed to violence' (quoted in Gibson, 2007, 292, 296). Toulmin's son Harry emigrated to America in 1793 as a consequence of such threats, and Toulmin and his congregation considered doing the same. It is reported that he upheld the 'rights of man' in his preaching and allowed a group of radicals, or 'democrats', to meet in his house and on one occasion, it is alleged, singing of the 'Marseillaise' was heard. In 1792 the London Constitutional Society despatched a hundred copies of Thomas Paine's *Letter to Dundas* for distribution (Lawrence, 1970, 40–2; Andrews, 2003, 134; Gibson, 2007, 292–7).

Stuart Andrews comments that Taunton was 'probably a more important Unitarian centre in the south west than Bristol', and it is clear that a Dissenting infrastructure in the town was well established by the mid-eighteenth century. Some two-thirds of the town's population were Dissenters. There was a Dissenting Academy founded in the 1670s by the Nonconformist minister Matthew Warren, where leading Dissenters such as Henry Grove and Thomas Amory studied. The Academy was widely viewed as an important centre of Commonwealth ideas of the 'Good Old Cause' and William Gibson comments that 'Taunton Academy graduates spread like spores through the Nonconformist and Dissenting congregations of the West Country, and further afield ... and for the most part, promoted reasonableness, moderation and tolerance among the congregations they served' (Gibson, 2007, 274). Visiting the town in 1769, Tobias Smollett commented approvingly on its close connections with 'Puritanism'. In the late eighteenth century the political life of Taunton was dominated by the clash between the Anglican town corporation and the party of Independent dissenters (Gibson, 2007, 268–97; Andrews, 2003, 133–4; Bradley, 1990, 351–4; see also Palmer, 1926, 5–8). Although Taunton's Dissenters suffered a decline in the late eighteenth century and the Academy closed in 1759, a strong bedrock of Dissenting traditions nevertheless remained for Coleridge.

In no sense then could Coleridge's rural retreat to Nether Stowey be regarded as a simple act of retirement from politics with Taunton and Toulmin's congregation a mere ten miles or so away. Coleridge developed a strong friendship with Toulmin and was a frequent guest at his home in Fore Street. In June 1797 he wrote to Estlin that 'the more I see of [Toulmin], the more I love him' (*CL*, i. 326) and in January 1798, after his acceptance of the Wedgwood annuity which freed him from becoming a salaried Unitarian minister at Shrewsbury or elsewhere, he expressed his determined wish to continue to 'preach often' and 'alternately to assist Dr Toulmin & Mr Howel, one part of every Sunday' while he remained at Nether Stowey (*CL*, i. 372). In 1798 Coleridge assisted Toulmin at the difficult time when his daughter drowned herself off the Devonshire coast, walking eleven miles to conduct the service on the Sunday instead of the distressed Toulmin (*CL*, i. 407, 408, 409). Coleridge's personal association with Toulmin, beginning in early 1797 after the delivery of the Bristol Lectures and the publication of *The Watchman* (1796), was probably too late to have any decisive influence on the nature of his dissenting publications; however, Toulmin had been a prolific writers of tracts and sermons from the 1770s, many of which Coleridge must have known and which may well have impacted upon his own and similarly historically grounded dissent.

Toulmin was an active Protestant Dissenter who 'made no bones of his radical Whig politics (Gibson, 2007, 295). In his works we see some of the rhetorical fire, power and energy that are almost entirely absent from Estlin's low-key, dry and scholarly publications. In his polemic against the

American War, for instance, Toulmin strikes a tone similar to Coleridge in *Conciones ad Populum* (1795): 'What promiscuous carnage! What mangled limbs! What hideous cries! Fields covered with ghastly corpses! Green pastures covered with human gore!' Toulmin likewise adopts the prophetic tone of the jeremiad, familiar to Coleridge and used with great power in *The Plot Discovered* (1795). Here is Toulmin:

> Be not too warm in congratulating yourselves; the glory of your triumph is tarnished with the sorrowful countenance and mourning garbs of orphans and widows – with the silence of your ports that used to hear the voice of merchandize – with the increased burdens which an exhausted treasury, multiplied taxes, and a diminished trade will entail on your posterity. The unborn may weep at the mention of victories in which their sire exulted. (Toulmin, 1776, 7–8; quoted in Andrews, 2003, 135)

Toulmin's numerous publications contributed to the Dissenters' campaigns against civil and religious disabilities, but what marks him out among the Dissenters – as it does Coleridge – is his attempt to ground his Unitarian Nonconformity in a tradition of historical struggle. In a series of publications Toulmin sought to identify the theological and historical origins of English Unitarianism. In 1777 he published his *Memoirs of the Life, Character, Sentiments, and Writings, of Faustus Socinus* describing the life and works of the first major Reformation theologian to espouse a belief in the full humanity of Jesus Christ, the sixteenth-century Italian, Faustus Socinus. Toulmin presents Socinus's ideas as the natural and inevitable consequence of the light shed by the Reformation. These ideas spread from Poland into Transylvania and were transmitted thence to Amsterdam and England. Toulmin describes the life and activities of the first Socinian or Unitarian preacher in England, John Biddle (Bidle), the man of 'excellent piety and virtue, and great learning' who formed the 'only Society of Socinians in England' at Gloucester. Toulmin tells how 'the adherents to Mr. BIDLE were called BIDELLIANS; but this name was lost in the more common appellation of SOCINIANS, or, what they preferred UNITARIANS'. For Toulmin, 'no names, how great or venerable soever' should determine judgement; their 'creed should be the submission of the soul to reason, argument and Scripture' (Toulmin, 1777, 278–9, 349). In 1791 Toulmin published his extended *Review of the Life, Character, and Writings of the Rev. John Biddle*, describing in much fuller detail the life and, especially, the persecution of Biddle by the Presbyterians under the Commonwealth, and his foundation of the first Unitarian congregation. Biddle 'gave the only scriptures a diligent reading; and made use of no other rule to determine controversies about religion, than *the scriptures*; and of no other *authentic interpreter*, if a scruple arose concerning the sense of the scriptures, than *reason*'. In the career of Biddle, Toulmin lessoned how 'bigotry' when 'armed with the power of the sword' becomes a dangerous thing: 'the alliance of the church with the state, gives the sting to this intolerant and baneful temper; and it matters little, whether the leaders in the church support the rank of bishops, or move only in the humble post of presbyters'. Toulmin's discussion of seventeenth-century Unitarianism is historically specific and sophisticated in its understanding of the political and religious disputes of the Commonwealth. He comments on how the Presbyterians took on the mantle of the bishops they had earlier banished:

> The conduct of the Presbyterians, during the short period, when they were in alliance with the supreme powers of this country, verifies the truth of these remarks. In reference to *their* measures, Milton had every reason to say with satirical poignancy, 'New presbyter is but old priest wrote large'. (Toulmin, 1791, 11, 53–4)

This historical awareness was deepened when Toulmin produced, in 1793 at the height of the French Revolution debate, a new and enlarged edition in five volumes of the Independent minister Daniel Neal's highly partisan *History of the Puritans from the Reformation in 1517 to the Revolution of 1688* (1732–8). Toulmin assiduously annotated Neal's *History* with copious notes demonstrating an extraordinary knowledge of the history of Protestant Dissent. Toulmin is, of course, also partisan. When discussing the 'unconstitutional' execution of Charles I he judges the king to have been guilty 'and the men whom he sought to crush appealed, in the justification of his death, to the first principles of justice, and the acknowledged purposes of human society'. Toulmin argues that Neal's work has 'a liberal cast; it is on the side of civil and religious liberty; it is in favour of the rights of Englishmen, against unconstitutional prerogative; it is in favour of the rights of conscience, against an imperious and persecuting hierarchy, whether Episcopal or Presbyterian' (Neal, 1844, ii. 96, 103).

Importantly, Toulmin's strong historical reading of Unitarianism as an integral part of the wider movement of Protestant Dissent dating from that great leftward sweep in theology of the Reformation was also firmly rooted in the locality of the West Country. This is apparent in his *History of Taunton* of 1791, a book that Charles James Fox consulted. Toulmin claims that Taunton may claim the reader's attention as few other towns in the kingdom 'have had a larger share in events of national importance' or can claim to be a theatre 'more adapted to give lessons, on liberty and virtue, to the rising generation' (Toulmin, *History*, 1791, 31–2, 56, 112, 114). The town's history presents 'a scene, which must instruct and affect every one, who has any idea what *liberty*, civil or religious, means: LIBERTY, that best birth right of Englishmen; and, next to Christianity, the most precious gift of heaven'. Toulmin describes the close and long-standing relationship between Taunton and Protestant Dissent, pointing out that a society of

Baptists had existed in the town since 1646. This society, however, persisted in maintaining the 'gloomy system of Calvinism, and the absurd notions of the Trinitarian scheme' until it adopted Unitarian notions in the eighteenth century. Taunton also contained a congregation of Quakers and Wesleyans, the latter meeting at the Octagon chapel in Middle Street. Toulmin tells how the town made a 'spirited stand' against the 'unconstitutional measures of Charles I' and provided firm adherents to the parliamentary cause, occasioning the displeasure of the restored Charles II who removed the town's royal charter and demolished its walls. He recounts the 'scenes of tumult, distress and blood' witnessed in the town's dramatic political history. Taunton was 'a place of considerable strength till the unhappy civil wars, in the reign of Charles I. when it became an object of vigorous struggle between the royal and parliamentary forces, which should possess its fortress: for it was considered as the key to the west of England'. Toulmin accuses the king of 'various arbitrary and oppressive measures', invading the privileges of Parliament and thus 'rousing the indignation of a free people'. He describes how Taunton changed hands twice during the war and how, besieged by Royalist armies, the townspeople remained firm to the parliamentary cause. Taunton was also notable in its enthusiastic support for the Monmouth rebellion in 1685 and suffered appallingly in its aftermath. The Duke entered the town to 'unusual demonstrations of joy' on 18 June, where he was proclaimed king. For Toulmin, Monmouth's uprising represented a 'meritorious attempt to rescue the nation from despotism' as things were then 'not sufficiently ripe' to 'effect so glorious a period to the designs of a popish and arbitrary prince; whose councils and government, evidently, were directed to the subversion of the protestant religion, and of our free constitution'. Caught up in the revenge of James II and the Bloody Assizes of Judge Jeffrys, Taunton was the 'theatre of his rage and cruelty' and the country 'overflowed with blood'. Not surprisingly, Taunton celebrated the 1688 revolution, which for Toulmin 'disarmed *despotism* ... In Religion it gave toleration: to our political constitution, it secured freedom.' Since that time, he adds, there has been in the town, 'a large party attached to the principles of the revolution' (Toulmin, *History*, 1791, 136, 145, 148, 149, 172).

Coleridge's West Country Dissent

In late May 1797 Coleridge preached a sermon in Toulmin's Mary Street chapel intended to awaken 'a Zeal for Christianity by shewing the contemptibleness & evil of lukewarmness' (*CL*, i. 326). In so doing, the tone of his sermon was exactly in accord with Toulmin's influential presence in Taunton. The singularity of Coleridge's political and religious dissent has long been noted, but much of this can be explained by viewing Coleridge's writings in the longer tradition of Protestant Dissent delineated or constructed in

Toulmin's publications and redactions of the writings of Socinus, Biddle, and Neal. In his Bristol pamphlet, *An Answer to 'A Letter to Edward Long Fox'* (1795), Coleridge lamented that 'the Law, the prophets, and the Gospel teach a series of doctrines so nearby bordering on some recent unpopular tenets, that it requires all the acuteness of beneficed interpreters to spriritualize them away into an harmless no-meaning' (*Lectures 1795*, 237). The 'unpopular tenets' Coleridge had in mind were, in part, those associated with his friend Joshua Toulmin.

At Bristol in 1795 Coleridge gave only three of his projected longer series of political lectures having, as he wrote to George Dyer in March, been 'obliged by the persecutions of Darkness to discontinue them' (*CL*, i. 155). Subsequently, he gave a course of 'Six Lectures on Revealed Religion, its Corruptions, and its Political Views'. They were probably delivered on Tuesday and Friday afternoons in the Card Room of the Assembly Coffee House in late May and early June (*Lectures 1795*, xxv–xxvi). In addition to those two series of lectures, Coleridge also delivered a 'Lecture on the Slave Trade' on 16 June (which he reprinted in the fourth number of *The Watchman* the following year). As well as the ten lectures that we are certain Coleridge delivered, there also exists a prospectus for six lectures comparing the English Revolution of the mid-seventeenth century with the French Revolution. Coleridge left Bristol for nearby Clevedon after his marriage to Sara Fricker on 4 October 1795, but he returned in November to take part in the opposition to the new repressive measures of Pitt's government, the Two Bills, which curtailed the freedom to meet to discuss political matters and extended the legal definition of treason. He gave his 'Lecture on the Two Bills' on 26 November and published it as the pamphlet *The Plot Discovered* in December 1795.

Coleridge's political position at this time was that of democrat, republican and dissenter, what was commonly referred to at the time as an 'English Jacobin' after the extremist French republican political faction, the Jacobins. Coleridge preferred the generic appellation of one of the 'Friends of Freedom', a term more accurately summing up his political position as one rooted in the traditions of English Protestant Dissent, rather than of French revolutionary politics. His political lectures certainly occasioned much opposition in the city. He wrote to Dyer that 'the opposition of the Aristocrats' was 'furious and determined' with 'Mobs and Mayors, Blockheads and brickbats, Placards and press gangs' conspiring against him (*CL*, i. 152). His attack on the war policy of the Pitt government is typical of much radical criticism of the time. More unusual is its tone, which, at times, approximates to that of a prophetic denunciation, similar to Toulmin's attack on the American war policy of Lord North. Coleridge argues that the government crackdown on radicals and its use of spies and informers have poisoned and corrupted the national psyche. Appropriating Proverbs 6:17–19, Isaiah 8:19, and Exodus 8:3, he writes:

There have been multiplied among us 'men who carry tales to shed blood!' Men who resemble the familiar Sprits described by Isaiah, as 'dark ones, that peep and that mutter!' Men, who may seem to have been typically shadowed out in the Frogs that formed the second plague of Egypt: little low animals with chilly blood and staring eyes, that 'come up into our houses and our bed-chambers!' These men are plenteously scattered among us: our very looks are deciphered into disaffection, and we cannot move without treading on some political spring-gun. (*Lectures 1795*, 60)

Coleridge also criticises the Established Church for its support of the war as anti-Christian. The religion it espouses is not that of peace, the religion of the 'meek and lowly Jesus' but that of 'Mitres and Mysteries, the Religion of Pluralities and Persecution' (*Lectures 1795*, 66–7). Coleridge's radicalism is thus based on an oppositional religious dissent that rejected the union of religious and political establishments for a purer form of Protestantism in which 'every true Christian is the Priest' (*Lectures 1795*, 68). In a letter to John Thelwall a year later Coleridge would claim that Christianity was 'a religion for Democrats', that 'which teaches in the most explicit terms the rights of Man, his right to Wisdom, his right to an equal share in all the blessings of nature' (*CL*, i. 282).

The 'Lectures on Revealed Religion' further developed the dissenting basis of Coleridge's politics, giving definition to his religious stance as a politically engaged Unitarian Christian and Protestant Dissenter. In the prospectus to the Lectures, Coleridge claimed that they were 'intended for two Classes of Men—Christians and Infidels' (*Lectures 1795*, 83). The two positions he thus wanted to combat were atheism and established Christianity. The Lectures set out to develop a form of religious radicalism which conforms to much contemporary Dissenting ideology as typified by its most important eighteenth-century spokesman, Joseph Priestley, upon whose works they heavily rely; however, Coleridge's particular brand of religious radicalism went far beyond that of middle-class Dissent of the 1790s. True to his Pantisocratic principles, Coleridge countenanced a redistribution of property, something that most propertied and commercial Dissenters would find thoroughly unpalatable. While clarifying Coleridge's theological position his Lectures also defined his political ideas – and, for most Dissenters, the two were inextricable. In *Conciones ad Populum* he had stressed the importance of the 'elect' reformers who were to guide the masses to political freedom by preaching the gospel to the poor. In the sixth lecture he appeals to the New Testament precedent of the small number of Apostles whom he compares to a grain of mustard seed and to the leaven in the meal. This Christian concept of an elect or faithful remnant informs both his ideas of Pantisocracy (with its twelve families) and his dissenting position (*Lectures 1795*, 229). The leaven and the mustard seed of the New Testament stand for the 'small but glorious band' of true friends of freedom who will gradually and peacefully transform society during the cold season of William Pitt's repressive rule.

It is, however, in his ideas concerning property that Coleridge departs most radically from both the Unitarian consensus and that of secular reformers like Thomas Paine and John Thelwall. Coleridge expressed his view to Thelwall that property was 'beyond doubt the Origin of all Evil' (*CL*, i. 214) and that Pantisocracy would make men virtuous by removing the temptation to accumulate. In the sixth lecture Coleridge refers explicitly to the example of the early Church in following Christ's example by keeping the community of property: 'In Acts ii. 44. 45 we read "And all that believed were together, & had all things in common – and sold their possessions & goods and parted them to all men, as every man had need".' This part of Christian doctrine, he adds, was soon corrupted. Coleridge also claimed that the Hebrew constitution enforced the equalisation of property, and argued that this was a wise and benevolent law because it prevented the concentration of power in too few hands: 'Property is Power and equal Property equal Power':

> [']The Land shall not be sold, for the Land is mine, saith the Lord, and ye are strangers and sojourners with me.['] There is nothing more pernicious than the notion that any one possesses an absolute right to the Soil, which he appropriates – to the system of accumulation which flows from this supposed right we are indebted for nine-tenths of our Vices and Miseries. The Land is no one's – the Produce belongs equally to all, who contribute their due proportion of Labour. (*Lectures 1795*, 125–7)

One wonders what the response of Coleridge's propertied audience was to this passage in his lecture. Coleridge actually wishes to go beyond the Jewish commonwealth's equalisation of property and argues for the 'abolition of individual Property' as 'perhaps the only infallible Preventative against accumulation' although he adds that the Jews were then too ignorant a people to achieve this (*Lectures 1795*, 128). The Lectures argue that universal equality and the abolition of individual property were the great objects of Christ's divinely inspired mission. In appealing to the texts of the Old and New Testament to justify his belief in the abolition of property, Coleridge was going much further than most of the radicals of the time were prepared to contemplate.

Coleridge's theory of property exceeded the revolutionary aspirations of Thelwall and Paine, or the propertied dissent of Priestley and the Unitarians. The nearest contemporary equivalents were the followers of the working-class radical Thomas Spence or the seventeenth-century Diggers led by Gerard Winstanley. The extent to which Coleridge would have wished to alter the relations of property in European states is not spelled out, but it would seem that the Pantisocratic project was an attempt to opt out of the social and political relationships of contemporary Britain and to build on a smaller scale an alternative polity that, like the leaven in the bread, would slowly construct another model of social and political organisation. Although Coleridge's faith in the equalisation of property in the Jewish theocracy or community of property in Pantisocracy did not last, many of the leading ideas of his Bristol and West Country radicalism would continue to figure in his later writings, albeit in transformed and adapted ways. Coleridge's characteristically idiosyncratic Protestant Dissenting ideas were thus shaped and forged by the contacts he made in the West Country, which deepened and strengthened the historical grounding of his Cambridge radicalism.

Bibliography

Andrews, Stuart, *Unitarian Radicalism: Political Rhetoric, 1770–1814* (Basingstoke: Palgrave Macmillan, 2003).

Bradley, James E., *Religion, Revolution, and English Radicalism: Nonconformity in Eighteenth-Century Politics and Society* (Cambridge: Cambridge University Press, 1990).

Brailsford, H. N., *The Levellers and the English Revolution* (London, 1961; rpt. Manchester, 1970).

Coleridge, S. T., *Notes, Theological, Political and Miscellaneous*, ed. Derwent Coleridge (London: Edward Moxon, 1853).

—— *S. T. Coleridge: Lectures 1795 on Politics and Religion*, ed. L. Patton and P. Mann, *Collected Works of Samuel Taylor Coleridge*, Bollingen Series 50, 1 (London: Routledge, 1971).

Ditchfield, Grayson M., 'Anti-Trinitarianism and Toleration in late Eighteenth-Century British Politics: the Unitarian Petition of 1792', *Journal of Ecclesiastical History*, 42 (1991).

Gibson, W., *Religion and the Enlightenment 1600–1800: Conflict and the Rise of Civic Humanism in Taunton* (Oxford and New York: Peter Lang, 2007).

Hill, C., *The World Turned Upside Down* (Harmondsworth: Penguin, 1972).

Holmes, R., *Coleridge: Early Visions* (London: Hodder & Stoughton, 1989).

Lawrence, B., *Coleridge and Wordsworth in Somerset* (Newton Abbot: David and Charles, 1970).

Leask, N., *The Politics of Imagination in Coleridge's Critical Thought* (London: Macmillan, 1988).

Little, B., *The City and County of Bristol: a Study in Atlantic Civilization* (London: Werner Laurie, 1954; rpt. Wakefield, 1967).

Morrow, J., *Coleridge's Political Thought: Property, Morality and the Limits of Traditional Discourse* (London: Macmillan, 1990).

Morton, A. L., *The World of the Ranters* (Oxford: Oxford University Press, 1970).

Neal, Daniel, *History of the Puritans from the Reformation in 1517 to the Revolution of 1688 ... Reprinted from the Text of Dr Toulmin's Edition* (2 vols, New York: Harper & Brothers, 1844).

Palmer, H. P., *Taunton: Its History and Market Trust* (Taunton: Goodman and Son, 1926).

Roe, N., *Wordsworth and Coleridge: the Radical Years* (Oxford: Clarendon Press, 1988).

Sandford, E., *Thomas Poole and His Friends* (London: Macmillan, 1888; rpt. Over Stowey: Friarn Press, 1996).

Seyer, S., *Memoirs Historical and Topographical of Bristol and its Neighbourhood from the Earliest Period Down to the Present Time* (2 vols, Bristol: Norton, 1823).

Stephenson, H. W., 'S. T. Coleridge and Unitarianism', *Transactions of the Unitarian Historical Society*, 5 (1932), 165–85.

Toulmin, J., *Memoirs of the Life, Character, Sentiments, and Writings, of Faustus Socinus* (London: J. Johnson, 1776).

—— *The American War Lamented. A Sermon preached at Taunton, February 18th and 25th 1776* (London: J. Johnson, 1777).

—— *A Review of the life, character, and writings of the Rev. J. Biddle who was banished to the Isle of Scilly in the Protectorate of Oliver Cromwell* (London: J. Johnson, 1791).

—— *The History of the Town of Taunton in the County of Somerset* (London: J. Johnson, 1791).

Underdown, D., *Pride's Purge: Politics in the Puritan Revolution* (Oxford: Clarendon Press, 1971).

—— *Somerset in the Civil War and Interregnum* (Newton Abbot: David and Charles, 1973).

Walford Davies, D., *Presences that Disturb: Models of Romantic Identity in the Literature and Culture of the 1790s* (Cardiff: University of Wales Press, 2002).

Watts, M., *The Dissenters: From the Reformation to the French Revolution* (Oxford: Clarendon Press, 1978).

White, D. E., *Early Romanticism and Religious Dissent* (Cambridge: Cambridge University Press, 2006).

7
Radical Bible: Coleridge's 1790s West Country Politics

Anthony John Harding

Radical appropriations of the Bible

Connections between Protestant Dissent and early expressions of Romanticism in England have been the focus of some important recent work in Romantic studies. Research on the periodicals founded or edited by Dissenters, the Joseph Johnson circle, the Warrington Academy circle, the Essex Street Unitarian Chapel, and prominent Dissenters such as Joseph Priestley, Richard Price, Anna Laetitia Barbauld, and others, has contributed a clearer picture of the extraordinarily active 'Dissenting' milieu within which the young S. T. Coleridge, and the writers with whom he established close friendships and often collaborated – Robert Southey, William and Dorothy Wordsworth, Charles Lamb, Charles Lloyd – formed such crucial relationships.[1] Research on radical politics in this period has also been greatly enriched by the work of cultural-materialist and new historicist scholars. In particular, cultural-materialist and new historicist critics, developing lines of enquiry first opened up by E. P. Thompson, have increasingly recognised the great diversity of the radical writing and political activity that took place in the years immediately following the French Revolution.[2] Noting this trend in historical scholarship, Marcus Wood in 1994 remarked on how it revealed 'the diversity of the social, intellectual, and geographical histories of radical organizations and individuals' (*Radical Satire*, 63).

In this essay, the focus is geographical, in that I particularly emphasise the West Country context of Coleridge's 1790s Unitarian radicalism, without losing sight of the active national networks within which West Country Unitarianism subsisted. My aim is to show that in developing a radical rhetoric rooted in Dissenting interpretations of biblical prophecy, Coleridge was adding his voice to those of prominent West Country Unitarians, particularly Joshua Toulmin of Taunton and John Prior Estlin of Bristol. By 'radical' here I mean that it attacked the anti-democratic principles and corrupt practices of the British parliamentary and governmental system of the time, and, further, that it questioned the alliance between property ownership and political power.[3] As Daniel White has pointed out, when Coleridge criticised the twin evils of property and commercialism he was setting himself at odds with both the values and economic infrastructure that were typical of late eighteenth-century 'rational Dissent', since Unitarian congregations in Bristol and elsewhere were dominated by members from the manufacturing and commercial classes (White, *Early Romanticism*, 120, 123). Estlin indeed owed his appointment at the Lewin's Mead Meeting to the banker and landowner Richard Bright; and John Cam Hobhouse, who was once head boy at the Stoke's Croft school (founded by members of the Lewin's Mead meeting), which was run on 'liberal and scientific lines' similar to those at the Warrington Academy, records that the Lewin's Mead Chapel 'was attended by the most influential merchants of the city, such as the Brights and the Castles and others of equal respectability'.[4]

This chapter therefore attempts to develop previous portrayals of the Dissenting milieu and radical millenarianism of the period, while laying more emphasis on West Country connections and relationships. Modern readers tend to think of a poem such as 'Religious Musings' (begun in London on 24 December 1794, and printed in the 1796 *Poems* at Joseph Cottle's press in Bristol) as a peculiarly Coleridgean product, that is, as personal or eccentric in its blend of religious and political hopes. In part, this is owing to the rather disparaging remarks Coleridge made many years later about the poem (in *Biographia Literaria*). But as Morton Paley shows, it was considered by many of his contemporaries to be a fine and very timely poem, in part because it drew on a range of reference and mixture of political and religious anxieties that would have been familiar to his intended audience (*Apocalypse*, 105, 108).

It is also important to point out how long-lasting was the impact of this early milieu on Coleridge's way of reading the Bible. For example, when in *Confessions of an Inquiring Spirit* (written between 1820 and 1824) he wants to question the idea that 'every word' of Scripture must be considered as 'dictated to the sacred *amanuensis* by an infallible Intelligence', he is adopting the term 'amanuensis' used by the prominent Unitarian scholar Gilbert Wakefield for the same purpose.[5] Equally, when he accepts 'with full belief' a scriptural declaration that 'the *Word of the Lord came*' to a prophet or other biblical personage (*Confessions*, 27), he is repeating the position taken by the West Country Unitarian Joshua Toulmin, who in a 1797 pamphlet drew his readers' attention to a 'mark of inspiration' distinguishing certain verses of the Bible, while denying that 'every word and syllable' must be received as inspired.[6] What Coleridge took from West Country Unitarianism – a blend of secular political engagement with devout attention to the New Testament call for a new form of human community, which was not at all incompatible with a rational-critical approach to the Bible – stayed with him for the rest of his life, despite changes in both his political and religious beliefs.

In the rest of this chapter I will, first, outline some relevant aspects of the culture of Unitarianism in late eighteenth-century England; then, give some examples of how West Country Unitarianism, in particular, exemplified this culture; and finally, examine some of the lectures and poetry Coleridge produced in 1794–7 to suggest how our sense of his work in this period might be enriched by investigation of these local connections. I want to emphasise the 'radical' reading of the Bible partly to make the case that it was exactly the sustained, historically informed engagement with the Bible encouraged by Unitarian ideology – the sort of close critical study that William Hazlitt describes his father as committed to – that contributed to the development of a new ethics of reading by such Romantic-era writers as Wollstonecraft, Coleridge, Wordsworth, Lamb, and Hazlitt.[7] After 1789 and the 'Declaration of the Rights of Man and Citizen' there was, for all who sympathised with the aims of the Revolution, a sense that one's thinking and reading ought to allow for the interests not just of one's own 'little platoon', but of all humankind; and for Unitarians in particular, reading the Bible *had* to be a critical activity, because it was thought to be a misunderstood and misrepresented text, a text that had been appropriated by worldly powers for impious, aggressive, and murderous purposes. The combination of the humanitarian and the critical in a single enterprise brought about a quiet but significant shift in the ethics of reading.

The Unitarian challenge, 1780–1794

Historians trace the origin of Unitarianism in England to 1662, when use of the Book of Common Prayer was imposed on English churches by Act of Parliament (the Act of Uniformity). Before this date, nearly 700 of the anti-episcopal ministers least willing to compromise – a number that included many Independents and Baptists – had already been ejected from their parishes by the 1660 Act for Settling Ministers.[8] In total, about 1,800 clergymen resigned their livings, rather than accept either a liturgy or a definition of the pastoral role decreed by government. This itself demonstrated how far-reaching was the action of the earliest reformers, who as the historian Euan Cameron puts it were engaged in 'setting up the authority of "the Word" *against* that of an institutional church which they later denounced as hopelessly corrupt and antichristian'. The so-called 'scripture principle' so dear to Protestants comes from the need to 'find a source of authority more impressive, more credible, and more venerable than "the Church" as then [*circa* 1520] perceived'.[9] In 1662, it seemed to many clergy that Parliament, by standardising the liturgy, was trying to deny the chief principle for which Luther, Melanchthon, Zwingli, Calvin, and other reformers had struggled, the primacy of Scriptural authority and the need for each believer to have the Bible speak directly to him.

The most conscientious of those clergy, including some whose views were not particularly 'puritan', resigned their livings rather than declare their full acceptance of the 1662 liturgy and subscribe to the Thirty-Nine Articles. John Spurr's study of the Church of England in the years following the Restoration gives the total number of clergy who were forced to leave their parishes between 1660 and 1663 (by either the 1660 Act for Settling Ministers or the 1662 Act of Uniformity, or both combined) as 1,760 (Spurr, *Restoration Church*, 43). Many of the congregations that were suddenly deprived of their clergy by the 'Great Ejection' formed themselves into new congregations, either on the Presbyterian model or as Congregationalist, Baptist, or Independent churches. Raymond Holt estimates that about 160 of those congregations that survived into the eighteenth century eventually became Unitarian.[10] More recently, scholars such as Stuart Andrews, Russell Richey, and Daniel E. White have added detail to this assessment, partly by pointing to the fluidity of denominational boundaries in the later eighteenth century, and partly by questioning received views of the complex relationship between Presbyterianism and Unitarianism. From a doctrinally orthodox perspective, the emergence of Unitarian congregations marked a decline from English Presbyterianism. Unitarians, however, saw themselves as representatives of a 'refinement of liberty', and as standing for 'humanitarian principles and the freedom of conscience'.[11] An alternative and (for Richey and White) more credible picture is that the 'Middle Way' associated with Richard Baxter, Edmund Calamy, Isaac Watts, and Philip Doddridge 'transformed the sectarian factionalism of Dissent's Puritan inheritance into a unified "community of Dissent"' (White, *Early Romanticism*, 38) out of which Unitarianism emerged. Andrews notes that in the 1780s and 1790s a number of former Anglicans, including several who were prominent scholars at Cambridge, such as William Frend and John Jebb, left the Anglican communion to affiliate themselves with Unitarian congregations (*Unitarian Radicalism*, 30). As Raymond Holt defines the Unitarians' own view of their history: 'A more open-minded study of Scripture led from Trinitarianism to so-called "Arianism" or Scriptural Unitarianism in its narrower sense, then to Humanitarian Unitarianism' (*Unitarian Contribution*, 306).

The crucial point for understanding Coleridge's Unitarian radicalism, however, is that within Unitarian communities the close, critical study of the Bible was not only tolerated, but actively encouraged. Rejection of the Book of Common Prayer – which enjoined the use of prayers addressed to the Trinity – was from this perspective the necessary consequence of the attentive study of Scripture. At a time when public worship was a matter of deep seriousness, all Protestant Dissenters had taken the risky step of refusing to have a form of worship imposed on them by Act of Parliament. Conscientious Unitarians shared with other Dissenters the penalties imposed by the Test and Corporation Acts, which prevented those who refused to receive the Sacrament 'according to the usage of the Church of

England' from holding public office in the service of the Crown, or certain civic offices, such as those of mayor or councillor.

A broadsheet publication of 1787, circulated in Bristol during the campaign for repeal of these punitive Acts, states as the first reason for seeking repeal that it is now 'universally acknowledged' that each man 'has an undoubted right' to judge religious matters for himself.[12] The second reason given for repeal is that 'The holy Sacrament of the Lord's Supper, being a matter purely of a religious nature ... ought not to be applied to the secular ends of civil societies' (*The Case*, 3). Unitarians went considerably further, however, by reading the Bible so carefully as to discover that (as they argued) it actually contained no authority for some of the key doctrines on which the Book of Common Prayer was based: the Trinity; original sin; the interpretation of the Communion service as anything other than a commemoration of Jesus's death; and the assertion in the Apostles' Creed that Jesus 'descended into hell'.[13] Indeed, a crucial argument often repeated by Unitarians was that these doctrines were not only unscriptural, but actually encouraged deism and atheism, since unbelievers would frequently cite these doctrines as reasons to reject the entire Bible.

The campaign of 1787 for repeal of the Test and Corporation Acts did not achieve its goal. (The Acts were finally repealed in 1828.) Nevertheless, several prominent churchmen, persuaded by the arguments of Wakefield, Priestley, Price, and other ministers and scholars, 'came out' as Unitarians in the 1780s and early 1790s. Andrews cites the example of John Disney, an Anglican clergyman who had hoped for reform of the liturgy but decided to resign his living in 1782 because 'many doctrines received as true by the church of England, in her articles and liturgy, were not only in no agreement, but in direct contradiction to what appeared to me to be the word of God'.[14] In 1793, Disney became minister at the Essex Street Chapel in London, an influential position. More closely related to Coleridge's circle were the Fellows at Cambridge colleges who were ejected for expressing views incompatible with Established Church doctrine: Thomas Fyshe Palmer, of Queen's College, Cambridge, John Jebb, of St. John's, and of course William Frend, of Jesus College (Holt, *Unitarian Contribution*, 116).

The view that Unitarianism was an undemanding, watered-down religion ignores the evidence that such men as Richard Price, Joseph Priestley, William Frend, Thomas Fyshe Palmer, and Gilbert Wakefield were every bit as fervent in their beliefs as the most committed of their Trinitarian opponents, and that (along with their fellow Dissenters) they faced civic penalties, and (unlike other Dissenters) the potential charge of blasphemy, for promulgating those beliefs. Gilbert Wakefield, sometime Fellow of Jesus College Cambridge, and later a lecturer in classics at the Dissenting Academy in Warrington, left the Church of England for reasons of conscience in 1779. In 1798 he was imprisoned in Dorchester Gaol for seditious libel, for his reply to Bishop Watson's *Address to the People of Great Britain*.[15] To preach in a Unitarian pulpit or even attend a meeting was to announce publicly one's opposition to the political and religious establishment.

Unitarians such as Wakefield concurred with the formulation of the German critic J. S. Semler: *'scriptura sacra continet verbum dei'* – Holy Scripture *contains* (not 'is') the word of God.[16] A large part of the Unitarian agenda had to do with using linguistic and textual analysis to pare away what they saw as the misunderstandings, interpolations, superstitious additions, and textual corruptions that clouded and confused the gospel message. Wakefield expresses it most vigorously in his 1781 *Essay on Inspiration*, arguing that in the first century or two after Christ 'the pacific Wisdom of the Gospel was made to administer, by a strange and deplorable Perversion, to Animosity and the inexorable Rage of Disputation' (*Essay*, 6). He appeals to the spirit of moderation – though his own language, where the Gospel is concerned, is not exactly moderate, as he expresses the 'ardent' wish 'to see the Foundations of CHRISTIANITY entirely disencumbered of that Mass of Rubbish, which IGNORANCE, ARTIFICE, and SUPERSTITION have heaped upon them, and restored to their pristine State of APOSTOLICAL SIMPLICITY' (*Essay*, 138).

Wakefield later engaged in an intense, even angry, pamphlet war with Samuel Horsley, then Bishop of St David's, in which Wakefield vigorously defended Richard Price and Joseph Priestley against Horsley's attacks. Wakefield quotes Horsley's defence of the alliance of church and state, and scornfully rejoins, 'What sort of *religion* must that be which requires "the concurrence of the *civil powers* to give it stability and strength?"'[17] More particularly, Wakefield mocks Horsley's claim that there can be no 'improvements' or progression in religious understanding: 'What is improvement in *theology*, but a fuller comprehension, a more clear perception, of the doctrines of revelation? Are not those doctrines to be collected from a detail of texts, accurately interpreted and impartially compared? Can the *whole* be known without a regular and minute acquaintance with all its *parts*? And will you be hardy enough to assert, that *we* of this day have not arrived at a better *interpretation* of the *scriptures* than our ancestors at the *reformation*? And what is the *theology* that is not founded on this *interpretation*, but *priestcraft* and *tradition*?' (*Address*, 10).

That the 'scripture principle' was still at work, vigorously and subversively, in Unitarian thinking, is also demonstrated by an anonymous tract, published in 1789, which the Cambridge University Library catalogue lists under the name of Joshua Toulmin of Taunton, noting however that it is 'sometimes attributed to John Disney'. The author quotes the admonition 'Thou shalt worship the Lord thy God, and him only shalt thou serve' (Matthew 4:10), and concludes that 'the worship of *two other* persons, is a merely human invention ... Upon this ground, I exhort you to leave the Church of England, – no longer to join in her religious services, – no longer to countenance her unscriptural practices.'[18] The closing pages of the tract cite several places in the Authorised Version where the translation allegedly misrepresents the meaning of the original Greek, slanting it towards a 'Trinitarian' interpretation.

This was the essence of the Unitarian challenge: not only rejection of the prayer book and rejection of the church and state alliance, but a critical reading of the Bible that emphasised the pacific message of the New Testament, and prized the 'apostolical simplicity' of primitive Christianity. When, therefore, the government enacted a law requiring the observance of solemn 'Fast Days' in support of the war against the French Republic – a war to which many of the population, probably a majority, were at this time opposed – Joseph Priestley, Gilbert Wakefield, and other prominent Unitarians denounced the law as both an encroachment on the hard-won liberty of individual conscience, and as a blasphemous abuse of the New Testament message. Unitarians were of course used to resisting interference by the state in religious functions. Priestley, addressing the Unitarian congregation of Hackney, East London, on 28 February 1794 – one of the days appointed by the government to urge the population to pray more fervently for the success of British troops fighting the French – used the occasion to proclaim a strong anti-war message.[19] The same month, Gilbert Wakefield published a stinging attack on the imposition of official Fast Days in support of what he saw as an unjust and imperialistic war: 'what fills up, in my opinion, the measure of our impieties, and leaves them incapable of aggravation, is, *the proclamation for a solemn fast*; to implore, truly, the assistance of the Almighty in destroying his own image, and desolating his own creation! No energies of language, that I have in store, can delineate *my* sense of this enormity, this sacrilegious profanation of religion.'[20]

Priestley made no secret of the fact that he saw the demise of the Catholic Church in France as a consequence of that church's alliance with a corrupt monarchy, and of its idolatrous doctrines; and he strongly hints that the Church of England may be the next to fall. 'What has more eminently contributed to destroy the earth, than the antichristian and idolatrous ecclesiastical establishments of Christianity, that have subsisted in these western parts of the world; many more persons having been destroyed by Christians, as they have called themselves, than by Heathens? And do we not see one, and one of the principal, of those establishments already, and completely, destroyed?' (*Present State*, 11).

West Country Unitarians were equally aware of being (as Priestley put it in his farewell sermon of 1794) 'a sect every where spoken against',[21] but proud of their Dissenting heritage and bold in challenging the status quo.

West Country Unitarianism, 1790–1800

Radical groups supporting parliamentary reform and opposed to the war with France had a strong presence in the West Country throughout the 1790s. Benjamin Flower's *Cambridge Intelligencer*, which maintained a consistent anti-government line from its beginning in July, 1793 – leading eventually to Flower's imprisonment in 1799 for having called the Bishop of Llandaff 'the Right Reverend time server and apostate' – was distributed from Tiverton and said to be the most popular radical paper in at least that part of Devon.[22] Coleridge had met Benjamin Flower while at Jesus College. Timothy Whelan has recently uncovered the story of Benjamin Flower's relationship with Eliza Gould, daughter of a tanner and Baptist deacon at Bampton, Devon. In 1794, Gould, then living at South Molton, became a distributor for the *Cambridge Intelligencer*, an enterprise that came at some social and financial cost as she was trying to run a school for young women. But she greeted with some enthusiasm the appearance of a Liberty Tree in Bodmin in 1795, commenting 'I firmly believe that Revolution is as much begun in England as ever it was in France' (Whelan, 'Politics, Religion, and Romance', 88–9).[23]

Joshua Toulmin's town of Taunton was a centre of Dissenting opinion, two-thirds of the inhabitants being Dissenters, though the Council was dominated by Anglicans. (Andrews notes that Taunton was probably a more important centre of Unitarian activity than Bristol (*Unitarian Radicalism*, 133).) Despite its strong condemnation of the Prayer Book liturgy, Toulmin's *An Exhortation* – if this pamphlet is indeed by Toulmin – is in line with Priestley's undertaking in his *Letter to the Right Honourable William Pitt* (1787) to use only rational persuasion, not violent resistance, to end the dominant position of the Established Church. His preaching breathed an air of quiet but resolute determination to uphold the 'apostolical simplicity' of the early communities. In a sermon on the first Christian communities (preached at Bridport in July 1788), he observes that 'The weapons of their warfare are spiritual', and urges his hearers: 'Your aim ... is to stand fast in the liberty, wherewith Christ hath made you free, and to recover Christianity from the gross corruptions, that have disguised and enervated it, to its original purity and simplicity.'[24] Toulmin was a consistent opponent of war. In 1776, he preached at Taunton a sermon, later published as a pamphlet, in which he pointed out not only the uncertain issue of the American war but the stubborn and inflexible attitude of the British government, which he blamed for provoking the conflict. It was 'a war, which, in all probability, will spread distress through every part of the *British* empire; a war to which we feel a particular aversion; a war which hath its own particular horrors and miseries'.[25] Consistent with this attitude, when Britain embarked on its war against France in 1793, Toulmin strongly disapproved and conscientiously tried to abstain from everything that implied support of it (Holt, *Unitarian Contribution*, 122–3).

John Prior Estlin first joined the Lewin's Mead Unitarian congregation in Bristol in 1770 as the minister's assistant; he was ordained to the ministry there in 1778 and stayed until forced by poor eyesight to retire, in 1816 or 1817 (Andrews, *Unitarian Radicalism*, 131). It was largely Estlin who brought about the transformation of Lewin's Mead from a liberal-Presbyterian to a Unitarian congregation, at the time when the old meeting-house was demolished and a new one built, in 1787–8.[26] Under his leadership, Lewin's Mead Chapel became one of the most influential Dissenting places of worship in Bristol, though (according to Andrews) it was not a centre for 'anti-government sentiment' to the extent that Taunton was, where two-thirds of the townspeople were Unitarians (Andrews, *Unitarian Radicalism*, 132, 135). Like Toulmin, and unlike the more apocalyptically minded Joseph Priestley, Estlin mostly emphasised the core Old Testament values of justice and mercy and the New Testament injunction to love thy neighbour, rather than millenarian prophecy. In his Christmas Day 1795 discourse, which is specifically aimed at answering Tom Paine's criticisms of religion in *The Age of Reason*, Estlin does echo Priestley's sentiment about the cataclysm in France being a possible sign of the millennium; but even in this pamphlet, his tone is reasonable and moderate. Estlin makes the case that Coleridge also makes in his 1795 Lectures for a close relationship between the core teachings of the Bible and the religion of reason: 'As there is a beautiful analogy between natural and revealed religion; as in fact they are the same, the latter only exhibiting clearer light, and more convincing evidence; as the difficulties which affect the one, affect also the other, so the arguments in support of both are drawn from the same source.'[27] He also eschews the use of any instruments other than persuasion and the duty to set an example by living a good life: 'Let the only weapons which we make use of in this contest be reason and argument, and … a life regulated by the precepts and example of Christ' (*Evidences*, 57). The characteristic Unitarian claim that there was a 'beautiful analogy' between natural and revealed religion, though it may have swayed some who would otherwise have become deists, left Unitarian opinion vulnerable to attack from conservative polemics such as those of the *Anti-Jacobin Review*, which as Nicholas Roe has shown (in *The Politics of Nature*) lost no opportunity to lump together rational Dissent with Painite deism and outright philosophical atheism.[28]

More than once in the early 1790s, Estlin preached on a text from the prophet Micah that later became one of Coleridge's favourite biblical mottoes, part of it being quoted in 'Effusion XXXV' (better known as 'The Eolian Harp'): 'what doth the Lord require of thee, but to do justly, and to love mercy, and to walk humbly with thy God?' (Micah 6:8). In a sermon preached in (probably) 1790 or 1791, Estlin applies this verse to the current state of European politics in a manner that is certainly in harmony with the Coleridge of the pastoral scenes in *Joan of Arc*, 'The Eolian Harp', and 'Reflections': 'The principal cause of the evils which now abound in the world, is the frequent violation of the laws of justice. It is this which occasions dark distrust, gloomy suspicion, and cautious reserve, and excites those who are governed by selfish principles, to repay fraud by fraud.'[29] In a later address on 'The Love of our Country', Estlin recommends a form of resistance that sounds almost Gandhian: true love of country, he suggests, means 'seeking the redress of grievances only by constitutional, legal and peaceful means' (*Sermons* [1802], 361). None of this should be taken to imply that Estlin was a compromiser, however. His 1795 Christmas Day discourse advocates a commitment to 'radical reforms in civil and religious institutions', to the eradication of war and slavery 'for ever', and to making 'man, in every instance, the brother and the friend of man' (*Evidences*, 47).

In a discourse delivered at the Lewin's Mead Chapel in 1797 that attempts to counter the atheism of the *philosophes*, Estlin puts forward a familiar Unitarian argument: that it is the superstitious beliefs imposed by the Established Church, the Catholic Church, and other denominations, that contribute most powerfully to the spread of atheism. In fact, he rather provocatively suggests that there is an analogy between state repression and the older churches' clinging to 'superstitious' beliefs: 'It is the *obstinate retaining* of *abuses* which is the cause of *violence* in the *civil* world, and the *general prevalence of superstition*, which is the prime cause of *infidelity* and a *disregard* to *God* in *religion*.'[30] A long 'Appendix' attempts to answer the colossal work of Charles François Dupuis, *Origine de tous les cultes, ou religion universelle* (7 vols, Paris, 1795), which purports to prove (among other things) that Jesus was a kind of sacrificial demigod, on the lines of Adonis, worshipped by the Phoenicians, or the Egyptian Osiris. According to John Beer, it may have been Coleridge who introduced Estlin to Dupuis's work.[31]

By 1797, many of the Dissenting groups that had adopted anti-war and anti-government political views were in retreat, and – as Peter Kitson observes – so far as a radical opposition still existed, the initiative had passed to the Painite, deistic, 'rights of man' wing of the movement. The 'rights of man' ideology had very different intellectual roots from the biblical traditions which West Country Unitarianism drew on.[32] Among those who continued to criticise the government, Unitarians were disproportionately represented: Gilbert Wakefield and Benjamin Flower were examples (Andrews, *Unitarian Radicalism*, 114). Toulmin wrote a vigorous defence of Unitarianism, delivered at Tiverton on 5 July 1797: *The Injustice of Classing Unitarians with Deists and Infidels. A Discourse*. This discourse reiterates the scriptural basis of Unitarian beliefs, and protests against the slander of associating Unitarians with deists and even with Muslims – an imputation that was given currency by Johnson's friend Mrs Hester Thrale Piozzi: 'WE make our appeal ... to the *Scriptures*; where the Unity of God is so clearly represented.'[33] Yet Toulmin, ever the reconciler and peacemaker, calls for 'forbearance and meekness' (*Discourse*, 34), even encouraging his reader to worship with other denominations, so long as services were not conducted on Trinitarian principles.

Coleridge and West Country radical Unitarianism

Coleridge was closely involved with both the political and the religious aspects of the Unitarian movement in the West Country, at a time when that movement was evidently energised by the anti-war campaign and the campaign for parliamentary reform. The preceding introduction to the public utterances of leading West Country Unitarians will have shown why it is important to see Coleridge's political and literary activities in context as an earnest, at times courageous, often original, but far from eccentric contribution to a significant regional political, ethical, and religious movement.

In 1795, Bristol was not only a busy commercial city but also a centre for political debate and philosophical enquiry; a place where, despite the inescapable presence of commerce – and of wealth generated by the slave trade, among other kinds of venture – a young democrat with new ideas might hope to find a receptive audience. Richard Holmes describes the attractions of Bristol for Coleridge:

> The public life of the city was sustained by several newspapers, publishing houses, theatres, Assembly Rooms, lecture halls in the Corn Market, a large municipal lending library, and research bodies like Dr Beddoes' Pneumatic Institute. Great national issues like the war with France, the slave trade, the breach with the American colonies, Pitt's increasingly draconian legislation against 'English Jacobins', and the questions of free speech and habeas corpus, were regarded as the personal responsibilities of the Bristol citizens. But lacking its own university, the city was an ideal arena for men from Oxford and Cambridge to attract immediate attention.[34]

John Prior Estlin and his wife were among the group of Bristol citizens who sponsored Coleridge's 'Six Lectures on Revealed Religion its' Corruptions and Political Views', delivered in Bristol between May and October, 1795. Among the others were Joseph Cottle and his brothers, and the wine merchant John Morgan and his wife.[35] It was also in Bristol – thanks to Thomas Beddoes, who had an extensive library of German works including works of biblical scholarship – that Coleridge first became acquainted with the new work in biblical scholarship, particularly that of Semler and Michaelis.[36]

Coleridge's Lectures belong squarely within the West Country radical Unitarian effort to indict the British establishment – both its religious and its political manifestations – for corruption, social injustice, and prosecution of an unnecessary war, while simultaneously answering the arguments of the Painites and atheist radicals who confused the irrationality of Trinitarian beliefs with the peaceable and rational teachings of both the Old Testament prophetic tradition and primitive Christianity. The word 'Corruptions' would signal to a contemporary audience that Coleridge wished to talk about the faith and practices of the first Christian communities, before this 'pure' Christianity had become tainted by the Gnostic and neo-Platonic doctrines brought into Asia Minor by Greek converts, especially those rich converts who had been educated in the Greek philosophical tradition. Coleridge's Prospectus further explains that the lectures are directed to an audience of 'Infidels' as well as believers, so that Infidels 'may not determine against Christianity from arguments applicable to its' Corruptions only'. The phrase 'Political Views' would have made it clear that Coleridge meant to expound a religion that took a strong, principled political stand, not one that disdained involvement with politics.[37] Both the reference to the 'corruptions' of Christianity and the allusion to its political relevance would have suggested connections with 'rational Dissent' or Unitarianism. More particularly, the word 'Corruptions' would remind Coleridge's Bristol audience of the work of Joseph Priestley (specifically, his *History of the Corruptions of Christianity*, 1782).

To say that Coleridge's thinking at this time was Unitarian and radical also necessarily involves saying that it is biblically based, because of the Unitarians' commitment to 'mental fight', communicating the biblical proclamation of justice, peace, and mercy. But there was no call to suspend rational thought when one opened one's Bible. Unitarianism was simultaneously engaged in critiquing, from a rationalistic perspective, most received ideas about the Bible, especially the notion that it was uniformly and unproblematically 'inspired', and that its pronouncements could therefore be received without attending to their historical context.

The question that sceptics and deists wished to have answered was essentially this: how can the modern age even begin to understand and believe a text containing so much that strains credulity? Biblical critics such as Michaelis and his English translator, Herbert Marsh, took on the task of developing a new way of interpreting the biblical record, sifting it to discover which parts were believable and which had to be considered imaginative elaboration or hyperbole. For those students of the Bible who were also believers, part of the difficulty was that this very task of developing new ways for the modern mind to extract the lasting spiritual meaning from the exotic, 'oriental' language and narrative was potentially at odds with the historical emphasis of the new approach. In principle, at least, historical-critical work, tending to highlight the different cultural milieus in which biblical narratives originated, was in conflict with biblical exegesis in the Protestant tradition, which still needed a concept of the 'unity' of the Bible.[38] Nevertheless, awareness of specific historical circumstances – such as the resistance to kingship under the Mosaic dispensation – could sometimes energise one's reading. This was certainly the case with Coleridge.

Coleridge draws on the work of Moses Lowman to show that the Hebrew Commonwealth was originally founded on egalitarian and democratic principles, and that the appointment of the first king, which took place early in the ninth century BCE, after the Israelites had pleaded with Samuel to authorise the institution of kingship in order to stave off chaos in the state, was regarded by Samuel himself, and by any careful student of the Mosaic dispensation, as a shockingly retrograde step, a compromise with sin and idolatry, and a political and moral error that would jeopardise Israel's right to be considered the Lord's chosen people. Lowman himself was answering a deistic attack on the Mosaic dispensation as 'arbitrary and oppressive'.[39] Coleridge adopts the same arguments in the 1790s to answer the attack on revealed religion in *The Age of Reason*. The crucial point here – an argument often deployed by John Milton and other seventeenth-century republicans – is that the Hebrew Commonwealth must have no king, because a king would be an idolatrous substitute for God, a false authority-figure coming between the nation of Israel and its real ruler, the Lord: 'the one true God was not only their God, and as such the only Object of their *Religion* and Worship, but he was the *King of Israel*, and so the proper political Head of that Nation' (192). Lowman paints a picture of an agrarian democracy that calls to mind some of Coleridge's most sanguine hopes for Pantisocracy. (Pantisocracy has been described by Nicholas Roe as a 'turbulent confluence of radical and imperialist ideologies, American travel accounts, the Hebrew commonwealth, and dissenting millenarianism', *Politics of Nature*, 46.) Under the Mosaic dispensation, Lowman argues, it was impossible for any individual to rise to a position where he could oppress his fellow subjects: 'The Wisdom of this Constitution is yet further observable, as it provided against all ambitious Designs of private persons, or Persons in Authority, against the publick Liberty' (Lowman, *Dissertation*, 48). The persistence of this wise constitution over the long term was guaranteed, first, by the equal division of property: Lowman undertakes some elaborate mathematical calculations, based on the north–south and east–west dimensions of Palestine, to prove that each household would have 16½ acres, with about 1¼ million acres retained for the Levites and the leaders of the twelve tribes. Lowman quotes Harrington's *Commonwealth of Israel* as source for some of these calculations (Lowman, *Dissertation*, 45). Moreover, the Assembly, which was both a civil and a military gathering, comprised two thousand representatives from each tribe, attending in rotation, so that, as Harrington puts it, 'the Advice and Consent of the Nation' (quoted, Lowman, *Dissertation*, 59) were consistently present in making decisions about national policy.

As Peter Kitson has shown in an important essay on Coleridge's *The Plot Discovered*, the biblical model of an egalitarian, democratic commonwealth exercised a powerful influence on Coleridge in the period immediately following the Treason Trials of 1794, and during the subsequent weakening of the radical movement after the Gagging Bills passed into law on 18 November 1795. *The Plot Discovered*, delivered as a lecture on 26 November 1795 and published early in December that year (Kitson, 'Electric fluid', 39), 'marks the movement of Coleridge's political ideas from one phase to another, as he abandons the millenarian aspects of his thought and concentrates more clearly on the ideal of the Commonwealth' (Kitson, 'Electric fluid', 37). Kitson shows that Coleridge's political thought in the writings of 1795 belongs in a 'tradition of radical religious and political dissent' originating in the 'leftward drift in theology occasioned by the Reformation'

(Kitson, 'Electric fluid', 37). This tradition regularly invoked John Milton, Algernon Sidney, and James Harrington; it was particularly encapsulated in James Burgh's *Political Disquisitions* (3 vols, 1774–5), which Coleridge borrowed from the Bristol library shortly before lecturing on the Two Bills.

It is worth re-emphasising, however, that Coleridge's political polemic was directed not only against the 'church and king' constituency but simultaneously against the anticlerical deism of Paine. Present-day readers are likely to have such an aversion to the concept of a theocracy – the term Josephus applied to the Jewish state – as to have difficulty understanding how theocracy can be reconciled with representative government. But the Commonwealth idea still had purchase among radical Dissenters, precisely because it *was* biblically based, a model of democracy instituted under Moses's magistracy, as contrasted with the Athenian model, ostensibly admired by most of the political class, which was not only pagan but – an equally disturbing feature for radicals – slave-owning. The Hebrews, on the other hand, were liberated slaves; and, as Lowman argued in *The Ritual of the Hebrew Worship*, the Jewish religious institutions (like the social ethic enshrined in the Levitical code) were 'a Type or Plan, a Shadow or Sketch, of the good Things to come in the Days of Messiah'.[40] A point that Coleridge makes repeatedly in the 1795 Lectures is that Paine's objections to the Levitical code of law make no allowance for the fact that the Israelites had only just emerged from generations of slavery, followed by forty years' wandering in the wilderness, and they were constantly being seduced by the attractions of the idolatrous cults practised by their neighbours. '[T]o govern well', Coleridge wrote in a notebook early in 1796, 'is to ... train up a nation to true wisdom & virtue' – a quotation from Milton's *Of Reformation* (1641).[41] The legislator's task was to provide for the training up of the people of Israel, whilst carefully guarding against the future emergence of despotism of an 'Oriental' kind.

Coleridge also found in early Christian writings many indications that the first Christian communities shared property in common. Those who had possessions would sell them, sharing the proceeds with other members of their church, so that every member of the community had sufficient provision. One of the most frequent criticisms of the Established Church made by non-believers and radical deists was that it gave the sanction of religion to gross inequalities of wealth. Coleridge is therefore trying to show that in its *original* form Christianity encouraged the sharing of property. His remarks about the dangers of commerce (in Lecture 6) were designed to prick the consciences of any Bristol merchants who happened to be among his audience, not only attacking the trade in goods acquired by acts of colonial aggression in India, Africa, or the West Indies – 'Not one thing necessary or even useful do we receive in return for the horrible guilt in which we have involved ourselves' – but advocating the abandonment of individual property altogether (*Lectures 1795*, 226, 228). As Daniel E. White has shown, in urging (on scriptural grounds) the abolition of property, Coleridge was going considerably further than either William Godwin or Joseph Priestley, and indeed further than other Socinian Dissenters: 'Coleridge means his audience to take him literally in his determination that, in addition to "loving kindness", Christians must preserve among themselves a "perfect Equality"' (*Early Romanticism*, 134). Doctrinally, Coleridge's version of the gospel was close to that of Estlin who had argued that 'as the laws of *christianity* are in fact the laws of *natural religion*, only explained with *peculiar clearness*, and enforced by *peculiar sanctions*, what is commanded by the one is commanded by the other, and what is inconsistent with the one is likewise inconsistent with the other' (*Sermons*, 360). However, Coleridge's interpretation of the Christian social ethic was far more explicitly radical than Estlin's.

Coleridge's poetry 1794–1797

There is a case to be made for listening to Coleridge's poetry of the mid-1790s with 'Unitarian' ears. For example, knowing that the verse from Micah quoted earlier was a favourite text of John Prior Estlin's – and perhaps a touchstone for a certain West Country Unitarian attitude of resolute, non-violent resistance to warmongering – helps us to realise that the conclusion to 'The Eolian Harp' is not an expression of pious obeisance, but a declaration of some political as well as religious significance. There are more obvious allusions to the cause of radical Unitarianism in many other poems: 'Effusion IV', first published in the *Morning Post* for 11 December 1794, laments the way that Joseph Priestley was driven into exile by 'RIOT rude', roused up by 'that dark Vizir', William Pitt.[42] And 'Religious Musings' takes a stand against all merely worldly authorities:

> Who the Creator love, created might
> Dread not: within their tents no Terrors walk.
> [. . .]
> This the worst superstition, him except
> Aught to desire, SUPREME REALITY!

> (*PW*, I. i. 177, 180, ll. 64–5, 132–3)

Though dated Christmas Eve, 1794, and clearly considered a poem on the Nativity, 'Religious Musings' manages to avoid conventional accounts of the Nativity and most of the usual images. Instead, in these lines from the 1796 *Poems* (they were removed in the 1797 printing), the birth is represented as a moment towards which the history of the world has been straining:

> Ah not more radiant, nor loud harmonies
> Hymning more unimaginably sweet

> With choral songs around th'ETERNAL MIND,
> The constellated Company of WORLDS
> Danc'd jubilant: what time the startling East
> Saw from her dark womb leap her flamy Child![43]

John Thelwall objected to the 'Della Cruscan' habit he thought Coleridge had taken on, of placing stress on 'adjectives and weak words', saying they gave him 'the earache', citing the last line here quoted as an instance ('flamy child!!!!' – see Coleridge, *Poetry and Prose*, 21n). Whatever we think of this visionary passage and Thelwall's objections, however, the poem tries to redirect our attention *away* from the Nativity scene towards the Jesus who ministered to others and suffered as a man, the 'Man of Woes' (*PW*, I. i. 174, l. 8).

The concern with the devastation and misery spread by war perhaps achieved its most powerful expression in 'The Visions of the Maid of Orleans', published in *The Morning Post* on 26 December 1796. This fragmentary piece, as Paul Magnuson remarks, 'is rather a prelude to Joan's visions than the visions themselves'.[44] But it does reconcile and develop the images of Joan as woman of the people and compassionate friend of the poor, and Joan as a type of prophet and Chosen One, 'Maid belov'd of Heaven', from his work with Southey on *Joan of Arc* (*PW*, I. i. 217). Joan, in 'The Visions … ', is a female David – with touches of Miriam and Deborah – a woman called from humble origins to be the saviour of her people.

Coleridge's expansion of the lines about Joan's calling introduces a new element, a horrific episode borrowed from a contemporary narrative about the campaign in northern France and the Low Countries between 1793 and 1795.[45] The anonymous Officer who tells this story describes how he came upon a dying man – actually a soldier – in a wagon, the exhausted and near-frozen horses unable to pull the wagon any further through the freezing January night. Coleridge transfers this scene to Joan's France, incorporating another even more affecting scene from the same narrative, of a young refugee mother who died of cold whilst nursing her infant. Coleridge turns the two descriptions into a story of a refugee family displaced by the invading English army. After bringing the dying man back to her father's home and hearing his story, Joan goes back to the hill from which she first saw the wagon and there has her first intimation of a call to heroic action. This is an instance of the kind of episode Wordsworth refers to in the 1800 'Preface' as demonstrating how 'the power of the human imagination is sufficient to produce such changes even in our physical nature as might appear miraculous'.[46]

Responding to a draft of the poem which he saw in February 1797, Charles Lamb objected to the jarring disparity between the high spiritual destiny Joan was to have and the emphasis on her humble origins: 'you are not going, I hope, to annex to that most splendid ornament of Southey's poem all this cock & a bull story of Joan the Publican's daughter'.[47] Lamb

was perhaps sceptical of the way the description of Joan's early communion with the spirit of wisdom could be meant to suggest parallels with
such figures as David and Samuel, who were also from lowly origins:

> From her childish days
> With wisdom, mother of retired thoughts,
> Her soul had dwelt; and she was quick to mark
> The good and evil thing ...
>
> (*PW*, II. i. 392, ll. 133–6)

When she is impelled to return to the hilltop after hearing the poor refugee's
story, the language again echoes biblical prophecy: 'a mighty hand / Was
strong upon her ... Thus as she toil'd in troubl'd ecstasy, / An horror of
great darkness wrapt her round, / And a voice utter'd forth unearthly tones'
(*PW*, II. i. 395–6, ll. 255–6, 266–8). This uncanny episode, which follows a
pattern that later informs the 'spots of time' in Wordsworth's 1799 *Prelude*,
is Coleridge's attempt to imagine – through the recreation of a traumatic
experience, that has called out all the young woman's feelings of compassion for human suffering – the state of mind in which an impressionable,
sensitive country girl *might* actually believe that an angelic messenger was
calling her to take on the mantle of a prophet and leader.

Lamb's aesthetic instincts may have been right, after all, in that the realistic
details of Joan's life at the inn – the 'rough-hewn bench', the 'gay sign-board',
and even the wagon with its half-dead horses, details that would have been
more at home in a poem by John Langhorne or George Crabbe – strike modern ears as absurdly dissonant with the words of the unearthly voice ('O thou
of the Most High / Chosen ...' (*PW*, II. i. 396, ll. 269–70)). Here, Coleridge's deep
interest in naturalistic explanations for our beliefs about the supernatural – all
the 'Wild phantasies' of the Laplander seeing the Northern Lights and hoping
his soul will join the 'happy spirits', which formed part of his 1795 contribution to *Joan of Arc* Book II – perhaps detract from a story about the emergence
of a French Miriam or Deborah. Wordsworth's story of the Pedlar's youth
avoids this jarring note by reducing the allusion to the Bible almost to a mere
parenthesis. Yet there is a fascinating idea here, one that is generated by reading the Bible with a critical, historicist eye while responding to the prophetic
call to act justly, resist tyranny, and show compassion towards those who suffer. Though initially discouraged by Lamb's criticisms, Coleridge did not lose
interest entirely but returned to the topic in 1814, revising the 'Visions' into
the poem we know as 'The Destiny of Nations: A Vision'. The lines about the
Laplander and the Greenland Wizard, suggesting more recent analogies for
some of the Old Testament imagery of angels and supernatural communications, as well as for Joan's voices, are still there: 'peopling air, / By obscure
fears of Beings invisible' (*PW*, II. i. 214).

In January 1797, about three weeks after publication of 'The Visions of the Maid of Orleans' and soon after moving to Nether Stowey, Coleridge wrote to Estlin asking for letters of introduction to Mr Howell, the Unitarian minister at Bridgwater, and Mr Toulmin of Taunton (*CL*, i. 301). The introductions were evidently successful. Both men were sufficiently impressed with Coleridge to invite him to preach to their congregations. As Coleridge reported to Estlin on one such occasion (with a peculiar mixture of affection, pride, and deference), 'I breakfasted with Dr Toulmin last Monday – the more I see of that man, the more I love him. I preached for Mr Howel the Sunday before – My sermon was admired – but *admired* sermons, I have reason to think, are not those that do most good' (*CL*, i. 326). These connections brought Coleridge close to the point of becoming assistant minister in Bridgwater, though without stipend; as is well known, he also preached at the Unitarian meeting in Shrewsbury, making an indelible impression on the young William Hazlitt. At this point, however, the offer of an annuity from the Wedgwoods made all plans of this kind redundant (*CL*, i. 387). Yet, in the spring of 1798 – some two months after his collaboration with Wordsworth on the *Lyrical Ballads* volume had begun – Coleridge was still willing to walk to Taunton and back again to conduct services for Toulmin.[48]

If the Stowey connections – most especially, Tom Poole, and William and Dorothy Wordsworth – had to some extent displaced Estlin from his role as one of Coleridge's chief mentors, and the relationship with Wordsworth was pulling Coleridge away from political and religious pursuits and towards literary and philosophical ones, the relationships he had formed in Bristol with the Estlins and the Morgans continued to be important for many years, as his letters demonstrate.

Conclusion

West Country radicalism, particularly the version developed by Coleridge in his lectures, in *The Plot Discovered* and *The Watchman*, in 'Religious Musings', 'Visions ...', and other writings of the period, exercised a strong attraction for John Thelwall, even before he settled at Llyswen Farm in the Wye Valley. In 1797, Thelwall visited Nether Stowey, arriving on 17 July. Soon after leaving Coleridge's household, he marked the occasion with a poem, 'Lines Written at Bridgwater', 27 July 1797:

> ... far from the strifeful scenes
> Of public life (where Reason's warning voice
> Is heard no longer, and the trump of Truth
> Who blows but wakes The Ruffian Crew of Power
> To deeds of maddest anarchy and blood)
> Ah! let me, far in some sequester'd dell

Build my low cot; most happy might it prove,
My Samuel! near to thine, that I might oft
Share thy sweet converse, best-belov'd of friends!– [49]

The demise of *The Watchman*, the conflicts in his relationship with Thelwall, the birth of his son Hartley on 19 September 1796, as well as his now-frequent conversations with Dorothy and William Wordsworth, were drawing Coleridge towards different forms of political and literary engagements. Retreating from the 'strifeful scenes / Of public life' in order to regroup seemed the wisest course, and if like-minded friends were able to join him in these 'sequester'd scenes', so much the better.

However, in the five or six years of his association and collaboration with leading Unitarians such as John Prior Estlin and Joshua Toulmin, Coleridge had received an intensive education in the kinds of rational enquiry favoured by eminent and influential Unitarian scholars, including enquiry into the historical context and the contemporary relevance of biblical prophecy. The years of his close association with Unitarian thinkers permanently changed his outlook. Though he would later repudiate Unitarian theology, so far as biblical studies were concerned he remained for the rest of his life an uncompromising and indefatigable 'inquiring spirit'.

Notes

1. The studies most immediately relevant to the concerns of this chapter are: Stuart Andrews, 'Coleridge and the "Truth in Christ": Bristol, 1795', *Coleridge Bulletin*, 19 (Spring 2002), 58–70, and *Unitarian Radicalism: Political Rhetoric, 1770–1814* (Basingstoke: Palgrave Macmillan, 2003); Felicity James, 'Coleridge and the Unitarian Ladies', *Coleridge Bulletin*, 28 (Winter, 2006), 46–53; Peter J. Kitson, '"The electric fluid of truth": the Ideology of the Commonwealthsman in Coleridge's *The Plot Discovered*', in *Coleridge and the Armoury of the Human Mind: Essays on his Prose Writings*, ed. Peter J. Kitson and Thomas N. Corns (London: Frank Cass, 1991), 36–62, and '"To Milton's Trump": Coleridge's Unitarian Sublime', in *Romanticism and Millenarianism*, ed. Tim Fulford (New York: Palgrave Macmillan, 2002), 37–52; Iain McCalman, 'New Jerusalems: Prophecy, Dissent and Radical Culture in England, 1786–1830', in *Enlightenment and Religion: Rational Dissent in Eighteenth-Century Britain*, ed. Knut Haakonssen (Cambridge: Cambridge University Press, 1996), 312–35; Victoria Myers, 'The Other Fraud: Coleridge's *The Plot Discovered* and the Rhetoric of Political Discourse', in *Romanticism, Radicalism, and the Press*, ed. Stephen C. Behrendt (Detroit: Wayne State University Press, 1997), 65–82; Morton D. Paley, *Apocalypse and Millennium in English Romantic Poetry* (Oxford: Clarendon Press, 1999); Nicholas Roe, *The Politics of Nature: William Wordsworth and Some Contemporaries* (2nd edition, Basingstoke: Palgrave Macmillan, 2002), chapter 4; Timothy Whelan, 'Politics, Religion, and Romance: Letters of Eliza Gould Flower, 1794–1802', *The Wordsworth Circle*, 36.3 (Summer 2005), 85–109, and 'Coleridge, the *Morning Post*, and Female "Illustrissimae": an Unpublished Autograph', *European Romantic Review*, 17.1 (2006), 21–38; Daniel E. White, *Early Romanticism and Religious Dissent* (Cambridge: Cambridge University Press, 2006). I am particularly grateful to the staff of Cambridge University Library, the Bristol

Record Office, and the library of the University of King's College, Halifax, for their assistance.

2. See especially Kevin Gilmartin, *Print Politics: the Press and Radical Opposition in Early Nineteenth-Century England* (Cambridge: Cambridge University Press, 1996); Timothy Morton and Nigel Smith, eds, *Radicalism in British Literary Culture, 1650–1830: From Revolution to Revolution* (Cambridge: Cambridge University Press, 2002); Richard Whatmore, 'British Radicalism in the 1790s' (review article), *History of European Ideas*, 31 (2005), 428–32; and Marcus Wood, *Radical Satire and Print Culture 1790–1822* (Oxford: Clarendon Press, 1994).

3. As Kevin Gilmartin remarks, 'The most disruptive implication of radical independence was its challenge to the intersection of property and power, a chief obstacle to the extension of political suffrage' (*Print Politics*, 33).

4. Pamela Bright, *Dr Richard Bright (1789–1858)* (London: The Bodley Head, 1983), 22, 24.

5. *Confessions of an Inquiring Spirit*, ed. H. N. Coleridge (London: William Pickering, 1840), 42–3. Compare Gilbert Wakefield, *An Essay on Inspiration considered chiefly with respect to the Evangelists* (Warrington: William Eyres, 1781), 24: '*Amanuensis* of the HOLY SPIRIT'.

6. 'The nature of the subject will, often, discriminate the divine communications. As "Thus saith the Lord", "The doctrine is not mine, but his that sent me", or any like phrase, will, wherever they occur, stamp the mark of inspiration'; Joshua Toulmin, *The Injustice of Classing Unitarians with Deists and Infidels* (London: Joseph Johnson, 1797), 14.

7. For Hazlitt's account of his father, see *Complete Works*, ed. P. P. Howe (21 vols, London: J. M. Dent and Sons, 1930–4), xvii. 110: 'After being tossed about from congregation to congregation in the heats of the Unitarian controversy, and squabbles about the American war, he had been relegated to an obscure village, where he was to spend the last thirty years of his life, far from the only converse that he loved, the talk about disputed texts of Scripture and the cause of civil and religious liberty.'

8. John Spurr, *The Restoration Church of England, 1646–1689* (New Haven: Yale University Press, 1991), 40–1, 43.

9. Euan Cameron, *The European Reformation* (Oxford: Clarendon Press, 1991), 136.

10. Raymond Holt, *The Unitarian Contribution to Social Progress in England* (2nd edition, London: Lindsey Press, 1952), 288.

11. White, *Early Romanticism and Religious Dissent*, 38, quoting Russell E. Richey, 'Did the English Presbyterians Become Unitarian?', *Church History*, 42 (1973), 61. White also points to theological differences between Arianism and Socinianism. Richard Price and Anna Laetitia Barbauld were Arians (that is, they held that Christ was a divine being, and existed before the Incarnation, but was subordinate to God the Father). Arians were, however, a minority among late eighteenth-century Unitarians.

12. *The Case of the Protestant Dissenters, with Reference to the Test and Corporation Acts* (n.p., 1787), 2. A copy of this publication is among the papers of the Lewin's Mead Unitarian Meeting at the Bristol Record Office. The preamble reviews the history of the legislation, suggesting that it was not intended to penalise any Protestant denomination, but only to keep Roman Catholics from taking political office.

13. These points of contention are from Gilbert Wakefield, *An Address to the Inhabitants of Nottingham* (London: J. Johnson, 1789), 8–13.

14. *Reasons for resigning the Rectory of Panton* (London: J. Johnson, 1782), 7, quoted by Andrews, *Unitarian Radicalism*, 47. Disney succeeded Theophilus Lindsey

as minister at the Essex Street Chapel, London, in 1793 (Andrews, *Unitarian Radicalism*, 49).

15. Holt, *Unitarian Contribution*, 120–1; Kitson, '"To Milton's Trump": Coleridge's Unitarian Sublime', 45; Andrews, *Unitarian Radicalism*, 3.
16. Thomas Albert Howard, *Religion and the Rise of Historicism: W. M. L. de Wette, Jacob Burckhardt, and the Theological Origins of Nineteenth-Century Historical Consciousness* (Cambridge: Cambridge University Press, 2000), 35.
17. Gilbert Wakefield, *An Address to the Right Reverend Dr. Samuel Horsley, Bishop of St. David's, on the Subject of An Apology for the Liturgy and Clergy of the Church of England* (Birmingham: Printed by J. Thompson, 1790), 37.
18. Anon. [Joshua Toulmin?], *An Exhortation to all Christian People, to refrain from Trinitarian Worship* (London: J. Johnson, 1789), 16. Cambridge University Library Syn.7.78.52 (3).
19. Joseph Priestley, *The Present State of Europe compared with Antient Prophecies; A Sermon, Preached at the Gravel Pit Meeting in Hackney, February 28, 1794, Being the Day appointed for a General Fast* (London: Printed for J. Johnson, 1794), 11. In some well-known lines, William Wordsworth recalled the experience of sitting in a church where others prayed for victory, while he 'sate silent': *The Prelude* (1805 text), 10.273; *The Prelude 1799, 1805, 1850*, ed. Jonathan Wordsworth, M. H. Abrams, and Stephen Gill (New York: Norton, 1979), 372.
20. Gilbert Wakefield, *The Spirit of Christianity, Compared with the Spirit of the Times in Great Britain* (London: Sold by Kearsley, 1794), 20–1.
21. Joseph Priestley, *The Use of Christianity, especially in difficult Times … Being the Author's Farewell Discourse to His Congregation* (2nd edition, London: J. Johnson, 1794), 7.
22. Quoted in Whelan, 'Politics, Religion, and Romance', 85. See also Andrews, *Unitarian Radicalism*, 153.
23. She met Flower in person only in 1799, however, after he had been committed to Newgate prison. By the end of the year, they were married (Whelan, 'Politics, Religion, and Romance', 105).
24. Joshua Toulmin, *The Conduct of the First Converts to Christianity, Considered and Applied, in a Sermon, Preached at Bridport, on the Tenth of July, 1788* (London: Printed by H. Goldney, and sold by J. Johnson, 1788), 5, 19–20.
25. Joshua Toulmin, *The American War lamented. A Sermon preached at Taunton, February the 18th and 25th, 1776* (London: J. Johnson, 1776), 2.
26. In 1843, the Lewin's Mead Congregation submitted a deposition to the House of Lords stating that the existing chapel had been built in 1788 on the site of an old Presbyterian meeting-house, and that 'The Society was Unitarian at the erection of the new Meeting-house'; O. M. Griffiths, 'Side Lights on the History of Presbyterian-Unitarianism from the Records of Lewin's Mead Chapel, Bristol', *Transactions of the Unitarian Historical Society*, 6.2 (October 1936), 124. Griffiths also says that Estlin's theology 'was certainly unorthodox' ('Side Lights', 117). Christopher James Thomas's brief history of the Lewin's Mead congregation also states that 'At the time the present chapel was erected, the congregation was avowedly a body of Unitarian Christians': *Some Account of the Rise and Progress of the Ancient Society of Protestant Dissenters, Worshipping in Lewin's Mead, Bristol* (Bristol: Stephens and Eyre, Printers, 1891), 20.
27. John Prior Estlin, *Evidences of Revealed Religion, and Particularly Christianity, Stated, With reference to a Pamphlet called The Age of Reason* (Bristol: Printed by N. Biggs, n.d. [1796]), 34.

28. Roe, *The Politics of Nature*, 76.

29. John Prior Estlin, *Sermons, Designed, Chiefly, as a Preservative from Infidelity, and Religious Indifference* (Bristol: Emery and Adams, sold by J. Johnson and T. Hurst, London, 1802), 44. This sermon cannot be dated precisely. Only a few bear specific dates, but they appear to be arranged in chronological order.

30. John Prior Estlin, *The Nature and the Causes of Atheism, Pointed Out in a Discourse, delivered at the Chapel in Lewin's-Mead, Bristol. To Which Are Added, Remarks on a Work, entitled Origine de tous les cultes, ou Religion universelle* (Bristol: Printed by N. Biggs, and Sold by J. Cottle ... and by J. Johnson, 1797), 25. As epigraph to this work, Estlin quoted fifteen lines from Coleridge's contributions to *Joan of Arc* (on which Coleridge collaborated with Southey), the passage in Book II beginning 'For what is Freedom, but the unfetter'd use / Of all the Powers which God for use had given?' There are substantive variants between this and the 1796 printed text (for which see *PW*, I, i. 210–12 (*Joan of Arc*, II. 13–18, 29–37)). Estlin's quotation prints 'has' for 'had' in line 2; after 'veil his blaze', ten lines beginning 'For all that meets the bodily sense ...', are omitted; line 15 of Estlin's quotation reads 'Creation dispossessing of its God'.

31. See John Beer, *Coleridge the Visionary* (London: Chatto & Windus, 1959), 213. On Dupuis, see also Anthony John Harding, *The Reception of Myth in English Romanticism* (Columbia, MO: University of Missouri Press, 1995), 33–5.

32. Kitson, '"The electric fluid of truth"', 38: 'the reform movement was soon to be in total disarray ... The decline of the more moderate Society for Constitutional Information at this time [following the 1794 Treason Trials] marks an end of a phase of radical politics ... This phase of thought also finds its expression in Coleridge's Bristol lectures, and, in a sad historical irony, it was being supplanted just as his radicalism reached its height. Soon pseudo-historical generalisations about Anglo-Saxon democracy and Commonwealth republican ideology would be replaced by emphatic avowals of deistic Paineite "rights of man philosophy", which were incompatible with Coleridge's scripturally based religious radicalism.'

33. Joshua Toulmin, *The Injustice of Classing Unitarians with Deists and Infidels. A Discourse Written with reference to Some Reflections from the Pens of Bishops Newton, Hurd, and Horsley, Doctors White, Knox, and Fuller, Mrs. Piozzi, and Others; and Delivered at Tiverton, July 5, 1797* (London: J. Johnson, 1797), 24.

34. Richard Holmes, *Coleridge: Early Visions* (London: Hodder and Stoughton, 1989), 92.

35. Lewis Patton and Peter Mann, 'Editors' Introduction', *Lectures 1795 On Politics and Religion*, ed. Lewis Patton and Peter Mann, *Collected Works of Samuel Taylor Coleridge*, Bollingen Series 50, 1 (London: Routledge, 1971), xxxv.

36. Elinor Shaffer, *'Kubla Khan' and The Fall of Jerusalem* (Cambridge: Cambridge University Press, 1975), 28.

37. *Lectures 1795*, 83. The 'Prospectus' exists in two versions: one is a manuscript draft, in Coleridge's hand, now in the Beinecke Library, Yale University; the other, a version given by Joseph Cottle, the Bristol printer who produced the 1798 *Lyrical Ballads*, in his *Recollections of Samuel Taylor Coleridge and Robert Southey* (London, 1847), 27–8. Cottle's version differs in minor respects from the manuscript. If Cottle struck off any printed copies of the 'Prospectus', they have not survived.

38. 'Historical critics', as Hans Frei says, 'were concerned with specific texts and specific historical circumstances. The unity of the Bible across millennia of differing cultural levels and conditions in any case seemed a tenuous, indeed a dubious hypothesis to

them'; Hans Frei, *The Eclipse of Biblical Narrative* (New Haven: Yale University Press, 1974), 7–8.

39. Moses Lowman, *A Dissertation on the Civil Government of the Hebrews* (2nd edition, London: J. Noon, 1745), 6.

40. Moses Lowman, *A Rational of the Ritual of the Hebrew Worship; in which the Wise Designs and Usefulness of that Ritual are Explain'd, and Vindicated from Objections* (London: J. Noon, 1748), 364.

41. *CN*, I. i. entry 110.

42. See editors' notes to this poem in *Coleridge's Poetry and Prose*, ed. Nicholas Halmi, Paul Magnuson, and Raimonda Modiano (New York: W. W. Norton, 2004), 14.

43. 'Religious Musings', *PW*, II. i. 231 (ll. 9–14 of the 1796 printed version). The point about the poem avoiding traditional Nativity imagery was made by David Fairer, in a paper given at the Coleridge Summer Conference, Cannington, July 2006.

44. Editor's note, *Coleridge's Poetry and Prose*, 125n.

45. *An Accurate and Impartial Narrative of the War, by an Officer of the Guards* (2 vols, 1795). See *The Watchman*, ed. Lewis Patton, *Collected Works of Samuel Taylor Coleridge*, Bollingen Series 75, 2 (London and Princeton: Routledge and Princeton University Press, 1970), 238n.

46. William Wordsworth, *Lyrical Ballads 1798*, ed. W. J. B. Owen (2nd edition, Oxford: Oxford University Press, 1971), 174.

47. Quoted, *Coleridge's Poetry and Prose*, 125n. For fuller discussion of Lamb's criticisms and Coleridge's reaction, see Paley, *Apocalypse*, 98–9.

48. *CL*, i. 407. Toulmin's daughter had just been drowned off the Devon coast, apparently during a fit of mental instability. For dating of the collaboration on *Lyrical Ballads*, see Holmes, *Early Visions*, 187.

49. John Thelwall, 'Lines, written at Bridgewater, in Somersetshire, on the 27th of July, 1797; during a long excursion, in quest of a peaceful retreat', *Poems chiefly written in Retirement* (Hereford, 1801; rpt. Oxford: Woodstock Books, 1989), 159.

Part III
Imagining the West Country

8

Wordsworth's 1793 Journey to the West Country and Wales

Carol Kyros Walker

When William Wordsworth set off on a summer journey to the west of England and Wales in late June 1793 he was twenty-three years old and worldly in the way of someone who had travelled on the continent. His younger sister Dorothy described him at this time as 'certainly rather plain than otherwise', adding that he 'has an extremely thoughtful countenance, but when he speaks it is often lighted up with a smile' (*Early Letters*, 95). Letters, poetry, and recollections provide the broad outline of where he visited between the end of June and 27 August when he arrived at the home of his friend Robert Jones in North Wales (see Figure 9). But there are gaps of time about which nothing is known. Mark Reed's chronology of Wordsworth's life is sprinkled with 'probably' for this period. Tracing the journey becomes the risky effort of joining what is known with conjecture about Wordsworth at a period before he met Coleridge, before he shared his life with his sister, before *Lyrical Ballads* confirmed his poetical career. It is a remarkably self-sufficient, capable, independent, psychologically rich person who steps out of the frame.

At the Isle of Wight

Wordsworth set off from London with a travelling companion, William Calvert, a friend from his days at Hawkshead Grammar School. Calvert, who preferred not to travel alone, had proposed they tour the west of England together. Having received a sizeable inheritance on the death of his father in 1791 (Moorman, 1968, 229–30), Calvert was in a position to cover the costs. As Dorothy phrased it, Calvert was 'a man of fortune ... who is to bear all the expenses of the journey and only requests the favour of William's company as he is averse to the idea of going alone' (*Early Letters*, 94). Wordsworth seized the opportunity, and the two Williams set out from London at the end of June. Their first destination, the Isle of Wight, was an indirect route to the West, and little can be documented about their time there. Lines from *The Prelude* (1805) recollect 'a sojourn / Through a whole month of calm and glassy days' (x. 296).

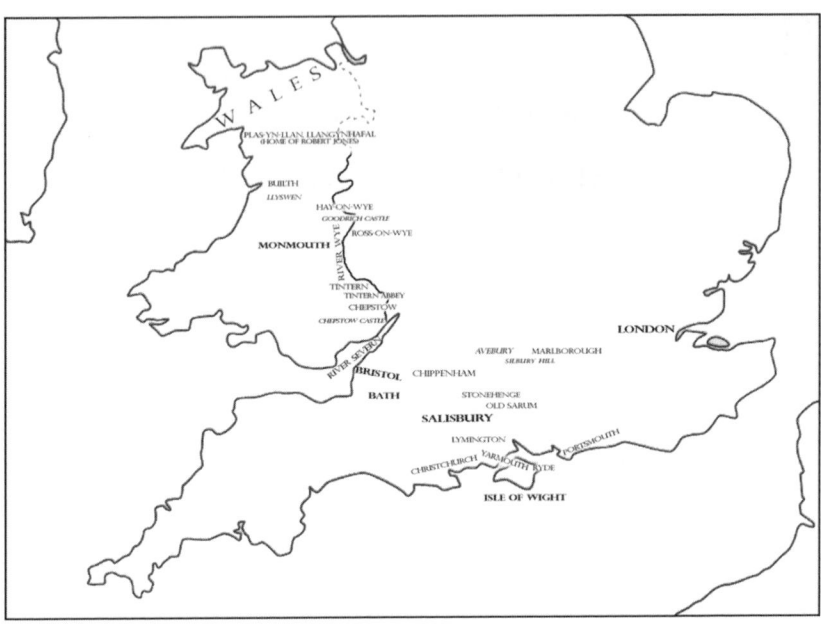

Figure 9   Wordsworth's journey to the West Country and Wales, summer of 1793, end of June to August.

The customary crossing then as now was from Portsmouth to Ryde. If they stayed in Ryde, they were well situated to observe warships in the Spithead channel. Kenneth R. Johnston, in his brilliant *The Hidden Wordsworth: Poet, Lover, Rebel, Spy*, argues compellingly that Wordsworth's motive for being there was to observe warships and to entertain the possibility of sneaking back to France. It is important to grasp this argument before proceeding further. Johnston emphasises that 'The naval arm of the British empire, the most powerful armed force in the world, was flexing itself as it had not done since the American war, for action against a much more dangerous and despised enemy' (1998, 343).

On 11 February 1793 England had declared war on France. Wordsworth was acutely aware of this on both political and personal levels. His bond to France was complicated. He had travelled through France in 1790 as part of his continental walking tour with his friend Robert Jones. In November the following year (with his degree from Cambridge having been awarded earlier, in January) he set off on another visit to France, probably not only to brush up his French language skills but to engage in the culture, which entailed embracing the Revolution. Another kind of embrace occurred while there: in 1792 he had an affair with Annette Vallon. Because his money had run out, he had to return to London, at an uncertain date in December 1792. However sketchy the dates, one fact is indisputable: he and Annette had conceived a child, and their daughter, Anne-Caroline, was born on 15 December and baptised in Orléans. England's declaration of war the next February made it impossible for him to return to visit his daughter and his lover. He had much to be concerned about as he began his journey on the Isle of Wight.

A poem attributed to this holiday, 'At the Isle of Wight, 1793', articulates two aspects of his sojourn on the Isle.[1] The poem articulates opposite aspects of his time on the Isle, and falls, accordingly, into two parts: an idyllic walk along the coastline, and a disturbing recognition that warships are poised to engage. From the sounds of the tide in the opening lines –

> How sweet the walk along the woody steep
> When all the summer seas are charmed to sleep;
> While on the distant sands the tide retires
> Its last faint murmur on the ear expires ...
>
> (1–4)

– to the sounds of cannon in the concluding lines

> But hark from yon proud fleet in peal profound
> Thunders the sunset cannon; at the sound
> The star of life appears to set in blood,
> And ocean shudders in offended mood,
> Deepening with moral gloom his angry flood.
>
> (15–19)

– the poem measures the extremes of emotion and the burden of worldly understanding Wordsworth needed to balance at this critical moment.

Wordsworth did not slip away to France this July. And clearly he did not spend the entire month watching the 'proud fleet'. If he continued to reconnoitre and, possibly, spy, he still had a luxurious stretch of time to be, with Calvert, the pair of tourists they set out to be, taking a gentlemanly approach to seeing what must be seen. The island offered many attractions. If they chose to keep very busy they could find most of the sites Thomas Gray listed for the Isle of Wight in his *Catalogue of the Antiquities, Houses, Parks, Plantations, Scenes in England and Wales*. Pursuing the 'Scenes and Situations' list in his book alone would have taken them over much of the island, which Gray measured as '60 M. round, 20 long, and 12 over' (1799, 53). Thomas Gray was singularly lacking in poetry as he listed what sites should be sought out on the island:

> The Needles (Rocks) and West End of the Isle seen from the Sea, with the Cavern.
> Freshwater (View from a Field there) S.S.W. of Yarmouth 6 M. and from the Gate of ditto.
> From Carisbrook Castle.
> From Ventnor's Cave.
> St. Lawrence's Cliffs, and its Situation.
> Blackgang Chine, near Chale.
> Fisherman's Cottage at Shanklin Chine.
> St. Boniface's Cottage, (Colonel Hill's) at Bonchurch, S. of Shanklin.
> Way from Cowes (by Water) up to Newport, and the Walk from Hurst-Stake to Newport.
> Shanklin Chine, on the S. E. Coast, N.N.E. of Dunchurch.
> Ashley Down (View of Brading Haven at High Water).
> Village of Rida, on the N. Coast, with Troublefield, (Col. Amherst's); Appleby, (Mrs. Roberts); and St. John's.
> Undercliff, S.W. of Dun-Nose, on the S.E. Coast.

If Wordsworth and Calvert wanted to tour at a more leisurely pace they could narrow this list. Carisbrook Castle, a 'must visit' today, was one of the great English castles, built in the twelfth century and renowned for its seventeenth-century inhabitant, Charles I, who was imprisoned here. They might have been drawn to examine the recent work by Capability Brown (Lancelot 'Capability' Brown) on the eighteenth-century mansion of the Worsley family, Appuldurcombe House. Wordsworth and Calvert, who would have known Capability Brown's Kew Gardens and Holland Park in London, may well have debated whether the gardens at Appuldurcombe were natural and indigenously English in appearance. Did they resemble French or Italian gardens? The scene would have generated aesthetic conversation. Do ha-has and follies compromise the effort to be natural? Can a natural appearance legitimately be brought about by landscaping, or are the terms mutually exclusive? Wordsworth would very likely be sorting out his views. Some years later, when established in Cumberland, he wrote his *Guide to the Lakes* articulating an aesthetic that favoured the preservation of the natural landscape, and encouraging and guiding travellers on how to see and appreciate it. In 1793, at the age of twenty-three, in an imaginary conversation with Calvert on the merits or defects of Capability Brown's work, a thought might well have been taking shape that would later be expressed by this pronouncement in the *Guide*: 'The rule is simple; with respect to grounds – work, where you can, in the spirit of Nature, with an invisible hand of art' (74).

Across Salisbury Plain

Wordsworth and Calvert very likely returned from the old Isle of Wight port town of Yarmouth to the mainland at Lymington, from which point they could have proceeded to Christchurch. In this scenario they would travel along the clear postal roads to Salisbury, stop for the night at a comfortable coaching inn like the still popular Red Lion, have a walk about town to visit the famed cathedral (see Figure 10), and head towards Old Sarum and the mysterious antiquities of Salisbury Plain. Accidents have a way of altering plans. Wordsworth's summer vacation took just such a dramatic turn somewhere near Salisbury. 'His tour was put a stop to by an accident which might have had fatal consequences', Dorothy Wordsworth reported to her friend Jane Pollard (*Early Letters*, 105). William and Calvert had been travelling in a small carriage called a 'whiskey', designed more for short jaunts about town than long-distance travel. 'Calvert's horse was not much accustomed to draw in a whiskey', Dorothy explained, 'and he began to caper one day in a most terrible manner, dragged them and their vehicle into a ditch and broke it to shivers' (*Early Letters*, 105). Despite this compressed account, which minimised the seriousness of what happened, the violence of the incident is evident. Did someone offer to help? Dorothy was reassuring:

Figure 10 Salisbury Cathedral.

Happily neither Mr. C. nor William were the worse but they were sufficiently cautious not to venture again in the same way; Mr. C. mounted
his horse and rode into the North and William's firm friends, a pair of
stout legs, supported him from Salisbury, through South into North
Wales, where he is now [30 August] quietly sitting down in the Vale of
Clwyd[2] ... (*Early Letters*, 105)

If Calvert's generosity remained consistent, at this critical point of separation he would have left Wordsworth sufficient funds to make it to Wales.
William's brother Richard, who was handling the family accounts, had
sent William five guineas (c. £5.25) for his holiday, and he would be stretching what was left of that sum for his unexpected pedestrian tour.

Salisbury Plain has a strange, ambiguous shape. In the late eighteenth
century, Gilpin, in his *Observations on the Western Parts of England* estimated
that '[i]t extends many miles in all directions, in some not less than fifty'
(1798, 82). To one early twentieth-century author the Plain incorporated
the city of Salisbury as well as the neighbouring village of Wilton. Ella
Noyes in *Salisbury Plain: Its Stones, Cathedral, City Villages, and Folk* identifies every road running through the Plain, beyond which they extend into
obscurity. Today travellers are warned about being run over by a tank in
parts of the Plain reserved for military manoeuvres. But there are no signposts announcing 'Salisbury Plain Begins Here' or 'Exiting the Plain'. Peter
Sager, in *The West Country: Wiltshire, Dorset, Somerset, Devon and Cornwall*,
gives the modern tourist the best preparation: 'If you look at a map of
Wiltshire, you will find a big bare patch in the middle. That is Salisbury
Plain. In reality, it is a vast green expanse undulating on and on as far as
the eye can see' (2000, 11).

If he followed the paths of earlier travellers Wordsworth would begin at
Old Sarum and proceed to Stonehenge. So Samuel Pepys made his way in
1668. After a night in Salisbury at the George Inn, having complained about
his bill Pepys went to tour the ruined castle and cathedral of Old Sarum and
then on to Stonehenge. From there he made his way to Bath, hiring a guide to
put him and his entourage in the right direction on passable roads. By the
late eighteenth century it was the authoritative and widely read Gilpin
that a first-time visitor to Salisbury Plain might depend upon for guidance.
Although his *Observations on the Western Parts of England* (1798) came out
five years after Wordsworth's visit, it glosses much of what Wordsworth experienced and alluded to in his poetry, and offers a reliable picture of what he
saw. His earlier *Observations on the River Wye* (1782) had completed the Wye
tour with a return to London, travelling west to east, crossing and commenting
on the upper part of Salisbury Plain.

The accident that put Wordsworth on a solitary pedestrian tour left
him near Old Sarum. At first sight it would have appeared to be a large,
elevated grassy circle of earth surrounded by a deep ditch. Gilpin was

surprised by it: 'Imagine the *ridge* of a hill falling into a *plain*; from the end of which a part having been artificially separated, forms a round knoll of about two thousand feet in diameter' (1798, 69). Gilpin's 'round knoll' is an Iron Age hill fort, with steep ramparts. Within the circle are the extensive ruins of a castle, built around 1070, and the precincts and grounds of a small cathedral, begun around 1075, with the bishop's palace and chapter house. The cathedral at Old Sarum had a short life: it was torn down in 1226, and the stone used to build the present Salisbury Cathedral two miles away.

Looking back to 1793 Wordsworth, in the 1805 *Prelude*, uses 'Sarum' as a synecdoche for the entire Salisbury Plain, seeing himself as 'a traveller at that time / Upon the plain of Sarum' (xii. 314–15). The passage begins with his walk:

> There on the pastoral downs without a track
> To guide me, or along the bare white roads
> Lengthening in solitude their dreary line,
> While through those vestiges of ancient times
> I ranged ...
>
> (xii. 315–19)

While he 'roamed' the Plain for '[t]hree summer days' (xii. 337), his claim that there was not a track to guide him was wide of the truth. There were tracks leading to the ancient sites on the Plain, and one of Turner's Stonehenge paintings shows a traveller on a clearly defined path. Emphasising direction-less wandering, Wordsworth's *Prelude* recollection leads inwards to a 'reverie' in which he sees 'A single Briton in his wolf-skin vest' (xii. 332), hears the rattling of spears, and glimpses flames where there is an altar upon which humans were offered in a sacrificial Druid rite. He finds

> Lines, circles, mounts, a mystery of shapes
> Such as in many quarters yet survive,
> With intricate profusion figuring o'er
> The untilled ground ...
>
> (xii. 339–42)

The images of his reverie shift to the realm of reality as the poet acknowl-edges he has been 'gently charmed' by an antiquarian's dream. Indeed the motif of reverie on the Plain has a precedent in William Stukeley, antiqua-rian and archaeologist, who in his seminal work *Stonehenge: A Temple Restor'd to the British Druids* reported: 'When you enter the building, whether on foot or horseback and cast your eyes around, upon the yawning ruins, you are struck into an exstatic *reverie*' (1740, 12).

Figure 11   Salisbury Plain. Stonehenge.

From Old Sarum to Stonehenge is an eight-mile walk and would have taken Wordsworth about two and a half hours, although if he truly could not find a track to follow, it might have been longer. Gilpin described how his wonder increased as he approached more closely to Stonehenge: 'Stonehenge, at a distance, appeared only a diminutive object. Standing on so vast an area on Salisbury Plain, it was lost in the immensity around it. As we approached, it gained more respect: and we could now trace a large ditch round the whole, confined within a gentle mound. But when we arrived on the spot, it appeared astonishing beyond conception' (1798, 77) (see Figure 11). The scene would have been to Wordsworth what it was to Gilpin, and Gilpin, in turn, was looking at Stonehenge through the eyes of the Stukeley, whose research on Stonehenge, as well as the other major stone circle of the Plain at Avebury, came out in 1740 and 1743 and strongly influenced the eighteenth-century travellers.

Stukeley attributed the origin, design, and spiritual character of Stonehenge to the Druids and regarded the whole site as a temple, complete with priests. Gilpin's mode was to report on the number of stones ('an hundred and forth') and the distinguishing characteristics of the outer circle and the inner circle. He noted how many stones were still standing in each circle. But he goes beyond measurements and numbers to acknowledge and reinforce Stukeley's theory that the Druids erected the temple and worshipped there.

Wordsworth no doubt walked around the two concentric circles of stone as Gilpin did and reflected on those early Britons whose calculations connected the constellations with the earth to align the stones with the magnetic north, a feat he considers in his *Prelude* reverie as an 'infant science, imitative forms / By which the Druids covertly expressed / Their knowledge of the heavens, and imaged forth / The constellations' (xii. 344–6). Although the widely accepted theory advanced by Stukeley was later proved wrong, Wordsworth's perception of Stonehenge, and any other circles he encountered, would have been affected by the prevailing notions of the time.

If strenuous, his time on the Plain was not altogether without pleasure, such as an afternoon rest in the grounds of Stonehenge. Recalling that summer over forty years later he wrote to his friend John Kenyon, 'Overcome with heat and fatigue I took my siesta among the Pillars of Stonehenge' (Noyes, 1958, 547). The duration of his visit to the Plain, according to his own varying reports, was three days, two days, or in this letter to Kenyon, 'a couple of days'. He describes his getting about as 'rambling', a term that suggests going in various directions by choice, not by default because of being lost or merely wandering aimlessly. An experienced long-distance walker, Wordsworth was well able to follow trails and find his directions naturally. His 'rambling' took him to Stonehenge efficiently enough and he might easily have continued on to Avebury, a little more than twenty-two miles due north, where he would find more stone circles celebrated by eighteenth-century antiquarians and archaeologists. If he proceeded towards Marlborough he would find Silbury Hill, a man-made mound, and if he went a little westward, Kennet Barrow, an extensive Neolithic burial chamber. 'All the plain, at least that part of it near Stonehenge, is one vast cemetery', Gilpin noted (1798, 84). Some years earlier, after his Wye valley tour, he had ridden past Avebury finding that '[e]verywhere we see tumuli, which were raised over [the ancient dead's] ashes; among which is Silbury Hill' (1782, 92). If Wordsworth in his few days on the Plain walked northwards to this area of burial grounds and stone circles he would also have found a main route to Bath and Bristol. Wallis's 1798 map of the *Post Roads of England and Wales* shows a road from Marlborough to Chippenham to Bath, then slightly northwest to Bristol.

Wordsworth's 'Salisbury Plain' poems

The major poetic outcome of the Salisbury Plain experience was a work that may be regarded as three poems in one: *Salisbury Plain, or A Night on Salisbury Plain*, written 1793–4, perhaps conceived in part before Wordsworth ever left London and very likely worked on while travelling; *Adventures on Salisbury Plain*, 1795–c.1799, which contained within it the tale of 'The Female Vagrant' that would be published separately; and *Guilt and Sorrow; or, Incidents upon Salisbury Plain*, 1841–2, which might itself be regarded as two poems. Stephen Gill has edited all three versions in his Cornell edition of *The Salisbury Plain Poems*. For this discussion I am using the latest, which is also the version of the poem Wordsworth decided to publish.

Guilt and Sorrow locates the subject of the poem, a sailor (a soldier in an earlier version, a generic traveller in the 1793–4 version) exactly where Wordsworth walked, 'on the skirt of Sarum's Plain' (1). The figure, stooped, 'with feet half bare', wearing a patched, faded red military coat that was beginning to shred, epitomised the human who, worn down by the circumstances of war and the dissolution of social order, has been reduced to vagrancy. Wordsworth draws on his own experience and his knowledge of others' to provide authenticity to the unfortunate sailor's setting and movements. Travellers who arrived to explore the antiquities on the Plain used the exceptionally tall spire of Salisbury Cathedral to guide them. As the depressed sailor moves deeper into the plain he realises that 'the distant spire, / Which oft as he looked back had fixed his eye, / Was lost ...' (21–3). The loss of this landmark casts the sailor into unknown territory where he must deal with his guilt and review his crime – meeting a traveller, robbing him, and then murdering him.

As he moves deeper into the Plain he finds himself alone except for the Bustard, the bird 'of those regions bleak / Shy tenant' (104–5). Other than the sheep, the shepherd and his dog, or the occasional 'solitary wagon winding round a distant hill' (88), the Plain appeared uninhabited, as Gilpin put it, 'totally void, though in a ruinous state, of every idea of picturesque beauty' (1798, 81). Gilpin claims the Bustard is 'the largest fowl we have in England' and 'leads his life in these unfrequented wilds, and studiously avoids the haunts of men, [and] the appearance of any thing in motion, though at a considerable distance, alarms him' (1798, 88). Wordsworth's poem bears out the characterisation: as the sailor approaches, the bird gives out a 'mournful Shriek' and exhibits 'strange affright' (106–7). Continuing his walk, the sailor comes to Stonehenge in a storm, and understands it as a place where human sacrifice took place. He cannot or will not seek refuge there, but presses on in the storm to a 'lonely Spital' (*Guilt and Sorrow*, 150), a sheltered resting place for travellers in the ruins of what was a place of religious worship. Taken together, the 'mournful shriek' of the bustard, the violent storm, darkness, terror, and, nearby, a mysterious body all contribute to the intense, Gothic atmosphere.

From this point onwards *Guilt and Sorrow* advances into a wider sphere as the vagrant woman tells her tale to the sailor, creating a story within a story. The landscape ranges from Cumberland to America, with country cottages that may be on Salisbury Plain but could be anywhere. The significance of the remainder of the poem lies chiefly in its voicing of Wordsworth's concerns about the ravages of war, war's effects upon the poor, and the displacement of human beings that results in vagrancy. In his 'advertisement, prefixed to the first edition' of the 1842 poem Wordsworth wrote:

The monuments and traces of antiquity, scattered in abundance over that region, led me unavoidably to compare what we know or guess of those remote times with certain aspects of modern society, with calamities, principally those consequent upon war, to which, more than other classes of men, the poor are subject. (Hayden, i. 118–19)

His days on Salisbury Plain surfaced again in Book Three of *The Excursion* (1814), entitled 'Despondency'. Here the setting and sound effects are recalled with a sense of awe comparable to that in *Guilt in Sorrow*:

> Not less than that huge Pile (from some abyss
> Of mortal power unquestionably sprung)
> Whose hoary diadem of pendant rocks
> Confines the shrill-voiced whirlwind, round and round
> Eddying within its vast circumference,
> On Sarum's naked plain— ...

(quoted from Hayden, ii. 143–8)

Stonehenge remained a powerful image. At a time in the poem when he self-consciously 'entertain[s] / The antiquarian humor' (134), he finds the ancient stones and monuments have a stabilising effect as symbols of what endures, objects that lift him from despondency.

To Bath, Bristol ...

'From that district [of Salisbury Plain] I proceeded to Bath, Bristol, and so on to the banks of the Wye, where I took again to travelling on foot', Wordsworth recalled in a note to Isabella Fenwick in 1843 (*Fenwick Notes*, 63), revealing an important fact – that he reached his next two destinations by mail coach or, possibly, a slower stage-wagon. From east to west at the northern part of the Plain the mail stopped at Marlborough, then in six miles at Caine, then in seven miles at Chippenham. Depending on where he finished his sightseeing, Wordsworth could have boarded a coach at any one of these stops, but to find the most reasonable fare he would have done well to begin his ride at Chippenham.

What Wordsworth anticipated on this thirteen-mile ride to Bath is hard to say. What he found on arrival was a stunning contrast in mood and visual impact to where he had just been. By the late eighteenth century Bath was a sophisticated, fashionable city. Its architecture, designed by John Wood the Elder (1704–75), and later his son, John Wood the Younger, born 1727, gave the city a uniformity of style that came to be known as Georgian and gave the term 'crescent' a new meaning. Wordsworth had moved from Druid stone circles to semi-circles that embraced the viewer with warm gold stones. The city was centred, as it always has been, on the Roman baths. Bathers from every walk of life came to take the waters hoping to cure ailments like rheumatism and arthritis. Away from the baths the town was a fashionable, and exclusive, social centre, largely because of the influence of Richard Beau Nash, bachelor, gambler, man-about-town, charmer of mistresses, arbiter of taste in dress and manners, omnipresent at places of pleasure. As everyone who has read Jane Austen knows, Bath was the place to be seen if a young lady needed to meet a suitor.

Beau Nash had died by the time Wordsworth arrived but the ambience of the city still reflected his panache. How many days Wordsworth remained in Bath and where he stayed cannot be known. He should have spent at least as much time here as he did on Salisbury Plain, if he wanted to tour the main sights of the town. Perhaps he stayed at The Greyhound, on High Street, where Coleridge, who would soon figure so importantly in his career, stayed on 2 December 1813. He could have stepped out of the inn, strolled to Bath Abbey, spent some time there and then walked to the Roman Bath. Here it would take him some time to ponder the development of the hot mineral springs, from Celtic and Roman times through the Saxon era, and up to the eighteenth century. It would have benefited him, following his walk on the Plain, to bathe in the warm water and then drink it, perhaps at the Pump Room. In the evening he could devote time to working on his Salisbury Plain poem, and the next day resume the pleasure of being a tourist, walking to the Poultney Bridge over the River Avon. There were John Wood the Younger's Royal Crescent and Wood the Elder's Queen Square to explore. However he spent the time, his presence in Bath made him a part of guidebook literature. An old Baedeker guide (1901) for Great Britain places him in distinguished company: 'Among the innumerable visitors of eminence in the 18th and early 19th cent. May be mentioned Chatham, Pitt, Canning, and Burke, Nelson, Wolfe, and Sir Sidney Smith, Gainsborough and Lawrence, Smollett, Fielding, Sheridan, Miss Burney, Goldsmith, Southey, Landor, Miss Austen, Wordsworth, Cowper, Scott, and Moore' (1901, 114). The editor forgot Coleridge! And, surprisingly, Gilpin, who pointed out what was worth seeing in Bath ('the parades, the baths, the rooms, and the abbey') and described the effect of the light as it struck the Crescent on a summer day: 'The whole seemed like an effort of nature to set off art; and the eye roved about in aston-ishment to see a mere mass of regularity become the ground of so pleasing a display of harmony and picturesque effect. The elliptical form of the building was the magical source of this exhibition' (1782, 92).

Even today local residents of the Bath–Bristol area, if asked the best way to get from one city to the next, will advise that there are two ways – one that is sce-nic and another that is colourless. 'We were told . . . ', Gilpin wrote in 1770, 'there are two roads between Bath and Bristol; of which the Gloucestershire road is the more picturesque. If so, we unfortunately took the wrong one' (1782, 91). It was roughly twelve miles to Bristol, and if Wordsworth was lucky his driver took the picturesque route. Bristol would have struck Wordsworth as distinctly different from Bath. It was a major port, with ships for global navigation as well as for plying routes to Ireland and the Mediterranean, America, the West Indies, and Africa. At this time of war, the British navy would have been in evidence. Bristol was also a city that flagged up prosperity and Wordsworth's first impressions would have been of substantial commercial buildings and well-built homes, some with a Dutch influence in design, a Cathedral, beautiful churches, well-endowed almshouses and streets congested with traffic. The walled medieval city was entered on Broad Street by a deep arched gateway, on top of which stood the spire of St John's Church (see Figure 12).

Figure 12   Bristol. Spire in the old city.

Bristol became a city charged with significance for Wordsworth, particularly his return visit in 1795 when he would remain for some five weeks meeting Coleridge and Southey. About his first visit in summer 1793 Wordsworth left no record of where he stayed or visited, though clearly this major city – a counterpart of London – inspired a desire to come back. Wordsworth very likely stayed at the White Lion Inn, Broad Street, listed for 1793 in *The King's Post* as 'one of the erstwhile [sic] great coaching establishments' (Tombs, 1905, 103). From his inn on Broad Street he was well placed to walk about the old city, where he would come upon the Exchange, an open-air court designed by John Wood the Elder whose work Wordsworth had already seen in Bath. Here, on Corn Street, was where the merchants of Bristol came to trade (corn, sugar, wool) and conduct their business. Four seventeenth-century brass pillars in front of the exchange provided surfaces on which to put their money and pay 'cash on the nail'. The expansive Guildhall opened onto Broad Street, and Corn Street led to Clare Street and St Stephen's Church, Gothic in style with a graceful spire which a visitor might look to for orientation. Perhaps Wordsworth noticed the bookshop on the corner of Corn Street and High Street – it was owned by Joseph Cottle, who five years later would become his publisher.

To see Bristol one must climb as well as stroll. For an overview the traveller would climb to the top of Brandon Hill. From here he could see the ships docked at the quays, and the homes and warehouses of wealthy Bristol merchants. One in particular, the home of John Pinney on Great George Street, was exceptionally fine and would figure in Wordsworth's life within two years. Wordsworth did not know Pinney in 1793, but if he gazed down on his fine residence on Great George Street and then looked beyond to the ships, he could piece together a story he surely had already heard – that the wealth in Bristol came from the slave trade. Pinney had made his money in the sugar trade and owned a plantation on Nevis in the West Indies, where he purchased and engaged slaves. He represented a genre of wealthy merchants in Bristol who, although honourable in their philanthropic support of civic causes, had prospered through slavery. Wordsworth would have noticed that not everyone in Bristol was white, and if he came down from Brandon Hill onto Great George Street he might have run into a black slave named Pedro Jones whom Pinney had purchased in Nevis and brought back to Bristol in 1783. From Great George Street Wordsworth could walk to what is now Park Street and make his way to College Green and Bristol Cathedral, passing, perhaps, a building at 25 College Street where Coleridge, Southey, and George Burnett shared living quarters in 1795. Near the Cathedral in today's Bristol sits the imposing Bristol Library, a reminder that there was a Bristol Library in King Street not far from this one, from which Coleridge and Southey regularly borrowed books.

There was another compelling ascent for Wordsworth – this time out of the Old City to the church of St Mary Redcliffe, more beautiful than the cathedral and commanding in a different way: '[I]ts spire, rising nearly 300 feet above the level of the road, is almost as fine as that of Salisbury, and its north porch is rich with most elaborate and complex decoration', wrote the early twentieth-century travel commentator Arthur Salmon in his *Heart of the West* (1922, 39). The attraction was not so much the architecture, however, as the church's association with Thomas Chatterton, the precocious and brilliant author of the 'Rowley Poems' who committed suicide in 1770 at the age of seventeen, depressed, disillusioned, starving, and alone in a garret in London. To Wordsworth and other Romantic poets Chatterton became a symbol of the misunderstood and unappreciated poet-genius, 'the marvellous Boy, / The sleepless Soul that perished in his pride' ('Resolution and Independence', 43–4).

The Sylvan Wye

The tide would have to be in and the winds calm before a ferryboat could safely navigate the Severn estuary to Wales at the Aust-to-Beachly crossing. The horses and cattle on board required securing and settling. If variations in temperature caused the kind of dense fog one encounters driving across the Severn Bridge in the morning today, the cautious boatman might delay. Certainly he would have to calculate in terms of the great range of the tide and swift current for which the Severn is noted. Once on land Wordsworth walked some two miles to Chepstow where his Wye Valley tour commenced.

After passing through Chepstow's stone archway and gate, Wordsworth could look up at the ruins of the massive castle, dating from 1066 and the Battle of Hastings. If Wordsworth wanted to tour the entire castle he would have to allow at least a day, starting with the round twin towers of the gate house, four floors high from ground to battlements, carrying on through the Lower Bailey, the Middle Bailey, the Great Tower, Gallery, the Upper Bailey, and at the farthest point, the Upper Barbican. There were wonderful perspectives of the River Wye, in turns swiftly flowing, winding, gently flowing, rounding bends, seen framed by pointed stone arches of windows or expanding from the open views along narrow upper walkways. He would have needed time to explore the castle grounds and then to walk away to see it in its total setting and understand how it fitted into the landscape – as a young J. M. W. Turner did when he visited in 1792 (Turner's watercolour was painted in the same year as Wordsworth's visit).

What tourists saw in and around castles was by no means as idyllic as Turner's painting. From about 1760 Chepstow Castle was a base for industry that included a nail factory, a glass blowing facility for the manufacture of bottles, and a malting kiln. A stable and a dog kennel also occupied the castle grounds. At Tintern an ironworks provided employment but not housing, so that some of the workers made their homes in the Abbey ruins.

Beggars tended to make their way to tourist sites, knowing that those fortunate enough to afford a summer tour might have some change to spare.

It was a walk of a little over five miles along the wooded banks of the Wye to Tintern and the Abbey. The poetic bounty of his journey had begun to come to him as he walked from Chepstow. It grew as he continued north to the end of his Wye Valley trip, and would be fully realised in the rich imagery of the poem written five years later, 'Lines Composed a Few Miles above Tintern Abbey, on Revisiting the Banks of the Wye During a Tour, July 13, 1798'.

Wordsworth's 1793 tour was on the pattern of Gilpin as well as the many tourists, middle-class and aristocratic, who came in increasing numbers to see what Gilpin had identified as picturesque scenes that included the castles and ruins. The classic tour started at Ross-on-Wye, twelve miles from Monmouth on the English side of the border, and proceeded on water with a boat down the River Wye. Wordsworth made his journey on foot in reverse direction, from south to north, roughly twenty miles. The views from a boat permitted a good perspective on the 'ornaments of the Wye', as Gilpin called them, putting them under four headings: 'ground, woods, rocks, and buildings' (1782, 26). Wordsworth was at a distinct advantage when he arrived at Tintern, for Gilpin bemoaned the fact that '[n]o part of the ruins of Tintern is seen from the river except the abbey church' (1782, 42). On land, Wordsworth could see everything (see Figure 13).

As the scholarly emphasis on Wordsworth's brooding over the war with France and his separation from his beloved Annette Vallon has increased, attention to his intense pleasure in nature and landscape – with a corresponding desire to find meaning in both – has diminished. Yet 'Tintern Abbey', which has relatively little do with the Abbey itself, offers ample evidence that there was considerable buoyancy and delight in his mood in summer 1793,

> when first
> I came among these hills; when like a roe
> I bounded o'er the mountains, by the sides
> Of the deep rivers, and the lonely streams
> Wherever nature led ...
>
> (66–70)

He qualifies this recollection by seeing himself as 'more like a man / Flying from something that he dreads, than one / Who sought the thing he loved' (70–2), yet returns to contemplate a nature that asks nothing of him but openness of spirit and clear sight:

> The sounding cataract
> Haunted me like a passion: the tall rock,

Figure 13   View from within Tintern Abbey.

> The mountain, and the deep and gloomy wood,
> Their colours and their forms, were then to me
> An appetite; a feeling and a love,
> That had no need of a remoter charm,
> By thought supplied, nor any interest
> Unborrowed from the eye.
>
> (76–83)

Though acknowledging that he has changed, that his relationship to nature has evolved, that he has heard the 'still, sad music of humanity' (91), Wordsworth wishes to pass on to his sister the gift of the total experience of the Wye, 'Knowing that Nature never did betray / The heart that loved her' (122–3). The elegant, ode-like poem of 1798 could never have been composed without the earlier, 1793 walk on which it so crucially depends. The process of composition itself bore testimony to the way the banks of the Wye demanded celebration: 'No poem of mine was composed under circumstances more pleasant for me to remember than this', Wordsworth recalled. 'I began it upon leaving Tintern, after crossing the Wye, and concluded it just as I was entering Bristol in the evening, after a ramble of 4 or 5 days, with my sister. Not a line of it was altered, and not any of it written down till I reached Bristol' (*Fenwick Notes*, 15).

After a walk of fifteen and a half miles up the banks of the Wye, he arrived at Goodrich Castle on a rocky hill on the border of England and Wales commanding a prospect of Herefordshire. The massive tower he would have come to first showed that in former times this had been a formidable border fortress. Ultimately, however, what was more important to him than this landmark was a diminutive person he met near the castle,

> ... a little cottage Girl:
> She was eight years old, she said;
> Her hair was thick with many a curl
> That clustered round her head.
>
> (4–7)

The child became the subject of 'We Are Seven', written in 1798. Wordsworth, in a lengthy note to Isabella Fenwick, recalls, 'The little Girl who is the heroine I met within the area of Goodrich Castle in the year 1793' (*Fenwick Notes*, 2). In 1841 Wordsworth returned to Goodrich Castle after nearly fifty years, with some hope of meeting her: 'It would have given me a greater pleasure to have found in the neighbouring hamlet traces of one who had interested me so much; but that was impossible, as, unfortunately, I did not even know her name' (*Fenwick Notes*, 4). As for the castle, it seemed to him in 1841 what it must have seemed in 1793 – 'a most impressive object'. Equally unforgettable must have been the church and churchyard in the hamlet near the castle, where the two siblings of the little girl were buried.

After Goodrich Castle Wordsworth's travels along the Wye involved long distances. One stretch that would be on his mind was the route to his final destination of the tour, Plys-Yn-Llan in North Wales where his friend Robert Jones lived. Builth and Hay-on-Wye were on his immediate route, and as he set out for Builth he faced a walk of forty-three miles. If he stopped for meals and rests to break up the journey, one pleasant retreat might have been the town of Llyswen, eleven miles before Builth. In the near future Llyswen would become significant to him as the place where the writer and radical John Thelwall had his farm – the 'Liswyn Farm' of 'Anecdote for Fathers'. From this point, between the Black Mountains and the Brecon Beacons, on a sunny August day the scenery would cancel out the fatigue. Builth today reflects a history of shepherds and cattlemen in the signs on shops, inns, and restaurants. At one end of the town the rhythmic call of an auctioneer carries over crammed stalls of sheep. More interesting to Wordsworth than the market-day crowds he would have found there was a particular fellow who became a study for the title character in his poem 'Peter Bell', written in 1798 and published in 1819. What attracted him to this stranger were qualities he recollected in later life: 'The countenance, gait, and figure of Peter were taken from a wild rover with whom I walked from Builth on the river Wye downwards nearly as far as the town of Hay' (*Fenwick Notes*, 17). Peter is a potter by trade ('Peter Bell', 170), aged 'two-and-thirty years or more' (206), whose roving through the country included Salisbury Plain: 'And well he knew the spire of Sarum' (212).

Wordsworth and Peter the rover apparently parted ways before reaching Hay-on-Wye, the potter, perhaps, having decided on somewhere else to vend his earthenware. In his wildest dreams Wordsworth could not have imagined what the town has become today – one vast used-book store in which, no doubt, are some scores of volumes of his own verse. Traces of Wordsworth's Hay-on-Wye require some effort to discover. Significantly, however, it was in his time a town that catered to coaching and was on a main postal route from England. As Wordsworth had now to plot his way to Jones's home, he had a reasonable option to expedite his journey in relative comfort. He could take a coach to Brecon, a hub of sorts for coach travel, which was linked to the turnpike north, and from there continue by coach all or part of the way to Jones's home. Alternatively, he could walk back to Builth, find the turnpike there, board a coach, walk, or combine feet and wheels. Riding or walking, from Hay all the way to Jones's home would be ninety-four miles.

However he accomplished the last leg of his journey, he had arrived at his destination by and conceivably before 30 August. There, with Robert Jones, his friend from his 1790 continental walking tour, Wordsworth was comfortably situated. As Dorothy told her friend Jane Pollard, William 'passes his time as happily as he could desire; exactly according to his taste' (*Early Letters*, 105).

Epilogue – up to 1798

Dorothy's joy in knowing her brother was with Jones was fuelled by her ardent desire to see him. A plan they shared was for him to meet her in Halifax for a visit, as they had not seen each other for three years. That reunion occurred, and there were better times ahead. William Calvert entered Wordsworth's life again in a financially significant way. His younger brother Raisley, who had inherited property near Keswick, offered Wordsworth 'a share of his income' for looking after him during his illness. When he died in January 1795 of tuberculosis he left Wordsworth a considerable legacy. The West Country retained a strong hold on him. In August 1795 he met Coleridge for the first time in Bristol, and his circle soon included Southey and Cottle, whose radical politics he shared. When Wordsworth and Coleridge published *Lyrical Ballads* in 1798, three of the poems in it – 'The Female Vagrant', 'We Are Seven', and 'Tintern Abbey' – had origins in his journey of 1793 ('Peter Bell' was considered but deferred). The 'Advertisement' to *Lyrical Ballads* contained a kernel of the democratic definition of poetry that he would articulate fully in the 'Preface' to the second edition of *Lyrical Ballads* (1800). The poems would 'ascertain how far the language of conversation in the middle and lower classes of society is adapted to the purposes of poetic pleasure'. So the voices of the little girl near Goodrich Castle, Peter the roving potter, and the vagrant woman of Salisbury Plain would echo down the years to the present.

Notes

1. Not published until 1940. See Hayden edition of Wordsworth's poems, Vol. I, 116. All quotations of Wordsworth's poetry will be from this edition, with the exception of *The Prelude*.
2. The home of Robert Jones, Plys-Yn-Llan, Llangynhafal, Denbigh.

Bibliography

Baedeker, Carl, *Great Britain: a Handbook for Travellers* (5th edition Leipzig: Karl Baedeker, 1901).

Gilpin, William, *Observations on the River Wye, and Several Parts of South Wales, &c. Relative Chiefly to Picturesque Beauty: Made in the Summer of the Year 1770* ([1782] London: Pallas Athene, 2005).

—— *Observations on the Western Parts of England, Relative Chiefly to Picturesque Beauty. To which are added, A Few Remarks on the Picturesque Beauties of the Isle of Wight* (London: T. Cadel Jr. and W. Davies, 1798). Eighteenth Century Collections Online. British Library book, http://galenet.galegroup.com.proxy.uchicago.edu

Gray, Thomas, *The Traveller's Companion, in a Tour Through England and Wales; Containing a Catalogue of the Antiquities, Houses, Parks, Plantations, Scenes, and Situations, in England and Wales, Arranged According to the Alphabetical Order of the Several Counties. A New Edition; to which are Added considerable Improvements and Additions* (London: G. Kearsley, 1799).

Johnston, Kenneth R., *The Hidden Wordsworth: Poet, Lover, Rebel, Spy* (New York and London: Norton, 1998).

Moorman, Mary, *William Wordsworth: the Early Years* (Oxford: Oxford University Press, 1968).

Noyes, Ella, *Salisbury Plain: Its Stones, Cathedral, City Villages, and Folk* (London and Toronto: Dent, 1913).

Noyes, Russell, 'An Unpublished Letter from Wordsworth to John Kenyon', *Modern Language Review*, 53.4 (October 1958), 546–7.

Reed, Mark L., *Wordsworth: the Chronology of the Early Years, 1770–1779* (Cambridge, MA: Harvard University Press, 1967).

Sager, Peter, *The West Country: Wiltshire, Dorset, Somerset, Devon and Cornwall* (London: Pallas Athene, 2000).

Salmon, Arthur L., *The Heart of the West: a Book of the West Country from Bristol to Land's End* (London: Robert Scott, [1922]).

Stukeley, William, *Stonehenge: A Temple Restor'd to the British Druids* (London: W. Innys and R. Manby, 1740).

Tombs, R.C. (ed.), *The King's Post. Being a volume of historical facts relating to the Posts, Mail Coaches, Coach Railroads, and Railway Mail Services of and connected with the Ancient City of Bristol from 1580 to the present time* (2nd edition, Bristol: W.C. Hemmons, 1905).

Wallis, John, *Wallis's New and Correct Map of the Post Roads of England & Wales* (London, 1798).

Wordsworth, William, *Guide to the Lakes* (5th edition, 1835), ed. Ernest de Selincourt (Oxford: Oxford University Press, 1982).

—— *The Early Letters of William and Dorothy Wordsworth (1787–1805)*, ed. Ernest de Selincourt (Oxford: Clarendon Press, 1935).

—— *The Fenwick Notes of William Wordsworth*, ed. Jared Curtis (London: Bristol Classical Press, 1993).

—— *The Prelude, 1799, 1805, 1850*, ed. Jonathan Wordsworth, M.H. Abrams, and Stephen Gill (New York and London: Norton, 1979).

—— *The Salisbury Plain Poems of William Wordsworth*, ed. Stephen Gill, Cornell Wordsworth Series (Ithaca: Cornell University Press, 1975).

—— *William Wordsworth: the Poems*, ed. John O. Hayden (2 vols, London: Penguin, 1977).

Wordsworth, William and Samuel Taylor Coleridge, *Lyrical Ballads, 1798* (Oxford and New York: Woodstock Books, 1990).

9
Coleridge in Devon

Graham Davidson

> I was reared
> In the great city, pent 'mid cloisters dim,
> And saw nought lovely but the sky and stars.

> *(PW*, I. i. 455, ll. 51–2)[1]

Thus Coleridge recalled his childhood as if it had all happened at school, in London. But, paradoxically, even in the poem from which these lines are taken, *Frost at Midnight*, there is a wonderful evocation of his native town, 'far in the West',

> ... my sweet birth-place, and the old church-tower,
> Whose bells, the poor man's only music, rang
> From morn to evening, all the hot Fair-day,
> So sweetly, that they stirred and haunted me
> With a wild pleasure ...

> *(PW*, I. i. 455, ll. 28–32)

a memory which awakes in him a hope, a longing, that someone from Ottery will appear in the classroom while he is pretending to study. Because he spent the first nine years of his life in Devon, he had many memories of his birth-place and the surrounding countryside. In effect, Coleridge had two childhoods, the first in Devon, and the second in London, and he looks back on these two periods in different ways: his general view is that leaving Devon resulted in his homeless wandering, his unsatisfactory relationships and lifelong sense of exile. Though one can hardly challenge the validity of personal feelings, I want to show that there is more continuity between these two lives than Coleridge was willing to admit, a continuity of unhappiness, the grounds of which were much the same in Ottery as they were in London. We will see that several early poems reflect the divided allegiances of his childhood, and that poems stemming from his

176

visits to Devon in the early 1790s mix contempt of the inhabitants with flirtatious verses for local beauties. Coleridge had a troubled relationship with his home in the West.

Exile in London

Coleridge was born at Ottery St Mary, Devon on 21 October 1772. For nine years, he had a childhood in Devon as normal as 'normal' ever is – he lived in one place, with a mother and father, and from nine other siblings, and three half-sisters, he found at least one brother, Frank, and one sister, Nancy, with whom he felt involved or engaged. But in October 1781, prefaced by William's death in 1780, this came to a sudden close. His father took Frank to join the Navy as a midshipman and thus robbed Coleridge of his closest companion – a brother and a friend, Coleridge called him after he heard of his death.[2] The evening he came home from Plymouth, happy with his achievement, the Rev. John Coleridge died of a heart attack. Under the impact of these two blows his youngest son's life changed radically. He was sent away in April 1782, to stay with his uncle in London, long before any school term began; the implication is that for some reason he was sent out of Devon months earlier than necessary. Not until July 1782 did he start going to school, first to the Christ's Hospital preparatory school in Hertford, where he was happy, in part because he had plenty of food, and then to Christ's Hospital in London, where he was much less happy, largely because he was 'half-starved'. However, the original plan had been to send him to Charterhouse, for the sons of gentlemen, not to Christ's Hospital, a school with a high proportion of sons of poor clergy. Coleridge became a Charity Boy, and Henry Crabb Robinson believed that this was Judge Buller's fault, who sent him to the Bluecoat School having first promised Charterhouse. It had a deleterious effect on Coleridge's relationship with his family, who were proud and

> thought themselves degraded by this; and refused to notice the boy in the school. He was, as it were, discarded for his misfortune. His brothers would not let him visit them in the school dress, and he would not (when he could) go in any other.[3]

Perhaps some of Coleridge's radicalism was catalysed by this incident; he developed a pride in the school, and partly out of his pride, and partly out of his family's discarding of him, he didn't go back to Devon again for seven years – that is between the ages of nine and sixteen. In London, we only have records of him meeting Luke and George throughout his school years. Although being sent away to boarding school while still only eight or nine was normal then, Coleridge, unsurprisingly, resented it. He felt that his family had deserted him, and it seems to have ruined his relationship with his mother. A lot of disparate things came together in this leaving of Devon: his losing of Frank, of his father, effectively losing his mother, and a deteriorating relationship with the rest of his family. No wonder he felt himself 'for eleven years together a poor, friendless Blue-coat Boy', as he told Ann Gillman in 1822 – though peculiarly forgetting the last three or four years of that time when, courting the Evans family, he was as happy as he ever was (*CL*, v. 258).

Coleridge's accounts of his childhood always return to this lifelong sense of exile, of being cast out from his homestead, his birthplace, 'the same Dwelling where his Father dwelt' – as he put it, with mild envy, to George, who in 1794 returned to Ottery to take up two of the Rev. John's three posts (*CL*, i. 311 n. 1). He told George that he had been 'too soon transplanted' for his soul to fix its 'first domestic loves'; and he frequently describes himself as an orphan, which he wasn't until 1809.[4] We might characterise the rest of his domestic life as an attempt to rediscover himself as a child, as someone to be looked after in other people's families – the Wordsworths', the Morgans', and the Gillmans' principally. As late as 1832, two years before he died, he was still comparing himself as a boy at Christ's Hospital with the boy at home in Ottery:

> I was sent for by Judge Buller – and placed in Christ's Hospital. O what a change! – Deprest, moping, friendless poor Orphan, half-starved/ at that time the portion of food given to the Blue-coats was cruelly insufficient, for those who had no friends to supply them – from 8 to 14 I was a playless Day-dreamer, an Helluo Librorum ... (*CN*, v. 6675)

But Coleridge's exclamation here, 'O what a change!', is an assertion that needs to be questioned. His external, forced exile can be seen to mask another kind of exile more deeply rooted – in Coleridge himself, in what he was as much as in what happened to him – and about which he tends to hide the truth from himself.

Exiled by reading

If he was half-starved in Christ's Hospital, food also had a significant place in his life in Ottery: Frank, Coleridge says,

> hated me, because my mother gave me now & then a bit of cake, when he had none – quite forgetting that for one bit of cake which I had & he had not, he had twenty sops in the pan & pieces of bread & butter with sugar on them from Molly, from whom I received only thumps & ill names.

What is odd about Coleridge's account of Molly's role in his upbringing is that he always believes that she is the cause of his lack of boyish exuberance – this passage goes on, relating Molly's treatment of him to an effect:

> So I became fretful, & timorous, & a tell-tale – & the School-boys drove me from play, & were always tormenting me – & hence I took no pleasure in boyish sports – but read incessantly. My Father's Sister kept an everything Shop at Crediton – and there I read thro' all the gilt-cover little books that could be had at that time ... and I used to lie by the wall, and mope – (*CL*, i. 347)

There is a lot of domestic disturbance here – he gets tit-bits from his mother, is thus hated by Frank and Molly, becomes a sneak, is timid and easily upset, and bullied by his father's students is packed off to his aunt in Crediton, where by himself he reads intensely, and thus gets depressed. Crediton is at least fifteen miles from Ottery, so the youngest Coleridge wasn't simply popping round the corner to visit his aunt; he was sent or taken there, presumably for some days at a time. Was it in order to be kept out of the way because he fitted in badly at home? Is this his first experience of a kind of exile, sent away because of his peculiarities, and the pressures on food and space in the family home? The unusual feature of his early years, his capacity to read, is isolating him from normal childhood activities. Despite describing his sister, Nancy, as his playmate, she is never mentioned in any of his narratives of his childhood; he is either sitting beside his mother, safe from Molly's attacks, or reading by himself, or fighting with Frank.

There is a key term in that passage linking what he was at Christ's Hospital with what he first had been at home in Ottery: 'Deprest, moping, friendless' runs the account of his life in Christ's Hospital in 1832, and 'I used to lie by the wall, and mope' he said in 1797 of his life in Devon. The moping is a result of intense reading, which disables Coleridge's physical activity for long periods. The boy in Crediton or Ottery finds no one to play with, is depressed, and is alone: it is one of the peculiar facts about Coleridge's childhood, that in the 'populous village' he never seems to have found a friend or to have belonged to a group or gang. Coleridge, in a big and busy family, had a peculiarly solitary childhood.

In the end it is hard to believe that Coleridge was 'driven from a Life in Motion to Life in thought and sensation' just because he was intimidated by Molly and Frank. His truly remarkable capacity to read was the unusual feature of his childhood. He says that he read because he couldn't play, but I think it nearer the truth to suggest that this ability to absorb himself in book after book, to find his life 'in thought and sensation', prevented him from playing or finding anyone to play with.

Moving from Devon to London made no difference to this trait. We have seen that in his aunt's shop in Crediton he 'read through all the gilt-covered little books that could be had at the time, & likewise all the uncovered Tales', so in London, introduced to a circulating library,

> I *read thro* the whole Catalogue, folios and all – whether I understood them or did not understand them – running all risks, in skulking out, to get the two Volumes which I was entitled to have daily ...

'Skulking out' means leaving the school premises without permission. Do we believe Coleridge when he says that he read the whole catalogue? It seems an extraordinary thing for a boy to do before he was 15, but the fact that he borrowed, and so probably read, two volumes a day suggests that we should not dismiss his claim as mere hyperbole.

But Coleridge was conscious that there was another kind of life, a life in motion, or action – the life a boy might be expected to lead – and every now and then, this would burst out of him. Thus in Devon, playing only by himself, he acted over what he had been reading and imagined himself, for instance, one of the Seven Champions of Christendom, 'cutting down the Weeds & Nettles' (*CN*, v. 6675). Or staying with his aunt in Crediton, to escape from his moping,

> my spirits used to come upon me suddenly, & in a flood – & then I was accustomed to run up and down the church-yard, and act over all I had been reading on the docks, the nettles, and the rank-grass. (*CL*, i. 347)

Much the same kind of acting out of the stories he had been reading occurs in London; James Gillman recounts how Coleridge got access to the circulating library:

> going down the Strand, in one of his day-dreams, fancying himself swimming across the Hellespont, thrusting his hands before him as in the act of swimming, his hand came in contact with a gentleman's pocket; the gentleman seized his hand, turning round and looking at him with some anger, 'What! so young, and so wicked?' at the same time accused him of an attempt to pick his pocket; the frightened boy sobbed out his denial of the intention, and explained to him how he thought himself Leander, swimming across the Hellespont. The gentleman was so struck and delighted with the novelty of the thing, and with the simplicity and intelligence of the boy, that he subscribed ... to the library, in consequence of which Coleridge was further enabled to indulge his love of reading.[5]

This was one kind of action, but there was another outlet to his reading – talking. Coleridge may have been an intense reader, but he was not passive, quiet, withdrawn – his passion for talking, perhaps as a substitute for action, developed early, and was first encouraged by his father when he took him visiting his parishioners.

Thus we might leave Coleridge's early years as Lamb saw him at fourteen or fifteen, just before he began to find real friendships at school, his sense of exile no longer troubling him, and about to embark on the happiest years of his life in the companionship of the Evanses. Lamb's vision of Coleridge depicts the life of reading, of thought and sensation, combining with a life of action, of delivering to the world the truths he was discovering; but even here he was talking because he had to talk – do something, entrance the chance passer-by – rather than address a particular person or group; his talking is a substitute for play, but it is a solo performance directed towards rather than involving companions:

> How have I seen the casual passer through the cloisters stand still, intranced with admiration ... to hear thee unfold, in thy deep and sweet intonations, the mysteries of Jamblichus or Plotinus ... or reciting Homer in his Greek, or Pindar, – while the walls of the old Grey Friars re-echoed to the accents of the *inspired charity-boy*![6]

This 'abstruse metaphysics' was then, and throughout his life remained, a refuge from emotions he did not want to confront; at times, philosophical discourse was to him a kind of play, an 'aye-babbling spring' whose 'fantastic playfulness' made 'a toy of Thought' (*PW*, I. i. 234, l. 57; 454, l. 23 and n.).

Coleridge was a lonely boy in Devon, before he was a lonely boy in London. Alienated by his intense reading both in Ottery and at Christ's Hospital, he had almost no physical life and no friends. If he was a visible and material exile in London, he was as much an inward and pyschological exile in Ottery, and what the boy was in Devon, he continued to be when at Christ's Hospital – until rescued by Middleton and the Evans family. Coleridge's sense of exile was strong, and justified, but it was as much born in him as bred by his circumstances.

Exiled from school – going back to Devon

In 1789, rising 17, Coleridge revisited Devon and Ottery for the first time in seven years, but we have no knowledge of how this first return affected him. There are recorded visits in 1791, 1792, and 1793, none in 1794 and 1795, and one in 1796. Although he occasionally returned in later years, it is the three years of 1791–3 that provide most interest.

In the summer of 1791 Coleridge left Christ's Hospital and, before going up to Cambridge, did something like a tour of his relations. He went to Exeter, where he would have met the Harts, 'wealthy druggists', whose daughter, Sara, was Luke's widow; Tiverton where James lived, the oldest surviving brother and head of the family; and Ottery in July and August, where his mother had lost her only daughter, Nancy, in March. By October he was ensconced in Jesus College. However, going to Cambridge seems to be the point at which he left behind him the three or four years of happiness he had experienced at Christ's Hospital. This second exile, from the relatively protected environment of Christ's Hospital, from the social comforts of the Evans family, and from Middleton's guardianship soon after he got to Cambridge, has some unhappy parallels with the first. His Ottery childhood closed with the death of William in 1780, the departure of Frank, and the death of his father. His Christ's Hospital childhood closed with the deaths of Luke and Nancy. Frank would die in 1792, though it would be a year before Coleridge knew of his death.

Although the sense of exile is much less marked at the close of this second period than the first, it is Coleridge himself who draws the parallels in two poems, 'An Anthem for the Children of Christ's Hospital', and 'Sonnet: On Quitting Christ's Hospital' (*PW*, I. i. 51–2, 54–5). The anthem is, as J. C. C. Mays points out, a poem full of praise for an institution of which his family were ashamed, and it makes no bones about the school's charitable foundation: his expectation is that the boys should be thankful for its care of them. The image of the school coming to the aid of a widowed mother with a brood of children to care for ('Cease, thou lorn Mother! cease thy wailings drear! / Ye Babes! th'unconscious sobs forego!' *PW*, I. i. 53, ll. 25–6) is a particularly emotive one for Coleridge, derived from recollection of how his family was plunged into poverty, and dependence on the goodwill of others, after the death of his father. For a boy who had spent much of his time hungry, lonely, and suffering unjust punishments – he told Godwin he was 'treated with contumely and brutality' at Christ's Hospital – this is an extraordinary tribute.[7]

Sometime in July or August 1791 Coleridge wrote his sonnet 'On Quitting Christ's Hospital', a poem which draws on the feelings of leaving home. It is a nice paradox that just as he was at, or travelling towards, his 'native seat' (a grandiose, or at least a gentleman's conception) he was writing a poem about leaving school as if that school were his home. His doubled childhood and divided allegiances could hardly be more clearly illustrated: the poem opens with, 'Farewell! Parental scenes! a sad farewell – / To you my grateful heart still fondly clings' and closes with,

> Lingring I quit you with as great a pang
> As when erewhile my weeping Childhood torn
> By early Sorrow from my native seat
> Mingled it's tears with her's – my widow'd Parent lorn!

> (*PW*, I. i. 54–5, ll. 11–14)

This is a neat and extraordinary comparison – a tribute both to his mother, to her distresses over the years, and to the school as a mother. He is leaving the school with as much regret as he left Devon.

The family's failure to visit him at Christ's Hospital, or to call him home in the holidays, contributed to Coleridge's sense that he didn't matter to them, and inevitably, the feeling rose in him that his family didn't matter to him. So in his returns to Devon, especially those of 1791 and 1792, what we see happening is not a recovery of lost childhood – a re-absorption into the family and community from which he had been exiled – but a growing sense of distance between himself and the people of Ottery. He summed up this feeling with some force in 1793, after hearing of Frank's death:

> I quitted Ottery, when I was so young, that most of those endearing circumstances, that are wont to render the scenes and companions of our childhood delightful in the recollection, I have associated with the place of my education – and when at last I revisited Devon, the manners of the Inhabitants annihilated whatever tender ideas of pleasure my Fancy rather than my Memory had pictured to my Expectation. I found them (almost universally) to be gross without openness, and cunning without refinement. (*CL*, i. 53)

That's a pretty severe indictment. It was written eighteen months into his residence at Cambridge, and he is still considering his time at Christ's Hospital 'delightful in the recollection'.

The scorn he felt for the inhabitants of his native seat is reflected in some of the poems he wrote in the summer of 1791. After leaving the coach at Cullompton, he made his way to Ottery via Plymtree, and pours his imprecations on the road – 'the damned Bog!' – by comparing this 'execrable way' to the 'sulphureous roads' used by 'the sad fiends' as they 'Took the first survey of their new abodes …' – thus suggesting that the inhabitants of Devon had something in common with Satan's followers (*PW*, I. i. 56–7). His 'Ode on the Ottery and Tiverton Church Music' begins with a dismissal of 'soul-dissolving Harmony' and the contrasting invocation of a 'Mightier Goddess …' – a goddess 'begot by Discord on Confusion', at a time when 'the Legion Diabolic / Compell'd their beings to enshrine / In bodies vile of herded swine' – suggesting that the natives of Devon are swine inhabited by devilish spirits heading for the cliffs (*PW*, I. i. 57–8, ll. 1, 16, 9–10). He feels the sacred might of this unnamed goddess working to the full pitch of her powers as her devotees

> Scrape, and blow and squeek and squall
> And while Old Otter's steeple rings
> Clappest hoarse thy raven wings![8]

There is nothing very kind in these comparisons, amusing though both poems are, and one feels, for instance, that Thomas Hardy might have found a different truth in the rustic music he heard.

Coleridge is in the kind of mood he describes as a consequence of his early reading and conscious intellectual superiority, when he experienced 'feelings of deep & bitter contempt for almost all who traversed the orbit of my understanding' (*CL*, i. 348). It is inspired by the kind of people, and his sense of their incompetence, that he discovers on his return visits to Devon. The affection that he remembers feeling *before* he returned to Ottery after his initial exile, his hope of seeing 'Townsman, or aunt, or sister more beloved' as he looked up in the classroom – that is all gone – they really are '*strangers*' to him (*PW*, I. i. 455, l. 42). The witty, unkind, and supercilious mood is also present in one other poem surviving from that summer, and combined with his undoubted appreciation of beauty in women, and its concomitant horror of ugliness, produced a twelve-line 'Epigram on My Godmother's Beard' (*PW*, I. i. 59–60). It opens with the couplet, 'So great the charms of Mrs Munday, / That men grew rude a kiss to gain' and closes with, 'To snatch a Kiss were vain (cried Pallas) / Unless you first should shave your beard' (1–2, 11–12). The squib was never published, but somehow it came to Mrs Munday's attention, and Coleridge records that it caused him to be struck out of his godmother's will. His willingness to circulate the poem is a sure sign of his lack of financial prudence, his contempt for 'sordid Wealth', and one of the many differences that marked him out from his brothers.

Summer 1792

Coleridge again returned to Devon this year, visiting Edward at Salisbury, James at Tiverton, and so making his way to Ottery. He had won a university prize for his Greek Ode on the misery of West Indian slaves, read publicly at Cambridge on 3 July. He was thus in confident mood as he began his visit to his relatives and home town. He had mocked their music-making abilities the previous year, and in 1792, his unkindness was more marked – the sheer ugliness of some of the people he met provoking his mirth. Thus the vicar of Ottery, Fulwood Smerdon, and his weighty wife – 'gross and round beyond belief, / A superfluity of Beef' (7–8) – are sneered at for 32 unrelenting lines:

> He, meagre Bit of Littleness,
> All Snuff, and Musk, and Politesse
> So thin, that strip him of his cloathing
> He'd totter on the Edge of Nothing ...

> (*PW*, I. i. 84–5, ll. 13–16)

Of the last quoted here, Coleridge noted in a letter to George, 'A good Line'. The poem is funny, but without a moment of compassion. He even printed it in the first edition of his 1796 poems – Smerdon was dead, but by the time he was preparing the second edition, he asked Cottle to take it out, noting that it was ludicrous and immoral (*PW*, I. i. 84, headnote).

Coleridge's only other letter in the summer of 1792 is also to George, some three weeks later at the end of August, and in Latin. Contempt and unkindness continue. His political differences with the leading lights of a Tory country town appear in his ironic remarks on Mr Hodge's 'ravenous hunger for news from France. The reports ... that we receive are very sad: the people of Paris were not burned alive when the city was captured, and Payne not cut to pieces at Canterbury when he was making his way to France.' He also makes fun of John Kestell, who believes he can do something for Frank:

> He has just come to meet me as I was walking down through the churchyard: 'Hallo! Mr. Samuel, how d'ye do! You know, I suppose, that Lord Shore ... whom the King has just made Governor-General of all India, is the husband of my son-in-law's sister ... I myself, ahem, will recommend him to the Governor-General very strongly, and I have no doubt but the Governor-General will deal with your brother's affairs in such a way that my recommendation, ahem, will be understood to be no ordinary one!' ... What a puffed-up creature! What pomposity! Our mother positively drinks in his long-winded speeches, and dreams of the most wonderful prospects. (*CL*, i. 41)

In one of those sad ironies of time, Frank's 'most wonderful prospects' had already ended with his suicide a few months before this letter – just one of the many tragedies and disappointments that Ann Coleridge endured. We can see how much Coleridge feels that his mother's ambitions are unrealistic, 'dreams' based on the unreliability of influence – and perhaps conscious that he had already lambasted those kinds of ambition in poems such as 'Dura Navis' and 'O Curas Hominum' – 'Pale Disappointment hangs her head / O'er darling Expectation dead!'[9]

His brother Edward either accompanied Samuel to Tiverton and then to Ottery, or met him there, as a substantial part of this letter to George describes Edward taking farewell of the inhabitants of their native town – in Latin verse. Coleridge depicts the scene with Hogarthian disgust:

> The flower of Ottery's manhood bewailed his departure: fat dirty Hobbs; and little weakly Smerdon, who is reduced to a shadow by the impudence of a disobedient wanton, and Kesell, who loves to draw out his words to extreme length, and multiply his 'ahems' in the middle of his sentences; and Hodge, who hates Tom Payne ... Yes, even bovine

Dorothy, even Miss Vaughan of the bleary eyes, even Miss Bacon mourns, on whose nose and cheeks many a pimple pastures, foul with oozing matter.

It's not a pretty picture, and presents the obverse of Coleridge's well-developed sense of female beauty. And it also depicts Edward as the leading social light of Ottery, both maidens and matrons throwing themselves at his feet. He was a handsome man, with a sharp sceptical wit, that probably appealed both to the town's socialites and to his younger brother – at least initially. In Salisbury they enjoyed each other's company, sizing each other up at the same time. Coleridge wrote to George: 'My Brother Edward is well – if you except a Punnomania ... his puns are very bad – of this he is conscious and therefore unwilling to allow Merit to those of others' (*CL*, i. 36). They also discussed George's health – more for their joint amusement than out of any compassion. Coleridge told George, 'I compared the carbuncle on your cheek, to the star of Venus passing over the disk of the Sun.' Edward improved upon this by comparing the defect 'to an ignis fatuus passing over a Dunghill' (*CL*, i. 37). One can't imagine George very amused, and he must have felt the animus in Edward's acerbic put-down.

Coleridge watched Edward work his admirers in Ottery, and immediately after the description of his leave-taking, told George:

> There is not the least doubt that Edward is a wit, seasoned with Plautine salt; and he will be likeable too, if he gives up that display of sham generosity, and would prefer reality to show. He would not attract the eyes of the rabble so much, but he would be more at harmony in himself. The satisfaction we gain from a quiet conscience is somehow lessened, when we accept as the reward of renown that which is got by mere ostentation. (*CL*, i. 41)

A much disturbed man, Coleridge could detect signs of disturbance in others – puns being one sign of a mind at odds with itself, and Hamlet the locus classicus. Edward is not at ease with himself, and so needs and enjoys the applause of the 'rabble' – that word another perspective on Coleridge's response to Ottery society.

Summer 1793

Coleridge appears in Devon this summer, the last of these yearly visits, in a very different mood – as a slightly dissolute flirt, writing flattering verses for local belles (*CL*, i. 60). His family know and disapprove of his irregular life at Cambridge, where he has made free with wine and women (though the intangibility of Mary Evans is haunting him) and his debts are mounting.[10]

Coleridge senses George's disapproval in particular, for George has not written to him, nor sent the money he desperately needed:

> I am fearful, that your Silence proceeds from Displeasure – If so, what is left for me to do – but to grieve? The Past is not in my Power – for the follies, of which I may have been guilty, I have been greatly disquieted – and I trust, the Memory of them will operate to future consistency of Conduct. (*CL*, i. 59)

He might like to think his follies past, but his conduct during the next year will become almost inexplicably erratic. He escapes from his immediate anxieties by first visiting his least reputable brother, Edward, where he spent six hours of a Monday drinking and disputing (*CL*, i. 57). Into the letter to George describing this he inserts an anacreontic poem celebrating his presentation of a moss rose to Miss Fanny Nesbitt, with whom Coleridge had shared a 'diligence' from Exeter to Tiverton – a very pretty girl, he thought. Miss Nesbitt appears to have accepted the gift warmly – for she put the rose in her bosom. Dick Hart, son of the wealthy druggist two of whose sisters married Coleridges, asked her if she wasn't afraid to put it there, as 'there might be Love in it'. We don't have her reply, but Coleridge responded immediately with a poem 'of the namby Pamby genus'.

'A Moss Rose'

Although this risks being a tendentious and salacious reading, it seems to me a sexually conscious poem. The opening lines – 'As late each flow'r that sweetest blows / I pluck'd, the garden's pride' (1–2) – not only refer to his habit of picking flowers from other people's gardens (cf. *CL*, v. 218), but may have a subliminal allusion to the sexual freedom he found in Cambridge – certainly it is not an uncommon metaphor. And what the poet saw – 'Within the petals of a Rose / A sleeping Love I spy'd' – is the image of a contented lover at rest within the bosom of his beloved. The next verse, however, suggests something slightly different:

> Around his brows a lucid wreath
> Of many a mingled hue;
> All purple glowed his cheek beneath
> Inebriate with dew.
>
> (*PW*, I. i. 93–4, ll. 5–8)

The 'lucid wreath' is of uncertain composition – is it the 'mingled hue' of a variety of flowers, or is it the blotched and mottled complexion of someone who has had too much to drink? Flowers themselves are associated less with

Cupid than Bacchus – especially the vine. Coleridge undoubtedly intends the reader to think of 'the impatient Boy' as Cupid, for at the end of the poem he deserts Venus for Nesbitt, but this figure is also a drinker – his cheek is purple, and 'inebriate with dew'. There is a minor Coleridgean obfuscation here – the cheek is inebriate rather than the sleeping love. And what is the dew? Will this become the 'honey-dew' of 'Kubla Khan'? The figure is sleeping off various forms of indulgence and pleasure. But there is also a subliminal image of the erect and eager phallus, inebriate with desire, in which case the dew is something else again.

Sleep and active desire are opposed states – but we might think that the desire is in the poet, and the sleeping love an image of this desire unfocused. This figure or image has to have a home – and thus the poet seizes 'th' unguarded Power' and places him on Fanny's breast. This action symbolises the poet's hope. Why else should he choose to disturb the sleeping figure and find another home for him? Once this figure discovers he has been moved, 'He struggled to escape awhile / And stamp'd his angry feet' (15–16). But as soon as he realises where he is – deep in Nesbitt's bosom, a 'soul-entrancing Sight' (17) – his impatience is subdued, and this subduing is the climax of the poem:

> He gaz'd, he thrill'd with deep delight
> Then clapt his wings for Joy.
> And – oh! he cry'd –

> (19–21)

We will hear of 'deep delight' again in 'Kubla Khan'. He finally determines to desert his first goddess – 'Another Love let Venus find' – and to 'fix his Empire' with lovely Nesbitt (24–5). He is relaxed, at home, and rests. The course of the poem is the course that Coleridge might have hoped his love for Fanny Nesbitt would take.

'Cupid turn'd Chymist'

Fanny Nesbitt seems to have replaced Mary Evans in Coleridge's affection during this summer of 1793, for there are four poems in which she is a key figure. Coleridge is capable of transferring his affection, if only temporarily, as he did in the sick ward in Christ's Hospital, when Jenny Edwards glided into his consciousness after he had begun his devotions to Mary Evans. Fanny Nesbitt's significance in Coleridge's story is that, briefly, she was a person whom he could have both loved and desired. But she is no Cambridge girl; and in Coleridge's mind she remains ever virtuous – indeed that was a considerable part of her attraction. And in 'Cupid turn'd Chymist', his second poem for her, the images of desire are combined with his icons of idealised love (*PW*, I. i. 94–6). Cupid mixes nectar and ambrosia in a cauldron heated by love-kindled flames to create 'a rich Elixir of Delight' (2). And then Coleridge, rather than Cupid one feels, adds in 'the magic Dews, which Evening brings, / Brush'd from th'Idalian Star by fairy wings' (5–6) – this is Venus, or the Evening Star, which had captured his imagination so early in life. But the qualities of this star and her magic dews are quite different from the traditional qualities of Venus – the 'tender Pledge of sacred faith', the 'gentler Pleasure of th'unspotted mind', and 'Hope, the blameless Parasite of woe' – which final and slightly discordant note indicates his mood darkening behind the façade of these flirtatious poems (7–8, 10). This mix of the sensuous, the sacred and the pure is the recipe for love, perfect love:

> The steaming Cauldron bubbled up in Sighs,
> Sweet Sound transpir'd, as when th' enamour'd Dove
> Pours the soft Murmurs of responsive Love.

> (12–14)

Coleridge likens the cooing of doves or pigeons to the sound of love-making, warm and responsive sounds he had no doubt enjoyed at Cambridge, but which he had yet to realise in any but 'loose' women. The bubbling potion though, called 'Kisses', does not as yet belong to any particular woman and Cupid divides it between the generic – the goddess of love, his 'Cyprian mother' – who is thus distinguished from the evening star – and the particular, Fanny Nesbitt, the local belle:

> With part the God his Cyprian mother blest,
> And breath'd on Nesbitt's lovely lips the rest.

> (17–18)

The frankness with which Coleridge admires and addresses Fanny may stem either from the possibility that he is not deeply involved with her, or because the poem is an adaptation of a Latin original by an Oxford student. But it turns out to be a useful poem when he wants to flatter. There are four different names assigned to the last line in various manuscripts – two are surnames – Nesbitt and Boutflower, and two are first or Christian names – Mary and Sara. Mary is Mary Evans (see Figure 14), and the manuscript contains some interesting variants which all suggest an intenser love for her; the 'cauldron' becomes a 'chalice' – thus demonstrating the holiness of the heart's affections – and the last line runs, 'And breath'd on Mary's lovelier lips the rest' – lovelier than Venus's (*PW*, II. i. 93–4). But when it came to printing the poem, in 1796, after his marriage, it is his wife who duly finds her name in the last line. It proved a poem for several occasions, as many of Coleridge's love poems do.

Figure 14   Joseph Allen, Mary Evans, at Wrexham in 1798 or 1799, some three or four years after her marriage to Fryer Todd. The painter Joseph Allen was probably brother to Robert Allen, with whom Coleridge, from the ages of 16 to 19, spent 'hours of Paradise ... in escorting the Miss Evanses home on a Saturday' (*CL*, V. 218).

'Absence: A Poem'

Coleridge left Tiverton around 3 August 1793, and travelled to Ottery. Fanny Nesbitt was left behind, and soon afterwards he wrote a long poem, which combines fulsome praise with regret at leaving her and Tiverton. It was initially entitled *Absence*, and later *Lines on an Autumnal Evening* (*PW*, I. i. 99–103). It is a poem largely free of the flirtatious innuendo characteristic of his two earlier poems for her. The earliest version opens with an address to imagination, his conception of which is very far from his mature definitions, and involves a kind of fairy world still part of country consciousness:

> Imagination! mistress of my lore!
> Where shall mine eye thy elfin haunt explore?

> Dost thou on yon rich cloud thy pinions bright
> Embathe in amber-glowing floods of light?
>
> (1–4)

which lightly anticipates some lines in the 'Eolian Harp' two years later (*PW*, I. i. 231–5). But in other versions of the poem, this opening question becomes an imperative requiring him not to use his imagination, or as he now more accurately terms the faculty, his fancy, simply to meditate on the landscape:

> O thou wild Fancy, check thy wing! No more
> Those thin white flakes, those purple clouds explore!
> Nor there with happy spirits speed thy flight
> Bathed in rich amber-glowing floods of light ...
>
> (*PW*, II. ii. 100–11)

'Those thin white flakes' will appear again in 'A Letter to ——' and 'Dejection'. The later versions of *Absence* redirect fancy from the studying of the appearances of nature to a lament for a lost or absent love – and in this respect it is precisely the movement of consciousness at the opening of the 'Dejection' poems: 'Ah! rather bid the perished pleasures move, / A shadowy train, across the soul of Love!' (see *PW* II. ii. 102). He may have been disappointed in love, and its pleasures may have perished, but he wants to revisit its origins, when the soul of love leapt out of 'Hope's trim bower'. Why? we might ask. And the question is not directly answered, except in that what follows is true love, as Coleridge imagines or fancies it. He wants to create what he has not realised in life. And the woman he creates, using what we might call the base-image of Fanny Nesbitt, is very much the kind of woman he creates in the Dejection poems. He calls on fancy:

> Aid, lovely Sorceress! aid thy poet's dream!
> With faery wand O bid the Maid arise,
> Chaste Joyance dancing in her bright blue eyes ...
>
> (14–16; see *PW*, I. i. 100 ; II. ii. 103)

In that phrase 'Chaste Joyance' (quite different from the responsive love created by Cupid's chemistry) we see the combination of two almost paradoxical powers – sensual joy, and purity of soul and mind – which combination Coleridge would make the hallmark of ultimate experience – the 'Joy, that ne'er was given / Save to the Pure, & in their purest Hour ...' ('A Letter to ——', *PW*, I. ii. 690, ll. 313–14). In this poem, he has bid fancy conjure up the maid ('*my love*'), and fancy does her work successfully: 'With raptur'd gaze the absent maid I view!' (20). Interestingly, and demonstrating the effort Coleridge made to clarify his earlier text, later versions suggest that his love has been reciprocated.

The first version contains an appeal that is missing in the later texts – 'Oh! bid her come in meek compassions's vest, / And heed the sigh that swells my secret breast!' (17–18). Compassion, and pity, are key words in Coleridge's vocabulary of human relationships. Having required fancy to turn away from the beauties of the landscape, and invoke the maid, her presence and her pity will create a language from the various sounds of nature, all speaking through her:

> With *her* along the streamlet's brink I rove,
> With *her* I list the warblings of the grove,
> And seems on ev'ry gale *her* voice to float
> Lone-whispering pity in each soothing note.
>
> (29–32)

The landscape, intially dismissed, now comes alive for the poet through the compassion of his muse – another feature of Coleridge's later poems for Sara Hutchinson.

This might seem an appropriate point for the poem to end. But his invocation releases the spirit and power of Coleridge's devotion – or, we might say, from this point on, he works his passage steadily away from reality. And unlike his earlier poems for Fanny, there is no jocular irony in his language – it is full of superlatives, seemingly sincere, but nonetheless surprising in the light of his love for Mary Evans:

> No lovelier maid does love's wide empire know
> No lovelier maid e'er heav'd the bosom's snow.
>
> (39–40)

Full snowy breasts, heaving with compassion, were one of the most exciting features of female beauty for Coleridge. But in praising Fanny's loveliness, his diction, though sensual, remains chaste and without double entendre:

> Love lights her smile – in joy's red nectar dips
> The opening rose, and plants it on her lips!
> Tender, serene, and all devoid of guile,
> Soft is her soul, as sleeping infants' smile!
>
> (45–8)

However, the ecstatic nature of this praise detaches him from her as a person – there is no sense of two people meeting and falling in love. And this detachment is reinforced in ll. 57–70, when he imagines, anacreontically, the various ways he might be present to her: did he have a wizard's rod, or the power of Proteus, 'A flow'r entangled arbour would I seem, / To shield my love from noontide's sultry beam' (59–60), which is honourable enough, but the passage moves on to imagining greater intimacies, and if the verse takes any risks with its chaste vision, it is in these lines:

> To fan my love I'd be the evening gale:
> Sigh in the loose folds of her floating vest,
> And flutter my faint pinions on her breast ...
>
> (64–6)

He is a cupid, fluttering at her breast to make her conscious of him. What is curious about Coleridge's praise of Fanny is that he cannot bring his own being into her presence – he has to transform himself into an arbour, a breeze, or the spangled skies, and sees her only through their presence. The Cambridge man, who used whores to satisfy his needs, is unable to realise that sensuality in his relationship with 'virtuous' women. It is a sad division in his soul.

His praise of Fanny is finished, but the poem still has some 35 lines to run, in the course of which she is completely forgotten. The final passage is a lament for his lost childhood. The transition from the one theme to the other is curious: he compares his waking from his dreams of Fanny to that of a savage who, having fallen asleep in the sunshine, wakes to a storm (a key word in his consciousness at the time), and

> So, tost by storms along life's wild'ring way,
> Mine eye reverted views the cloudless day,
> When, Isca! on thy banks I joy'd to rove,
> While hope with kisses nurs'd the infant love.
>
> (79–82)

The landscape Coleridge here evokes is not that of the nettles in Crediton churchyard, but a romance landscape, 'cloudless', uncorrupted by lost innocence, 'Where love a crown of thornless roses wears', and memory 'feeds the lambent flame of joy!' (89, 92). But it is a landscape from which he feels himself banished:

> No more the sky-larks melting from the sight
> Shall thrill the attuned nerve with pure delight:
> No more shall deck thy 'pensive pleasures' sweet
> With wreaths of sober hue my evening seat!
>
> (93–6)

The sober philosopher, 'with Learning's meed not unbestowed', steadily and staidly seeking love as the reward of a devout life, has been driven out of his imagined paradise – the edenic, cloistered countryside – by the stormy and bewildering powers discovered within himself, to which he has given too much licence. He takes leave of a landscape that we feel he may just have begun to notice for the first time, with a kind of backward glance that Adam and Eve gave to their happy seat:

> Scenes of delight! my aching heart ye leave,
> Like those rich hues that paint the clouds of eve!
> Tearful, and sadd'ning with the sadden'd blaze,
> Mine eye the gleam pursues with wistful gaze,
> Sees shades on shades with deeper tints impend,
> Till chill and damp the moonless night descend.

> (101–6)

Those are the last lines of a poem in praise of Fanny Nesbitt, and they combine two lost worlds – of love, and of innocent childhood – overwhelmed by the storms of life. It is as if he is saying goodbye to any hopes he might have had of experiencing a union of body and soul, of sense and spirit – and it produces a feeling of exile.

'Songs of the Pixies': the faery way of writing

Coleridge was still at Ottery in September 1793, and sometime that month 'conducted a party of young Ladies' to the Pixies' Parlour, an excavation on the bank above the river Otter, just outside Ottery – the walk there from the centre of town takes some twenty minutes (see Figure 15). When the party arrived, one of their number, 'elegantly small, and of complexion colourless yet clear ... was proclaimed the Fairy Queen' (see *PW*, I. i. 107–12 and headnote).

If ever there was a poem of the namby-pamby genus, this would seem to be it. So why did he continue to print, and revise as late as 1834, a poem he frequently dismissed and never praised? Probably for reasons similar to those that made him work and rework *Absence* – both poems evoke a quality of consciousness that he believed, even by the age of 22, he had lost, or was discovering he had lost in this, his last extended visit, to Devon. He was revisiting both the childhood he had never had, and, through the flirtations of this summer, the nature of a perfect love, first glimpsed in Mary Evans, that would never be his. The losses of love and childhood are combined in these poems.

This consciousness is centred around the word 'faery'. Its association with a lost world is evident in a poem he would write for Mary Evans a year later,

Figure 15   The Pixies' Parlour, Ottery St. Mary.

in the summer of 1794: *The Sigh* opens, 'When Youth his faery reign began / Ere Sorrow had proclaim'd me man ... Then', he says to Mary, 'I heav'd the painless SIGH for thee!' (*PW*, I. i. 127, ll. 1–2, 6). This time of youth, of painless sighs, Coleridge dates very precisely, from 15 to 19, the era of poetry and love, before the dissolutions of Cambridge.

Coleridge's use of the term 'fairy' or 'faery' is a way of describing the real but unperceived, of distinguishing the spiritual from the material, and is based on the superstitions of his home county. Thus he justifies his writing 'Songs of the Pixies' by reference to the local belief that they are 'a race of beings invisibly small – harmless or friendly to man' and that the Pixies' Parlour is where they retreat from the sultry heat of the midday sun.

The course and function of the poem is to proclaim Miss Boutfleur 'our Faery Queen', a phrase which not only reminds us of *A Midsummer's Night's Dream*, but also of Spenser's Virgin Queen. Miss Boutfleur's pixie or faery nature is at one with Coleridge's vision of womanhood:

> For lo! attendant on thy steps are seen
> Graceful EASE in artless stole,
> And white-rob'd PURITY of Soul

> With HONOR's softer mien:
> MIRTH of the loosely-flowing Hair,
> And meek-ey'd PITY eloquently fair
> Whose tearful Cheeks are lovely to the view
> As snow-drop wet with dew.
>
> (96–103)

Taken together those capitalised personifications are his idea of what she is, and include not only the all-important 'PITY', but also graceful 'EASE' and 'MIRTH'. Mirth is another significant word in Coleridge's lexicon, representing a kind of sensual exuberance – exemplified here in her loosely flowing hair, a sweet disorder in the tress – that takes us back to Herrick and Lovelace reacting against the tight codes of Puritanism and linking Coleridge to the cavalier spirit.[11] The last two lines are a chaste echo of the more erotic 'All purple glowed his cheek beneath / Inebriate with dew' of *The Moss Rose*, and it says something about Coleridge that he cannot let Miss Boutflower's cheeks rest in this chaste condition – he has to flush her out, so to speak. 'Unboastful Maid!' he calls her at the beginning of the last verse, and one feels she might have been a quiet person, not openly responsive to Coleridge. Her beauty and stillness are a challenge to him, and noting her lily-pale complexion he ends the poem by suggesting that before next spring,

> We'll tinge with livelier hues thy cheek,
> And haply from the nectar-breathing Rose
> Extract a BLUSH for LOVE![12]
>
> (*PW*, I. ii. 749–50, ll. 109–11)

But the cool, stately little Miss Boutflower remained unmoved. The kind of woman that Coleridge wants, the pure statue becoming the warm wife, is the myth that he never really escaped from, but as he got older, he realised the rarity of his dream – 'there are Mirandas and Imogens, a Una, a Desdemona, out of Fairy Land – rare, no doubt; yet less rare, than their Counterparts among men in real life' (*CL*, v. 183).

Coleridge has come to this faery bower to have the various miseries of his life eased by the pixies' 'soothing Witch'ries' (47). And this emphasis on himself appears in his telling not of the party arriving at the parlour, but as if he came, or was accustomed to coming, on his own. The pixies speak of him as 'A youthful BARD, "unknown to fame"' (38) whom Indolence and Fancy have induced to seek them out – indolence and imagination being two elements traditionally constitutional of a poet: but this bard is simultaneously a philosopher, for as well as the Faery Queen, he 'Wooes the Queen of solemn Thought' (39) – a sentiment much like that in *Absence*, 'I came with Learning's meed not unbestowed'. Coleridge often carries the dignity of formal knowledge with him, even into the bowers of love. Standing in front of the cave, without any consciousness of the rest of the party, he 'heaves the gentle mis'ry of a Sigh / Gazing with tearful eye' (40–1), the two lines Coleridge damned as Della Cruscan. But what he sighs for here is not the loss of Mary Evans, but 'Many a rudely-sculptur'd Name / To pensive MEM'RY dear!' (43–4). The sighting of these names is sufficiently important to Coleridge for him to mention it in the preface to the poem: on the outer sides of the Pixies' Parlour

> there are innumerable Cyphers, among which the author descried his own Cypher and those of his Brothers, cut by the hand of their Childhood. At the foot of the Hill flows the River Otter. (*PW*, I. i. 108)

It was only a few months earlier, in February, that Coleridge had learned of Frank's death (*CL*, i. 53, 55). The mood here, as in the letter to George, is not the anguish of weeping afresh, but more the melancholy of rediscovering the losses of his childhood. Those carved initials would have reminded him either of brothers he never knew, Jack and William, or of brothers of whom he had seen very little as he grew up, whom he had yet to learn to love, and felt little inclination to do so. Thus reminded of brothers he never knew, or lost to him, or for whom he has no brotherly feeling, he will have felt again his detachment from his family, detached not by his own will, but by his being sent out of Devon so early in life.

In relation to his childhood, the pixies do one particular thing for him, they teach him the value of play. Verses six and seven of this poem have play at their heart – '... thro' mystic ringlets of the vale / We flash our faery feet in gamesome prank', and '... with quaint music hymn the parting gleam / By lonely OTTER's sleep-persuading stream' (63–4, 69–70). Verse seven concludes, 'For mid the quiv'ring Light 'tis ours to play, / Aye-dancing to the cadence of the stream' (89–90). The pixies persuade him, or he persuades himself through his creation of the pixies, that dancing, singing and 'wildly-working Dreams' (77) are all the stuff of the freely moving imagination. This is the adult learning to play as the child never did.

The dreams and hopes of childhood are woven into this poem, faery dreams that throughout his life will counterpoint the harsh realities of his childhood. But the pixies also witness what is beyond 'the grosser ken of mortal sight' (54), the subject of 'the visionary hour', woodland courtships in which love is reciprocated – and in ways typically Coleridgean: the enamoured rustic talks, the maiden's breast heaves, and the electric dart evokes a gentle response:

> Along our wildly-bower'd, sequester'd walk
> We listen to the enamour'd Rustic's Talk;
> Heave with the heavings of the Maiden's Breast

> Where young-eyed Loves have built their turtle nest,
>   Or guide of soul-subduing Power
> Th' electric Flash, that from the melting Eye
> Darts the fond Question and the soft Reply ...

(56–62)

The pixies find Cupid is still nestling in breasts, but the game seems to be played out happily, and there is no sense that the rustic has to imagine himself as the wind, or the spangled skies to get a lodging in the abode of love. This is probably the last poem Coleridge wrote in Devon, and it speaks of a visionary world of maidenly beauty, of fulfilled love, and of a childhood much desired but never known.

'Sonnet: to the River Otter'

In the landscape of this festive play, the Otter features in two verses, inducive of sleep in one, and providing the dance rhythms in the other. He seems to have thought of the Otter as a childhood companion, and in a sonnet probably written between 1793 and 1796, addresses it with affection in the opening line: 'Dear native Brook! wild Streamlet of the West!' (*PW*, I. i. 299–300, l. 1), and associates it with the kind of childhood we never hear of in his letters to Tom Poole or his note to James Gillman:

> What happy, and what mournful hours, since last
> I skimm'd the smooth thin stone along thy breast,
> Numbering its light leaps! yet so deep imprest
> Sink the sweet scenes of childhood, that mine eyes
>   I never shut amid the sunny ray
> But strait with all their tints thy waters rise,
>   Thy crossing plank, thy marge with willows grey,
> And bedded sand that vein'd with various dies
> Gleam'd through thy bright transparence!

(3–11)

This vision of the Otter is therefore of a kind with that of the pixies – not the childhood he had, but the childhood he wanted. The last line of this sonnet – 'Ah! that once more I were a careless child!' – does not speak as honestly as the letters and notes for we have seen that the cares of childhood were great upon him. But the Otter and surrounding countryside as a landscape symbolic of the untroubled child, living a happy family life, quiescent in Coleridge much of his life, was revived in his later years. In 1825, he writes in response to his nephew Edward's account of a visit to Ottery:

It has been no small comfort to me to follow you in spirit along the Banks of the Otter, and over the Hills & Vales adjacent, and to return with you ... to the social Table, the Chat, the Music, and the group of happy Faces and affectionate Hearts ... (*CL*, v. 489)

Edward's experience reminds Coleridge of something that ought to belong to childhood, rather than something his childhood realised. And this is curiously characteristic of him in his later years. In 'Youth and Age', he speaks of a time when he was young, verse and hope were his, and 'Life went a maying / With NATURE, HOPE, and POESY'; except for his school courtship of Mary Evans, it would be difficult to find such a time in Coleridge's life. And as he lay dying, 'without expectation of a speedy release', he commented how strange it was that 'very recently by-gone images, and scenes of early life, have stolen into my mind, like breezes blown from the spice-islands of Youth and Hope'.[13]

Was he, in the comfort and security of the Gillmans' home, able to contemplate the childhood he had never had, but for which he had always longed? Perhaps, but what we can be sure of is that Coleridge's life was a series of exiles; from Ottery, from Christ's Hospital, even from Cambridge; and from Mary Evans, from his wife, from Sara Hutchinson – those key and failed relationships marking in him the division between the life of the senses and the life of the intellect. It is a condition he lamented all his life, keeping him from ever having a home, and is typified in 'Constancy to an Ideal Object', when he addresses his '*living* Love', his 'dear *embodied* Good' – the visionary woman, part mother, part lover, who combines the truths of philosophy with the power of poetry:

> Ah! loveliest Friend!
> That this the meed of all my toils might be,
> To have a home, an English home, and thee!

> (*PW*, I. ii. 777–8; ll. 11–12, 16–18)

Notes

1. See also *PW*, I. ii. 682, ll.63–4: '(Alas! for cloister'd in a city School / The Sky was all I knew of Beautiful)'.
2. *CL*, i. 55; it is possible the brother and the friend are two different people, but if so it isn't clear who the friend is.
3. *Henry Crabb Robinson on Books and their Writers*, ed. Edith J Morley (3 vols, London: J. M. Dent, 1938), i. 105.
4. Coleridge as orphan: e.g. *CL*, iii. 103, 105, and *CL*, i. 61 for Hartley as an orphan.
5. James Gillman, *The Life of Samuel Taylor Coleridge* (2 vols, London: Pickering, 1838), i. 22.
6. 'Christ's Hospital Five and Thirty Years Ago', in *The Works of Charles and Mary Lamb*, ed. E. V. Lucas (7 vols, London: Methuen, 1903–7), ii. 21.

7. Bodleian Libary, Abinger Dep. c. 604/3, 2.
8. *PW*, I. i. 58, ll. 28–30. Mays believes this poem contrasts the 'well-managed church music at Tiverton' with the music at Ottery, 'which was provided by an untrained orchestra'.
9. *Coleridge: the Early Family Letters*, ed. James Engell (Oxford: Clarendon Press, 1994), 64, n.14.
10. Nearly £150, according to Griggs: see *CL*, i. 59, n.1.
11. Cf. Alan Rudrum, 'The Royalist Lyric', in *The Cambridge Companion to the Writing of the English Revolution*, ed. N. Keeble (Cambridge: Cambridge University Press, 2001), 181ff.
12. Cf. 'The Kiss and the Blush', *PW*, I. ii. 749–50.
13. *Table Talk Recorded by Henry Nelson Coleridge (and John Taylor Coleridge)*, ed. Carl Woodring, *Collected Works of Samuel Taylor Coleridge*, Bollingen Series 75, 14 (2 vols, London and Princeton: Routledge and Princeton University Press, 1990), ii. 296 and n.; cf. *CL*, vi. 705, 10 July 1834.

10
Southey's West Country

Lynda Pratt

On 29 August 1803, Robert and Edith Southey completed their packing and left their home city of Bristol. Their departure was prompted by personal tragedy: the death of their only child from hydrocephalus. As Southey explained to his younger brother:

> all is over & poor Margaret in heaven ... the blow has gone to my very heart, & made me often think those the happiest who have none but themselves to care for.
>
> Joe [Southey's dog] is left with Biss ... John Morgan & his wife have been uncommonly kind in their attention to us. they have got a home for the cat. Hort houses my lumber at the Red Lodge whither he is removed. it is a dreary business packing up. the worst I ever had yet ... this place & every thing about it is haunted. I cannot escape the recollection & the very image of her.[1]

The Southeys' destination was Greta Hall, Keswick, then occupied by Edith's sister Sara, her husband Samuel Taylor Coleridge and their three children. It was to become their home for the remainder of their lives. In exchanging Bristol for the Lakes, Southey was leaving behind the city in which he had been born and spent much of his first three decades. It was a city which by 1803 had long been a spectral place, haunted by the ghosts of a dead daughter, mother, cousin, and father, and by the monitory shade of Thomas Chatterton, summoned up by the teenaged Southey in 'Bristol Church-Yard', one of his earliest surviving poems.[2] Southey was also leaving the city and the wider geographical region which had been at the very centre of his literary life, both as subject and as professional hub for his dealings with other writers, publishers, printers, and booksellers.

Southey's career was to be marked out by English regional geography and mapped onto provincial spaces. The hasty, tragic relocation of 1803 was to have a significant, and at the time unseen, impact on his reputation. In the early 1800s, Southey was known to contemporaries as a prolific, controversial, West Country poet. He was, as David Rivers explained, 'Of the City of Bristol'.[3] By the time of his death forty years later, he was labelled as a prolific, controversial member of the Lake School, alongside Coleridge and Wordsworth. The 'Lake' Southey was authorised and enshrined for posterity in the verses Wordsworth composed for a public memorial, placed in the ancient church of St Kentigern's, Crosthwaite:

> Ye vales and hills, whose beauty hither drew
> The poet's steps and fixed him here ...
> His joys, his griefs, have vanished like a cloud
> From Skiddaw's top ... [4]

The verses are an attempt to tag Southey culturally – to pigeonhole him as a 'Lake' writer, though one cast in a very different mould from Wordsworth himself. Yet they overlook the contingencies of literary history, the inconvenient (to Wordsworth) fact that Southey's residence in Keswick came about by unhappy accident rather than design. As a result they obscure Southey's earlier regional affiliations – his connections to Bristol and the West Country, his birthplace and the cradle of his literary ambitions. This is a tendency that has largely continued to the present day. Although the current resurgence of Southey's reputation has exposed the problems inherent in defining him as a 'Lake' writer, his earlier, West Country identity has been largely overlooked in preference for a reassessment of his engagement with the colonial and exotic.[5] There is no doubt that Southey is a key figure in the development of Romantic discourses of race and empire. However, he is much more than this. The specifically English, regional aspects of his career are also important indicators of Romantic period culture. This chapter will restore Southey to the West Country and offer a reading that counters both Wordsworth and much recent criticism. It will suggest that although Southey ceased to live in Bristol from 1803, he did not leave it behind and that his West Country connections link his early and late career. In so doing, it will consider how such an act of cultural remapping impacts on understanding of his writings and of the relationships between regional, national and global Romanticism.

I.

Southey was proud of what he once described as 'our western country', and of staking claim to his regional heritage.[6] He was born in his father's shop in Wine Street, Bristol on 12 August 1774. His ancestry was, as he later emphasised, firmly rooted in the West Country. His father's family originated from Wellington, Somerset, where his 'great, great, great grandfather ... was a great clothier ... and had eleven sons who peopled that part of the country with Southeys'.[7] His mother's paternal ancestors, the Hills, were also Somerset-bred, living and dying 'respectably and contentedly upon their own lands in the beautiful vale of Ashton'.[8] Southey did not share their fate. His place of residence post-1803 was fixed – he moved into Greta Hall and lived there until his death in 1843. His earlier life was very different, characterised by mobility. As a child he moved between Bristol and Bath, shuttling between the homes of his parents and fearsome maiden aunt, Miss Tyler. This peripatetic existence did not cease once he was an adult. Between 1794 and 1803 Southey lived on occasion in London, Oxford, Dublin, Spain, Portugal, and the Hampshire village of Burton. Although the majority of his time was spent in the West Country, even there he had no fixed home, living in a series of rented houses in Bath, Bristol, and the village of Westbury-on-Trym. The West Country as an ambivalent space – simultaneously ancestral and impermanent, fixed and somewhere to pass through – was only emphasised by the numerous walking tours Southey took across it, both by himself and in the company of others.

Southey's accounts of these tours provide important evidence of his interaction with his West Country environment, the ways in which he viewed the landscape and the purposes to which he put it. In January 1797, for example, he went to see the Mesolithic skeletons recently discovered at Aveline's Hole, near Burrington Combe, Somerset. He described what he found in two narratives – a private letter to his patron, Charles Wynn, and a public one to the *Monthly Magazine*, where it appeared under the signature 'B.':

> The entrance to the cavern is by a steep descent: from the irregular manner in which the skulls lie, it appears, that the bodies were thrown down carelessly; and I am confirmed in this opinion, by observing, that though the cavern extends one hundred and thirty feet, there are no bones farther in than a body thrown from the aperture would have fallen; none of the smaller bones remain. The skulls are incrusted with Stalactydes, and crumble away when an attempt is made to remove them.[9]

Southey offered his periodical observations as an 'authentic account', in contrast to the more 'exaggerated' speculations found elsewhere in the press, bolstering it with information about other similar discoveries in the area, at Nimlet and Budcombe. He also encouraged readers to provide him with further information 'at what period these modes of sepulture were common'. His public letter is, though, more than an exercise in popular antiquarianism. It reveals the connection between his personal experience of a place and his professional endeavours.

Southey's West Country was inextricably linked to writing. The first decade of his career was founded on the West of England as a centre of literary production and distribution. His first two collections of *Poems* were issued by local publishers: respectively, Richard Cruttwell in Bath, 1795; and Joseph Cottle in Bristol, 1797. The latter also commissioned and published Southey's *Letters Written During a Short Residence in Spain and Portugal* (1797) and *Joan of* Arc (1796 and 1798). The first edition of *Joan* was, indeed, intended as a testament to the capacity and production values of regional publishing. Cottle ordered new type and fine paper in order to produce the 'handsomest book that Bristol had ever yet sent forth'.[10] He also struck off special, larger copies of *Poems* and *Letters* for Southey to distribute to friends. Even later in the 1790s, when Cottle's business failed and Southey moved to the London firm of Longman and Rees, these local book-production connections were not severed. Rees had himself been a bookseller in Bristol and continued to make use of regional printers. It was the provincial firm of Biggs and Cottle which printed Southey's third collection of *Poems* in 1799, and subsequent new editions of this and the 1797 collection in 1800 and 1801, the second edition of *Letters Written During a Short Residence in Spain and Portugal* (1799), both volumes of the *Annual Anthology* (1799 and 1800), the Islamic romance *Thalaba the Destroyer* (1801), and in 1803 his edition of Chatterton and translation of *Amadis of Gaul*. Southey's sense of the valuable professional resources found in Bristol and its environs sharpened when, in autumn 1802, he flirted with the idea of a move to a house in the Vale of Neath, in South Wales. One attraction was its proximity to a canal, with 'regular vessels to Bristol ... a fine conveyance for books'.[11] Indeed, when he did move to Keswick, Southey missed his friends, pets, books (which had been stored in Bristol) and 'James the bookseller'.[12] His lament suggests that, at least in the early months, he found that being a poet resident in the Lakes was a professional loss rather than a gain.

The West Country provided Southey with more than easy access to the mechanics of literary production. It also allowed him to engage in cultural networks. In the mid-1790s, Cottle's shop in Bristol was a meeting place for local literati and a repository for their works-in-progress. A copy of Southey's *Madoc*, for example, seems to have been kept there and, as a result, even when unpublished, the poem had some currency in local literary circles.[13] Southey's participation in regional networks was also manifested in his appearances in and contributions to publications by fellow local authors. His dedicatory poems to Amos and Joseph Cottle appeared in 1797 and 1798, respectively; and in 1799 his responses to nitrous oxide were documented by Thomas Beddoes.[14] His commitment to and central role in Bristolian culture emerges most clearly in the *Annual Anthology*, published in 1799. The volume, intended by Southey as the first of a series, proclaimed its local origins and internationalist ambitions. It was the appropriation of a German model, *Almanacks of the Muses*, by an English, regionally based writer. Printed by the Bristol firm of Biggs and Cottle (who were also designated as the recipients of any future contributions), the first *Annual Anthology* contained a series of poems on West Country subjects: a sonnet on Stonehenge (by 'the late ROBERT LOVELL'); Humphry Davy's 'Ode to St Michael's Mount' and an extract from his unfinished 'Mounts-Bay'; and Joseph Cottle's inscription 'Copied from the Wall of the Room in Bristol

Newgate, where Savage died'.[15] In addition to Davy, Lovell, and Cottle, the volume included contributions by other Bristol-based authors, including Amos Cottle, Thomas Beddoes and Southey himself.

As the contents of the *Annual Anthology* suggest, for Southey the West Country was not just a site of literary production and networking. Its places, people, history, and legends played a significant part in the poetry he produced in the first decade of his career. Between 1795 and 1803 he published a series of poems about West Country subjects. These included inscriptions 'For a Cavern that overlooks the River Avon', 'For a Tablet at Silbury Hill', 'For a Monument at Taunton', 'For the Ruins of Glastonbury Abbey', 'For a Monument At King William's Cove, Torbay', and 'For a Monument at Corfe Castle' (see Figure 16). There were ballads on 'St Michael's Chair And Who

Figure 16 The ruins of Corfe Castle, subject of a Southey inscription. From Francis Grose, *The Antiquities of England and Wales* (8 vols, London, 1772–6), ii. [1].

Sat There' and 'The Well of St Keyne'; and sonnets on 'Corston', Lansdown Hill in Bath, and Porlock Vale in North Somerset. Some of his West Country poems – notably 'The Circumstance On Which the Following Ballad is Founded Happened Not Many Years Ago in Bristol', 'The Sailor who had served in the Slave-Trade', 'The Cross Roads', and 'The Ass and His Master. A Circumstance Lately Related in the Provincial Papers' – engaged with recent events in Bristol and the nearby town of Stroud, focusing in particular on the condition of the poor, the alienated and dispossessed. Others, such as 'The Old Woman of Berkeley', invoked local legends. A further group, including an ode to 'The Martins', 'A Morning Landscape' and 'Night', drew upon Southey's experience of West Country homes and landscapes.

The sheer number of poems emerging from, and relating directly or obliquely to, Southey's West Country experience is testimony to the impact of the region upon him. Moreover, his reaction to it was diverse. Southey's responsiveness to landscape, his ability – sharpened by his reading of William Lisle Bowles – to fuse the picturesque with the personal, was acknowledged by his contemporaries. He was, noted George Dyer in 1797, 'remarkable for his powers of description, and for exciting the softer feelings of benevolence'.[16] This is seen very clearly in his 'Inscription for a Cavern that overlooks the River Avon':

> Enter this cavern Stranger! the ascent
> Is long and steep and toilsome; here awhile
> Thou mayest repose thee, from the noontide heat
> O'ercanopied by this arch'd rock that strikes
> A grateful coolness: clasping its rough arms
> Round the rude portal, the old ivy hangs
> Its dark green branches down, and the wild Bees,
> O'er its grey blossoms murmuring ceaseless, make
> Most pleasant melody. No common spot
> Receives thee, for the Power who prompts the song,
> Loves this secluded haunt. The tide below
> Scarce sends the sound of waters to thine ear;
> And this high-hanging forest to the wind
> Varies its many hues. Gaze Stranger here!
> And let thy soften'd heart intensely feel
> How good, how lovely, Nature! When from hence
> Departing to the City's crouded streets,
> Thy sickening eye at every step revolts
> From scenes of vice and wretchedness; reflect
> That Man creates the evil he endures.[17]

Centred on what Southey called 'my cavern' in the Avon Gorge, near Clifton, these lines offer a poeticised south west.[18] The nature inscription, appropriated from Mark Akenside, allows him to move from private to public meditation, to blend the picturesque with the hortatory. It had an immediate impact, eliciting responses from both Coleridge ('This Lime-Tree Bower My Prison') and Wordsworth ('Lines Left Upon a Seat in a Yew-Tree').[19] Wordsworth, and Coleridge's poems represent in their own right powerful and influential ways of engaging with a locality. Southey too was capable of writing in a similar vein: the 'calm ... interrupted by such stirring sounds / As harmonize with stillness' and 'hill and vale and wood' of 'Night', published in the *Morning Post* in 1798, echo the 'calm, that ... disturbs meditation' and 'Sea, and hill, and wood' of Coleridge's 'Frost at Midnight'.[20] However, as David Simpson points out, Southey is fundamentally more 'elusive' and less given to 'wholeness' than his peers.[21] His response to the West Country is more diverse, historically conscious and therefore different from that of Wordsworth and Coleridge. That does not mean that it is less significant or worthy of consideration – but rather indicates that there was more than one way of seeing, that Romantic period writers responded in varied ways to their environments.

II.

In 1799 Southey embarked on a short walking tour of an area often seen as Coleridge's poetic ground – the North Somerset coast near Porlock, at one end of what since 2005 has been called 'The Coleridge Way'. Coleridge had previously described the countryside around Porlock going towards Linton and Linmouth as full of 'woods and waterfalls, not to speak of ... august cliffs, and the vast valley of stones, all which live disdainful of the seasons'.[22] Southey had hoped to take a similar route, travelling from Porlock along coastal paths towards the Valley of the Rocks. However, his guide did something else, something unexpected. As Southey recorded:

> The man was stupid. He conducted me over the hill instead of taking the road nearer the channel, where there are many noble scenes; and what there was remarkable in the barren, objectless track we went he did not point out. I thus lost the Danish encampment where Hubba beseiged Oddune. We past the spot where Kenwith Castle stood; but for which fortress and its gallant defender, the efforts of Alfred might have been in vain, and the tide of our history have flowed in a different channel.[23]

Southey was well-versed in David Hume's *History of England* and knew that in travelling inland from Porlock he was walking through a barren but historically resonant landscape. He was passing the place where in the ninth century Oddune, Earl of Devon, had routed the invading Danes, 'pursued them with great slaughter', killed their leader Hubba and 'got possession of the famous *Reafen* or enchanted standard, in which the Danes put great confidence'.[24] Oddune's victory had in turn given new heart to Alfred the Great, who went on to win a great victory at the Battle of Edington and unite the Wessex nation. Walking through North Somerset in 1799, Southey had invasion and national disintegration on his mind – at an inn in Porlock the evening before passing Kenwith, he had recalled Mother Shipton's gloomy prophecy that 'Porlock Bay / Should old England Betray'.[25] His preoccupation is understandable given the threat posed by revolutionary France and, indeed, Southey was not unusual in drawing parallels between the contemporary situation and the Danish invasions of the ninth century. Joseph Cottle and the Poet Laureate Henry James Pye both did the same thing, writing patriotic epics about Alfred the Great.[26] Southey did not write a national epic, but this does not mean that he was inattentive to English history. What is striking from his 1799 account is his annoyance at the guide's failure to guide, to point out historical landmarks. He was horrified at the prospect that he might have passed unknowingly over spots of overwhelming national significance, places where, if a castle had not been defended and a battle not won, the entire history of the nation would have been different.

In mapping out his own imaginative landscape, Southey was not as 'stupid' as his guide. His West Country was a signposted one – in which the traveller had places of importance pointed out for them. Southey later described 'local history' as consisting of *'every thing* about a parish that can be made interesting, – all of its history, traditions & manners that can be saved from oblivion'.[27] In the 1790s, the poetic vehicle he used most consistently for engaging with 'local history' was the inscription. The West Country inscriptions he produced in this period indicate what he found 'interesting' about the region, marking out a series of historically significant sites – including, Corfe Castle, where King John imprisoned and tortured his opponents; Taunton, where the notorious 'bloody' Judge Jeffreys had pronounced his verdicts on participants in Monmouth's rebellion; the landing place at Torbay, Devon, where 'by the People call'd' William of Orange 'came, to take the Crown the People gave';[28] and the 'Ruins of Glastonbury Abbey' –

>   the holiest spot
> That Britain boasts; here was it, Legends say,
> JOSEPH, who stood beside the cross of Christ,
> Taught her rude dwellers first the lore of life …
>   …   Has thy heart
> Leapt at the songs of Britain's peerless Knights,
> LANCELOT, and PELLENORE, and LAMORACK?
> Here rest his mortal relics, round whose board
> The heroes sat, ARTHUR, heroic King,
> The prowest Monarch, he whose deeds adorn
> The country's ancient annals. Dost thou love

Thy country, and the freedom once her boast?
Here was it, in these moors, that ALFRED lay.
Like to the couching lion, and beheld
Th'invading Danes, and rush'd to victory.
This fabric, Englishman! may emblem well,
The noble structure of the laws he built,
Like this majestic once, and ruin'd now![29]

Southey signposts Glastonbury as 'the holiest ground in England', a place of both local and national significance to 'the religionist, the patriot, and the lover of romance'.[30] His poetic mapping of the West Country erects 'inscriptions to perpetuate the memory of any remarkable event, or deed', to cherish patriots, to upbraid tyrants and to commemorate the 'spot on which any memorable struggle for the welfare, or liberty of mankind had occurred'.[31] In so doing, Southey, himself the product of provincial literary culture, revitalises the inscription for a time of national and international crisis. He turns it into a vehicle for political, social, and cultural commentary, showing how 'powerful incentives to virtue, to patriotism, to intellectual perfection' can be found in a West Country appropriated for the radical cause.[32]

In the 1790s and early 1800s, Southey's West Country was rooted in a radical appropriation of local and national history. His handling of local legends was partial and dictated by his republican politics. For example, he acknowledged the literary potential of Brutus, the Trojan hero who according to local legend had landed at Totnes in Devon, but he refused to engage with it, passing the subject on to friends such as Humphry Davy.[33] Southey felt, perhaps, that a poem about the founder of a dynasty of English kings was ill-suited to his own republican politics. He might also have been deterred by the failure of Alexander Pope and William Browne in tackling the same subject or by the knowledge that another Bristol poet, Ann Yearsley, had got there before him, publishing 'Brutus', an epic fragment, in 1796.[34]

Southey was also aware of the West Country as a place latent with counterfactual historical possibilities – speculating, as on his 1799 walk from Porlock, about what would have happened if history had followed other trajectories. The same held true for its literary possibilities. What Southey did not choose to write about the West Country is in many ways as significant as what he did. Although he realised that 'England should be the home of an Englishman's poem', the West Country was not reimagined in his epics or romances.[35] His explorations of North Somerset did not, unlike those of Coleridge and Wordsworth, result in a plan along the lines of 'The Brook': 'a subject ... that should give equal room and freedom for description, incident, and impassioned reflections on men, nature, and society'.[36] Southey's West Country did, though, feature in several projected but unwritten poems. These include: an 'inscription by the lime-kiln', to recall the spot in Bristol where in 1795 a poor man had fallen asleep and suffocated; an inscription on a suicide at Sea-Mills; eclogues on Southey's grandmother's home in Bedminster and the felling of the 'long road-elms on the common near Wellington'; and a 'deeply interesting poem of domestic feelings' on his Somerset forefathers.[37] There was also an inscription on 'Kenwith Castle', reminding the reader of what might have happened if the castle had after all fallen to Danish invaders.[38] Another projected West Country poem, but this one on a much larger scale, owed its origins to the same 1799 tour of North Somerset that had inspired the Kenwith inscription.

In August 1799, leaving his 'stupid', historically illiterate guide behind, Southey had walked to the Valley of the Rocks. His reaction to what he saw there was recorded in a letter to Humphry Davy. It was

> strange & magnificent which ought to have filled the whole neighbour-hood with traditions of giants & devils & magicians. but I could find none – not even a lie preserved ... & there my conjectures rested – or rather took a new direction to the Preadamite Kings, the fiends who married Diocletians fifty daughters – their giant progeny – old Merlin & the builders of the Giants Causeway. For the next Anthology I project a poem on our Clifton Rocks.[39]

What is striking is how Southey responds to the mythic associations of the site, and segues from this into the cultural codification of those myths in Milton's 'History of Britain'.[40] His disappointment at finding none of these traditions preserved within the 'whole neighbourhood', at the failures of the local populace to maintain and transmit indigenous stories, explains his final reaction – a proposal for a poem not on the Valley of the Rocks but on the more local (to Southey) geological formations of the Avon Gorge, near Clifton and Bristol. These were also known as 'St Vincent's Rocks', and a sketch in Southey's *Common-Place Book* suggests what his 'fine local poem' might have done:

> It might begin by saying why I ought to celebrate them. The camp, my cavern, the legend of the building to which there leads no path, Cook's folly and its tale, the suicide at Sea-Mills ... Chatterton. Bristol, too, might have its fame. And Ashton might be mentioned. The hot wells, and those who come to die there.[41]

This brief note for an unexecuted poem sums up Southey's engagement with the West Country. It demonstrates how the place that witnessed Southey's birth as a writer was made up of the interplay between a series of complex elements: regional landscape; personal experience ('my' cavern, the ances-tral site of Ashton); local history (the Roman camp at the top of the Avon Gorge);[42] local legends (the tale of a local man called Cook who, terrified of snakes, locked himself up at home, only to be bitten by a viper hidden in a

Figure 17   Philip James De Loutherbourg, *Part of the Avon Gorge at Clifton, with a Kiln on the Cliff Edge* (1786 or 1800) © Tate, London 2009. In the 1790s Southey had thought of commissioning De Loutherbourg to illustrate his works. Both St Vincent's Rocks and Bristolian lime-kilns were the subjects of later proposed, but unwritten, poems by Southey.

stack of fire-wood);[43] present events (a man who in 1797 drowned himself in the Bristol docks and left behind a journal inscribed on the walls of his room);[44] and literature (the ever-present spectre of Chatterton). It shows that for a young, ambitious poet, the West Country was full of potential – a territory to be written about and a place central to local, and indeed national, history and identity (see Figure 17).

III.

Southey's move to Keswick in 1803 represented a decisive and deliberate physical break with his West Country past. Although he did revisit Bristol, notably in 1808 when he met Walter Savage Landor, he never lived there again. Yet a physical disconnection was not the same as an emotional or professional one. In terms of his literary career, Southey never broke with or repudiated his West Country days, and in the years following his move to Keswick, he continued to return to the poetic productions of his earlier years.

So what did he do? Southey passed over some West Country poems, especially those first published in the *Morning Post*. He neither revised them nor included them in the collected editions of his self-styled 'minor', i.e. shorter, poems published in 1805, 1815, 1823 and 1837–8. Others, however, took on what might be described as a West Country afterlife, and were revised and republished throughout the remainder of his career. Southey's revisions were as varied as the types of genre he had engaged in when writing about the West Country. His two Cornish ballads 'The Well of St Keyne' and 'St Michael's Chair' underwent a transformation, not in the actual text of the poems but in their paratexts. When first published in the *Morning Post* on, respectively, 3 December 1798 and 27 April 1799, neither poem had an epigraph. This did not remain the case. When 'The Well of St Keyne' was republished by Southey in the 1799 *Annual Anthology*, it was accompanied by a new headnote, derived from Thomas Fuller's *History of the Worthies of England* (1662):

> *I know not whether it be worth the reporting that there is in Cornwall, near the parish of St. Neots, a Well arched over with the robes of four kinds of trees, withy, oak, elm, and ash, dedicated to St. Keyne. The reported virtue of the water is this, that whether husband or wife comes first to drink thereof, they get the mastery thereby.*[45]

The epigraph makes it clear – as had not been the case in the *Morning Post* version – that the ballad that follows plays out as comedy a specifically Cornish 'rustic superstition' that

> If the husband of this gifted Well
>   Shall drink before his wife,
> A happy man thenceforth is he
>   For he shall be master for life.
>
> But if the wife should drink of it first
>   God help the husband then![46]

The quotation from Fuller thus geographically locates a poem whose local connections had previously been implicit rather than explicit. Southey did not stop here. His concern with embedding the regional affilia-tions of his ballad continued, and when he came to revise 'The Well of St Keyne' for republication in his 1815 *Minor Poems*, he expanded the Fuller headnote into a five-and-a-half-page compilation of information distilled from Carew's *Survey of Cornwall* (1723), Serenus Cressy's *Church History of Brittany* (1668), and William Owen's *Cambrian Biography* (1803).[47] His other Cornish ballad 'St Michael's Chair' was similarly altered. Although it appeared without any paratextual materials in the *Annual Anthology* (1799), *Metrical Tales* (1805), and *Minor Poems* (1815 and 1823), when revised for inclusion in Southey's final, self-canonising *Poetical Works* (1837–8), a new headnote was added, a two-page quotation from John Whitaker's 1804

Supplement to Richard Polwhele's *History of Cornwall*.[48] This made it explicit that Southey's blackly comic ballad of marital strife drew upon a legend connected to St Michael's Mount in Cornwall, and not to any other place named after the saint. This practice of annotation, of giving a popular and populist form cultural authority, connects Southey's ballads to those collected by Thomas Percy and Joseph Ritson. Yet by ensuring that his ballads were '"*well-authenticated*"', something he had publicly found lacking in Wordsworth's 'Goody Blake and Harry Gill', Southey also pulled their regionality into greater focus.[49]

Southey's investment in the annotated, regional ballad highlights potential connections with the seemingly more elite genres deployed in his annotated, avowedly internationalist epics, suggesting subtle linkages between 'The Well of St Keyne' and the revisionist epic *Madoc*. Southey's inscriptions took a different route. He had always been convinced that the genre literally spoke for itself – that it conjured up place and past without any need for authorial mediation in the form of notes or prefaces. As a result, his inscriptions had never been heavily annotated, often lacking any notes at all. Indeed, at exactly the point when he was adding headnotes to his ballads, Southey stripped any residual paratextual material from his West Country inscriptions. 'For a Monument at Silbury-Hill', for example, had originally included a footnote, derived from Paul-Henri Mallet's *Northern Antiquities* (1770), on the burial practices of the 'Northern Nations'. This was removed in 1815 and nothing was put in its place.

However, he did more than this. Southey composed relatively few new ballads after his move to Keswick, but the inscription remained an important vehicle for him until the end of his writing life. He built upon the foundations laid during his West Country years, producing two entirely new sequences – an incomplete series on the Peninsular War and three inscriptions for Thomas Telford's Caledonian Canal linking the east and west coast of Scotland:

> Athwart the island here, from sea to sea,
> Between these mountain barriers, the Great Glen
> Of Scotland offers to the traveller,
> Through wilds impervious else, an easy path,
> Along the shore of rivers and of lakes,
> In line continuous, whence the waters flow
> Dividing east and west. Thus had they held
> For untold centuries their perpetual course
> Unprofited, till in the Georgian age
> This mighty work was plann'd, which should unite
> The lakes, control the innavigable streams,
> And through the bowels of the land deduce
> A way ... [50]

As his hymn to Telford's achievements shows, in his later years Southey used the inscription to valorise contemporary feats of engineering and their impact on the landscape, be it regional, national or, as in his Peninsular War poems, international. In so doing, he extended the genre's reach and potential as a potent commentary on the connection between a locale and the ancient and recent past.

IV.

On 24 October 1836, Southey and his eighteen-year-old son Cuthbert left their Lake District home for a seventeen-week tour. Their travels were centred in the West Country. In Bristol, they visited Joseph Cottle, now long retired from publishing and working as an odd-job man in a school run by his sisters. They went from there to Bremhill, where they stayed with William Lisle Bowles; to Taunton, where they visited Southey's eighty-six-year-old aunt Mary; to Nether Stowey, where they stayed with Thomas Poole; to Sir Thomas Acland's residence near Exeter; to the home of Southey's old school friend Nicholas Lightfoot at Crediton; and finally to the house of Southey's nephew, Derwent Coleridge, at Helston in Cornwall. The weather was not always favourable. Southey and his son witnessed the effects of the 'great hurricane' of 29 November 1836 on the sea at Dawlish, and the 'great snow' of late December prevented an expedition onto Dartmoor.[51] So why did Southey, aged sixty-two and in only moderate health, undertake such an arduous journey?

His reasons were personal and professional. As he explained to Margaret Holford Hodson, he would show Cuthbert 'the scenes of my childhood & early youth' and take the opportunity of examining William Cowper's 'letters to Mr Bagot, which the possessor invites me to do under his roof, tho he will not risque their transmissal any where else'.[52] Editing Cowper rekindled a long-cherished plan to write a poem modelled on *The Task* and, for this, the time Southey spent in Bristol would, he claimed, be especially useful:

> In all likelihood this may be my last visit to the scenes of my youth, – & as I have long meditated a reflective poem (as desultory as the Task, & yet with the same pervading unity,) for which Bristol should afford title & ... starting ground, – there is this additional reason for wishing to see them once more.[53]

Southey's idea for a poem about Bristol came to nothing and it was added to the catalogue of his unwritten West Country projects. Within eighteen months his health had completely collapsed, forcing him to abandon writing. Yet his turning (or rather returning) in the closing years of his writing life to the idea of a poetic celebration of the place of his birth and his birthplace as a writer, is evidence of the continued importance that Bristol and indeed the West Country as a whole had for him. This significance also echoes through the project Southey began on his arrival back in Keswick in February 1837: a collected edition of his poetry.

This was Southey's chance to set his 'house in order', to present himself to posterity.[54] When he compiled this final collection, Southey ensured that the productions of and about his West Country years featured prominently: including poems about Silbury Hill, Taunton, Corston, Porlock, and Bristol and its environs, as well as numerous others produced during his residence in the West of England. The 1837–8 edition is a last attempt by Southey to reclaim – to take possession of – his own literary and regional past. Moreover, its mixed economy – the combination of epic and ballad, of poems on epochal events such as the battle of Waterloo and on local incidents such as the funeral of a hated Bristol Alderman – presses Southey's claim as a writer produced by and writing for a culture to whom the international, the national, *and* the regional all matter.[55]

Southey himself is currently being repossessed – his significances to Romantic period writing revealed and reinterpreted. It is important to recognise that such acts of reclamation involve revisiting and remapping *all* his poetic territories and that in so doing, the landscape of Romantic period culture is itself refined. The new Southey criticism should, then, inhabit not just the exotic domains of *Thalaba* and *The Curse of Kehama*, but also the haunted streets of Bristol and the history-infused fields, hills, and coast of Robert Southey's West Country.

Notes

1. R. Southey to T. Southey, 29 August 1803, British Library, Add MS 30927.
2. Bodleian Library, Oxford, MS Eng. Poet. e. 10.
3. D. Rivers, *Literary Memoirs of Living Authors of Great Britain* (2 vols, London: R. Faulder, 1798), ii. 372.
4. *Southey: the Critical Heritage*, ed. L. Madden (London and Boston: Routledge & Kegan Paul, 1972), 416.
5. See, for example, C. Bolton, *Writing the Empire: Robert Southey and Romantic Colonialism* (London: Pickering and Chatto, 2007).
6. R. Southey to T. D. Lamb, [c. 31 July 1792], Houghton Library, Harvard, bMS Eng 265.1 (34).
7. R. Southey to J. May, 26 July 1820, *Life and Correspondence of Robert Southey*, ed. C. C. Southey (6 vols, London: Longman, Brown, Green and Longmans, 1849–50), i. 3. Hereafter *Life and Correspondence*.
8. R. Southey to J. May, 1 August 1820, *Life and Correspondence*, i. 10.
9. *Monthly Magazine*, 3 (February 1797),114–15; see also, R. Southey to C. W. W. Wynn, 29 January [1797], National Library of Wales, MS NLW 4819D.
10. R. Southey, *Poetical Works, 1793–1810*, gen. ed. L. Pratt (5 vols, London: Pickering and Chatto, 2004), i. 201.
11. R. Southey to E. Southey, 23 September [1802], *New Letters of Robert Southey*, ed. K. Curry (2 vols, New York and London: Columbia University Press, 1965), i. 289.
12. R. Southey to C. Danvers, October 1803, *Selections from the Letters of Robert Southey*, ed. J. W. Warter (4 vols, London: Longmans, Brown, Green and Longmans, 1856), i. 242.

13. It was, for example, referred to by the lawyer James Losh and poet Romaine Joseph Thorn; see L. Pratt, 'Revising the National Epic: Coleridge, Southey and *Madoc'*, *Romanticism*, 2.2 (1996), 161 n.4.
14. A. S. Cottle, *Icelandic Poetry* (Bristol: J. Cottle, 1797), xxxi–xlii; J. Cottle, *Malvern Hills, a Poem* (London: T. N. Longman, 1798), xiii–xv; T. Beddoes, *Notice of Some Observations Made at the Medical Pneumatic Institution* (Bristol and London: T. N. Longman and O. Rees, 1799), 11.
15. R. Southey, *The Annual Anthology* (Bristol and London: T. N. Longman and O. Rees, 1799), [i], 146, 172–6, 281–6, 279–80. Hereafter, *Annual Anthology*.
16. G. Dyer, *The Poet's Fate, a Poetical Dialogue* (London: G. G. and J. Robinson, J. Johnson and J. Debrett, 1797), 27 n.
17. R. Southey, *Poems* (Bristol and London: J. Cottle and G. G. and J. Robinson, 1797), 57–8.
18. R. Southey, *Common-Place Book*, ed. J. W. Warter (4 vols, London: Longman, Brown, Green and Longmans, 1849–50), iv. 196.
19. See L. Pratt, 'The Literary Career of Robert Southey, 1794–1800', DPhil thesis (2 vols, University of Oxford, 1998), i. 79–84.
20. R. Southey, 'Night', *Morning Post*, 26 September 1798, ll. 1, 2–3, 6; S. T. Coleridge, *Fears in Solitude, Written in 1798, During the Alarm of an Invasion. To which are added, France, an Ode; and Frost at Midnight* (London: J. Johnson, 1798), 19.
21. D. Simpson, 'Locating Southey', *Eighteenth-Century Studies*, 41.4 (2008), 566.
22. S. T. Coleridge to J. Cottle, [early April 1798], *CL*, i. 403.
23. *Common-Place Book*, iv. 520.
24. D. Hume, *The History of England, from the Invasion of Julius Cæsar to the Accession of Henry VII* (2 vols, London: A. Millar, 1762), i. 57.
25. *Common-Place Book*, iv. 520.
26. J. Cottle, *Alfred, An Epic Poem in Twenty-Four Books* (1800) and H. J. Pye, *Alfred; An Epic Poem, in Six Books* (1801).
27. R. Southey to A. E. Bray, 26 February 1831, University of Rochester, MS AS727. Bray responded, addressing her *A Description of the Part of Devonshire Bordering on the Tamar and the Tavy* (1836) to Southey.
28. 'Inscription. For a Monument at King William's Cove, Torbay', *Morning Post*, 23 April 1799, ll. 3–4.
29. 'Inscription. For the Ruins of Glastonbury Abbey', *Morning Post*, 12 October 1798, ll. 1–4, 7–20.
30. R. Southey to E. Southey, 19 May 1799, *New Letters*, i. 194.
31. Nathan Drake, *Literary Hours, or Sketches Critical and Narrative* (Sudbury: J. Burkitt, 1798), 81.
32. Drake, *Literary Hours*, 82.
33. *Common-Place Book*, iv. 17.
34. R. Southey to G. C. Bedford, 12 May 1805, *New Letters*, i. 383. A. Yearsley, *The Rural Lyre; A Volume of Poems* (London: G. G. and J. Robinson, 1796), [1]–27. See also, L. Pratt, 'Tea and National History? Ann Yearsley, John Thewall and the Late Eighteenth-Century Provincial English Epic', in *Peripheries of the Enlightenment*, ed. R. Butterwick, *Studies in Voltaire and the Eighteenth Century* (Oxford: Voltaire Foundation, 2008), 272–5.
35. *Common-Place Book*, iv. 17.
36. *Biographia Literaria*, ed. J. Engell and W. J. Bate, *Collected Works of Samuel Taylor Coleridge*, Bollingen Series 75, 7 (2 vols, London and Princeton, NJ: Princeton University Press and Routledge & Kegan Paul, 1983), i. 195–6.

37. *Common-Place Book*, iv. 192, 199.
38. *Common-Place Book*, iv. 200.
39. R. Southey to Humphry Davy, [4 September 1799], Royal Institution, London, Davy MSS, 27 B/1.
40. John Milton, 'History of Britain', *The Works of John Milton, Historical, Political, and Miscellaneous* (2 vols, London: A. Millar, 1753), ii. 2–3.
41. *Common-Place Book*, iv. 195–6.
42. William Barrett, *The History and Antiquities of the City of Bristol* (Bristol: W. Pine, 1789), 11. Southey's father was a subscriber to Barrett's book (xiv).
43. For Cook's folly, see Rev. George Heath, *The New Bristol Guide* (Bristol: R. Edwards, 1799), 182.
44. *Monthly Magazine*, 4 (October 1797), 321–3. For Southey's interest in this 'dreadful' case see his letter to J. May, 2 November 1797, Cornell University Library, Southey MSS.
45. *Annual Anthology*, 229.
46. *Annual Anthology*, 231.
47. R. Southey, *Minor Poems* (3 vols, London: Longman, Hurst, Rees, Orme and Brown, 1815), iii. 153–8.
48. R. Southey, *Poetical Works* (10 vols, London: Longman, Orme, Brown, Green and Longmans, 1837–8), vi. 69–70. Hereafter *Poetical Works*.
49. R. Southey, review of [S. T. Coleridge and W. Wordsworth], *Lyrical Ballads* (1798), *Critical Review*, 24 (October 1798), 200.
50. *Poetical Works*, iii. 163.
51. R. Southey to J. Cottle, 9 May 1837, *New Letters*, ii. 467.
52. R. Southey to Margaret Holford Hodson, 7 October 1836, Huntington Library, HM 2378.
53. Southey to Hodson, 7 October 1836.
54. R. Southey to Margaret Holford Hodson, 1 March 1837, *New Letters*, ii. 466.
55. 'The Alderman's Funeral', *Poetical Works*, iii. 47–53.

11
Romantic Hydrography: Tide and Transit in 'Tintern Abbey'

Damian Walford Davies

Ever since Marjorie Levinson in *Wordsworth's Great Period Poems* (1986) gave us a portrait of a disingenuous poet who in 'Lines written a few miles above Tintern Abbey' 'artfully assembled'[1] an idealised locus through strategies of displacement and sublimation, commentators have animatedly exchanged views on the poem's geographic and psychic *emplacement*. Sensing that 'Tintern Abbey' 'is an especially difficult work to situate', Levinson sought to 'reconstruct' a 'scene of composition' and reveal the components of an 'observed scene'[2] in order to lay bare Wordsworth's bad faith, his occlusion of the social and his flight into the mind. The landscape above, at, or below Tintern Abbey has been combed in the service of various arguments for and against Levinson's brand of deconstructionist historicism.[3] Despite the clamour of voices, however, the poem's *situatedness* – its *localness or locatedness* in the Wye Valley – has remained stubbornly intact. In part, this is no doubt due to the poem's powerfully presentist modality (its timeshifts notwithstanding), and its sense of a real landscape empirically apprehended: 'The day is come when I again repose / Here, under this dark sycamore'.[4] Indeed, the debate as to the locus of the poem's 'origins', conducted mainly within a New Historicist frame, has fetishised a static paradigm of the relation between poem and landscape, despite the acknowledgement that Wordsworth and Dorothy were energetically on the move from 10 to 13 July 1798.

Though attuned to Wordsworth's anxious sense of 'shifting geographical configurations and changing history', Michael Wiley has emphasised the way in which 'Tintern Abbey' 'brings narrative to a pause at a carefully situated spot and historical moment'. Wordsworth is seen to take 'his famous meditative "stand"', adopting a 'stationary position', even as he speaks of 'both an extended region, ranging from a spot upriver of the rural Abbey ruins to urban areas, and an extended span of time'.[5] Specifically concerned to 'resolve the location' of the poem, David Miall identifies its geographical and imaginative nodal point in the vicinity of Symonds Yat, north of the abbey – a scene whose 'particular configuration', Miall argues, provides an

218

imaginative paradigm for the rest of the poem as 'nature itself models how nature can be understood as a ground for human experience'.[6] Recently, James M. Garrett has recognised how Wordsworth's 'narrative' depends 'on movement through space and time', despite the 'stationary quality' of the poem, which 'gives the illusion of standing still upon a single spot of earth'.[7] But while a number of critics have valuably sought to chart the poem's various 'movements' – meditative, syntactical, structural – such 'motion' has been narrowly conceptualised as an intra-textual phenomenon. And so, despite its 'vagrant' currents, 'Tintern Abbey' has remained grounded in the Wye Valley – and thus, I suggest, delimited.[8] One might say that attempts to recover the originary 'scene' of the poem (elided or not) represent a modern critical incarnation of the obsessive picturesque debate in contemporary guides and tours regarding the most advantageous position from which to achieve a view of Tintern Abbey itself.[9] Further, I suggest that continued critical haggling over the poem's precise location along a corridor of around 22 miles (say from Chepstow to Goodrich) succumbs to the very Romantic Ideology that so much commentary on 'Tintern Abbey' has sought to expose and explode.

My aim here is to replace the 'static' model of composition identified above with a more kinetic conception of the poem's multiple locations. I suggest that the poem is dynamically constituted by motion through the various topographies of its composition. Thus we are able to see 'Tintern Abbey' not merely as a poem of the Wye and of walking, but also as a 'tidal' utterance of the Severn Estuary, the Avon, and the West Country, even as a 'suburban' utterance of Bristol. I argue that the poem is crucially conditioned by tidal action, in both literal and figurative senses, and my hydrographic reading seeks to reveal the poem's response to and calibration of actual water depths and speeds of flow. Indeed, composed at the end of the very decade in which, like the 'national work' of the Ordnance Survey,[10] hydrography was officially and professionally recognised in Britain (Alexander Dalrymple became the first Hydrographer to the Admiralty in August 1795[11]), the poem is itself a hydrograph, a verbal chart of the littoral, riverine, inter-tidal, estuarine, and marine topography over which it can be seen to move, and a textual inscription of the various border crossings that Wordsworth negotiated during its peripatetic composition. In addition, a tidal hermeneutic allows us both to confirm and to contest some of the assumptions of New Historicist readings of the poem. Over and above its supposed pantheism, its 'pictures of the mind', 'Tintern Abbey' represents a compelling psycho-geographical chart.

The composition history – one might say composition geography – of 'Tintern Abbey' during the period 10–13 July 1798 is not easily recovered since Wordsworth left us with 'alternate recollections' of the process.[12] According to the Isabella Fenwick note, he began the poem 'upon leaving Tintern, after crossing the Wye' on 13 July, and 'concluded it just as [he] was entering Bristol in the evening, after a ramble of 4 or 5 days' with Dorothy. Wordsworth added: 'Not a line of it was altered, and not any part of it written down till I reached Bristol.'[13] However, in a letter of September 1848, the Duke of Argyle informed the Rev. T. S. Howson that Wordsworth had told him that 'he had written *Tintern Abbey* in 1798, taking four days to compose it, the last 20 lines or so being composed as he walked down the hill from Clifton to Bristol'.[14] Further contradictory evidence appears in Christopher Wordsworth's *Memoirs of William Wordsworth* (1851):

> We crossed the Severn Ferry, and walked ten miles further to Tintern Abbey ... The next morning we walked along the river through Monmouth to Goderich [*sic*] Castle, there slept, and returned the next day to Tintern, thence to Chepstow, and from Chepstow back again in a boat to Tintern, where we slept, and thence back in a small vessel to Bristol.[15]

Crediting the evidence of the Fenwick note, John Bard McNulty in 1945 drew the logical conclusion that 'Tintern Abbey' was composed partly – indeed, mostly – on board the 'small vessel' that carried Wordsworth 'across the Severn Estuary and up the River Avon to Bristol'[16] – an intriguing possibility that critics have not pursued. Even the 'orthodox' critical position – which takes its cue from Mary Moorman's 1957 biography and Mark L. Reed's meticulous 1967 chronology in accepting the itinerary outlined in the *Memoirs* and in assuming that the poem was 'probably' begun on 11 July as Wordsworth walked north to Goodrich and completed on the evening of 13 July[17] – entails the recognition that 'Tintern Abbey' was partly composed on river and estuary water, both eddying with tidal currents. This fact, I suggest, has 'no trivial influence' ('Tintern Abbey', l. 33) on our understanding of the poem. In the argument that follows, I accept the 'received' interpretation, sketched above, of Wordsworth's movements and of the chronology of the poem's composition.

The Wye Valley: shifting scape, kinetic space

A notable feature of contemporary tours of the Wye Valley is the way in which the landscape itself is conceived as motile, and movement is established as crucial to an aesthetic appreciation of the scenery. This is observable not merely in those tours describing the fashionable boat trip from Ross through Monmouth to Chepstow, in which one would expect motion to constitute a defining aspect of tourists' experience of the Wye. Contributing to this sense of the shifting nature of the terrain was the status of the Wye Valley as uncanny frontier land and borderspace, and of the Wye and the Severn as literally fluid lines of demarcation (or rather areas 'constantly undergoing processes of both fixing and blurring'[18]) between Wales and the West Country, and between Gloucestershire and Monmouthshire. Legally and culturally, Monmouthsire itself, of course, has always been a 'debatable'[19] land of hybrid identities and ambiguous cultural allegiance, described by William Coxe in his *Historical Tour in Monmouthshire* (1801) as 'the connecting link between England and Wales; as it unites the scenery, manners and language of both'.[20] Observing that in Monmouthshire 'all are *home* views, even where the whole Estuary of the Severn forms a part of the enchanting scene, and the points of the Horizon are the Hills of Glocester [*sic*] and Somerset'[21] (my emphasis), David Williams in his *History of Monmouthshire* (1796) offers a choice illustration of how a borderscape, both *heimlich*/homely and *unheimlich*/other, is experienced as uncanny.

Describing the famous Piercefield walks, south of Tintern, Coxe remarks on the effect of the interrupted vistas created by the mazy Wye, not, as one might expect, in terms of discontinuity, but rather in terms of uncanny transition, sinuous doubling and cultural conveyance:

> The screen of wood prevents the uniformity of a bird's eye view, and the imperceptible bend of the amphitheatre conveys the spectator from one part of this fairy region to another without discovering the gradations … hence at one place the Severn spreads in the midst of a boundless expanse of country, and on the opposite side to the Wy [*sic*]; at another, both rivers appear on the same side … Hence the same objects present themselves in different aspects and with varied accompaniments; hence the magic transition … from the mild beauties of English landscape to the wildness of Alpine scenery.[22]

Charles Heath's popular cento of passages from contemporary tours, *The Excursion Down the Wye from Ross to Monmouth*, first published in 1796, warns the prospective tourist that 'the attention is not suffered to pause long on a particular object, so rapid are the attractions on each bank'.[23] When elements of the landscape were found to 'occur' too tamely, tourists craving the Picturesque had recourse to an imaginative stage-managing of the scene, designed to secure a more dramatic debouching of the natural and built environment into open sight. Thus Richard Colt Hoare sought the theatrical thrill of the kinetic as he boated down the Wye:

> Chepstow castle comes in sight. I could wish the banks before it on the left were covered with wood, as it appears in part only over a narrow neck of land not in a very advantageous point of view; whereas it would break on the sight most nobly and surprize every beholder if it could possibly be hidden till the boat turns the angle.[24]

The proximity of 'break' and 'neck' conspires to offset a sense of leisurely enjoyment and relaxed connoisseurship with a suggestion of radical, exhilarating speed.

Complementing this conception of the Wye as a dynamic chronotope[25] was an acute awareness on the part of tourists of the motion of the river itself and of its tides. Charles Heath's *vade mecum* combines basic hydrography, geology, and poetic discourse as it draws tourists' attention to 'the variety of the current' and to the Wye's water music:

> here, deep, majestic, slow; – there, huddling and brawling over a wide expanse of pebbles; – and now again, foaming over ragged strata of projecting rocks, or eddying round the huge fragments that have fallen from the neighbouring heights ... the pensive wanderer ... admiring, through its transparent stream, the successive strata of sand, of gravel, and of rock, over which it flows, has his ear regaled, in a few hundred paces, with all the varieties of plaintive sound, from the faintest murmurings to the sullen roar.[26]

William Gilpin was also concerned to articulate how the varying speeds of flow, the eddyings and agitations caused by rocks, weirs, cascades, and the contrary actions of flood-tide and river flow, imparted a corresponding motion to the surrounding landscape, animated in a kinetic continuum:

> In all the scene we had yet passed, the water moving with a slow, and solemn pace, the objects around kept time, as it were, with it ... But here, the violence of the stream, and the roaring of the waters, impressed a new character on the scene: all was agitation, and uproar ...[27]

Visitors were also alive to the changing 'complexion' of a river that, to a distance of around two miles north of Tintern, was affected by tidal action. A. M. Culyer, travelling past the limit of the tidal stream in 1807, noted that south of Tintern, the water 'lost that fine transparency, which had distinguished its smoother parts above Llandogo',[28] while Henry Skrine, standing on the Gloucestershire side of the Severn Estuary a few years later, was attuned not only to the 'new beauties' of the riverscape near the Severn's confluence with the Wye south of Chepstow (see Figure 18), but also to the way in which the estuarine water was becoming 'more and more influenced by the tide'.[29] As R. J. Fertel has argued, Wordsworth's footnote to the opening movement of 'Tintern Abbey' that ends with the phrase 'With a sweet inland murmur' – 'The river is not affected by the tides a few miles above Tintern' – marks his empirical awareness (Fertel calls it a 'humble recognition') that 'sweet' – that is, 'fresh' – water 'would murmur and roll differently from salt water'.[30] The line, and the note, signal a sensitivity to riverine and estuarine tidal action that interfuses the poem as a whole and provides an interpretive paradigm that allows us to chart in 'Tintern Abbey' the fluxes and refluxes of Wordsworth's 'tidal' sensibility. Levinson's statement that 'Tintern Abbey' is 'a transitioning, a liminal poem, delivered by a man who

Figure 18 Amelia de Suffren, *From Piercefield Walks* (the junction of the Wye and Severn); aquatint, May 1802.

situates himself at a junction of inland waters and ocean tides'[31] (a position he would adopt again at the end of the 'Intimations' ode: 'Hence, in a season of calm weather, / Though inland far we be, / Our souls have sight of that immortal sea / Which brought us hither') is a valuable insight. My concern is to examine the ways in which the poem itself registers the pull of bodies of water that are, at the same time, bodies of knowledge and feeling.

'Streaming infrashapes'

Wordsworth, McFarland remarks, was 'virtually hypnotized by the idea of running water'.[32] Critics have long recognised the centrality of the paradigm of the stream to Wordsworth's imagination, and analysis of the form and characteristic movements of 'Tintern Abbey' has often, unsurprisingly, invoked and internalised metaphors of flow. Seeking to understand Wordsworth's identification of the poem as fundamentally 'odal' – 'I have not ventured to call this Poem an Ode; but it was written with a hope that in the transitions, and the impassioned music of the versification would be found the principal requisites of that species of composition'[33] – Stuart

Curran speaks of the poem's 'dialectical transition[s]' and the 'course' of its argument; 'no movement in the poem is without counterflow', he remarks, and 'Everything Wordsworth celebrates must be *eroded*'[34] (my emphasis) – as if the speculativeness of the poem's current is wearing away its banks and bedrock of certainty and hope. Pamela Woof's reading emphasises 'The river-like flow, the flux and re-flux that is the movement of the poem'; Wordsworth's rhythms are felt to 'surge onwards'.[35] Identifying 'Tintern Abbey' as 'a living embodiment of the movement of a stream', McFarland has argued that the poem 'overlie[s] a streaming infrashape' (as, he suggests, does the longer Romantic lyric generally). He detects in the general 'flow' of the poem – sustained by enjambment, polysyndeton and apposition – an 'ineluctable' current, and describes syntactic and conceptual movements as local 'eddies' and 'streams'.[36] Though clearly recognising that riverflow powerfully infuses the structure of the poem, these critics are concerned with the symbolic, intra-textual resonances of the phenomenon, rather than with the ways in which the poem, as a physico-verbal cartograph, bears traces of Wordsworth's contact with shifting river- and estuary-scapes. A hydrographic reading of 'Tintern Abbey' that emphasises the particularity of the flow conditioning the propagation of its syntactic and conceptual tides must deploy a new technical vocabulary in order to chart Wordsworth's 'hydrodynamic' responsiveness. The fact that some reaches of 'Tintern Abbey' were without doubt composed on water legitimises a bathymetric 'sounding' of the poem. Such a reading answers Franco Moretti's call for a pioneering 'literary geography' that 'choose[s] a unit' of a text, 'find[s] its occurrences', and then 'place[s] them in space'[37] in order to analyse how geography shapes the verbal ground of a literary work. Thus my charting of 'Tintern Abbey' extends Moretti's experimental, experiential criticism, which makes 'systematic use of maps',

> not as metaphors, and even less as ornaments of discourse, but as analytical tools: that dissect the text in an unusual way, bringing to light relations that would otherwise remain hidden.[38]

Charting 'Tintern Abbey'

The precise hydrography informing Wordsworth's tidal imagination in 'Tintern Abbey' can be extrapolated with astonishing precision, employing data generated by XTide open source Tidal Prediction software, which uses tidal algorithms developed by the US National Oceanic and Atmospheric Administration. Each graph in Figure 19 shows the height in metres of the flood and ebb-tides in the Severn Estuary (Avonmouth being the tidal gauge) over 24 hours, the four graphs, taken together, covering the period 10–13 July 1798.[39] The dark- and light-shaded areas under the tidal curve denote the flood- and ebb-tides respectively, and the dark and light zones above the curve mark night and day. This data set enables us to deliver 'Tintern Abbey' from the prison-house of the Wye Valley (an incarceration perpetuated by New Historicist debates), and to read it as a poem responsive to plural topographies. If my charting of Wordsworth's geographical position in relation to the contours of 'Tintern Abbey' appears dogmatic – another inscription of the acts of emplacement cited above – the reader should bear in mind that the boundaries drawn between the poem's movements are necessarily approximate and therefore permeable and negotiable. As Schimanski and Wolfe remind us, borders are not only 'divides' but 'joins, fuzzy areas, overlaps, in-between zones'[40] in textual as in topographical terms; as Lamont and Rossington argue, a border is always a 'notional line, inviting discussion as to what it separates and what are the possibilities and consequences of crossing it'.[41]

The boat carrying Wordsworth and Dorothy across the 'Old Passage' over the Severn from Aust to Beachley on 10 July 1798 would most probably have waited for low tide's 'slack water' – 'The time at high or low water when the tide is not flowing visibly in either direction' (*OED*) – which occurred at 10.32 a.m. (see Figure 19, Graph 1). Disembarking at Beachley, they headed north, crossing the remnants of Offa's Dyke – the ancient boundary between Mercia and Wales – near Sedbury, before proceeding up on the Gloucestershire side of the Wye, near or even on Offa's Dyke in places, and crossing the river (whose southward flow was by now contending with the flood-tide, its fresh water increasingly interfused with estuary salt) to Tintern and into Monmouthshire. Thus before he began to compose 'Tintern Abbey', Wordsworth had negotiated a number of significant, and palpable, borders, and I suggest that such 'passages' are a feature of 'Tintern Abbey' as a whole.

Wordsworth travelled north on the Monmouthshire/Welsh side of the river on 11 July, past the limit of the tidal stream, hence his footnote to the first 'passage' of the poem. It is on this day that he is likely to have begun composing 'Tintern Abbey'. For some two miles north of Tintern, his journey that morning would have been attuned to the harmonics of an ebbing tide (see Figure 19, Graph 2). There is a sense in which the persistent enjambment of the opening 23 lines of the poem enact the *downward* tidal ebb and the natural *southward* flow of the Wye. That recognition aligns the motivated flow of the poem-river with the direction of the 'ebbflow' of reading itself, thus drawing the reader southwards as the location of the poem tracks northwards – a psycho-geographical counterflow that is there also in Wordsworth's 'present' act of recalling his past ('Once again / Do I behold these steep and lofty cliffs …'). 'Thoughts of more deep seclusion' (l. 7) is Wordsworth's first inscription of an awareness of – and an anxiety about – *depths* in the poem, submerged in synaesthetic collocations. Developing his insight that 'Space acts upon style' in an analysis of Sir Walter Scott's fiction, Moretti suggests that

> Although the novel usually has a very low 'figurality' … near the border, *figurality rises*: space and tropes are entwined; rhetoric is dependent upon space.

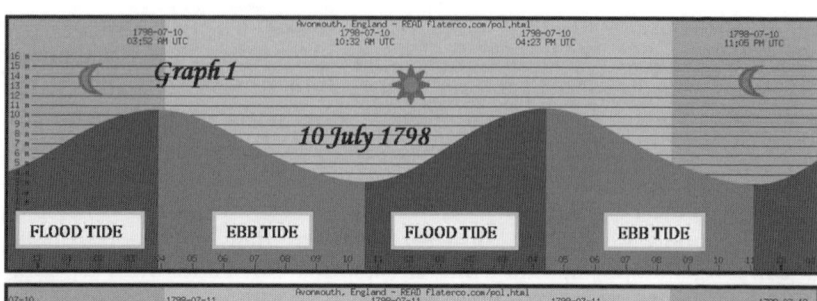

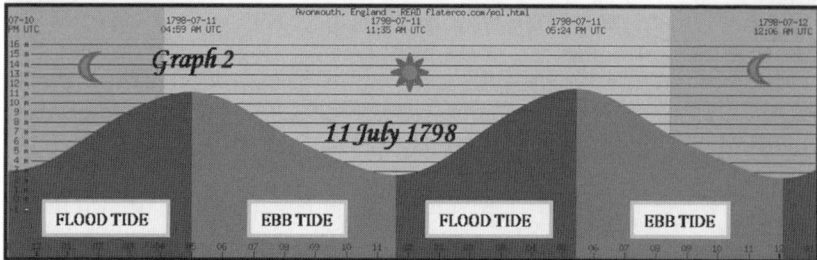

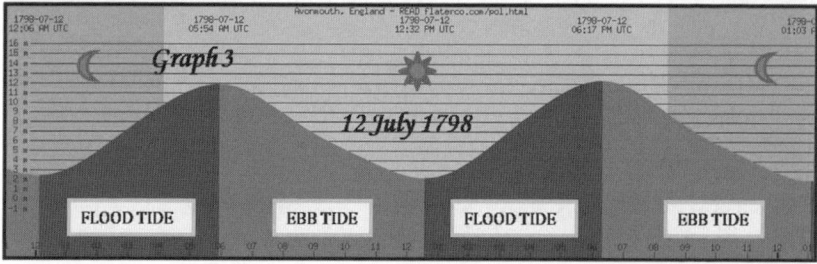

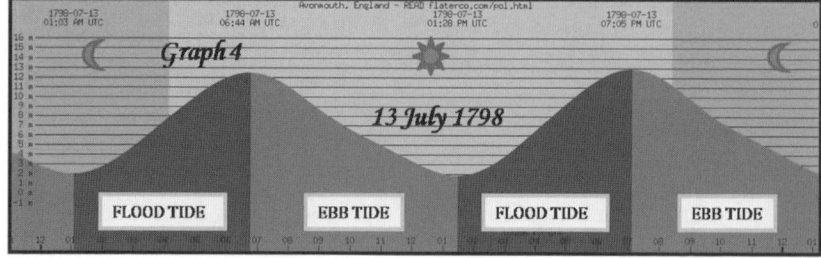

Figure 19   XTide (version 2.10) open source tidal prediction (centred on Avonmouth) for 10–13 July 1798; http://www.flaterco.com/xtide.

An 'impact' with a border generates a 'figural leap'.[42] Wordsworth's much-debated 'vagrant dwellers' and his hermit-figure (ll. 21–3) – unconscionable (as some would have it) sublimations of 'actual' knowledge – may, in Moretti's paradigm, signal the figural 'leap' occasioned by Wordsworth's negotiation of two further borders on 11 July – the crossing of the Wye at Monmouth and the entry into Herefordshire, south west of Symonds Yat. Indeed, the opening paragraph of 'Tintern Abbey' as a whole displays a deepening commitment to the figural. Though the crossing of county boundaries (to which contemporary tours were remarkably sensitive[43]) hardly compares with the much anticipated and famously 'missed' border crossing inscribed first as deflationary disappointment and then as imaginative release and insight in Book 6 of *The Prelude*, it may nevertheless have motivated the 'crossings' from the 'analytical predicates'[44] of the poem's opening to the metaphorics that, for so many critics, mark an occlusion of socio-political 'reality'.

The half-line break at line 23 visually denotes a 'border crossing' as both poet and poem strike into new topographical and textual territory, marking the morning of 12 July, as Wordsworth and Dorothy cross back into Monmouthshire and proceed down to Tintern, past the tidal limit near Bigswear bridge. Their journey coincided towards midday with the last of the ebb-tide and the incipient flood-tide (12.32 p.m.; see Figure 19, Graph 3). Wordsworth's composition begins to be affected by an awareness of turning tides, especially since at this point he and Dorothy would have made the decision to proceed to Chepstow and return that afternoon to Tintern by boat on the Wye. The tide's inescapable dialectic makes itself felt in the emotional and syntactic countermotions of the passage, as the lines 'cast doubt on all their positive affirmations by being shadowed by negative words and prefixes, by a modifying "perhaps" or an "I trust" or by verbs in a "may have", subjunctive mode that allows doubt to enter', as Pamela Woof has observed.[45] Wordsworth now measures his deep debt to the Wye Valley's 'forms of beauty' specifically within a hydrodynamic paradigm. Memory's 'sensations sweet' ('sweet' resonating again, as in line 4, with the sense of 'fresh' as opposed to 'saline') operate physiologically as the motion of fluids: 'Felt in the blood, and felt along the heart, / And passing even into my purer mind / With tranquil restoration'; and again: 'the motion of our human blood / Almost suspended' (ll. 29–31, 45–6). Those phrases 'Almost suspended' and 'in the blood' (where, as has often been noted, '*along* the blood' would be expected[46]) are poised between motion and stasis, the adverbial qualification and prepositional *frisson* conspiring perfectly to embody the sense of slack water between the motion of ebb- and flow-tides, when water is itself almost 'laid asleep / In body' (ll. 46–7). In addition, as Wordsworth nears Chepstow, the poem's preoccupation with literal depths deepens, and increasingly clear views of the Severn Estuary give rise to a bathymetry of the spirit – 'the deep power of joy' (l. 49) – that will intensify from this point.

Having reached Chepstow, Wordsworth and Dorothy are likely to have waited until an hour or so after low water at 12.32 p.m. (see Figure 19, Graph 3) so as to use the afternoon flood-tide to convey them to Tintern back up the Wye. The river was now brackish, the incoming tide whirling against the flow of its current. This enables us to identify the energising paradox at the heart of the final compositional movement of 12 July (ll. 50–8). Wordsworth claims that imaginative returns to the 'sylvan Wye' have provided a healing counterforce to 'the fretful stir / Unprofitable and the fever of the world' (ll. 53–4). The increasing flood-tide eddying against the riverflow in an area characterised by an extreme tide differential (noted by contemporary tourists) provides a paradigmatic example of fretful stirring, consonant with the poem's many counterflows, its generic instability ('the oscillation between sonnet and ode', as Philip Cox has argued[47]), and its status as impassioned impromptu.[48] In other words, the Wye is both the epitome of, and the antidote to, febrile agitation.

The paragraph break between lines 58 and 59 is yet another border for Wordsworth and the reader to cross. I suggest it is now the early morning of 13 July; Wordsworth, beginning the longest section of the poem, crosses the Wye at Tintern from Wales/Monmouthshire into England, and as Pamela Woof notes of this movement of the poem (her own critical idiom taking Moretti's 'figural leap'), 'Future, past and present swirl and jockey in the mind.'[49] Negotiating stretches of Offa's Dyke once more as he and Dorothy accompany the morning's ebb-tide to the sea (see Figure 19, Graph 4), Wordsworth conjures past, present and future selves and meditates on mutability, a stone's throw from a river whose switchback waters are the very medium that has enabled him – albeit fitfully, given their changing complexion – to 'see into the life of things'. Figurality rises again as Wordsworth criss-crosses the border-tump of the dyke: 'when *like* a roe'; 'more *like* a man'; 'Haunted me *like* a passion' (my emphases) – three similes in the space of ten lines. And nearing the sea and his point of embarkation for Bristol (either Chepstow or, most likely, Beachley), Wordsworth is again moved to take bathymetric soundings: 'by the sides / Of the *deep* rivers', 'the *deep* and gloomy wood' (my emphases; ll. 69–70, 79). The time of departure in the 'small vessel' approaches, and Wordsworth's reflections on loss and recompense (ll. 86–9) at the landing pier at Beachley are inter-tidal thoughts, motivated by the dramatic displacement in the estuary close to low tide and by its altered water music – 'the still, sad music of humanity, / Not harsh nor grating, though of ample power / To chasten and subdue' (ll. 92–4). The paradox of 'still … music' again captures the 'stand of the tide' at slack water with delicate precision.

And now, sometime around 12.30 p.m. on 13 July (see Figure 19, Graph 4), Wordsworth and Dorothy embark on their journey south across the estuary, so as to catch the last pull of the ebb-tide to assist their passage to the mouth of the Avon. 'Tintern Abbey' is, for the first time, composed on open water, now subject to the convolutions of estuarine tidal currents and to the 'confluent waves'[50] propagated at the Wye's 'embouchure'[51] into the Severn – an area known for its extremely fast tidal currents (see Beechey's striking hydrographic map of 1846, Figure 20). The famous poetic passage on which Wordsworth now embarks responds fully to the physical sensations of the

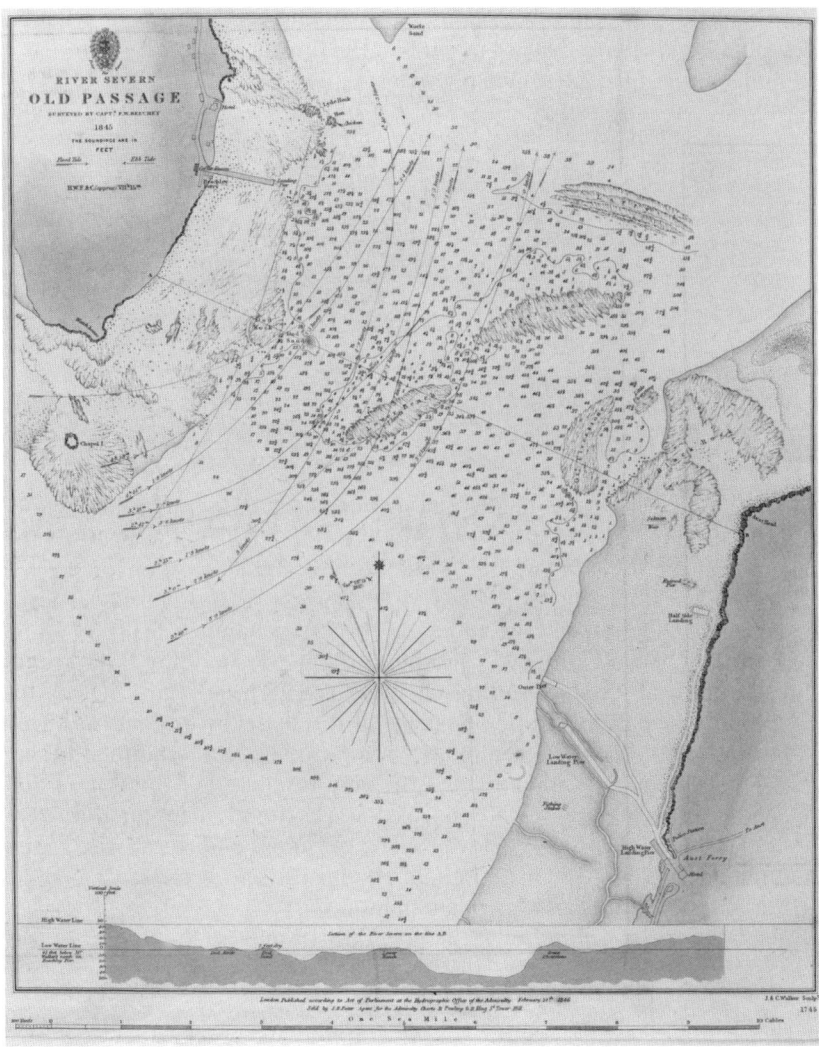

Figure 20   River Severn Old Passage, Surveyed by Captain Beechey; J. & C. Walker sculpt.
(London: Hydrographic Office, 1846). 'Shows drying and submerged banks and
rocks, soundings, direction and speed of tidal flows ... Panel at bottom shows vertical
section of River Severn to 100 feet below high water line.'

estuarine passage on which he has just embarked; Pamela Woof notes that
the lines generate an 'upward movement *propelled* by simple "ands"'; 'We
are *swept* ... into a holding together' (my emphases).[52] Once again, the
critic's evaluative idiom is itself swept up with tidal motion and emotion.

Wordsworth may couch his observations in the past tense, but what he describes is experienced *now* – in, and as, the flow of the estuary, before it is sublimated into pantheist metaphysics:

> And I have felt
> A presence that disturbs me with the joy
> Of elevated thoughts; a sense sublime
> Of something far more deeply interfused,
> Whose dwelling is the light of setting suns,
> And the round ocean, and the living air,
> And the blue sky, and in the mind of man,
> A motion and a spirit, that impels
> All thinking things, all objects of all thought,
> And rolls through all things.[53]
>
> (ll. 94–103)

Simply stated, the passage stands as a remarkable description of tidal action; the motion and the spirit are those of the tides. This is the heart of the poem's pantheist hydrography. With the offing (that portion of the sea 'at a distance from the shore beyond anchorages or inshore navigational dangers', *OED*)[54] now visible, and as he *feels* the channel's depth of water beneath him, Wordsworth takes another bathymetric sounding as he attunes himself physically to 'something far more deeply interfused'. Indeed, his description of 'nature and the language of the sense' as 'The *anchor* of my purest thoughts' (l. 110; my emphasis) betrays an anxiety regarding the very *need* – now, here – for anchors. It is the very instability of the element on which he is moving that conditions his desire at this moment for groundedness: 'Therefore am I still / A lover of the meadows and the woods, / And mountains; and of all that we behold / From this green earth' (ll. 103–6). 'Tintern Abbey' is a shipwreck poem manqué.

Separated at the beginning of the poem's final movement –

> Of all my moral being.
>
> Nor, perchance …

– the two halves of line 112 are a visual trace of the channel into the Avon. The flood-tide is now increasing (see Figure 19, Graph 4), carrying the vessel up the Avon towards Bristol. This turn for home marks the turn to Dorothy, Wordsworth's other 'anchor', and to her companionable form, the tide-governing moon (l. 135). But that turn is troubled: 'Nor, perchance, / If I were not thus taught, should I the more / Suffer my genial spirits to decay' (ll. 112–14). The negatives, the ambivalence of 'Suffer', and the peculiarity of the conception that 'spirit' can 'decay' (pantheist immanence of spirit notwithstanding) all identify these lines as a site of anxiety.

So it is: as the boat was carried between Dungball island (later dredged away) and the Avon Battery and its nearby barracks at the mouth of the river, Wordsworth would have passed between two gibbet-masts, clearly marked on the 1830 Ordnance Survey map (see Figure 21). Whether or not bodies were displayed on them on 13 July 1798, they put Wordsworth in mind of punishment and perishability.[55] Their presence both makes the turn to Dorothy as an emotional sheet-anchor all the more explicable, and reveals the fragility of that act. The echo of Psalm 23 ('Yea, though I walk through the valley of the shadow of death, I will fear no evil; for thou art with me') in the next line – 'For thou art with me' – maps this entrance to the Avon as literally 'the valley of the shadow of death', as opposed to the 'green pastures' of the Wye and its (less than) 'still waters'. A destabilising irony infuses the subsequent reference to 'this fair river' – actually a deathly Avon at flood-tide rather than a verdant, psalmic Wye. Coasting on an increasingly fretful flood between two gallows, Wordsworth needs to feel that he can elevate 'joy', 'quietness and beauty', 'lofty thoughts', 'chearful faith', 'blessings' and 'healing thoughts' above 'evil tongues', 'Rash judgments', 'the sneers of selfish men', and 'greetings where no

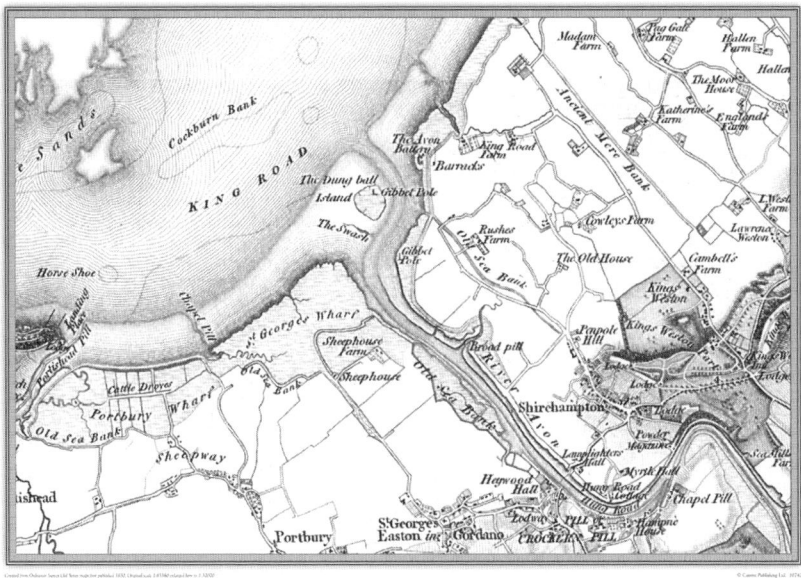

1830 - Old Series

Figure 21 Detail of the 1830 Ordnance Survey ('Old Series') map of Avonmouth, showing the two 'gibbet poles' at the entrance to the Severn Estuary, one on 'The Dungball Island', and the other below it on the north shore. © Cassini Publishing Ltd; www.cassinimaps.com.

kindness is'. Indeed, haunting this boat's return to port with its freight of 'wild eyes' and its emotional cargo of betrayal, judgement, and remedial blessings is the narrative of that other sailor at the mercy of wind and tides: the ancient mariner. The references to 'evil tongues', 'Rash judgments', 'the sneers of selfish men' and 'greetings where no kindness is' (ll. 129–31) may also have been motivated by Wordsworth's contact with the estuary pilots ferrying him home – men described by Richard Warner (who had been ferried across the Severn less than a year earlier, and whose account of his journey Wordsworth had just read), as being 'as rude, turbulent, and violent, as the æstuary they navigate; each individual resembling the Stygian ferryman, described by Virgil'.[56] It is a troubling analogue, since it transforms Warner, and the Wordsworth who remembers him, into dead men.

Disembarking probably at one of the many quays along the Avon, and walking down to Bristol through Clifton, Wordsworth's immediate contact with the tide ceases. And yet the anxious eddies of the mind to which streaming water has given rise continue. The suburban villas of affluent, expanding Clifton provide him with archetypes of ideal (and conservative) inner spaces – 'thy mind / Shall be a mansion for all lovely forms, / Thy memory be as a dwelling-place / For all sweet sounds and harmonies' (ll. 141–3). These structures – material first, before they are transformed into metaphors – are bulwarks against future 'solitude, or fear, or pain, or grief', defences against unwelcome thoughts not merely of Wordsworth's demise in 'after years' ('If I should be, where I no more can hear / Thy voice'

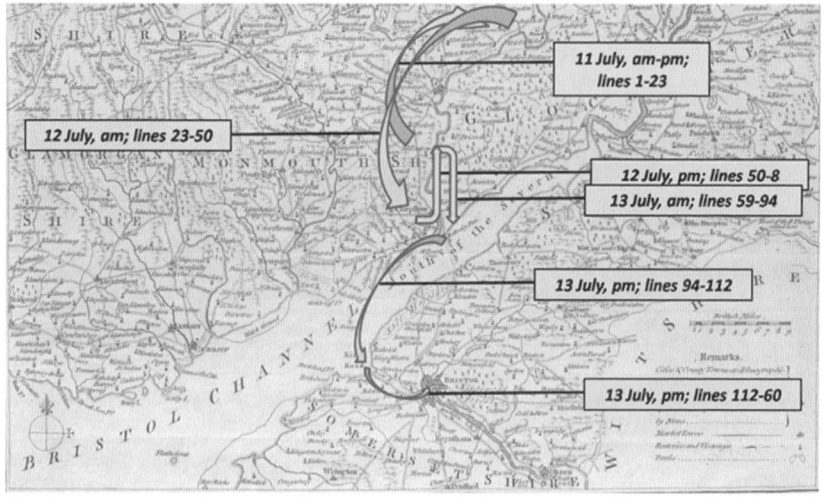

Figure 22   Charting the composition of 'Tintern Abbey', 11–13 July 1798, against Thomas Kitchin's *Map of the Rivers Severn and Wye* (London: R. Baldwin, 1782).

(ll. 148–9), but also of his chilling proximity to 'Rash judgments' and death in Paris at the end of 1792 (the 'poor mistaken and bewildered offering' of Book X of *The Prelude*). '[T]his delightful stream', 'these steep woods and lofty cliffs, / And this green pastoral landscape' (ll. 151, 158–9) are now those of Clifton Gorge to Wordsworth's right, not those of the Wye. Wordsworth, I suggest, is at this point fully conscious of these uncanny foldings and doublings, of what one might call shadow-chronotopes. This 'moving' poem is characterised by chronological and geographical displacements more radical than those figured by paradigmatic New Historicist readings. The poem's values are in flux, just as the poem itself is; 'Tintern Abbey' is *about* the slippage between the apparent and actual referents of its insistent demonstrative adjectives ('this', 'these'). Taking the poem-as-hydrograph out of the critically overdetermined space of the Wye Valley – or rather allowing it to take *us* out of the Wye Valley (see Figure 22) – is to recognise it as amphibious and kinetic, as a profoundly material product of physical sensation. That materiality survives at the very heart of the poem's imaginative transformations in the form of tidal movements that ensure that 'Tintern Abbey' cannot ever petrify into the dogma of the transcendent, or fossilise into the parenthesis of the local. Thus, like the tides, it continues to propagate.

Notes

1. Marjorie Levinson, *Wordsworth's Great Period Poems: Four Essays* (Cambridge: Cambridge University Press, 1986), 32.
2. Levinson, *Wordsworth's Great Period Poems*, 55, 39, 41.
3. See, for example, Thomas McFarland, *William Wordsworth: Intensity and Achievement* (Oxford: Clarendon Press, 1992), 1–33, and Charles J. Rzepka, 'Pictures of the Mind: Iron and Charcoal, "Ouzy" Tides and "Vagrant Dwellers" at Tintern, 1798', *Studies in Romanticism*, 42.2 (Summer 2003), 155–85.
4. Lines 9–10; *Lyrical Ballads and Other Poems, 1797–1800*, ed. James Butler and Karen Green (Ithaca: Cornell University Press, 1992), 116. All quotations from 'Tintern Abbey' are taken from this edition, hereafter *LB*.
5. Michael Wiley, *Romantic Geography: Wordsworth and Anglo-European Spaces* (Basingstoke: Palgrave Macmillan, 1998), 70.
6. David Miall, 'Locating Wordsworth: "Tintern Abbey" and the Community with Nature', *Romanticism on the Net*, 20 (November 2000), http://www.erudit.org/revue/ron/2000/v/n20/005949ar.html, accessed 16 January 2009.
7. James M. Garrett, *Wordsworth and the Writing of the Nation* (Aldershot: Ashgate, 2008), 159.
8. One exception is Andrew Bennett's thoughtful discussion of the tensions in 'Tintern Abbey' between 'composition' (associated with rural perambulation) and 'writing' (as grounding 'urban' condition); see *Wordsworth's Writing* (Cambridge: Cambridge University Press, 2007), 42–57.
9. Compare William Gilpin's remarks in 1770 with those of Richard Colt Hoare in 1797: William Gilpin, *Observations on the River Wye, and Several Parts of South Wales, &c. Relative Chiefly to Picturesque Beauty* (2nd edition, London: R. Blamire, 1789), 47: 'were the building ever so beautiful, incompassed as it is

with shabby houses, it could make no appearance from the river. From a stand near the road, it is seen to more advantage'; The *Journeys of Sir Richard Colt Hoare through Wales and England, 1793–1810*, ed. M.W. Thompson (Gloucester: Alan Sutton, 1983), 83: 'It looks very well from the opposite side of the river.'

10. See Rachel Hewitt, '"Eyes to the Blind": Telescopes, Theodolites and Failing Vision in William Wordsworth's Landscape Poetry', *Journal of Literature and Science*, 1.1 (2007), 5–23; Rachel Hewitt, 'Wordsworth and the Ordnance Survey in Ireland: "Dreaming O'er the Map of Things"', *The Wordsworth Circle*, 37.2 (2006), 80–5; Ron Broglio, 'Mapping British Earth and Sky', *The Wordsworth Circle*, 33.2 (2002), 70–6; and Wiley, *Romantic Geography*, 143–76.

11. See http://www.canfoh.org/Intro&Hist/history_of_hydrography.htm, accessed 16 January 2009, and Andrew S. Cook's *Oxford Dictionary of National Biography* article on Dalrymple, http://www.oxforddnb.com/view/article/7044, accessed 16 January 2009.

12. See Donald E. Hayden, *Wordsworth's Travels in Wales and Ireland* (Tulsa: University of Tulsa, 1985), 27.

13. *The Fenwick Notes of William Wordsworth*, ed. Jared Curtis (London: Bristol Classical Press, 1993), 15.

14. Quoted in *LB*, 357.

15. Christopher Wordsworth, *Memoirs of William Wordsworth* (2 vols, London: Edward Moxon, 1851), i. 117.

16. John Bard McNulty, 'Wordsworth's Tour of the Wye: 1798', *Modern Language Notes*, 60.5 (1945), 293.

17. See Mary Moorman, *William Wordsworth: A Biography. The Early Years, 1770–1803* (Oxford: Clarendon Press, 1957), 402, and Mark L. Reed, *Wordsworth: The Chronology of the Early Years, 1770–1799* (Cambridge, MA: Harvard University Press, 1967), 243. Donald E. Hayden remarks that 'As to questions about the actual date of composition, I think we cannot do better than to follow Reed's suggestions ... This scheme balances Wordsworth's comment that he began the poem as he left Tintern on 13 July with his other comment that he took four days to compose it'; *Wordsworth's Travels*, 32. The one unresolved issue seems to be how far Wordsworth and Dorothy sailed up the River Avon on 13 July before disembarking and walking down the hill from Clifton to Bristol; see McNulty, 'Wordsworth's Tour of the Wye', 291, and Hayden, *Wordsworth's Travels*, 30.

18. *Border Poetics De-limited*, ed. Johan Schimanski and Stephen Wolfe (Hamburg: Wehrhahn Verlag, 2007), 13.

19. Border crossings and the 'debatability' of geographical, historical, and disciplinary boundaries in the Romantic period are at present very much at the forefront of an increasingly devolved Romanticism. See *Romanticism's Debatable Lands*, ed. Claire Lamont and Michael Rossington (Basingstoke: Palgrave Macmillan, 2007), and *Romantic Border Crossings*, ed. Jeffrey Cass and Larry Peer (Aldershot: Ashgate, 2008).

20. William Coxe, *An Historical Tour in Monmouthshire* (2 vols, London: T. Cadell and W. Davies, 1801), i. 1.

21. David Williams, *The History of Monmouthshire* (London: H. Baldwin, 1796), 9. A number of tours remark on the cross-border, trans-county vistas afforded by elevated spots along the Wye Valley and Severn Estuary – for example, T. H. Fielding's *A Picturesque Description of the River Wye* (London: Ackermann & Co., 1841), 32: 'the eye wanders to the distant horizon, as it follows the retiring lines of the blue lands of Somersetshire'.

22. Coxe, *An Historical Tour in Monmouthshire*, ii. 401–2.
23. Charles Heath, *The Excursion Down the Wye from Ross to Monmouth* (Monmouth: C. Heath, 1808), no pagination.
24. *The Journeys of Sir Richard Colt Hoare*, 83.
25. For a suggestive discussion of the operations of a 'tidal chronotope' in Joseph Conrad's *The Heart of Darkness*, see *Border Poetics De-limited*, 217–34.
26. Heath, *The Excursion Down the Wye*, no pagination.
27. Gilpin, *Observations on the River Wye*, 25.
28. A.M. Culyer, *Recollections of a Visit to Llanbeder [sic] in the County of Brecon with Remarks on an Excursion down the River Wye from Ross to Chepstow* (1807); unpublished manuscript tour, National Library of Wales MS 784A,125.
29. Henry Skrine, *Two Successive Tours Throughout the Whole of Wales, with Several of the Adjacent English Counties* (London: J. Turner, 1812), 5–6.
30. See R.J. Fertel, 'The Wye's "Sweet Inland Murmur"', *The Wordsworth Circle*, 16.3 (1985), 134–5.
31. Levinson, *Wordsworth's Great Period Poems*, 46.
32. McFarland, *Intensity and Achievement*, 40.
33. The note was added to the 1800 edition of the *Lyrical Ballads*; LB, 357.
34. Stuart Curran, *Poetic Form and British Romanticism* (Oxford: Oxford University Press, 1986), 76–7.
35. Pamela Woof's 'Introductory Essay' in Robert Woof and Stephen Hebron, *Towards Tintern Abbey: A Bicentenary Celebration of 'Lyrical Ballads', 1798* (Grasmere: The Wordsworth Trust, 1998), 53, 52.
36. See McFarland, *Intensity and Achievement*, 38–40, 47, 51–2, 55.
37. Franco Moretti, *Graphs, Maps, Trees: Abstract Models for a Literary Theory* (London: Verso, 2005), 53.
38. Franco Moretti, *Atlas of the European Novel, 1800–1900* (London: Verso, 1998), 3.
39. For this set of data and many invaluable discussions, I am deeply grateful to Dr Robert Barber, Associate Director of the Centre for Microfluidics and Microsystems Modelling in the Computational Science and Engineering Department at Daresbury Laboratory, Warrington, UK. Regarding the choice of Avonmouth (rather than, say, Beachley) as the data source, Barber notes that 'Avonmouth constants' provide 'a better chance of predicting "historical tides" since the longer data sets used to compute the Avonmouth harmonic constituents ['the harmonic elements in a mathematical expression for the tide-producing force, and in corresponding formulae for the tide or tidal current; each constituent represents a periodic change or variation in the relative positions of the Earth, Sun and Moon'] will probably lead to more stable harmonic constants ['The amplitudes and epochs of the harmonic constituents of the tide, or tidal current at any place'] and therefore better predictions ... XTide predictions for Avonmouth have used 19 years of input data and the subsequent analysis extracted 82 constituents, and the 40 constituents of highest amplitude were then retained for tidal prediction' (personal correspondence). The definitions in square brackets are taken from http://www.waterlevels.gc.ca/english/glossary/H.shtml, accessed 16 January 2009.
40. *Border Poetics De-limited*, 13.
41. *Romanticism's Debatable Lands*, 5.
42. Moretti, *Atlas of the European Novel*, 43, 44.
43. See, for example, *The Journeys of Sir Richard Colt Hoare*, 82 (at Goodrich): 'Division of the two counties a hedge running in a straight direction up the hill; on the

Hereford side fern and wild ground, on the Monmouth side copse wood and tim-
ber. A little further on the left the counties of Hereford and Gloucester are divided
by a little brook'; and 97: 'Follow the road to Crickhowell for about four miles
and enter Brecknockshire, the crossing marked by a boundary stone near the
roadside'; and Culyer, *Recollections of a Visit to Llanbeder*, 104 (near Welsh Bicknor,
south east of Goodrich): 'Having passed the Church, the Boatmen shewed us a
Rock lying in the bed of the river called the County rock, as marking the boundaries of the three Counties of Monmouth, Hereford & Gloucester – from this Point,
the right bank lies in Herefordshire & the left in Gloucestershire.'

44. Moretti, *Atlas of the European Novel*, 44.
45. Woof, Introductory Essay, *Towards Tintern Abbey*, 52.
46. See Christopher Ricks, *The Force of Poetry* (Oxford: Oxford University Press,
1987), 121.
47. See Philip Cox, *Gender, Genre and the Romantic Poets* (Manchester: Manchester
University Press, 1996), 55–6.
48. See J. Bard McNulty, 'Self-Awareness in the Making of "Tintern Abbey"', *The
Wordsworth Circle*, 12.2 (1981), 97–100.
49. Woof, Introductory Essay, *Towards Tintern Abbey*, 54.
50. Fielding, *A Picturesque Description of the River Wye*, 32.
51. *The Journeys of Sir Richard Colt Hoare*, 96.
52. Woof, Introductory Essay, *Towards Tintern Abbey*, 55.
53. David Miall remarks that Wordsworth's 'sense of a "motion" or "spirit" that "rolls
through all things"' is 'reminiscent of the rolling Wye'; see note 6 above. My
contention is that we are dealing with physical *sensation* rather than with a more
abstract 'sense' – fundamentally motivated by, not merely figurally 'reminiscent
of' moving (estuarine, not riverine) water.
54. For an interpretation of the offing as a 'figure of the border', see *Border Poetics
De-limited*, 217–34.
55. The Avonmouth gibbets may also be said to ghost the 'mouldering' 'gibbet-mast'
that Wordsworth was to describe the following year in one of the famous 'spots
of time' in the Two-Part *Prelude*; see Part 1, ll. 288–327.
56. See Richard Warner, *A Walk through Wales, in August 1797* (Bath: R. Cruttwell,
1798), 9–10. As Duncan Wu notes, 'When [Wordsworth] and Dorothy were in
Bath during July [1798], just before setting off on their Wye tour, they ate several meals in Warner's company'; *Wordsworth's Reading, 1770–1799* (Cambridge:
Cambridge University Press, 1993), 143.

12
The Road Not Taken: Robert Bloomfield's Wye Valley and the Poetic Imagination

Tim Fulford

When Robert Bloomfield took a tour of the Wye Valley and the Welsh borders in 1807, he was already established as the best-selling 'pastoral poet' of the age – far better known than Wordsworth and Coleridge, whose *Lyrical Ballads* his own *Farmer's Boy* (1800) outsold by twenty to one. Indeed, in the eyes of contemporaries, it was Bloomfield, rather than the two West Country and Lakeland poets we now call 'Romantics', who had revived both landscape verse (the dominant poetic genre in the 1700s) and Rural Tales (the title of his second, 1802, collection) for the new century. But he had not done so by harvesting the already-poetic landscape of the Wye Valley, which hundreds of tourists had already traversed and which Uvedale Price and William Gilpin had made the epitome of picturesque beauty. For although Bloomfield admired the work of John Dyer, who had imagined the Marches as Siluria – a culturally unique zone in which, since Roman times, British history had been rooted into the landscape (see Goodridge, 1995, 1) – it was, nevertheless, the flatter area of Suffolk that inspired his poetry. Suffolk because it was there, in a small village, that Bloomfield had spent his boyhood and there, in that same small village, that his family still lived. Bloomfield himself, however, did not: his rural poetry detailed his Suffolk youth from a distance; it was a new kind of Georgic not just because it spoke of a world of rural work from the perspective of a labourer rather than a landowner but also because it spoke from the city. Bloomfield's were poems for the new urbanising Britain because they remembered the country from the position of a villager who had, as so many thousands did in the early nineteenth century, emigrated to London. And they did so from a world of sweated labour: Bloomfield's boyhood was an emotion recollected not in tranquillity but in the workshop; he composed verse in his head whilst labouring for hours a day as a shoemaker in an East End garret.

If Bloomfield's poetry gives the lie to Wordsworth's fear (expressed in the Preface to *Lyrical Ballads*) that mechanical labour corrupts, by its very repetitiveness, the taste of the labourer, it nevertheless displays many of the same characteristics as Wordsworth's own verse – a matter not of mutual influence but of similar responses to times in which a commercial and manufacturing culture left many people deracinated and yearning for a half-remembered place of origin – a childhood land in which the power of capital had not yet disturbed the culture or the consciousness. These similar responses included the organisation of verse according to the work-rhythms of shepherds and labourers, the penning of rural tales based on popular ballads and songs, and the addressing of poems to favourite landscapes. Not surprisingly, Bloomfield was an early supporter of Wordsworth's poetry: he had read 'Tintern Abbey' by 1802; like Wordsworth moreover, he sent his new volume to Charles James Fox, the great Whig parliamentarian and enthusiast for pastoral verse, whose political authority resided on his claim to represent the ordinary people.

Despite the similarities, Bloomfield occupied a different position from Wordsworth. Whereas the latter was a Cambridge University gentleman, Bloomfield was a self-educated journeyman. And whereas Wordsworth came into his poetic self by travelling into the already-poetic West Country, Bloomfield arrived at his by dwelling on his former home, the largely unpoetic East England (which had not been previously identified by travellers, tourists, and poets as hallowed ground). Bloomfield, that is to say, had to *make* his locality an authentic site from which Englishness could be derived without the aid of a prior tradition in art and letters on which Wordsworth, near Tintern on the much-toured Wye, could draw. He did so so successfully that, by 1806, his name was being used to market one of the first ancestors of the coffee-table books that, today, picture Wordsworth's Lakeland and Hardy's Wessex. *Views in Suffolk, Norfolk and Northamptonshire Illustrative of the Works of Robert Bloomfield* was a lavish collection of engravings made from specially commissioned sketches of places that featured in the poems: clearly, Bloomfield had turned the obscure villages of his youth into verbal portraits that the middle-classes were prepared to pay to consume visually.

In making Suffolk a place in which a labourer's participation in a traditional rural Englishness could be celebrated, Bloomfield satisfied the pastoral desires of urbanites with sufficient disposable income to buy lavish publications – an expanding market in the early nineteenth century. He also attracted the patronage of the local Whig landowners whose ideology committed them to the idea that they held obligations towards the 'lower orders' who worked on their estates. And it was these men, seizing on Bloomfield's poeticisation of an area much of which they owned, who propelled him into renown. Renown led in turn to independence from the need to labour at his trade, but brought stresses of its own, which were to make Bloomfield disenchanted both with London and with the Suffolk villages of which he was now publicly the poet.

Disenchantment with London stemmed initially from gentlemen's desire to satisfy their curiosity and meet the shoemaker who wrote poetry – to advise him as to his reading, gaze at him, or, worse, expect him to judge their poetry. Resenting becoming a spectacle, Bloomfield could neverthe-less ill-afford to displease his social superiors. He gave up shoemaking and moved out of his East End garret so as to be able to receive polite people's visits with less embarrassment. But he still found even well-intentioned patronage intrusive: in 1803 the Duke of Grafton found him a place at the Seal Office, but the work was so highly pressured it made Bloomfield desperate:

> I expected a busy day at the Seal Office; and so I found it with a vengeance. I had eat no breakfast, and the Mob of Lawyers made me perfectly savage: at One o'clock we shut the Office, but shut in between 40 and 50 people, and did not get through the Work for 3 quarters of an hour after one. I then ... took another 3 hours' Mobbing at the Office, having seald dur-ing the day nearly 1100 Writs! by far the busiest day ... that have occurrd for eight years past. Returnd to my sick house, tired and insufferably disgusted ... – to crown all, a young Man in the neighbourhood fourced on me a M:S. book of poems for me to read and to give my judgment of, which accorded with the feelings of the moment, being a doleful string of Elegies as black as midnight – This I shall call Black Friday – Another trifle had displeased me. I had found in the Morning Chronicle a bit of news put there by some fool or other that 'Bloomfield the poet has been recently appointed to a *handsome* situation in the Seal Office in the Temple, thus he has not courted the Muses unsuccessfully!' ... – tis use-less to be angry, but if the Asses that meddle with another mans business before they know it were buried three times as deep as your poor Wife, I would not were [i.e. wear] black for them. – ... Extreem publicity begins to be more and more disgusting to my feelings, and these boobys make it worse. – ... my cough plagues me, and I have no time to write down my Rhimes, I have enough on my mind to craze a saint ... (Letter 103 of *The Letters of Robert Bloomfield*: to George Bloomfield, 29 February 1803)

A different kind of pressure was exerted by Lord Buchan, who in 1802 invited Bloomfield to his salon of artists but expected him to recite his own verse in front of the fashionable ladies and gentlemen there: moved to tears by his own verse-tale as he did so, Bloomfield was mortified with embarrass-ment, a feeling compounded when, in 1806, Buchan moved to publish his letter of apology without seeking his permission. He ever after took care to avoid social occasions on which he would be expected to sing for his supper as a peasant poet.

Still more depressing were the demands of his Suffolk patron Capel Lofft, the literary gentleman who had, after being shown the manuscript of *The Farmer's Boy* by Bloomfield's elder brother George, overseen its publication. Lofft was a peremptory yet insecure man who, as Bloomfield became successful, began to insist that his own prefaces and notes to the poetry editions must be included in prominent positions. He needed the association with Bloomfield, in fact, to establish his own reputation as a disinterested foster-father of genius and erudite arbiter of taste. But the prefaces and notes were embarrassing, featuring fulsome praise and cranky grandstanding. Bloomfield's publishers and friends wanted them removed. The resulting dispute lasted years, left Bloomfield feeling both guilty and ill-used, and led, in May 1806, to his alienation from George, whom he accused of toadying to Lofft. Since George, who now lived in Suffolk, had been his closest family member, the father-figure who had brought him up in London, the affair was personally traumatic as well as professionally delicate. Afterwards, Bloomfield rarely went to his native village or home county again.

To escape London and Suffolk, Bloomfield took to the hills. When he climbed Box Hill, Surrey, in 1803, during a solitary walking tour, it was the first time he had been in hill country, having previously, like most of the labouring classes, been confined to the fields and the shop where he worked:

> Having been harrassd by too much thinking and too many trivial engagements, and an employment that I shall never like, I determined that I would respire one mouthfull of real country air if possible and I know at the same time that pollution of smoke reaches ten miles round the Metropolis. I had heard much of Leithe Hills and of Box Hill in the neighbourhood of Dorking ... Remember that I am no Welshman, therefore to me these Hills are Cader Idris's and Snowdens. – (Letter 106 of *The Letters of Robert Bloomfield*: to George Bloomfield, 17 April 1803)

The tour put Bloomfield in the position of a Romantic for the first time: a solitary walker travelling as a social, aesthetic, and moral antidote to the effects of modern urban life upon him. It led to no published writing, only to private correspondence, but it made him all the more eager to go west in 1807 when a tour of Wales was suggested by his friend Mary Lloyd Baker of Uley in Gloucestershire.

Lloyd Baker, née Sharp, had written a fan-letter to Bloomfield in 1803. This led to a correspondence and to Bloomfield's warm reception in Lloyd Baker's extended family circle of sisters, aunts, and uncles, based near London and in Northamptonshire. The Sharps were radical Whig gentry (Granville Sharp, the anti-slavery and anti-cruelty campaigner, was Lloyd Baker's uncle) who neither wished to interfere in his publications nor make him recite verses in public. They had no designs upon him, though he remained conscious of their difference in class, power, and education and knew that he could never reciprocate their invitations to their houses. But Bloomfield enjoyed the ladies' attention and readily made his way to Uley, to take the tour in the company of Lloyd Baker, her husband the local landowner, and their friends the Coopers (relatives of the radical surgeon Astley

Cooper). Together, the party then embarked on an elongated version of the already-popular tourist route: they went by road from Uley to Ross, then by boat along the Wye, alighting at Tintern, where Bloomfield's response to the famous ruin was a little different from Gilpin's and Wordsworth's: he neither wished for a mallet to break some of the gables and make the abbey more picturesque nor averted his gaze from the beggars and ironworks that clustered around. Instead, moved too deeply to sit and sketch the arches as his companions did, he 'gave vent to my feelings by singing for their amusement and my own the 104th Psalm' (*Journal of a Tour Down the Wye*, p. 19). The 104th Psalm thanks the Lord for creating the earth. In the King James version Bloomfield knew, it evokes pastoral valleys such as that in which Tintern stands:

He sendeth the springs into the valleys, which run among the hills.
They give drink to every beast of the field: the wild asses quench their thirst.
By them shall the fowls of the heaven have their habitation, which sing among the branches.
He watereth the hills from his chambers: the earth is satisfied with the fruit of thy works.
He causeth the grass to grow for the cattle, and herb for the service of man: that he may bring forth food out of the earth.

(Psalm 104:10–14)

Bloomfield declared of his performance 'though no "fretted vault" remains to harmonize the sound, it soothed me into that state of mind which is most to be desired' (*Journal of a Tour Down the Wye*, 19). 'Fretted vault' is a quotation from the 'Elegy Written in a Country Churchyard' by Thomas Gray (himself a Wye tourist): 'Where thro' the long-drawn aisle and fretted vault / The pealing anthem swells the note of praise' (ll. 39–40). For Bloomfield, then, the pastoral valley and ruined church call forth a poetic act of worship, poetry being the mode which he feels to be profound enough to express his love of nature and its creator. This act, he knows, is over-determined: he sees the abbey and imagines his Psalm-singing in relation to Gray's portrait of the country church as a place where the act of commemoration acquires value. He is self-consciously following in Gray's versesteps, quietly claiming poetry as a deeper, more pious, response to Tintern than the picturesque sketches that tourists were expected to make.

The Tintern visit was brief: with the tide ebbing, the party embarked again for Chepstow, and went thence by road to Abergavenny, where they climbed the Sugar Loaf mountain. On to Brecon and Hay-on-Wye, making sketches at every castle and ancient monument they encountered. Then to Hereford, Malvern, Worcester, and Cheltenham and so back to Uley.

Visiting the Wye as a labourer-poet taken up by well-meaning patrons, and as a tourist expected to sing for his tour, Bloomfield found himself in a new and precarious position. Mostly, he enjoyed it, since, precisely because he had been tied to his trade in a way gentlemen poets never were (even poor and radical ones like Wordsworth and Coleridge), he had never before travelled west of London. Nonetheless, his new and, to him, anomalous position, a visitor rather than a Londoner recollecting his native Suffolk, led him to commence an innovative kind of work – a conventional tour poem (*The Banks of Wye* (1811)) that was, like Wordsworth's Duddon sonnets of this period, to accompany a prose guide with accompanying sketches made at picturesque spots. As such, the project, like Wordsworth's *Guide to the Lakes*, was a new, hybrid, genre, the guidebook as rewritten by the poet to feature his own verse as well as illustrations that represented the region as a place of aesthetic value. Bloomfield hoped to take advantage of his popularity as a topographical poet and of the Wye's renown as a picturesque location, building on the success of the *Views in Suffolk, Norfolk and Northamptonshire* by feeding the public's ever-increasing desire for lavishly illustrated books.

Bloomfield began the making of his Wye-book while still basking in the warmth of the new experience and the attention paid him by the ladies of the party. His letters show him taking his new roles as artist and tour guide very seriously, seeking sketches and verse from Mary Lloyd Baker and promising her a private view of his work:

> But of all this I will write more in due time. And you will here probably ask yourself, what does he mean by due time? Why I mean that when you have fulfilld *your* promise, and sent me your Wye Scetches to copy, and the said copying is done. I mean to have the pleasure of exhibiting to you and them my whole triple-page'd Journal, Drawings, prose, and rhime.
>
> Since my return I have spent an evening at Fulham, very delightfully. Mr and Mrs Owen, and a Sweedish Gentleman, *the Baron De Gear* ... The Sweed talkd of the scenery of the Baltic, Mr O talk'd of the Alps, and of the passage of mount St Gotherd &c, – and I – What could I talk about? – The *Wye*, to be sure! (Letter 216 of *The Letters of Robert Bloomfield*: to Mary Lloyd Baker, 2–5 October 1807)

Once he received the sketches, Bloomfield set about recreating the tour on paper:

> I have succeeded beyond the former estimate of my own self approving vanity, and the proof that I posess that latter article, is my telling you so. They are all done by Candle light! These long winter evenings are all in my favour, and you may figure to yourself the solid oak of my old Table bearing on his back half the Castles in Wales, besides my two elbows, and

all the paraphernalia of drawing! Remember that though I am in general pleased with my own performances I percieve that some of my trees are amazingly like a pile of Cheshire Cheeses. And one in particular, I was hamper'd with, it seem'd to have a determination to resemble a large Oil Jar with a handle, but I cut the handle off, and, it became as good a tree as the rest, aye and as good as some that I have seen at Sadler's Wells. (Letter 217 of *The Letters of Robert Bloomfield*: to T. J. Lloyd Baker, 18 November 1807)

Mildly flirtatious letters of this kind were Bloomfield's way of prolonging a relationship that was valuable to him: Lloyd Baker's admiration, and that of her sisters and aunt, gave him confidence without intimidating him (as the patronage of noblemen tended to do). He flourished in a feminine circle, enjoying being humorous for their benefit, unbuttoning as he could not to others outside his class, but knowing, all the same, that his value to these ladies depended upon his amusing them. He was, nonetheless, careful to show the ladies' powerful husbands that he needed their help too, consulting Thomas Lloyd Baker and his friend Bransby Cooper about histories of Monmouthshire in preparation of the prose section of the book.

Despite Bloomfield's diligent effort, his Wye-book never appeared in the intended tripartite prose/poetry/picture format. Back in London, away from the Lloyd Baker/Sharp circle, afflicted by financial difficulties and sinking into depression, he found work slowing up. It was not until February 1811, after many months' practice at turning his rough sketches into finished drawings and much research into local history, that he sent the Wye-book to his publishers, Vernor and Hood, only to hear that that they were now 'averse to the costly and fashionable stile of publishing' and would produce only a smaller-scale volume with no more than four illustrations (letter 256 of *The Letters of Robert Bloomfield*: to Mary Lloyd Baker, 16 January – 2 February 1811). Their decision may have been an early indication of the financial difficulties that would bankrupt the firm after Hood's death in 1811. At all events, it made the book they did publish in that year a far less appealing production, containing only Bloomfield's Georgic verse and a few engravings after his sketches. Nevertheless, *The Banks of Wye*, now more straightforwardly a poetry publication, was a substantial work, albeit not one for which the public was looking from a poet they liked for his tales of village life. Two centuries later, however, we can finally reconstitute the Wye-book that Bloomfield originally prepared, by comparing the published poem with the prose journal (printed posthumously in 1824), restoring deleted passages and autograph sketches from manuscript, and investigating hitherto unpublished letters.

Reconstituted, Bloomfield's Wye-book can be seen to have made a distinctive response to the tour that was, at the same time, a departure in his own oeuvre – despite its affiliation to the conventional genre of the tourist poem and guidebook. In part this was, as Tim Burke has noted, a matter of Bloomfield's sympathetic understanding of the work of the rural labourers that he now witnessed, in passing, as a leisured tourist – an understanding that subverts the unthinking aestheticisation of labour that often character-ises the picturesque. The informal prose journal shows Bloomfield chatting long with a shoemaker friend in Ross; discussing the price of cider with their Welsh guide; noting that the Welsh girl who served their meal at Tintern was glad to see them go. Everywhere, he is immediately interested in the people who work the landscape, regarding them as authorities on it as important as the guidebooks, aesthetic treatises, and county histories. His viewpoint comprehends not just the viewing stations built by local landowners such as Valentine Morris but also the cracks of the floorboards in his inn-cham-ber, through which he peeps at the ostlers and maids breakfasting together below.

Had the tripartite Wye-book been published, Bloomfield would have inau-gurated a new kind of many-voiced travel writing. Even the verse that was published, however, defines more directly and forcefully than ever before the new purpose of touring the Wye: not the education of taste in rules of aesthetic judgement (as in Price and Gilpin) but the mental restorative that holiday-escape into natural beauty offered an urban middle-class otherwise chained to the account-book and the office.

> Wait not, (for reason's sake attend,)
> Wait not in chains till times shall mend;
> Till the clear voice, grown hoarse and gruff,
> Cries, 'Now I'll go, I'm rich enough.'
> Youth, and the prime of manhood, seize;
> Steal ten days absence, ten days ease;
> Bid ledgers from your minds depart;
> Let mem'ry's treasures cheer the heart;
> And when your children round you grow,
> With opening charms and manly brow,
> Talk of the Wye as some old dream,
> Call it the wild, the wizard stream;
> Sink in your broad arm-chair to rest,
> And youth shall smile to see you bless'd.

(*The Banks of Wye*, book IV, ll. 401–14)

Here the Wye is a consolation of age: taking a longer view than Wordsworth at Tintern, Bloomfield sees the river, recreated virtually in memory and talk, as reviving, in an otherwise sedentary figure, a younger and livelier self. It confers a blessed experience of wildness that is also a token of masculinity: the father, defined by domesticity, is cheered in himself and admired by his children because recollecting his experiences of 'the wizard stream' conjures into being the 'manly brow' of his 'prime of manhood'.

Figure 23 Martin's Tower, Chepstow Castle, from Robert Bloomfield, *The Banks of Wye, a poem in four books* (London: the author, Vernor, Hood and Sharpe, 1811).

Bloomfield is ambivalent about the picturesque. His Wye-book was to feature engravings after his and his friends' sketches. His prose journal records them sketching at every castle they visited (see Figure 23). At Tintern, however, sketching was not a deep enough response to place and, as he concludes his verse tour, he offers only faint praise of Gilpin. Artists may learn from the Wye, he declares, but by encountering nature's forms and rhythms rather than by applying artificial criteria and apparatus:

> Artists, betimes your powers employ,
> And take the pilgrimage of joy;
> The eye of genius may behold
> A thousand beauties here untold;
> Rock, that defies the winter's storm;
> Wood, in its most imposing form,
> That climbs the mountain, bows below,
> Where deep th'unsullied waters flow.
> Here *Gilpin*'s eye, transported, scann'd
> Views by no tricks of fancy plann'd;
> *Gray* here, upon the stream reclined,
> Stored with delight his ardent mind.

(*The Banks of Wye*, book IV, ll. 415–26)

Gilpin is 'transported' when he looks at nature unguided by fancy or pre-determined ideas. Bloomfield's role model is, instead, the poet Gray, who absorbs delight by letting his ardent mind repose on the water, as if in meditation.

How to recline upon the stream was a question for Bloomfield's own representation of the tour. His poetic endorsement of natural form led to a problem that was not resolved in the published *Banks of Wye*, a problem to which the tripartite Wye-book would have presented a novel solution. The problem concerns his own medium: whether nature's forms and rhythms are always so neatly harnessable within the polite diction and conventional rhyming couplets of the tour poem. Had the poem been combined with the colloquial first-person prose journal and the amateur sketches, then its obtrusion of formality upon the reader would have been seen to be only one version of the journey, in dialogue with more informal responses which, without it, might themselves have seemed too slight and private for publication. Standing alone, the published poem seemed stilted, lacking the animation of *The Farmer's Boy* because Bloomfield did not speak for the Wye landscape as his own – known as a place marked on his body and mind by work in its fields. The original verse-manuscript, however, shows that Bloomfield recognised this difficulty and found an original way to overcome it, for it begins more in a comic-heroic than a polite manner with a prelude about a giant called Scoop, who had fashioned the hills and dales of the Gloucestershire country in which the Lloyd Bakers lived:

> When Time's young curls embower'd his brow
> And infant streams began to flow,
> Huge giant Scoop with spade in hand,
> And all the Island at command,
> With puffing breath and monstrous stride
> Came thundering on by Severn's side.
> Fancy still hears his foot rebound,
> When *Stinchcombe* trembled at the sound.
> Here Cambrian mountains caught his eye
> Towring to meet the distant sky
> Jealous he mark'd them one by one
> And dreading ~~much to be~~ sore the work out-done
> 'Out-done' he cried, ''Tis true I'm warm'
> But this bright prospect nerves my arm
> I too the mountain pile can rear
> Outdone, there shall be just such here.'
> Then stript at once to set about it,
> (Look at the spot and who can doubt it,)
> But, at the moment he was speaking
> His limbs were stiff, his back was aching,

For *Mendip*, and the western shore,
The marks of recent labours bore:
Weary he rested, full of pain,
By *Nympsfield*, on the upland plain,
And with a gnashing envious smile
There stuck his spade upright the while,
And chang'd his mind. – Then sprewing first,
O'er Severn's Vale a cloud of dust,
Again he pluck'd it from the ground,
The crumbling earth flew wizzing round;
Then dashing sternly to and fro,
He cut a casual hole or two;
In one of which (a sweet one truly)
Some modern pigmies built up Uley
And *Owlpen*, by the dark wood side,
Which none can find without a guide.
And here, the happy natives stroll
Around their green illshapen Bowl,
A Bowl all zigzagg'd round about
With one large gap to let them out.

(British Library Add. MS 28265 ff. 48–9)

With their deliberately clunky rhymes ('truly/Uley'), slangy diction ('wizzed' 'zigzagg'd') and undignified account of the country's origin as a giant's casual whim of imitating the hill country of Wales, these opening lines undercut their own pretensions to the heroic. They also present a compliment to Bloomfield's gentlemanly (and womanly) patrons, in which deference is pre-empted by humour. As a beginning to a four-book landscape poem, they are highly unorthodox, a versification of the tongue-in-cheek humour of Bloomfield's correspondence with Lloyd Baker. They are playful, revealing the poet's enjoyment of his own ability to fictionalise, to tell it like it's not – and in this they reflect the West Country's status as a charming holiday place, an escape from Bloomfield's London cares and from his branding as a Suffolk labourer poet. Yet for all that, they do concern themselves with labour, as Bloomfield so often did: funny though they are, they show the giant working up a sweat digging. Polished, knowing, and displaying a flexible deployment of Butler's Hudibrastic cocktail of octosyllabic couplets, phrasal verbs, and casual diction, Bloomfield's light verses still suggest, however jokily, that the country depends on backbreaking toil – a point quietly made later in the poem when the tourists in their pleasure-boat glide effortlessly past bent-backed gleaners in the fields. Bloomfield's West Country was not a holiday-land for everyone.

As different from Wordsworth's 'Tintern Abbey' as they are from Gilpin's *Observations*, Bloomfield's lines on Scoop reveal a cultivated, accomplished, well-read poet entertaining his patrons; they also suggest that he was worldly enough to know that the Cotswolds were not, after all, the Andes (which he had celebrated as sublime peaks in the unpublished poem 'To Immagination') and that, therefore, describing them in pious and solemn terms would only lead to bathos. Nevertheless, getting the tone right was a vexing matter for him, and as the tour became a more and more distant memory, and the flirtatious feminine circle receded from his grasp, he worried about whether the opening was appropriate for a piece intended for public consumption. Revealingly, it was when Mary Lloyd Baker wrote to him during the course of another West Country tour she was making (of Cheddar Gorge) that, in the light of her intimate attention, he again became enthusiastic about the lines, writing in reply

> [t]he Cheddar Cliffs have taken up a nook in my heart, and imagination scratches a picture of her own, like an old Hen in a garden.
>   I had taken a momentary dislike to Old Scoop, but you strengthen my original feeling and I begin to think that He may be a personage not *altogether* to be ridiculed. I have a great mind to keep him alive. (Letter 245 of *The Letters of Robert Bloomfield*: to Mary Lloyd Baker, 31 October– 1 November 1809)

In the end, *The Banks of Wye*, to its detriment, appeared without Old Scoop: the lines fell prey to Bloomfield's anxiety (evident in the more sober main body of the poem) about his qualifications to write in the style of and from the position of a leisured gentleman – a position in which the trip put him for the first time. He internalised the perceived doubts of his patrons, Lofft and Thomas Park, literary gentlemen who edited poetry for magazines, and consulted other friends too: it seems none of these men, arbiters of conventional taste, saw the opening as serious enough. Effectively, as another letter to Mary reveals, Bloomfield's was too feminised as well as too playful a discourse to meet male expectations about the proper language for topographical poetry:

> Since you saw or heard any part of my Journal, and I think I remember *how far* I had then proceeded in my amusement, much alteration has taken place in the plan and divisions &c. As I advanced I began to conceive that it might even eventualy be renderd fit for publication, and this perswasion set me about a thorough examination and revision. I concieved that it was, owing to the careless and hasty manner of its early composition, much too hudibrastic, and contain a vast deal of useless matter which might give way to the superior graces of nature, or to unbridled fancy. I had finished it, as I thought, according to this plan, last summer; and I had the joint opinion of my *then* companions, Inskip, himself a poet, and a man of strong mind, and my host, Mr. Weston of Shefford, Beds,

and as he has read and thought more than any man I ever found in his station of life, and his age, and is an enthusiast in poetry, with a memory truly astonishing considering his mutifarious reading, I consider him highly capable of detecting what were blemishes in a harum scarum story like mine, – We read it for the purpose of criticizing closely, We all doubted the propriety of Giant Scoop in the outset of the piece, yet all agreed that the ridiculous thought was not without merit, only perhaps out of place. Previous to this I had shown it to Mr Rogers, author of 'The pleasures of memory', and he, even then, in its ruder state, said that it would probably be well recieved if published, but that it was evident that I had not taken the pains with it which might be taken. I then wrote the whole out again with great emendations, in which state Mr. Lofft gave the opinion which I very barely stated to you. I took his hints and the others in conjunction, and wrote *the whole out again*, still in the mending way with additions and curtailments, and in this new dress, without the personage above mentioned, Scoop, I submited the piece to the calm, judicious, and candid Mr Park of Hampstead (He had seen the giant long ago and said nothing in his praise, which I know how to understand) He was decidedly of opinion that the thing would do me credit, and at the same time pencil'd his doubts and remarks. With this encouragement I *once more* wrote out the whole; gave the brat a name; and offer'd it to My Bookseller. I know of nothing which can *now* retard its ultimate appearance before the world. (Letter 256 of *The Letters of Robert Bloomfield*: to Mary Lloyd Baker, 16 January – 2 February 1811)

Being new to the tour-poem and of inferior class to his readers, Bloomfield did not dare to be facetious and mock the public's cultural expectations of such a book and of the place it described. Abandoning his hudibrastic lines, he left out the most characteristic and individual of his poetic voices, submitting to male arbiters of taste rather than reproduce in public the verse inspired by his chatty, female correspondents. The deletion was a variation of what had previously happened with 'To Immagination': when Lofft wanted to revise that poem to render it more properly sublime and lyrical, Bloomfield had given it over. Not having the confidence to maintain his own version against Lofft's heavy-handed coercion, and reluctant to lose his independent voice, he had chosen not to finish it for publication at all. What was lost in this new excision from *The Banks of Wye*, however, was an idiosyncratic response to the West Country that remade the poetic traditions in which that region had previously been compassed and that questioned the conventional pieties of the gentlemanly tour. Without this response, and lacking the prose journal and extensive illustrations intended for the tripartite publication, *The Banks of Wye* was a slighter and less original book than first planned, although it did contain a few engravings derived from sketches made in situ (Figures 24 and 25).

Figure 24   New Wear on the Wye, from Robert Bloomfield, *The Banks of Wye, a poem in four books* (London: the author, Vernor, Hood and Sharpe, 1811).

The abandonment of the tripartite Wye-book and the excision of Old Scoop revealed that Bloomfield was unable to continue in a direction in which his writing took comic flight away from his homeground. That homeground was both his strong resource and, by 1811, the pale within which his patrons wished to confine and define him as Suffolk poet and nothing else. In this sense, Bloomfield's West Country offered an (in the end not taken) opportunity for him to escape the category of local labouring-class writer, an opportunity to claim, as Wordsworth already had when touring the Wye, the status of poet of innovatively voiced imagination. This lost opportunity is all the more to be regretted because *The Banks of Wye* that Bloomfield did publish contained, despite its often stilted verse, a brilliant meditation on the mind's relationship to place and time. Bloomfield had read and admired *Lyrical Ballads*: his Wye poem may eschew the first-person self-analysis of Wordsworth's Tintern lines, but it nevertheless also considers the effects on the reflective mind of recalling a spot marked out by both natural beauty and human history. In climactic verses on ruined Raglan castle, once the last stronghold of the Royalists in the Civil War, Bloomfield first evokes the triumph of nature over man's achievements, however violent and heroic they once were:

Figure 25 Van Mountain, near Brecknock from the Priory Woods, from Robert Bloomfield, *The Banks of Wye, a poem in four books* (London: the author, Vernor, Hood and Sharpe, 1811).

Majestic Ragland! Harvests wave
Where thund'ring hosts their watch-word gave,
When cavaliers, with downcast eye,
Struck the last flag of loyalty:
Then, left by gallant Worc'ster's band,
To devastation's cruel hand
The beauteous fabric bow'd, fled all
The splendid hours of festival.
No smoke ascends; the busy hum
Is heard no more; no rolling drum,
No high-toned clarion sounds alarms,
No banner wakes the pride of arms;
But ivy, creeping year by year,
Of growth enormous, triumphs here.
Each dark festoon with pride upheaves
Its glossy wilderness of leaves
On sturdy limbs, that, clasping, bow
Broad o'er the turrets' utmost brow,
Encompassing, by strength alone,

> In fret-work bars, the sliding stone,
> That tells how years and storms prevail,
> And spreads its dust upon the gale.

> (Book III, ll. 19–40)

The ivy embraces the stone; as the castle moulders, the plant prospers, until the monuments of martial valour are encased in a 'wilderness of leaves' and the sounds of human life give way to the stifling constriction of the creeper. These are sophisticated verses that demonstrate how much could still be achieved in the Augustan rhyming couplet. Partly this is a matter of allusion: Milton's serpent Satan is not far behind the snake-like plant that 'with pride upheaves' itself at the tower's expense. It's also a result of lexical vividness, rhetorical insistence, and syntactical energy creating urgency: Bloomfield pressures his reader to feel awed and threatened by a nature that, in the figure of the ivy, represents the triumphant and vampiric power of death, supporting itself on the works of mankind. This is a post-Edenic fallen world, where nature is both beautiful (as in the glossiness of the leaves) and menacing because time, death, and – in Miltonic terms – sin are fundamental to its growth. It is a world, too, in which nature and humanity (here represented by historical monuments to human deeds and achievements) are at odds.

It is now that Bloomfield ventures a meditation on time, history, and nature that is akin to Wordsworth's and that may represent his response to reading *Lyrical Ballads*:

> The man who could unmoved survey
> What ruin, piecemeal, sweeps away;
> Works of the pow'rful and the brave,
> All sleeping in the silent grave;
> Unmoved reflect, that here were sung
> Carols of joy, by beauty's tongue,
> Is fit, where'er he deigns to roam,
> And hardly fit – to stay at home.
> Spent *here* in peace, – one solemn hour
> ('Midst legends of the Yellow Tower,
> Truth and tradition's mingled stream,
> Fear's start, and superstition's dream)
> Is pregnant with a thousand joys,
> That distance, place, nor time destroys;
> That with exhaustless stores supply
> Food for reflection till we die.

> (Book III, ll. 41–56)

'[O]ne solemn hour / ... / Is pregnant with a thousand joys' is verbally close to Wordsworth's 'One impulse from a vernal wood / May teach you more of man, / Of moral evil and of good, / Than all the sages can' from 'The Tables Turned', although for Bloomfield it is the encounter with nature's overwhelming of humanity's works, rather than solely with its beauty, that makes visiting the spot so endlessly educative. The surprising word here is 'joys': as in Wordsworth's 'Tintern Abbey' the visitor unexpectedly derives joys from a scene that should, because it reveals the passing of time, produce melancholy. This is, then, no simplistic sightseeing event, no mere touristic picturesque, but a complex response that finds, as the paradoxical one/thousand phrasing suggests, a plenum of emotions and thoughts from a brief encounter. These emotions and thoughts are joys, despite the evidence of destruction that causes them, because they fertilise a human activity that turns out to be less vulnerable to time than castles and towers are – the activity of reflection that vivifies the mind and restores the past in memory and that, though it may die with us, survives in the form of 'legends' and tradition – the stories, songs, and poems that we make and that others repeat after us. And these, implicitly, renew the 'carols of joy' that long-dead denizens of the castle once sang with 'beauty's tongue'. This, of course, is an implicit poetic; Bloomfield, in the poem he is deriving from his visit and that we are now reading, is adding another turn to the traditions, legends, and songs that allow us to redeem from oblivion the works of the past – and redeem ourselves as consciousnesses destined for oblivion. Carolling joyfully in the poem, he retrieves the songs of yore from the ivy's clutches. As a response to a Wye-tour this is as profound, but not as self-foregrounding, as Wordsworth's, to which it compares in its intimation of the ability of the human mind to overcome time's depredations when that mind, fertilised by an encounter with a temporally shaped landscape, is prompted to reflect upon itself and assert its power of song.

Profound though it is, Bloomfield's response to Raglan remains isolated, lost in a poem of occasional brilliance that was published without its more original lines and without the prose journal and sketches that should have accompanied it. Bloomfield missed a chance, owing to his booksellers' reluctance and his own inhibiting consciousness of what was proper for a labourer-visitor writing at the touring-gentry's behest. As a result it was easy to neglect the merits of his Wye: literary criticism, although idealising a fellow nature-poet's imaginative response to the Wye Valley, damned the poem with faint praise. In the twentieth century, Bloomfield's reputation dwindled to nothing. If, after Wordsworth's 'Tintern Abbey', the Wye was a critical testing ground for Romantic poetry, then Bloomfield failed the test. His deleted lines on Old Scoop, now published for the first time, show us both that this failure was not of his own making and that Wordsworth's egotistical sublime was not the only way to bring into being a new and distinctive response to landscape. Bloomfield's comic sublime was also an innovative and individual discourse – an implicit celebration of tourism as a social amusement which the sober and intense Wordsworth could not have made, but which still allowed for meditations on nature as intense as that prompted by Raglan. As such, it was a discourse that we, as well as he, are the poorer for not having pursued: the romantic West Country, a place of beauty, pathos, and legend from Wordsworth to Thomas Hardy, would have been a more completely human place for its inclusion.

Bibliography

Bloomfield, Robert, *The Farmer's Boy* (London: Vernor and Hood, 1800).

—— *Rural Tales, Ballads and Songs* (London: Vernor and Hood, 1802).

—— *The Banks of Wye, a Poetical Journal. A Poetical Journal. Aug. 17. 1807.* British Library Add. MS 28265.

—— *The Banks of Wye, a Poem in Four Books* (London: Vernor, Hood and Sharpe; Longman, Hurst, Rees and Orme, 1811).

—— *Journal of a Tour Down the Wye*, in *The Remains of Robert Bloomfield* (2 vols, London: Baldwin, Cradock and Joy, 1824).

—— *The Letters of Robert Bloomfield and his Circle*, ed. Tim Fulford and Lynda Pratt, *Romantic Circles* online edition.

Brayley, E. W., *Views in Suffolk, Norfolk and Northamptonshire; Illustrative of the Works of Robert Bloomfield* (London: Vernor, Hood and Sharpe, 1806).

Burke, Tim, 'Colonial Spaces and National Identities in *The Banks of Wye*: Bloomfield and the Wye after Wordsworth', in *Robert Bloomfield: Lyric, Class, and the Romantic Canon*, ed. Simon White, John Goodridge, and Bridget Keegan (Lewisburg: Bucknell University Press, 2006), 89–112.

Dyer, John, *The Fleece: a Poem in Four Books* (London, 1757).

Gilpin, William, *Observations on the River Wye and Several Parts of South Wales* (London, 1782).

Goodridge, John, *Rural Life in Eighteenth-Century English Poetry* (Cambridge: Cambridge University Press, 1995).

—— '"That Deathless Wish of Climbing Higher": Robert Bloomfield on the Sugar Loaf', in *Wales and the Romantic Imagination*, ed. Damian Walford Davies and Lynda Pratt (Cardiff: University of Wales Press, 2007), 161–79.

Price, Uvedale, *An Essay on the Picturesque as Compared with the Sublime and the Beautiful: and on the Use of Studying Pictures for the Purpose of Improving Real Landscape* (2 vols, London, Hereford, 1794).

Wordsworth, William, *Lyrical Ballads, with Other Poems* (London: Longman and Rees, 1800).

Part IV
In Pursuit of Spring

13

'The Outset of Life': Shelley, Hazlitt, the West Country, and the Revolutionary Imagination

Michael O'Neill

In 'the outset of life', William Hazlitt muses, tellingly more than half way through 'My First Acquaintance with Poets', 'our imagination has a body to it' (ix. 104).[1] Hazlitt's imagination vividly embodies his 'first acquaintance' with Coleridge and Wordsworth in the essay, bathing it in an unsentimental glow of affection and rapture, even as his later disillusion finds expression. The result is a remarkable account of an affective and intellectual trajectory central to the Romantic period: bliss at the 'outset', subsequent disenchantment. In the essay Hazlitt writes with the subdued passion of the principled dissenter, who has not sold his political soul for a mess of Tory pottage, but he also writes with real and brilliant empathy: 'the sense of a new style and a new spirit in poetry came over me' (ix. 104), a 'new style and a new spirit' imprinted on the lineaments of the countryside round Alfoxden.

Romantic and revolutionary dawns broke in the west for Shelley, too, whose *Queen Mab*, first mentioned by the young poet in December 1811, seems to have taken a major step towards final completion in the summer of 1812 when he spent July and August in Lynmouth, near Barnstaple in Devon. The Shelley party, including Elizabeth Hitchener, left Lynmouth in haste on 28 August, after Shelley's Irish servant Daniel Healey (or Hill) had been arrested at Barnstaple (on 19 August) for distributing the poet's *Declaration of Rights*. Shelley could not pay the £200 fine, which meant that Healey had to spend six months in prison. During his stay at Lynmouth, Shelley wrote to Thomas Hookham: 'I enclose also by way of specimen all that I have written of a little poem begun since my arrival in England. I conceive I have matter enough for 6 more cantos … The Past, the Present, & the Future are the grand and comprehensive topics of this Poem. I have not yet half exhausted the second of them.'[2] By then, following his 'arrival in England' from Ireland to Wales in early April 1812 (or from Wales to England in late June), Shelley appears to have drafted, in the view of Donald H. Reiman and Neil Fraistat, 'approximately four of a projected ten cantos'.[3] Clearly the stay at Lynmouth was poetically productive. Edward Dowden asserted many years ago: 'The poetical mood was not likely to pass away when Shelley found himself at Lynmouth, still amid hills and rushing brooks [as when he was in Wales], and now in presence of the ever-changing sea.'[4] Belletristic this may now sound, but Shelley's time in Lynmouth was a crucial phase during a time of intense speculation and poetic experimentation; the effect of the West Country scenes leaves its impression on Shelley's poetry of the time. *Queen Mab* still remains a work ripe for attention to its imaginative and explosive attempt to reignite revolutionary fires, the extinction of which so disheartened Hazlitt.

No poet among the Romantics was more conscious of a 'new spirit in poetry' than Shelley. In his greatest shorter poem, 'Ode to the West Wind', he prays that the wind might 'Drive my dead thoughts over the universe / Like withered leaves to quicken a new birth' (63–4),[5] while he writes in his peroration to *A Defence of Poetry*: 'It is impossible to read the compositions of the most celebrated writers of the present day without being startled with the electric life which burns within their words' (701). Here the wording repeats the phrasing used in the earlier *A Philosophical View of Reform*, except that Shelley now depicts himself as 'startled with' rather than 'startled by' (647), arguably pointing up the involuntary 'startling' induced by 'the electric life' of the writings produced by his contemporaries, a life unsentimentally celebrated in Hazlitt's *Spirit of the Age*. Shelley's readiness to respond to the 'compositions' of others is at the centre of his own creativity and aligns him with the capacity for creative and critical relishing that Hazlitt calls 'Gusto', that is, 'power or passion defining any object' (ii. 79).

The present chapter explores how, with a Proustian subtlety, Hazlitt gives us a picture of the complex of feelings induced in him by reflecting on his first, unforgettable acquaintance with poets. It seeks, moreover, to link Hazlitt's celebration of a 'new style and a new spirit' to Shelley's Lynmouth-based explorations. This will involve parallels and suggestive comparisons rather than the tracing of a direct influence. Hazlitt and Shelley make a piquant pairing: they should have been allies, but Hazlitt reserves some of his most dazzling scorn for Shelley's own pyrotechnics. Leigh Hunt, who took principled exception to Hazlitt's first major attack on Shelley, in the *Table Talk* essay 'On Paradox and Common-Place' in which the poet features as a 'philosophic fanatic' (vi.130), later recalled, as Nicholas Roe reminds us, 'someone telling him that Shelley had "cut up" Hazlitt at Godwin's'.[6] But Hazlitt's hostility seems to run more deeply than personal grudge will allow, and this chapter will finish with a brief coda on the final lack of concord between the two men.

I.

Final lack of concord is almost a guarantee of authenticity in and for Hazlitt. Hazlitt's arguments '*in favour of the Natural Disinterestedness of the Human Mind*', to quote the subtitle of his 1805 work *An Essay on the Principles of*

Human Action, bear most impressive fruit in Keats's notion of '*Negative Capability* that is when man is capable of being in uncertainties, Mysteries, doubts, without any irritable reaching after fact & reason'.[7] They may have influenced Shelley's account of the sympathetically outgoing work performed by the imagination in *A Defence of Poetry*. Yet Hazlitt's practice as an essayist criss-crosses between being carried out of himself into the feelings of others and decisively complicating that negatively capable process by refusing to quiet the restless, aggressive impulse to impose his own perspective. Hazlitt's disinterestedness is a complex process that does not claim a superhuman ability to transcend personal feeling. The author who speaks, however wryly, of a 'secret affinity, a *hankering* after evil in the human mind' in 'On the Pleasure of Hating' (viii. 118) was never likely to fall in love with a Utopian politics. Hazlitt's very ability to admire an ideological foe, such as Burke, strikes Tom Paulin as illustrating 'the disinterested ability to appreciate the arguments of an enemy', 'one of the fundamental values', according to Paulin, that Hazlitt 'acquired from his Unitarian upbringing'.[8] Yet Hazlitt's admiration for Burke is less a question of appreciating an argument than of responding to the power of a personality. His prose relishes Burke's performance rather than his paraphrasable points. For Hazlitt in 'On the Prose-Style of Poets', Burke's style

has the solidity, and sparkling effect of the diamond: all other *fine writing* is like French paste or Bristol-stones in the comparison. Burke's style is airy, flighty, adventurous, but it never loses sight of the subject; nay, is always in contact with, and derives its increased or varying impulse from it. It may be said to pass yawning gulfs 'on the unstedfast footing of a spear:' still it has an actual resting-place and tangible support under it – it is not suspended on nothing. It differs from poetry, as I conceive, like the chamois from the eagle: it climbs to an almost equal height, touches upon a cloud, overlooks a precipice, is picturesque, sublime – but all the while, instead of soaring through the air, it stands upon a rocky cliff, clambers up by abrupt and intricate ways, and browzes on the roughest bark, or crops the tender flower. The principle which guides his pen is truth, not beauty – not pleasure, but power. (viii. 7–8)

Tom Paulin brilliantly reminds us, apropos those colourless 'Bristol-stones' (quartz crystals found near Bristol), that the West Country allusion serves to recall the fact that Burke was MP for Bristol, but lost his seat when asserting 'the principle that a member of parliament must vote according to his conscience, not according to the wishes of his constituency'. He notes, too, both the overt allusion to *Henry IV, Part 1* (I. iii. 193), where the 'unstedfast footing of a spear' evokes Hotspur's and, by implication, Burke's 'wildly impolitic' nature, and the covert allusions to Godwin's *St Leon* and Caesar's encomium on Antony in *Antony and Cleopatra* when 'the barks of trees thou brows'd' (I. iv. 66). This latter allusion serves, as Paulin argues, to remind us that there is 'a mighty general shadowing' Hazlitt's symbol of the chamois (Napoleon).[9] One might read these allusions as Hazlitt's refusal to conceal his own complicated view of Burke: that is, his prose is not simply a negatively capable medium through which the 'airy, flighty, adventurous' force of Burke's writing makes itself felt. David Bromwich has ingeniously argued for a reconciliation of Hazlitt's belief in disinterestedness and his understanding of the mixed motives at work in human beings, especially the contest that can take place between the admiration for power and the impulse towards sympathy.[10] And, like Burke's, Hazlitt's own style 'has an actual resting-place and tangible support'; yet that 'resting-place' and that 'support' can often seem to be nothing other than his own convictions and determination that others should appear as he wishes them to appear. Like Burke's prose, Hazlitt's 'never loses sight of its subject', yet this 'subject' is not necessarily to see the person as he was but as he appeared to Hazlitt to be. Thus, the allusion to Antony that Paulin points out works, as Paulin does not observe, to explain the tenacious hold that Burke has over Hazlitt: if Antony fleetingly brings Napoleon to mind, the effect is to remind us of Hazlitt's admiration for the French Emperor, while Caesar's praise – itself at odds with his antagonism towards Antony elsewhere in the drama – might prove 'disinterestedness' or it might suggest, rather, the reluctant yet inevitable admiration that Antony/Burke inspires. Above all, the passage brings out the strong drive in Hazlitt's portraits to make his subjects affirm a leading characteristic, a drive that is of the first importance in considering his account of the major Romantic poets.

There is in Hazlitt a recoil from abstraction that suggests he will find it difficult to devote his writing to the espousal of libertarian ideals. It is easier for him to mock Wordsworth's apostasy, for example, than to articulate a new or updated Declaration of Rights. What evokes his finest prose is an embittered nostalgia, expressed in his essay on Wordsworth's *The Excursion*, for the 'glad dawn of the day-star of liberty ... when France called her children to partake her equal blessings beneath her laughing skies'. This passage betrays in its very idiom a sharp recognition that 'that season of hope ... is fled with the other dreams of our youth, which we cannot recal' (ii. 120). Those 'equal blessings' beneath the 'laughing skies' convict themselves in their very utterance of something idealised, pastoral, and literary. This is not to deny the affective power of Hazlitt's longing for that 'day-star of liberty', nor the edge of his contempt for those (such as the author of *The Excursion*) who have taken to the penning of 'Birth-day and Thanksgiving odes, or the chaunting of *Te Deums* in all the churches of Christendom' (ii. 120).

Yet Hazlitt is a writer in whom different feelings twist round one another. The very image of the 'day-star of liberty', for example, suggests a steady permanence, the light of the sun. But it also intimates the fate of stars in daylight, namely, that they will fade and be seen no more. That 'day-star', along with the 'dawn' in which it manifested itself, has both 'fled' and 'left behind it traces, which are not to be effaced' (ii. 120), a sequence of ideas and images that bears acutely on the way in which Shelley words the central experience of *The Triumph of Life*. In this poem, Shelley's elegy for the fate of Romantic desire, stars – like ideals – pass into an all too common light of day, but they bequeath traces of their presence. Rousseau, central to Hazlitt, too, appears as the quintessential representative of Romantic desire, and is haunted by a beautiful 'shape all light' (352), his own 'day-star of liberty'. Like Hazlitt's day-star, Shelley's shape offers the promise of a new 'day': 'like day she came, / Making the night a dream' (392–3); like Hazlitt's day-star, she is eclipsed by an effacing, destructive light that turns her into a waning star, traces of whom are not utterly effaced: 'And the fair shape waned in the coming light / As veil by veil the silent splendour drops / From Lucifer' (412–14), and yet Rousseau is able to go on to say, 'So knew I in that light's severe excess / The presence of that shape' (424–5), even if it is a 'presence' that borders on the verge of absence, 'The ghost of a forgotten form of sleep' (428). Shelley might almost be writing his poetic gloss on Hazlitt's prose elegy for revolutionary ideals and even speaks the same or a similar language of 'traces' (see 337) and 'erasure' (see 406).

Neither Hazlitt nor Shelley deplores the failure of the Revolution in naïvely emotional terms. For one thing, *The Triumph of Life* never allows its dream-vision to be interpreted as a point-by-point allegory of recent history. For another, it evokes the bafflement of understanding and mimes the bewilderment of disillusion, but it does not supply an absolutely sure explanation. Attempts to explain seem only to raise more questions than they solve; questions themselves, with their air of striking to the heart of things, only catalyse further visions, new uncertainties. Hazlitt, too, asserts his allegiance to 'the day-star of liberty', but he associates it in the same sentence with the 'airy, unsubstantial dream' and the near-absoluteness of Wordsworthian loss, quoting the lines from the *Intimations Ode* that begin 'What the radiance, which was once so bright, / Be now for ever taken from our sight' (quoted ii. 120). Yes, those lines will turn into an assertion that finds 'Strength in what is left behind' (183),[11] but Hazlitt knows the near-tragic quasi-fact that human beings are destined always to lose their dearest dream. The pull towards this conviction shows itself throughout his prose in its many moments of recollection of past happiness, with their concomitant, implicit sense of present loss, redeemed only by the reclaiming work done by his prose. It shows, too, in such passages as the wry, sad, hilarious lament for lost friendships in 'On the Pleasure of Hating'. The sustaining of revolutionary ideals has somehow to occur in a world in which human beings are not equal to their best and brightest speculations, since they occupy a sphere in which, as if ruled by a gravitational law, emotions obey a cyclical and dispiriting rule as each heavily punctuated clause begets its hating neighbour: 'We hate old friends: we hate old books: we hate old opinions; and at last we come to hate ourselves' (viii. 120–1). Keats's 1819 flare of distaste for perfectibilinarian notions has, one might feel, a grounding in his reading of Hazlitt: 'in truth I do not at all believe in this sort of perfectibility', he writes to the George Keatses; 'the nature of the world will not admit of it – the inhabitants of the world will correspond to itself' (ii. 101). 'The inhabitants of the world will correspond to itself': the 'world', being what it is, makes us who we are, Keats asserts in a pointed rebuke to those who believe that they might transcend what even Shelley at his most enthusiastically Godwinian recognises as obstacles: 'chance, and death, and mutability' (*Prometheus Unbound*, III. iv. 201). This idea is not the premise for reactionary conservatism on Keats's part, who will go on to commend the notion of the 'world' as '"The vale of Soul-making"'. 'Intelligences' come into existence and are made souls 'by the medium of a world like this' (ii. 102). But it reveals a robust dislike of facile optimism, an optimism that affects to transcend or ignore or annul the presence in life of 'Pains and troubles' (ii. 102).

Hazlitt, along with Keats, dislikes in Shelley, not wholly fairly, the traces of such optimism, but before considering Hazlitt's response to Shelley it is relevant to note that in his subtly entangled response to Wordsworth and Coleridge he is addressing former friends who have shaped his identity and with whom he quarrels the more intensely because of their influence over him. From the first word of its title, 'My First Acquaintance with Poets' speaks of personal experience. The essay's structure and tone balance between initial stirrings and the long vistas of retrospection that beguilingly refuse to overwhelm its subject. Cunningly, the essay begins with origins and primal allegiances: 'My Father was a Dissenting Minister at Wem in Shropshire; and in the year 1798 (the figures that compose that date are to me like the "dreaded name of Demogorgon") Mr Coleridge came to Shrewsbury, to succeed Mr Rowe in the spiritual charge of a Unitarian Congregation there' (ix. 95). The seemingly factual sentence plays the part of a prologue to a swelling theme. It brings on to the essay's stage the *dramatis personae* of Hazlitt's imaginative awakening, the central theme of the essay. They include Hazlitt's father, the poetically, personally, and politically revolutionary year 1798,[12] the *ur*-figure of Demogorgon (possibly brought to Hazlitt's attention by Shelley's *Prometheus Unbound* as well as by *Paradise Lost*, II. 964–5), and the mentor par excellence, Coleridge, poetry displacing theological zeal. It will end with a comic but telling allusion to Wordsworth's *Hart-Leap Well*, 'But there is matter for another rhyme, / And I to this may add a second tale' (quoted ix. 109), to which Shelley probably also refers at the close of his witty epyllion *The Witch of Atlas* (669–70). In both essay and epyllion the allusion forges a link with Wordsworth and opens a gap between his work and his successors; in both cases, it asserts an ongoing creative energy. Hazlitt has just turned the tables on armchair, Utopian radicalism by way of an anecdote involving Charles Lamb:

It was at Godwin's that I met him [Lamb] with Holcroft and Coleridge, where they were disputing fiercely which was the best – *Man as he was, or man as he is to be.* 'Give me,' says Lamb, 'man as he is *not* to be.' This saying was the beginning of a friendship between us, which I believe still continues. (ix. 109)

Holcroft and Coleridge stage the classic argument of the times: between conservative and Utopian perspectives. Lamb, puncturing pretension, takes us into the carnivalesque, anarchic realm of comedy where a turn of phrase annihilates the fixities of ideology. Discipleship (where Coleridge was the master) has passed into undemanding but vigilant friendship. Yet if the friendship with Lamb seems won at the cost of estrangement from Wordsworth and Coleridge, the final quotation from *Hart-Leap Well* functions in a complex way. It concludes the first part of Wordsworth's poem, and Wordsworth does, indeed, 'add a second tale', or, at any rate a 'Part Second' which concludes with an admonitory 'lesson' (173) that twines itself round the trellis of modified millenarianism as Wordsworth speaks of 'the coming of the milder day' (171). Concealed in Hazlitt's closing allusion, then, is the possibility of such a 'coming'. Wordsworth is quoted to serve Hazlitt's ends. Wordsworth's 'milder day' might have been at a remove from his earlier, more democratic aspirations, but it will suffice as an unmentioned vanishing point towards which Hazlitt's essay streams.

This is not to suggest that the essay effects some sentimentalising rapprochement. But, true to the essay's fascination with 'likeness' and its endorsement of a fisherman's remark that 'we have a *nature* towards one another', seen by Coleridge as illustrating Hazlitt's 'theory of disinterestedness' (ix. 108), affinity as well as difference inheres in Hazlitt's subsequent as well as first acquaintance with the poets. Coleridge, too, earns an allusive salute at the close of the essay's penultimate paragraph, preparing us for the final reference to Wordsworth. In a delicately worked *mise-en-abîme*, Hazlitt writes with what might be termed meta-mnemonic subtlety:

The next day we had a long day's walk to Bristol, and sat down, I recollect, by a well-side on the road, to cool ourselves and satisfy our thirst, when Coleridge repeated to me some descriptive lines from his tragedy of Remorse; which I must say better became his mouth and that occasion better than they, some years after, did Mr Elliston's and the Drury-lane boards, –

Oh memory! shield me from the world's poor strife,
And give those scenes thine everlasting life. (ix. 108)

The scene shifts between literary recollection and symbolic suggestions, as the two pedestrians sit 'by a well-side on the road, to cool ourselves and satisfy our thirst'. Holcroft had been found guilty by Coleridge (with

Hazlitt's evident approval) of 'barricadoing the road to truth' (ix. 100), yet Coleridge himself betrayed 'instability of purpose' 'by shifting from one side of the foot-path to the other' (ix. 100–1, 100). In the essay's final return to Coleridge, the two men seek to 'satisfy' their 'thirst' beside the 'road', Hazlitt once again divining a common desire for meaning and significance, and reaffirming the value of 'memory' in giving early 'scenes' 'everlasting life' in his own prose. As he quotes Coleridge's invocation to memory, he may imply, too, the impossibility of being shielded from 'the world's poor strife'.

Coleridge, like Hazlitt's father, lives a life that is a dream, even if 'No two individuals were ever more unlike than were the host and his guest' (ix. 98). Indeed, the father's 'glimmering notions', produced in response to the 'Bible, and the perusal of the Commentators', have a distinctly millenarian tinge: they may seem strange, arcane, even religiose, but they serve as veiled 'types, shadows' of the revolutionary epoch and the mental experience they bear witness to has a value denied to ordinary modes of perception: 'though the soul might slumber with an hieroglyphic veil of inscrutable mysteries drawn over it, yet it was in a slumber ill-exchanged for all the sharpened realities of sense, wit, fancy, or reason' (ix. 98). Here Hazlitt seems to offer a parallel to *The Triumph of Life*, which begins with an account of the Poet experiencing a visionary trance whose indefinability is carefully defined, a 'strange trance' 'Which was not slumber, for the shade it spread // Was so transparent that the scene came through / As clear as when a veil of light is drawn / O'er evening hills they glimmer' (29, 30–3). Yet both writers set 'trance' and dream against 'the sharpened realities' that come in the wake of what both refer to as 'life'.

If Coleridge is both the medium towards realising and a siren-voice luring away from an awareness of such 'realities', Hazlitt's relationship with him is a voyage of self-discovery. At the outset of this essay about 'the outset of life', Hazlitt cuts across factual narration with a powerful tribute to Coleridge, held gratefully responsible for ensuring that the younger man's 'understanding' 'did not remain dumb and brutish' and 'found a language to express itself' (ix. 96). In Hazlitt's *Great Gatsby*-like mode of narration, where the older Carraway voice evokes and judges his former self, the 'outset of life' is a liminal stage when 'We are in a state between sleeping and waking, and have indistinct but glorious glimpses of strange shapes' (ix. 104). That last phrase might easily slip, if metrically regularised, into a Shelleyan poem, and serve there as a speculative beacon of ultimate hope. In Hazlitt's case, these glimpses are the more tantalisingly impermanent because they were of realities, but realities that have now vanished into a temporal virtuality which can be recovered only through prose evocation. His essay sways between moods and perspectives. On the one hand, it delights in anticipation: so, Hazlitt is buoyed up by the thought '*I was to visit Coleridge in the Spring*' (ix. 102). On the other hand, it is heavy with retrospection, sometimes expressing itself as a general law of the human mind ('As we taste the pleasures of life, their spirit evaporates, the sense palls; and nothing is left but the phantoms, the lifeless shadows of what *has been*!' (ix. 104)), sometimes related to the practice of writing ('I can write fast enough now. Am I better than I was then? Oh no!' (ix. 101)). Superbly resistant to ideological pigeonholing, the essay holds possibilities and limits in suspension; adverse judgements marry grateful recognitions, and the essayist himself is at the centre of the experiencing process. By the close, the West Country, with its *'Valley of Rocks'*, arbours, inns with delicious breakfasts, and 'dark brown heaths overlooking the channel', with sights recalling Coleridge's 'spectre-ship in the *Ancient Mariner*' (ix. 107, 106), is both real and allegorical of the imagination's right to possess a kingdom of its own: one that, Hazlitt suggests through his tenaciously recollecting and arranging art, ought to extend its sway over society at large.

II.

The young Shelley distributed a *Declaration of Rights* during his stay in Lynmouth; a copy was found floating in a bottle near Milford Haven, one of the 'Vessels of Heavenly medicine', no doubt, which Shelley apostrophises in his 'Sonnet: On Launching Some Bottles Filled with *Knowledge* into the British Channel'. Shelley in the West Country brings us face to face with what might be called the *ur*-principles of the Romantic revolutionary imagination. There is the uncompromising sense that reason, art, and eloquence exist for the betterment of humanity. In *Declaration of Rights*, released in August 1812 though printed in Ireland in March of that year, Shelley rehearses the fundamental tenets of his thinking, thinking that draws on Godwin and Paine for its views of government as at best a necessary evil, for its commitment to 'unrestricted liberty of discussion' since 'falsehood', as Shelley says in a flashingly brilliant use of a metaphor found also in Byron's *The Giaour* (first edition 1813), 'is a scorpion that will sting itself to death', and for its dismissal of any Burkean notion of society as a contract between the living and the dead.[13] For Shelley, 'The present generation cannot bind their posterity' (Murray, 58).

What is keenly evident and, indeed, quasi-Hazlittean is the courage which Shelley displayed in asserting his revolutionary ideals at a time when those ideals were hugely out of fashion. A nation engaged in war with Napoleon was in no mood to tolerate dissent or libertarianism. Shelley not only defied such intolerance in his own person; he also defended the right of others to publish heterodox opinion, sending in July and August 1812 various printed copies of his *Letter to Lord Ellenborough*, in which he mounts an impassioned attack on the decision by Lord Ellenborough to sentence the bookseller Daniel Isaac Eaton to eighteen months' imprisonment (including time in the pillory) for publishing *The Age of Reason: Part the Third*, attributed to

Tom Paine and deemed blasphemous. Experiencing the *'perilous pleasure of becoming the champion of an innocent man'* (Murray, 62), as he puts it in his Advertisement, Shelley was, indeed, putting himself in the way of peril (the pamphlet would used against him during the Chancery trial in 1817 over custody of his children by Harriet). The *Letter*, read by E. B. Murray as 'the first sustained example of Shelley's mature style' (356) has in common with Hazlitt's fiercest productions an uncompromising readiness to pick up the gauntlet thrown down by the poet's adversaries. Its cadences support its conviction of the right and duty to speak out:

> Falsehood skulks in holes and corners, 'it lets I dare not wait upon I would, like the poor cat in the adage,' except when it has power, and then, as it was a coward, it is a tyrant; but the eagle-eye of truth darts thro' the undazzling sunbeam of the immutable and just, gathering thence wherewith to vivify and illuminate a universe! (Murray, 64)

The opposition between skulking falsehood and eagle-eyed truth allows of no shade of grey. Yet the same essay refers to the need to be guided 'thro' the labyrinth of life' (65), and the passage above anticipates Shelley's lament in *A Defence of Poetry* that 'we "let *I dare not* wait upon *I would*, like the poor cat in the adage"', Lady Macbeth's taunt again drawn on, this time to regret the fact that 'We want the creative faculty to imagine that which we know' (695). The Shelley of 1812 is less preoccupied by the gulf between imagining and knowing, a gulf which his greatest work explores and seeks to span. But even in the passage quoted above, the mental processes associated with 'truth' are active and engaged, and make us aware of the need to experience and convey it: to gaze at the 'immutable and just', and to gather from that gaze 'wherewith to vivify and illuminate a universe!' The unspecific nature of 'wherewith' suggests less that the gazer will emerge from the encounter with the 'immutable and just' as some bearer of encoded absolutes than that he or she will incorporate into his or her thinking and feeling materials and energies which can be used, first, to revive, then to 'illuminate', 'a' rather than 'the' universe. Truth, we might extrapolate from Shelley's imagery, will be a dynamic process, one involving many cooperating minds, each recreating the world in the light of new insights and recognitions.

More generally, if Hazlitt in 'My First Acquaintance with Poets' looks back, the Shelley of 1812 anticipates. His mode is essentially apocalyptic rather than elegiac, even when retrospection is at work. These summer months, when he was in the West Country, are deeply significant in poetic terms. Linked to the work on *Queen Mab* are reflections in the blank verse poem 'To Harriet' ('It is not blasphemy to hope'), which Dowden speculated was written in Lynmouth, partly because the poem contains strong echoes of *Tintern Abbey*, the scene of which the Shelleys would have passed on their way to Devonshire. Dowden enjoined himself to 'Note the traces' of Wordsworth's poem,[14] and the poem is derivative of Wordsworth in its syntax and phrasing, but strikingly Shelleyan in its concern with lyric subjectivity. The revolutionary self, not for the last time in Shelley's work, is cast as a 'lone spirit' (7) and subject to the 'Dark Flood of Time' (58), even as he hopes it will whirl him on to 'the space / When Time shall be no more' (9–10) (quoted from *CPPBS*). Above all, he appeals for a sustaining of 'the dear love / That binds our souls in soft communion' (46–7), a sustaining that requires 'the stretch of fancy's hope' (30), as though it might, in fact, not be possible. Love and politics mirror one another: the perfect society will, the poem implies, reflect the lovers' 'soft communion', and yet tensions that drive Shelley's later poetry may already be present: after all, the emotional 'binding' he longs for also sounds confining; the poem's cumulative and seemingly rhetorical questions, about, for example, whether the poet may ever 'learn to doubt / The mirror even of Truth' (57–8), tangle themselves up in self-doubting phrases that suggest the possibility of doubt, if not of 'Truth', then of Shelley's capacity to apprehend it, or of Harriet's readiness to support his pursuit of it.

In 'A retrospect of Times of Old' (quoted from *CPPBS*), probably written during his stay in Devon, Shelley produced a poem that, as Dowden noticed, has 'much in common with those earlier pages of "Queen Mab," which picture the fall of empires, and celebrate the oblivion that has overtaken the old rulers of men and lords of the earth'.[15] The poem fast-forwards through history with Shelley's characteristically millenarian eagerness; of the horrors that went into the composing of 'gore-emblazoned Victory' (57), Shelley writes, despatching them with rhythmic verve: 'All, all have faded in past time away! / New Gods, like men, changing in ceaseless flow, / Ever at hand as antient ones decay' (67–9). The prospect of eternal recurrence just glimmers here, in an anticipation of the closing chorus of *Hellas*, but the poem puts its faith in hope for a better future. Hope itself begins to take on a degree of complex uncertainty in 'The Voyage' (quoted from *CPPBS*), a poem in which narrative complicatedness captures the angularity of revolutionary perspectives: the poem is especially fine for the way in which it balances the 'Spirit's visioned solitude' (61), and the dignified trust attributed to 'seafaring men' in Necessity (or 'the Soul of Nature', 108) as 'Blind, changeless and eternal in her paths' (109), against the grim realities of human cruelty (recorded in the visionary's dream) and the horror of conscription visited upon a sailor.

In its vehemence of contempt for those who 'have appropriated human life / And human happiness' (267–8), 'The Voyage' reasserts a conviction in the essential rights deriving from the fact of being 'human'. *Queen Mab*, in the four cantos that Shelley seems to have drafted by 18 August 1812, probably including cantos 2 to 4, blends evocations of West Country seascapes, 'the wild ocean's echoing shore' (ii. 2), with indictments of 'human pride', figured in the collapse of empires (canto 2) and the transience of tyrannical power (canto 3), and of 'War ... the statesman's game, the priest's delight' (iv. 168). The writing's pointedness about how political wrongs are abetted by the abuse of language is formidable, anticipating both the nominalist scepticism of *Hymn to Intellectual Beauty* and the way in which rings are run round orthodoxy in *Prometheus Unbound*: 'They have three words: – well tyrants know their use, / Well pay them for the loan, with usury / Torn from a bleeding world! – God, Hell, and Heaven' (iv. 208–10). These, the opening lines of a passage (up to 220) which was one of four extracts from the poem 'specified in the indictment for blasphemous libel ... against Clark's original piracy' (*CPPBS*, 557) in 1821, illustrate Shelley's sense of tyranny as an interlocking mechanism in which state religion bolsters policies based on inequality, greed, and violence. The cold-eyed ferocity of the writing, its iambic rhythms steely with purpose as they register a voice intent on having its anti-establishment say, is impressively sustained. Things as they are in contemporary political terms contrast with things as they might be in a world whose only constant is dynamic process: 'Throughout this varied and eternal world / Soul is the only element, the block / That for uncounted ages has remained. / The moveless pillar of a mountain's weight / Is active, living spirit' (iv. 139–43).[16] Such an 'active, living spirit' recalls the beliefs of 1790s radicals for whom spirit and matter are interfused in a truly active universe, one on which human institutions might model themselves. A virtual voice in the wilderness, Shelley sought to reaffirm this vision, steeped in Enlightenment values yet vibrant with Romantic revolutionary ardour, in his 1812 West Country writings.

III.

Hazlitt was critical of contemporary poets for their self-centredness. Wordsworth displayed 'a systematic unwillingness to share the palm with his subject' (ii. 328), where 'systematic' suggests that he did so out of settled conviction. Southey 'bows to no authority: he yields only to his own wayward peculiarities' (vii. 216). Byron, 'who in his politics is a *liberal*, in his genius is haughty and aristocratic' (vii. 135–6). Thus, Hazlitt's criticisms of Shelley, principally in 'On Paradox and Common-Place' and in his review of *Posthumous Poems*, are not *sui generis*; they reflect an abiding mistrust on Hazlitt's part against a wilfulness he sees as part of poetic genius. In 'On Paradox and Common-Place' he asserts that poets 'make bad philosophers and worse politicians' since 'They live, for the most part, in an ideal world of their own' (vi. 132). Such an 'ideal world' is where Shelley, above all other poets for Hazlitt, conducts us – and it is all the worse for being an 'ideal world' or Utopia that emerges from the 'metaphysical crucible' (vi. 130) of the poetry, a crucible in which Shelley puts everything about which he wishes to speculate. 'He is clogged', writes Hazlitt sardonically, by 'no dull system of realities' (vi. 130). Or again, 'Spurning the world of realities, he rushed into the world of nonentities and contingencies, like air into a *vacuum*.' Lurking beneath these firework displays of virtuoso brilliance lies ego; Shelley 'became the creature of his own will', 'wasting great powers by their application to unattainable objects' and leaving us with a poetic style that affects as 'a passionate dream, ... a confused embodying of vague abstractions'.[17]

Hazlitt puts the case against his fellow revolutionary Romantic with ruthless one-sidedness. Leigh Hunt sought to redress the balance, and landed some shrewd blows, bringing into the open the gap between Hazlitt's professed belief in disinterestedness and the production of 'twenty articles to show that the most disinterested person in the world [Shelley] is only a malcontent and fanatic', and defending Shelley's use of 'will' to embody the fact that 'the hope of reformation is not everywhere given up'. These are fine insights, as is Hunt's shrewd and delicate understanding of the relationship between the 'real' and the 'ideal' in Shelley. As Hunt notes, his friend's poetry can be read as an attempt to 'do the whole detail of the universe a sort of poetical justice, in default of being able to make his fellow-creatures attend to justice political'.[18] Shelley, one might wish to add, was more various in his poetic endeavours, more dynamic in his vision, and more wide-ranging and far-seeing in his political and spiritual vision than Hazlitt was able to discern. But if it is the essence of the revolutionary imagination to engage in permanent contest, yet to transform the terms of contestatory debate in the light of an imaginative drive for betterment, we can only be grateful for the intersecting legacies bequeathed by both Hazlitt and Shelley: legacies brooded over and kindled into being through their encounters with the West Country.

Notes

1. Unless indicated otherwise, Hazlitt is quoted from *The Selected Writings of William Hazlitt*, ed. Duncan Wu (9 vols, London: Pickering & Chatto, 1998). As here, volume and page numbers are supplied parenthetically.
2. *The Letters of Percy Bysshe Shelley* (2 vols, Oxford: Clarendon Press, 1964), i. 324.
3. *The Complete Poetry of Percy Bysshe Shelley* (2 vols to date, Baltimore: Johns Hopkins University Press, 2002–), ii. 492. Hereafter *CPPBS*.
4. Edward Dowden, *The Life of Percy Bysshe Shelley* (new edition, London: Kegan Paul, 1909), 143.
5. Unless indicated otherwise, Shelley's poetry and prose are quoted from *Percy Bysshe Shelley: the Major Works*, ed. Zachary Leader and Michael O'Neill (Oxford: Oxford University Press, 2003; corrected edition 2009).
6. Nicholas Roe, *Fiery Heart: the First Life of Leigh Hunt* (London: Pimlico, 2005), 331.
7. *The Letters of John Keats*, ed. Hyder E. Rollins (2 vols, Cambridge, MA: Harvard University Press, 1958), i. 193.
8. From Introduction, William Hazlitt, *The Fight and Other Writings*, ed. Tom Paulin and David Chandler, intro. Tom Paulin (London: Penguin, 2000), xvii.
9. Introduction, William Hazlitt, *The Plain Speaker: the Key Essays*, intro. Tom Paulin, ed. Duncan Wu (Oxford: Blackwell, 1998), x, xi, xii–xiii.

10. See David Bromwich, *Hazlitt: the Mind of a Critic* (New Haven: Yale University Press, 1983), esp. 101.

11. Quoted from the reissued Oxford Major Works edition, ed. Stephen Gill (Oxford: Oxford University Press, 2008).

12. See Tom Paulin, *The Day-Star of Liberty: William Hazlitt's Radical Style* (London: Faber, 1998), 133–5, for the suggestion that 1798 here alludes to the Irish Rising.

13. Quoted from *The Prose Works of Percy Bysshe Shelley, Volume I*, ed. E. B. Murray (Oxford: Clarendon Press, 1993), 57. Hereafter 'Murray'.

14. Quoted in Percy Bysshe Shelley, *The Esdaile Notebook: a Volume of Early Poems*, ed. Kenneth Neill Cameron (London: Faber and Faber, 1964), 217.

15. Dowden, *Life*, 143.

16. This edition retains the full stop after 'remained' in Shelley's first 1813 printing.

17. Quoted from Hazlitt's unsigned review of Shelley's *Posthumous Poems* (1824) in *The Edinburgh Review*, July 1824, in Theodore Redpath, *The Young Romantics and Critical Opinion, 1807–1824* (London: Harrap, 1973), 390, 389, 388.

18. From Leigh Hunt's *Lord Byron and Some of his Contemporaries* (1828), in Redpath, *The Young Romantics*, 407, 408, 409–10, 410.

14

'Over the Dartmoor Black': John Keats and the West Country

Nicholas Roe

The death of John Keats's father, Thomas Keates, on the night of Saturday, 14 April 1804, was as mysterious as the beginning of his short life. Over the two centuries since that April night, no one has been able to say where Thomas came from. There are apparently no baptism records for him: perhaps he was a Dissenter, possibly, as Robert Gittings came to suspect, he was illegitimate.[1] Thomas left no will, and no legacy in his favour from a relative has come to light. Even his name proves elusive, scattering into Keates, Keats, Keast, Keate, Keat, Keighte, Keyte, Keet, Keit, Kight, Kite, Kates, Kett, Cate, and Cade.

When Keats heard the news of his father's death he was an eight-year-old pupil at Enfield School. It proved to be the first in a series of losses that shaped his life as a poet who understood that '[t]hat which is creative must create itself'.[2] In his poems and letters Keats says nothing about his parents and forebears beyond observing, in an acrostic poem for his sister-in-law, that the family name 'Keats' was created in song, 'Enchanted . . . the Lord knows where'. Likewise, 'Keats' the poet was embodied for his friends by the strange magic of his own words: the painter Benjamin Haydon recalled how Keats used to recite *Endymion* in a 'half chant', as if his physical presence and the process of enchantment produced by the rhythms of his verse mutually manifested one another.[3] Charles Cowden Clarke also noticed how Keats seemed actually to grow as he recited poetry: 'He *hoisted* himself up, and looked burly and dominant, as he said, "what an image that is – '*sea-shouldering whales!*'"'.[4]

Keats's poetry has always been read in terms of his 'place', both social and geographical. Responding to the *Blackwood's* critics who linked Keats's voice to the disreputable 'Cockney' spheres of London, nineteenth-century commentators identified him with an otherworld of 'magnificent and universal sensuousness' – at once everywhere and nowhere.[5] Keats's aesthetic relocation, isolating him from the 'reality' Richard Woodhouse recognised as his principal subject, was one reason for recent new historicist endeavours to return him to contemporary social and political contexts.[6] This chapter attends to other senses of 'place' in Keats by investigating locations and environments in which Keats lived and wrote, or was rumoured to have done. It explores ideas of his origins that had currency among his family and friends, and speculates on how his poetry may have been shaped by the possibility of the family's West Country ancestry. Amy Lowell dismissed Louis Holman's collection of places associated with Keats, by observing '[t]here's nothing so silly as to try to date a poet's work geographically'.[7] On the contrary, Keats in his poems was particularly responsive to the sense of place. To follow him through the English landscape is also to track the paths and byways of his imagination as they diverge, converge or intersect in the restless process of self-creation.

At Lulworth Cove – two centuries back

According to family tradition Thomas Keates was a native of the West Country. Keats's sister, Frances, heard the story from Eleanor Jones, the wife of her guardian Richard Abbey: 'I was told when a child', she recalled aged eighty-three, 'that my father was a native of Lands End Cornwall.'[8] The villages of Madron and Sennen have been mentioned as possible locations, although Keatses were widespread in Cornwall in the eighteenth and nineteenth centuries. When I visited the churchyard at St Neot, under Bodmin Moor, I discovered the tombstone of a Thomas Keast and close to him the grave of a William Rawlins – a proximity that Hardy would have relished. The poet's friend and biographer Charles Brown avowed that '[h]is father was a native of Devonshire'.[9] Perhaps Thomas was one of the mariner Keates who plied the coast between Penzance, Plymouth, and London.

Thomas Keates has also been traced to Dorset, following Joseph Severn's recollection that in late September 1820 the *Maria Crowther*, en route for Rome, had put in to the Dorset coast. From Wednesday 20 to Wednesday 27 September, the brig was battered by equinoctial storms and hurricane force winds, until the weather abated over the last three days of the month.[10] They moored at Portsmouth on the 28th, enabling Keats to pass his last night in England with the Snook family at Bedhampton, then set sail on the 29th. When the wind again turned contrary, it seems likely that they landed on the Dorset coast on Saturday 30 September or Sunday 1 October, and Keats with Severn went ashore. When they came back on board, if Severn can be believed, Keats made a holograph of his sonnet 'Bright star' on a blank page of the 1806 *Poetical Works of William Shakespeare*.[11] That Severn knew the sonnet was not originally composed on this occasion appears from his letter to Charles Brown, 19 September 1821, asking, 'do you [know] the sonnet beginning – "Bright star – would I were stedfast as thou art" – he wrote this down in the ship.'[12] Severn later changed his account of the Dorset landing and 'Bright star', and it is worth registering at the outset that Keats 'wrote [the poem] down' and Severn suspected Brown might know it already. Possibly he was aware of Brown's transcriptions of Keats's poems, in which a quite different version of 'Bright star' appears under the title 'Sonnet (1819)'. This formed the text for its first publication, titled 'Sonnet. (*From the unpublished Poems of John Keats*)', in *The Plymouth and Devonport Weekly Journal*, Thursday 27 September 1838, where it appeared in the top left hand corner of an inside page.[13]

Severn's first public recollection of the Dorset landing was in a letter to *The Union Magazine*, published in February 1846 with a facsimile of the 'Bright star' sonnet reproduced from the Shakespeare *Poetical Works*.[14] 'The present exquisite Sonnet was written under such interesting circumstances that I cannot forbear making them public', Severn tells us:

> Keats and myself were beating about in the British Channel in the autumn of 1820, anxiously waiting for a wind to take us to Italy, which place, together with the sea-voyage, were deemed likely to preserve his life; for he was then in a state of consumption which left but the single hope of an Italian sojourn to save him. The stormy British sea, after a fortnight, had exhausted him; and on our arrival off the Dorsetshire coast, having at last the charm of a fine and tranquil day, we landed to recruit.

Severn goes on to explain how the landing in Dorset 'recruited' Keats, and in so doing initiated a myth about his origins in which poetry and place were drawn together:

> The shores, with the beautiful grottoes which opened to fine verdure and cottages, were the means of transporting Keats once more into the regions of poetry; – he showed me these things exultingly, as though they had been his birthright. The change in him was wonderful, and continued even after our return to the ship, when he took a volume (which he had a few days before given me) of Shakespeare's Poems, and in it he wrote me the subjoined Sonnet, which at the time I thought the most enchanting of all his efforts. Twenty-five years have passed away, and I have by degrees (in the love I bear to his memory) placed it in my mind as amongst the most enchanting poetry of the world.
>
> After writing this Sonnet, Keats sank down into a melancholy state, and never wrote again, save one painful letter on the same subject as the Sonnet – ...[15]

'Echoing grottos, full of tumbling waves / And moonlight' are associated in *Endymion* with sleep and a 'silvery enchantment' that 'calm'd to life again' (I. 453–64). Severn had heard Keats read *Endymion* in 1817 and possessed his own copy of the poem, and it is possible he consciously recollected those lines in describing how the grottoed shore encountered 'as though his birthright' rapt Keats 'into the regions of poetry'. So it was that Keats 'wrote ... the ... Sonnet ... and never wrote again'. While not suggesting that 'Bright star' originated here, the passage embraces ideas of birth, a native place, renewed creativity and, finally, an 'enchanting' sense of completion as the scene of 'birthright' forms the backdrop to what has become Keats's last poem.

From Severn the story was transmitted to Richard Monckton Milnes, who gave it a different slant:

> He landed once more in England, on the Dorchester coast, after a weary fortnight spent in beating about the Channel: the bright beauty of the day and the scene revived for a moment the poet's drooping heart, and the inspiration remained on him for some time even after his return to the ship. It was then that he composed that Sonnet of solemn tenderness —
>
> 'Bright star! Would I were stedfast as thou art,' &c.*
>
> and wrote it out in a copy of Shakespeare's Poems he had given to Severn a few days before. I know of nothing written afterwards.[16]

Milnes' asterisk alerted readers to 'See the Literary Remains' where 'Bright star', headed 'Keats's Last Sonnet', closed the second volume.[17] Milnes had based his printed text of the poem on Keats's holograph in the copy of Shakespeare's *Poetical Works*, and as an alternative to the closing line gave in a footnote, 'Another reading: – Half-passionless, and so swoon to death', drawn from the separate transcript of the poem by Charles Brown.[18] Brown had sent Milnes his transcripts of Keats's poems and his manuscript 'Life of John Keats' in March 1841, for use in preparing *The Life, Letters, and Literary Remains*.[19] That Milnes was aware of Brown's different version of the poem, titled 'Sonnet (1819)', did not sway his judgement that on landing in Dorset in October 1820 Keats had *composed* the sonnet, and that there was 'nothing written afterwards'.

Harry Buxton Forman's edition of Keats's *Poetical Works* (1883) quoted Milnes's account from 1848 and once again reproduced the facsimile of 'Bright star' from the Shakespeare *Poetical Works*.[20] In the interim, Milnes had published a new edition of his book in 1867, altering his account of the Dorset landing to intimate that he knew 'of nothing composed' after 'Bright star', further underlining the supposition that the sonnet had been originally composed on that occasion.[21] This idea rapidly gained ground, and in late nineteenth-century editions of the poems 'Bright star' was routinely titled 'Keats's Last Sonnet'.[22]

Severn had known in 1821 that the sonnet did not date from October 1820 but understandably, as many years passed, that awareness had dimmed. In 1873, aged seventy-nine, he presented an account in his autobiography 'My Tedious Life' that consolidated the myth of original composition:

Ariving on the Doncaster coast Keats was persuaded to land with me & for a moment he became like his former self, he showed me the splendid caverns & grottos with a poets pride as tho' they had been his birthright & when we returned to the ship he wrote for me in a vol of Shakespeare's Poems that magnificent sonnet … I am not aware if this was not the first transcript of this fine Poet[r]y for it seemed inspired by our recent visit to the seacoast – I believe certainly that this sonnet was the very last poetical effort the poor fellow ever made …[23]

'Doncaster coast' is crossed out in the manuscript and 'Dorchester' pencilled above by a later hand – the mistake is typical of Severn, whose 1820 'Journal of the Voyage' had 'Dundee Ness' for 'Dungeness'.[24] His idea that 'Bright star' was Keats's 'last poetical effort' echoes his own letter to *The Union Magazine*, while his new suggestion that the sonnet 'seemed inspired by our recent visit' falls in with Milnes's supposition that it was then 'composed' and gives the story the imprimatur of the man who had accompanied Keats.

'My Tedious Life' was unpublished when Sidney Colvin's and W. M. Rossetti's two biographical studies of Keats appeared in 1887, fixing the location of the landing as Severn had not done. First, Colvin's version:

> They landed on the Dorsetshire coast, apparently near Lulworth, and spent a day exploring its rocks and caves, the beauties of which Keats showed and interpreted with the delighted insight of one initiated from his birth into the secrets of nature. On board the same night he wrote the sonnet which every reader of English knows so well; placing it, by a pathetic choice or chance, opposite the heading of a *Lover's Complaint*, on a blank leaf of the folio copy of Shakespeare's poems … These were Keats's last verses.

And here is Rossetti:

> The last verses which Keats ever wrote formed the sonnet here ensuing. He composed ['Bright star'] late in September 1820, after landing on the Dorsetshire coast, probably near Lulworth, and returning to the ship which bore him to his doom in Italy; and he wrote it down on a blank page in Shakespeare's Poems, facing 'A Lover's Complaint'.[25]

It is not clear where Colvin's and Rossetti's ideas of Lulworth came from: possibly both writers took Lulworth, a well-known site of picturesque beauty, as the readiest point of reference, and from then on the locality 'near Lulworth' was fixed as fact.

Five years after Colvin's and Rossetti's books Keats, Severn, and the *Maria Crowther* sailed into the treacherous currents of William Sharp's *Life and Letters of Joseph Severn* (1892), where the anecdote from 'My Tedious Life' was quoted and further elaborated:

Off the Dorset coast the schooner one day lay becalmed, and Keats ventured ashore with his friend. 'For a moment', says the latter, 'he became like his former self. He was in a part that he already knew, and showed me the splendid caverns and grottos with a poet's pride, as though they had been his by birthright. When he returned to the ship he wrote for me on a blank leaf in a folio volume of Shakespeare's "Poems", which had been given him by a friend, and which he gave to me in memory of our voyage, the following magnificent sonnet' ... 'This', says Severn, 'was the very last poetical effort the poor fellow ever made'.[26]

Severn's 1846 remark about Keats's 'birthright' has been firmed-up in Sharp's version, so that when Keats landed on the 'Dorset coast' he became like his 'former self ... in a part that he already knew'. Having set the scene Sharp allows Severn to sketch Keats's 'very last poetical effort', a poem both original and conclusive, in a setting that was familiar from the poet's early life and where he set foot in England for the last time.

At the dawn of the twentieth century a cluster of associations had gathered around Keats's and Severn's Dorset landing:

- They had landed on the Dorset coast at or near Lulworth Cove in late September or early October 1820.
- It was then that Keats wrote out the 'Bright star' sonnet in Shakespeare's *Poetical Works* (Severn, 1821; Severn, 1846; Colvin, 1887), or actually composed it (Milnes, 1848; Milnes, 1867; Severn, 1873; Rossetti, 1887; Sharp, 1892).
- 'Bright star' was the last poem Keats wrote (Severn, 1846; Milnes, 1848; Milnes, 1867; Severn, 1873; Colvin and Rossetti, 1887; Sharp, 1892).
- The landscape of the Dorset coast appeared 'as though [Keats's] birthright' (Severn, 1846, 1873; Sharp, 1892); he was 'in a part he already knew' (Sharp, 1892).

All of these associations, suppositions, and fictions are gathered into Thomas Hardy's encounter with Keats, the commonplace and the extraordinary, in his poem 'At Lulworth Cove a Century Back':

> Had I but lived a hundred years ago
> I might have gone, as I have gone this year,
> By Warmwell Cross on to a Cove I know,
> And Time have placed his finger on me there:
>
> '*You see that man?*' — I might have looked, and said,
> 'O yes: I see him. One that boat has brought
> Which dropped down Channel round Saint Alban's Head.
> So commonplace a youth calls not my thought.'

'*You see that man?*' — 'Why yes; I told you; yes:
Of an idling town-sort; thin; hair brown in hue;
And as the evening light scants less and less
He looks up at a star, as many do.'

'*You see that man?*' — 'Nay, leave me!' then I plead,
'I have fifteen miles to vamp across the lea,
And it grows dark, and I am weary-kneed:
I have said the third time; yes, that man I see!'

'Good. That man goes to Rome — to death, despair;
And no one notes him now but you and I:
A hundred years, and the world will follow him there,
And bend with reverence where his ashes lie.'

As an afterthought Hardy added the date, '*September* 1920', and this note:

> In September 1820 Keats, on his way to Rome, landed one day on the
> Dorset coast, and composed the sonnet, 'Bright star! Would I were stead-
> fast as thou art'. The spot of his landing is judged to have been Lulworth
> Cove.[27]

With Keats 'look[ing] up at a star, as many do', Hardy's poem represents the
culmination of the nineteenth-century tradition that located the composition of 'Bright star' at Lulworth. Five years earlier Colvin had published
in the *Times Literary Supplement* a note that used Brown's transcript to
prove that the sonnet 'in a slightly different form, was work of an earlier
date'. The point was repeated in Colvin's full-length biography of 1917.[28]
Numerous critics and biographers since Colvin have debated the moment of
its composition, variously fixing the date between 1818 and 1820. Over the
same period Sharp's claim that Dorset was 'a part that [Keats] already knew'
has received intense scrutiny that shows no sign of abating. In 1922 Amy
Lowell alluded to 'Keats's intimacy with the Dorsetshire coast'; seventy-five
years later that locality was revisited, with fresh suggestions, by Andrew
Motion.[29]

Thomas Hardy and the horse-dealing Keatses

In April 1914 Sidney Colvin wrote to a Truro newspaper, *The West Briton*,
inviting information about 'the family name Keats ... [and] any record of a
Thomas Keats who is likely to have been the poet's father, or any record of
a family from which he is likely to have sprung'.[30] He received a considerable response, some of it discouraging: the Cornish historian J. Hambley
Rowe searched widely for records of Keats/Keast names in local parish
registers, and found 'no evidence of a decisive character'.[31] On 18 April *The*

Times republished the *West Briton* letter. It was noticed by Thomas Hardy, who also received a letter from Colvin about Severn's claims. He replied on 14 June 1914:

> We have been weighing probabilities in the question of the 'splendid caverns & grottoes' of Severn, that you write about, & have come to the conclusion that he must mean 'Durdle Door', close to Lulworth Cove. ... Why we think it must have been Durdle Door is that it impressed my wife just in the same way when she first saw it as a girl.

Colvin accepted Hardy's suggestion and his 1917 biography introduced Durdle Door – the arch of limestone that strides seawards to the west of Lulworth – along with the rocky cleft of Stair Hole, closer to the Cove itself.[32] The Dorset landing and its location at or near Lulworth Cove reappear in all twentieth-century biographies of Keats, with some variations on possible locations including Studland Bay and Holworth.[33]

Thomas Hardy was intrigued and speculated about other places for Keats's landing, at isolated Worbarrow Bay to the east of Lulworth ('but it is difficult to find') and remote Cave Hole, Portland ('difficult of access except at low & quiet tides').[34] Ranging through his own imaginative domain of Wessex, Hardy had also been drawn back to memories of his early childhood and his father. 'I am sending some Keats names that I jotted down when you wrote to the papers', Hardy tells Colvin: 'They are useless, I fancy, which is why I did not send them earlier. However here they are. I knew personally all the persons mentioned, & used always to be struck by their resemblance to the poet.'[35] The 1851 England census shows that a carrier named William Keates and his family lived next door to Hardy's childhood home at Higher Bockhampton, and Hardy adds in a follow-up note to Colvin: 'some 40 years ago my father told me that the K—s of this neighbourhood came of a family of horse-dealers, who lived in the direction of Broadmayne'.[36]

The horse-dealers of Broadmayne passed directly into Colvin's biography ('Mr. Thomas Hardy tells me of a Keats family sprung from a horsedealer of Broadmayne ...'[37]) and thence to another biographer, also on the trail of the Dorset Keatses, who regarded Hardy's suggestion as 'most plausible'. Amy Lowell had written 'at once' to Hardy's second wife, Florence Dugdale, who replied on 29 July 1922. 'Mrs. Hardy's letter is a little fuller in detail than Sir Sidney's account', Lowell tells her readers, 'and the detail gives the matter a more likely possibility.' With Sir Sidney squashed, Lowell quotes from her own more copious source:

> there was a family named Keats living two or three miles from here, who, Mr. Hardy was told by his father, was a branch of a family of the name living in the direction of Lulworth, where John Keats is assumed to have landed on his way to Rome (it being the only spot on this coast answering

to the description). They kept horses, being what is called 'hauliers', and did also a little farming. They were in feature singularly like the poet, and were quick-tempered as he is said to have been, one of them being nicknamed 'light-a-fire' on that account. All this is very vague, and may mean nothing, the only arresting point in it considering that they were of the same name, being the facial likeness, which my husband says was very strong. He knew two or three of these Keatses.[38]

Shortly after this correspondence a picturesque article in *The Times* entitled 'Hardys and Keatses' cited a riot near Dorchester, Christmas Eve 1827, when the Fordington Mummers attacked the Bockhampton Band. Among the Bockhampton contingent were one John Hardy and three of the Keates clan – Joseph, William, and Charles. 'It is impossible to escape the feeling', the article says, 'that Mr. Hardy knew more than he told when he was reminiscent to inquiring friends … of a possible clue to the ancestry of Keats.'[39]

The tradition of Keats's Dorset ancestry lingered on as recently as 1962, as did the details of the Hardys' accounts:

> While I was organist at Upwey church (1927–1929) there were living in the village a Mr. and Mrs. Wakeley. He was a retired blacksmith, and she before her marriage was a Miss Keats from Broadmayne. I always understood that she was related to the poet Keats … Also, rather curiously, there are or were a family of 'horse-dealers' named Keats in that area.[40]

While it is unlikely that we shall ever know what Hardy's horse-keeping hauliers looked like, their trade identified them as plausible kin for the Thomas Keates who in the 1790s became Head Ostler of the Swan and Hoop livery stable at Moorfields. If Hardy's suggestion was right, Thomas had moved to London but continued in the horse trade. Other branches of the Keats family had a facial resemblance to the poet, as we shall see, and in the absence of more conventional documentary sources one should not discount such likenesses – assuming that they can be demonstrated.

At the mid twentieth century Robert Gittings made strenuous efforts to refine the search, zooming-in on Sharp's suggestion that Keats 'already knew' the Dorset coastal area and proposing as possible forebears of the poet several nests of Keatses at Broadmayne, Owermoigne, and Holworth, all villages on the road that led eastward from Dorchester to Lulworth and onwards to Poole and Corfe Castle.[41] In an article from 1958, Gittings thought he had got his man:

> The name Keats … is fairly generally distributed along the South Coast, but a search of parish records in this strip of coastline gives some interesting results. Studland and Lulworth both have Keatses during the poet's lifetime, though in the latter place the more usual seems to have

been Cates with a C: but it is in the parish of Owermoigne, farther west towards Weymouth, and including the hamlet of Holworth and the fine bay of Ringstead, that the Keatses seem to have been something more than a 'little clan'.[42]

Gittings brings forward a John Keats, born 'about 1755' who by 1803 was living at Owermoigne – some five or six miles from Dorchester – where he was employed as a turf and furze-cutter and as 'some sort of carter and haulier'. This John Keats fits the Hardys' idea that the Keatses who resembled the poet were 'hauliers', although Gittings concedes that the 'connection must remain only a possibility'. Still, the 'main points' were the numbers of Keatses in this area of the Dorset coast; the fact that Keats's father worked with horses; and 'the strong physical and temperamental likeness between this family and the poet, observed by Thomas Hardy, who "used to notice such things"'.[43] Gittings later distanced this possibility, noting in an appendix to his biography of Keats merely that 'Thomas Hardy informed Colvin and Mrs. Hardy informed Amy Lowell ... that a family called Keats in the East Dorset village of Broadmayne bore a facial and temperamental likeness to the poet. Although no Thomas Keats was baptised in any Dorset parish in 1773 or early 1774 except one in Fordington (Dorchester) very early in 1773',[44] the road that led from Hardy's Dorchester to Corfe Castle and Poole held other Keats associations.

Hannen Swaffer (1879–1962) the journalist, critic, socialist, and spiritualist traced his forebears through his grandmother Eliza Hannen (born 23 March 1814) to her father Samuel Keats, a stonemason of Corfe Castle said to have been distantly related to the poet. A photograph of Samuel survives, inscribed 'Samuel Keats, 1st cousin of the poet'. It shows no resemblance to Keats although his interest in statuary, Druid circles, and his evocation of Saturn, 'quiet as a stone', might form some acknowledgement of Samuel's 'kindred hand'. Eliza's cousin Amelia Keats was born at Poole, 28 June 1820, the daughter of Elizabeth and Charles Keats, a victualler. When she died on Christmas day, 1917, at Wirtemberg Street, Clapham, Amelia Spicer (née Keats) was reported to be 104 years old, a 'step-sister' of the poet who kept his portrait over the fireplace in her sitting-room. Amelia seems to have confused her birthday with her cousin's and there is nothing to bear out her story of being the poet's 'step-sister' (which is not to rule out a family link of some kind during the nineteenth century).[45]

Just as the passing of Amelia, 'the last Miss Keats', was reported in Clapham, news came to the Boston Keatsian, Fred Holland Day, that the 'entrancingly beautiful' dancer Mildred Keats, star of the silent movie 'Queen of the Sea' (1918) strikingly resembled the poet. Sought out by Day, Mildred claimed that 'to the personal knowledge of her grandfather (Thos. Keats, b. Cornwall Eng in 1837, and now [1921] living in Portland, Ore., aged 84) who *was named after the poet's father*, Thomas Keats the father of the poet came from Cornwall Eng. Miss Keats' grandfather was born less than a square away from the house in which the poet's father was born.' Day made no note of where exactly in Cornwall the 'square' that separated the birthplaces of Mildred's two Thomas Keatses could be found. Mildred Keats went on to star on Broadway in the 1920s, and her claim of a family link to John Keats seems to have been little more than that.

Apart from the landing in September/October 1820, the nearest that Keats is known to have come to Cornwall and Dorset was on his journey in early May 1818 from Teignmouth to London with his brother Tom, when the mail coach followed the route from Honiton through Axminster and Bridport to Dorchester, then turned north east to Blandford and Salisbury. At Carisbrooke on the Isle of Wight, April 1817, from 'the little hill close by' he could see the whole of the north of the island, and across the Solent to the coastline extending westwards to Poole, Studland Bay, and Lulworth.[46] At Winchester, August–September 1819, Keats was living close to the Wiltshire/ Dorset border. On the face of it, these separate instances do not amount to much, yet when taken together Keats's various migrations from London 1817–20 show a marked westward tendency, to the Isle of Wight (April 1817; June–August 1819); to Teignmouth (March–May 1818 and, wishfully, May 1819[47]); to the Chichester–Bedhampton area (January 1819); to Winchester (August–October 1819). Furthermore each of these visits coincided with major phases of composition: *Endymion* (Isle of Wight, April 1817); *Isabella* and the verse epistle 'Dear Reynolds' (Teignmouth, March–May 1818); *The Eve of St Agnes* (Chichester–Bedhampton, January 1819); *Lamia* and *Otho the Great* (Isle of Wight, June–August 1819); *Lamia, Otho the Great, The Fall of Hyperion* and 'To Autumn' (Winchester, August–October 1819). Although it proved mistaken, the supposition that Keats's final Dorset sojourn also stirred a 'poetical effort' in 'Bright star' fitted an established pattern of poetic composition in Keats – a pattern, moreover, that apparently responded to the magnetism of the West Country held by family tradition to have been associated with his forebears.

Haberdasher Keats; Bookseller Keats; Sheriff Keats; Admiral Keats

Besides Keats's sister Frances, other Keatses connected with the poet traced their ancestry to the far west. We know that the poet's father, and therefore Keats himself, had a relative named Elizabeth, and apparently a young cousin, Joseph Keats, a London haberdasher.[48] This haberdasher's son, Joseph Henry Keats, was born around 1816 and in later life set up as a bookseller in Brighton where he became acquainted with Bryan Waller Procter ('Barry Cornwall'). Writing in 1858, Procter takes up the story:

> I said Mr Keats, you bear the name of a very fine poet' — 'Yes, sir'; (he answered) 'I was a second cousin of Mr Keats. I have more than once talked about him, with Mr Leigh Hunt'. — 'Well I know Mr Leigh Hunt

very well and I knew Mr Keats the poet also'. 'Ah! — I am related also to Mr Sheriff Keats —' 'I don't know him' (I replied) 'but you may depend upon it the poet was the greatest man ...'[49]

In claiming kin as a 'second cousin' to the poet, bookseller Joseph Keats identified his father (the haberdasher) as a cousin of the poet's father, Thomas, and Joseph's and Thomas's parents as siblings who shared a common ancestor. Bookseller Keats also said he was related 'to Mr Sheriff Keats' and, if we can believe him, so were the poet and his father. Mr Sheriff Keats was Frederick Keats, Sheriff of London 1856–7, a direct descendant of John Keats (1745–88), vintner of Newport Pagnall, and his wife Ann Mower (d. 1829) who were married at St George's, Hanover Square, 7 January 1777. Their sons, Thomas Mower Keats (born 1778) and Joseph Keats (born 1783), owned hatter's businesses within yards of each other at 14, The Poultry and 74, Cheapside – addresses known to John Keats, who in 1816 lived with his brothers at 76, Cheapside.[50] Thomas Mower Keats married Fanny Fortnum, and it was their son, Frederick (1807–65), who became Sheriff of London on Tuesday, 30 September 1856. On that occasion *The Times* reported that Sheriff Keats was descended from 'an ancient and honourable family in the west of England'.[51] If that was true, then so were the hatter Keatses of Cheapside and – assuming here that Procter's report is reliable – so were John Keats the poet and his father Thomas.[52] A mid-Victorian photograph of Frederick in his Sheriff's gown closely resembles the poet's compact figure, as if this might be a middle-aged John Keats, Poet Laureate, at his installation after Wordsworth's death in 1850. Frederick also resembles the stocky presence of another relative boasted in *The Times*, who was 'one of the most distinguished admirals of the navy': Sir Richard Goodwin Keats.[53] And Admiral Richard returns us, more or less, to the West Country.

What high windows show

Sir Richard Goodwin Keats, hero of numerous naval actions during the Napoleonic wars, highly regarded by Nelson, was born on 16 January 1757 at Chalton, Hampshire, the eldest son of Rev. Richard Keats (of a Devonshire family) and his wife Elizabeth. Richard's birthplace is significant in that, as we have seen, John Keats was drawn repeatedly to this part of England – to Chichester, Bedhampton, the Isle of Wight, and to Winchester where Richard Goodwin Keats was educated. In *John Keats: the Living Year* Robert Gittings argued that Keats's attendance at the consecration of Lewis Way's chapel at Stansted Park on Monday, 25 January 1819, provided him with images for Madeline's room in *The Eve of St Agnes*. According to Gittings, stanzas 24 and 25 –

> A casement high and triple-arch'd there was,
> All garlanded with carven imag'ries

> Of Fruits, and flowers, and bunches of knot-grass,
> And diamonded with panes of quaint device …

(208–11)

– are 'an almost exact description of the windows opposite which Keats spent two or three hours in Stansted Chapel'.[54] The resemblances, first pointed out by Mary Moorman, are indeed striking, as are Keats's possible links with Lewis Way. The Ways came from a family at Bridport, Dorset; Ways had been prominent at Guy's Hospital; and Keats's friends Woodhouse and Reynolds were acquainted with the owner of Stansted.[55] Keats and Brown had recently visited Chichester to stay with the parents of Charles Wentworth Dilke, and had moved a dozen miles westward to the Old Mill House, Bedhampton, the home of Dilke's sister Letitia and her husband John Snook. Was it merely curiosity roused by the advertisement in the *Sussex Weekly Advertiser* –

> THE CONSECRATION of the CHAPEL in STANSTED PARK, will take place on Monday, the 25th instant, (being the holiday of the Conversion of St. Paul) …

– that induced Keats and Brown to make the five-mile up-hill journey on a wet Monday morning, 'in a chaise behind a leaden horse', to keep company with 'the Right Rev. the LORD BISHOP of St. DAVID's, or the Honourable and Right Rev. the LORD BISHOP of GLOUCESTER'?[56] Keats's views about the bishops' 'bare-faced oppression and impertinence' are well known, and can hardly have been much of an encouragement for him to attend this consecration of a chapel dedicated to the conversion of the Jews.[57] He reported that the ceremony was 'not amusing', that he began to 'hate Parsons', and that he was ill for some time afterwards – 'my own fault of exposing myself to the Weather'.[58] His presence at Stansted Chapel seems strange, unless he was drawn there by the local Keats associations. Stansted Park is just three miles from Chalton, where Richard Goodwin Keats had spent his childhood. Of course it can be argued that three miles might as well be three hundred miles: Keats was not in Chalton itself, and there is no evidence that he was consciously tracking down a place associated with a possible relative. However, it is not *im*possible: Lieutenant Midgley John Jennings, Keats's heroic uncle, had been badly wounded at the Battle of Camperdown, 11 October 1797. As a serving officer in the marines he would certainly have known of and very likely talked about Richard Goodwin Keats's exploits aboard his most famous command, the *Superb*, and, anyway, Keats can hardly have missed the numerous references to Captain Keats in *The Times* and *Examiner*. While there is nothing more explicit to link Keats's presence at Stansted-by-Chalton with Captain Keats of the *Superb* it is significant that, once again, his travels and patterns of poetic composition coincided with Keats presences that in this instance apparently extended to an actual family link of some kind.

That there was another building known to Keats with a 'casement high and triple-arch'd' seems to have been overlooked. This was the schoolhouse at Enfield, the large seventeenth-century mansion built of rich red brick where John Ryland and John Clarke established their school in 1787. The façade was moulded into fanciful designs of flowers and pomegranates with cherubs' heads peeking over niches.[59] Above this, protruding from the tiles, were three latticed windows – in this case, truly 'high' *and* 'triple arched', and as Keats recalls in *The Eve of St Agnes,* 'All garlanded with carven imageries / Of fruits, and flowers' (209–10). Here Midgley John Jennings was educated before he entered the marines and, shortly afterwards, Keats and his brothers George and Tom. According to a school friend, 'Jennings their sailor relation was always in the thoughts of the brothers & they determined to keep up the family reputation for courage.'[60] Perhaps the 'triple-arch'd' windows of Stansted Chapel reminded Keats of the 'high and triple arch'd' windows of his school – the windows, probably, of the rooms where the boys slept in small dormitories. It's possible that there was also another association, drawing in his sailor relations and the mysterious origins of the family, that carried Keats back to the memory of schooldays behind these famous lines, written shortly after Keats's visit to Stansted Chapel:

> The boisterous, midnight, festive clarion,
> The kettle-drum, and far-heard clarionet,
> Affray his ears, though but in dying tone: –
> The hall door shuts again, and all the noise is gone.

> (258–61)

According to Charles Cowden Clarke, Keats said the final line '"came into my head when I remembered how I used to listen in bed to your music at school"' – a memory that speaks in part of the reassuring community he joined at Enfield.[61] A record of such first causes of great art would be 'enchanting', Clarke adds, without indicating how the schoolboy became the poet of *The Eve of St Agnes* who, like Shakespeare in *Twelfth Night,* mingles warmth and chill, merriment and melancholy as Porphyro and Madeline meet by moonlight.

The 'dying tone' of Keats's music was almost certainly suggested by the 'dying fall' of Orsino's opening speech in *Twelfth Night,* and it allows the moonlit scene of romance associated with happy schooldays to invoke the sombre memory of his father's death as he returned from an evening of merriment like the one in *The Eve of St Agnes.* Occurring less than a year after Keats entered Enfield School, the death of his father on the night of

14 April 1804 so tempered Keats that his memory of merrymaking and music fled acquired the finality of that grim monosyllable: 'gone'. Underlying the sumptuous imagery and rich textures of *The Eve of St Agnes* is a memory of the loss that had set the schoolboy Keats on the path to become a poet and also, perhaps, thoughts of remoter ancestors now out of reach, enchanted 'o'er the southern moors' where Porphyro and Madeline are, likewise, 'gone: ay, ages long ago' (370).

Coda

Jean Haynes, the distinguished genealogist who devoted more than fifty years to the pursuit of Keats family associations, responded to my enquiry about Keats's 'step-sister' Amelia Spicer:

> I am afraid this is old stuff. I researched this claim and others, like that of Hannen Swaffer, another relative, and although one gets back to Dorset many times, the Keatses in, say Corfe Castle, are legion, and those in Poole connected with the Newfoundland fisheries – mentioned by Keats – the notes I have on their wills do not give any conclusive connection with the poet's father. I looked at the registers in the churches in Poole and Corfe back in the 1960s. Amelia Spicer lived in S. London and her ancestry went back to a stonemason, Samuel Keats. There was also a Charles Keats of Poole. Richard Church mentioned the Hannen Swaffer claim but, until, as one of my other correspondents on this theme said once, a will is found where the writer says, 'my brother/cousin/uncle Thomas Keats of the Swan and Hoop, Moorgate' surfaces, I don't see how he can be identified ——
>
> I feel sure [Keats] knew Dorset and Devon. His letters from Teignmouth – where we often went on holiday on his account – hint that he had relatives there. I did go to visit an old lady there the god-daughter of the Captain Tonkin mentioned by Keats. She was in her late eighties about 1955 so I don't know how old the Captain could have been.
>
> Sorry I can't help further on this. There are a lot of people on the internet claiming connection largely through sharing the name, which is also common in Staffs. I wrote an article for the Society of Genealogists magazine about a year ago hoping it might stir up some response, but – no joy.

Until evidence emerges as to who Thomas Keates was, and where he came from, Keats's West Country forebears must remain a matter of conjecture based on Fanny Keats's recollections in old age, and anecdotal evidence that links the poet with Sheriff Keats, Admiral Keats, and 'an ancient and honourable family in the west of England'. Still, while the Dorset Keatses are ubiquitous yet elusive, there remains the evidence of Keats's imagination traced briefly in this essay. This suggests that for Keats there was some kind of attraction, magnetism, or 'enchantment' about England's West Country that coincided with family traditions and affected his imaginative life and physical movements around England, 1817–20. Perhaps it was not a matter of chance, then, that as Porphyro and Madeline make their escape Keats's first thought was to send his lovers to an ancient, ancestral dwelling further west than Dorset or Devonshire – in Cornwall, or the far-flung point where the West Country meets the sea, at Land's End:

> 'Let us away, my love, with happy speed:
> There are no ears to hear or eyes to see ...
> Put on warm clothing, sweet, and fearless be,
> Over the Dartmoor black I have a home for thee'.[62]

Notes

1. Typescript of 'Standing Apart', BBC Radio 3 programme broadcast 23 February 1971, in the Robert Gittings archive at West Sussex Record Office, Chichester, West Sussex Record Office, Add Mss 42, 137, page 6.
2. *Letters of John Keats*, ed. Hyder Rollins (2 vols, Cambridge, MA: Harvard University Press, 1958; 1972), i. 374, hereafter *LJK*.
3. *The Keats Circle*, ed. Hyder Rollins (2nd edition, Cambridge, MA: Harvard University Press, 1948; 1969), ii. 143, hereafter *KC*.
4. Charles and Mary Cowden Clarke, *Recollections of Writers* (1878; Fontwell: Centaur Press, 1969), 126, hereafter *RoW*.
5. David Masson, 'The Life and Poetry of Keats', *Macmillan's Magazine* (November 1860), rpt. in *Keats: the Critical Heritage*, ed. G. M. Matthews (London: Routledge, 1971), 381.
6. For Woodhouse, see *The Manuscripts of the Younger Romantics*, gen. ed. Donald H. Reiman, *John Keats*, ed. Jack Stillinger (7 vols, New York and London: Garland 1985–8), volume iv; 'Poems, Transcripts, Letters, & c. Facsimiles of Richard Woodhouse's Scrapbook Materials in the Pierpont Morgan Library', 240.
7. Houghton Library, Holman MS Am 800. 48, 'Notes by Edna Bowne Holman (Mrs. L. A. H.) of remarks by Amy Lowell during first interview between her and my father'.
8. Fanny Keats's draft recollections about the origins of the Keats family, pencilled on a letter from Harry Buxton Forman of 1 February 1886; Houghton Library, MS. Eng. 1509. 71.
9. Sidney Colvin, *John Keats: His Life and Poetry, His Friends, Critics and After-Fame* (London: Macmillan, 1917), 3; Charles Brown, *Life of John Keats*, ed. Dorothy Hyde Bodurtha and W. B. Pope (London, New York, and Toronto: Oxford University Press, 1937), 40. Robert Gittings surveyed possible West Country backgrounds in 'Keats's Father', *The Mask of Keats: a Study of Problems* (Melbourne, London, and Toronto: Heinemann, 1956), 82–7, and 'Appendix 2' in his biography, *John Keats* (London: Heinemann, 1968), 441–2.
10. *The Times* and *The Morning Chronicle*, 20–29 September, reported that in the Channel the 'wind changed to south-west, and blew a hurricane'; 'extremely squally, the wind blowing very hard S.S.W'; 'rough passage' and 'high seas'.

11. See the authoritative account in Jack Stillinger, *The Texts of Keats's Poems* (Cambridge, MA: Harvard University Press, 1974), 228–30.

12. Letter dated 19 September 1821, *Joseph Severn Letters and Memoirs*, ed. Grant F. Scott (Aldershot and Burlington: Ashgate, 2005), 172.

13. *The Plymouth and Devonport Weekly Journal* (27 September 1838). *The Texts of Keats's Poems*, 229, and see also *The Manuscripts of the Younger Romantics*, gen. ed. Donald H. Reiman, *John Keats*, ed. Jack Stillinger, volume vii, 'The Charles Brown Poetry Transcripts at Harvard', 62.

14. Severn had told Charles Brown that Keats 'wrote ['Bright star'] down in the ship' in a letter, 19 September 1821, *Joseph Severn Letters and Memoirs*, 172.

15. 'Sonnet by the Late John Keats', *The Union Magazine*, 1.2 (February, 1846), 157.

16. *The Life, Letters, and Literary Remains of John Keats* (2 vols, London: Moxon, 1848), ii. 72.

17. *The Life, Letters, and Literary Remains of John Keats*, ii. 306.

18. See *The Texts of Keats's Poems*, 229.

19. *KC*, ii. 51, 98.

20. *The Poetical Works and Other Writings of John Keats*, ed. Harry Buxton Forman (4 vols, London: Reeves and Turner, 1883), ii. 361–2. Forman also had access to and reproduced an extract from Severn's letter to Brown, 19 September 1821; see iv. 366–7.

21. *The Life and Letters of John Keats: a New Edition* (London: Moxon, 1867), 304.

22. Milnes had so titled the poem in 1848; see also *Poetical Works of John Keats*, ed. W. T. Arnold (London: Kegan, Paul, Trench and Co., 1888), 345; *Poetical Works of John Keats*, Chandos Classics Series (London and New York: F. Warne, 1892), 344.

23. 'My Tedious Life', *Joseph Severn Letters and Memoirs*, 640–1.

24. See William Sharp, *The Life and Letters of Joseph Severn* (London: Sampson Low, Marston and Co., 1892), 54–5, and facsimile reproduction at this point.

25. Sidney Colvin, *Keats*, English Men of Letters Series, ed. John Morley (London and New York: Macmillan, 1887), 201–2; William Michael Rossetti, *Life of John Keats*, Great Writers Series, ed. Eric S. Robertson (London: Walter Scott, 1887), 114.

26. Sharp, *The Life and Letters of Joseph Severn*, 54–5.

27. *The Complete Poetical Works of Thomas Hardy*, ed. Samuel Hynes (3 vols, Oxford: Clarendon Press, 1982–5), ii. 371, 513.

28. *Times Literary Supplement* (18 February 1915), 55; Colvin, *John Keats: His Life and Poetry*, 493.

29. Andrew Motion, *Keats* (London: Faber and Faber, 1997), 3–5.

30. *The Times* (18 April 1914), 6.

31. The responses to Colvin's *West Briton* enquiry survive in 'Research Papers of Sidney Colvin', London Metropolitan Archives, at K/MS/03/195. J. Hambley Rowe searched the registers of parish churches at Callington, St Columb Major, St Dominick, Antony East, St Cleer 'where Keasts persisted from 1603–1759', Madron, Gulval, Phillak, Gwithian, Ladock, and St Allen.

32. Hardy to Sir Sidney Colvin, 14 June 1914, *The Collected Letters of Thomas Hardy*, ed. Richard Little Purdy and Michael Millgate (7 vols, Oxford: Clarendon Press, 1978–87), v. 31.

33. See Gittings, *John Keats*, 414.

34. *Collected Letters of Thomas Hardy*, v. 31 and note.

35. *Collected Letters of Thomas Hardy*, v. 31.

36. *Collected Letters of Thomas Hardy*, v. 31.

37. Colvin, *John Keats: His Life and Poetry*, 4.

38. Florence Emily Hardy to Amy Lowell, 22 July 1922, The Houghton Library, Harvard University, bMS Lowell 19 (561): 7 Letters to Amy Lowell; [1914]–1922. See also the letter in Amy Lowell, *John Keats* (2 vols, London: Jonathan Cape, 1924), i. 6.

39. 'Hardys and Keatses: Two Dorset Families. (By a Correspondent)', *The Times* (28 February 1928), 19.

40. J. D. Walder to Jean Haynes, 6 November 1962, 'Research Papers of Jean Haynes', London Metropolitan Archives, K/MS/04/028.

41. Gittings, 'Keats's Father', 85.

42. Robert Gittings, 'Keats and Lulworth Cove', *Keats-Shelley Memorial Bulletin*, 9 (1958), 16–20.

43. Gittings, 'Keats and Lulworth Cove', 20. It is not made clear that the family of John Keats of Owermoigne was the family alluded to by Hardy.

44. Gittings, *John Keats*, 441–2.

45. See Tom Driberg, *'Swaff': the Life and Times of Hannen Swaffer* (London: Macdonald, 1974), 5–6. Irene Swaffer to Jean Haynes, 26 March 1962, Haynes research papers at the London Metropolitan Archive, K/MS/04/028/1; John Lyall to Jean Haynes, 8 October (no year), Haynes research papers at the London Metropolitan Archive, K/MS/04/028/1; Gittings, *John Keats*, 442.

46. *LJK*, i. 131.

47. *LJK*, ii. 112–13.

48. Jean Haynes, 'Elizabeth Keats', *Keats-Shelley Memorial Bulletin*, 9 (1958), 21.

49. Jean Haynes, 'Keats's Paternal Relatives', *Keats-Shelley Memorial Bulletin*, 15 (1964), 27–8; Edmund Blunden, *Leigh Hunt: a Biography* (London: Cobden Sanderson, 1930), 331; Gittings, 'Keats's Father', 80–1.

50. Joseph Keats the hatter died 13 January 1819, and the following summer 'a woman in mourning call'd [on Keats], — and said something of an aunt of ours' (*LJK*, ii. 237). Was this caller the late Joseph's widow Elizabeth, also known as 'Betsy', who in 1804 had helped at the Swan and Hoop after Thomas Keates's death?

51. 'The New Sheriffs', *The Times* (1 October 1856), 10.

52. Thomas Mower Keats's son Frederick was Sheriff of London in 1856. His West Country ancestry was reported in *The Times* (1 October 1856), 10. See also Gittings, 'Keats's Father', 81.

53. 'The New Sheriffs', *The Times* (1 October 1856), 10.

54. *John Keats: the Living Year 21 September 1818 to 21 September 1819* (1954; London: Heinemann, 1978), 80.

55. See Phyliss G. Mann, 'New Light on Keats and his Family', *Keats-Shelley Memorial Bulletin*, 11 (1960), 33–8.

56. *Sussex Weekly Advertiser; or, Lewes and Brighthelmstone Journal* (Monday, 18 January 1819). A similar advertisement appeared in the *Hampshire Chronicle and Courier* (Monday 18 January 1819); *LJK*, ii. 62.

57. *LJK*, i. 178.

58. *LJK*, ii. 37.

59. When the schoolhouse was demolished in 1872, the façade was taken to the Victoria and Albert Museum, where it is still on display.

60. *KC*, ii. 164.

61. *RoW*, 143.

62. *The Manuscripts of the Younger Romantics*, gen. ed. Donald H. Reiman, *John Keats*, ed. Jack Stillinger, volume vi., 'The Woodhouse Poetry Transcripts at Harvard', 223.

15
Going Westward: William Wordsworth, Thomas Hardy, and Edward Thomas

Saeko Yoshikawa

'What, you are stepping westward?'

In 1795 William and Dorothy Wordsworth abandoned London and travelled westward, visiting Bristol, where they may have encountered Samuel Taylor Coleridge for the first time, and then onward into deepest Dorsetshire, to Racedown Lodge. Here, after a long personal struggle, in which the French Revolution and Wordsworth's estranged lover Annette Vallon were implicated, and which may have involved a mental crisis or breakdown, Wordsworth found solace in the genial landscape and gained a new self-awareness as a poet. Here he composed *The Borderers* and began to write 'The Ruined Cottage'. Life at Racedown consisted of composing, gardening, and walking – Wordsworth ordered four pairs of shoes 'of the very strongest kind double soles and upper leathers' (*Letters, Early Years*, 155) to cope with the local tracks and lanes. They walked over the nearby hills, including William Crowe's Lewesdon Hill, and Wordsworth was soon thinking of 'exploring the country westward' (*Letters, Early Years*, 168). In summer 1797, they made just such a journey across country to Alfoxden, at the foot of the Quantock Hills in Somerset, their 'principal inducement' being 'Coleridge's society' (*Letters, Early Years*, 190) at Nether Stowey. But the landscape and topography of the Quantocks also fascinated them: 'There is everything here; sea, woods wild as fancy ever painted, brooks clear and pebbly as in Cumberland, villages so romantic' (*Letters, Early Years*, 189), Dorothy wrote to Mary Hutchinson on 4 July 1797. Many of Wordsworth's poems for *Lyrical Ballads* (1798) were composed during walks with Coleridge and Dorothy over Quantock's 'airy ridge': between July 1797 and July 1798, Wordsworth's lifelong bearings as a poet were established in this quarter of England's West Country. This essay develops the Wordsworthian pattern of poetic beginnings at the Quantocks, by way of suggesting and sketching similarities in the lives and careers of two later poets who were physically and imaginatively drawn to the West Country: Thomas Hardy and Edward Thomas.

Wordsworthian wests

Although it has nothing to do with the English West Country, Wordsworth's 'Stepping Westward' – composed on a tour of Scotland in 1803 – offers a helpful steer in considering the poet's westerly longing. The poem grows from a memorable greeting from a local inhabitant: '*What, you are stepping westward?*' Struck by the phrase, the traveller-poet starts to speculate about the meaning of his travelling westward. With the east 'all gloomy to behold' (10), the western sky is still 'glowing' (22) and seems to draw him onwards to a further journey:

> Yet who would stop, or fear to advance,
> Though home or shelter he had none,
> With such a Sky to lead him on?
>
> ('Stepping Westward', 6–8)

Soft, courteous, and powerful, the greeting uttered beneath the bright expanse of the western sky brings a kind of exaltation, seeming to give him a 'spiritual right' (15) to advance 'through the world that [lies] / Before [him] in [his] endless way' (25–6). As so often in Wordsworth an otherwise trivial incident proves to be a kind of blessing, as if stepping westward were 'A kind of *heavenly* destiny' (12).

The 'Glad Preamble' that opens the thirteen and fourteen-book *Prelude* has a similarly exalted effect:

> Oh there is blessing in this gentle breeze,
> That blows from the green fields and from the clouds
> And from the sky;
> .....
> The earth is all before me – with a heart
> Joyous, nor scared at its own liberty,
> I look about, and should the guide I chuse
> Be nothing better than a wandering cloud
> I cannot miss my way.
>
> (*The Prelude*, 1805, i. 1–3, 15–19)

This passage is usually attributed to Wordsworth's journey towards Grasmere in 1799, less often to the trek to Racedown in 1795.[1] Whichever it may have been, the lines describe a westering movement that gradually takes on the heightened significance of a blessed 'spiritual right' like the traveller in 'Stepping Westward'. The 'Glad Preamble' contains no details that might anchor it to a specific locality, whereas Wordsworth's memories of the Quantocks were more forthcoming about the place and the poetry it inspired:

That summer, under whose indulgent skies,
Upon smooth Quantock's airy ridge we roved
Unchecked, or loitered 'mid her sylvan coombs,
Thou in bewitching words, with happy heart,
Didst chaunt the vision of that Ancient Man,
The bright-eyed Mariner, and rueful woes
Didst utter the Lady Christabel;
And I, associate with such labour, steeped
In soft forgetfulness the livelong hours,
Murmuring of him who, joyous hap, was found,
After the perils of his moonlight ride,
Near the loud waterfall; or her who sate
In misery near the miserable Thorn;

(The Prelude, 1850, xiv. 397–409)

Here Wordsworth recalls roving with Coleridge and Dorothy along the Quantock Hills. He evokes the openness, freedom, and the sense of motion unchecked along the 'airy ridge', and then continues downwards and inwards, ''mid sylvan coombs', to trace the paths of imagination that led to 'The Ancient Mariner', 'Christabel', 'The Idiot Boy', and 'The Thorn'. The effect is to suggest that the Quantock contours are continuous with the visionary landscapes of the poems – all four of which are explicitly located in the area of these Somerset hills.

Although there is no description of the sea in this *Prelude* passage, the word 'Mariner' suggests its presence and indeed Coleridge's poem locates the Mariner's 'own countrée' in a scene not unlike the little port of Watchet, a few miles away from the Quantocks. For Wordsworth, as for Coleridge, the sense of the sea at a distance carried intimations of infinity and eternity. From Racedown Lodge, they could 'see the sea 150 or 200 yards from the door, and at a little distance [had] a very extensive view terminated by the sea seen through different openings of the unequal hills' (*Letters, Early Years*, 161). The 'extensive view' mentioned here describes very accurately the vistas of sea glimpsed between hills from the summit of Pilsdon Pen and it's clear that Wordsworth was often drawn closer still:

My walk over the hills was charming. I could hear the murmuring of the sea for three miles; of course I often stopped listening with pleasing dread to the deep roar of the wide weltering waves. (*Letters, Early Years*, 154)

This is from Wordsworth's letter to William Mathews in October 1795. Here the sound of the sea reminds him of one of his favourite poems, James Beattie's *Minstrel* (he quotes from memory from Book I, stanza liv) – and he actually requests a copy of the poem in the same letter. *The Minstrel*, subtitled

'The Progress of Genius', in many respects offered a model for Wordsworth's own version of the autobiographical poem, *The Prelude*. Beattie's influence on the 'dedication scene' (*The Prelude*, 1805, iv. 330–45) and the 'sea of mist' scene from Mount Snowdon (*The Prelude*, 1805, xiii. 42–59) is clear and in both instances the distant sea contemplated from a summit brings a sense of spiritual uplift.

In Somerset, too, Alfoxden House was located within two miles of the sea at Kilve. From the house, Wordsworth and Dorothy had a view across woods and meadow-country to the Bristol Channel, and Wordsworth enjoyed walking over the hills with their more extensive prospect of the sea. A constant presence in day-to-day life, the sea also forms a sublime background in many of the poems written at this time. The narrator of 'The Thorn' climbs a hill in order to 'view the ocean wide and bright' (182); the old man in 'Old Man Travelling' is walking to the port of Falmouth to take a 'last leave of [his] son, a mariner' (18); in 'We Are Seven' two of the seven siblings have gone away to sea; and in 'Anecdote for Fathers' the image of 'Kilve's delightful shore by the green sea' indicates the mood of the poem. While firmly based in a local terrain, each poem opens through a glimpse of the sea to suggest wider possibilities and horizons – across the Atlantic, where Coleridge's idealistic community of Pantisocracy had been projected.

This sense of expansiveness came back to Wordsworth when he, with his family, returned to the West Country after forty-three years in the spring of 1841, at the occasion of his daughter Dora's marriage to Edward Quillinan. He revisited Tintern Abbey, Goodrich Castle and the Wye, Alfoxden, Nether Stowey, and the Quantock Hills – all of them old haunts of Coleridge, Dorothy, and himself. Mary Wordsworth called this revisitation 'our *pilgrimage*' (*Letters, Mary Wordsworth*, 245), and it was a pilgrimage that reawakened memories which were to unfold in a series of detailed autobiographical recollections. He began to retrace the composition of his poems and recount the biographical stories behind them – a process that led to what are now known as the 'Fenwick Notes'.

Perhaps the most striking of the 'Notes' is the one relating to 'We Are Seven' in which Wordsworth details geographical information behind the poem, and mentions 'one of the most remarkable facts in [his] poetic history and that of Mr. Coleridge' (Curtis, 1993, 2): the origin of 'The Ancient Mariner' and the first conception of *Lyrical Ballads*. Casting back nearly half a century, Wordsworth recalls that he and Coleridge 'agreed to defray the expence of the tour by writing a Poem', and he continues: 'Accordingly we set off and proceeded along the Quantock Hills, towards Watchet, and in the course of this walk was planned the Poem of The Ancient Mariner' (Curtis, 1993, 2). The note suggests that the expedition was made as a kind of research trip prior to the poem's composition: perhaps they decided on their route along the 'Great Road' that crosses the westerly ridge of the Quantocks in order to provide materials for a poem that in its closing verses would give a wide perspective of 'light-house', 'Hill', and 'Kirk'. They could as easily have taken the lower road that goes around West Quantoxhead, but from there they would have been unable to see the 'harbour-bay ... clear as glass' to which Coleridge's mariner eventually returns. When Wordsworth came back in 1841, years after Coleridge's death, it was as if the locality and landscape seemed to claim the poems they had inspired, while stirring Wordsworth himself to fresh creativity. The 'Fenwick Notes' are Wordsworth's *Biographia Literaria*, prompted by this late revisit to the West Country.

Thomas Hardy's 'Place on the Map'

A native of Dorset, Thomas Hardy was a westward traveller, too. Like Wordsworth, the westerly journey Hardy made in his youth brought new possibilities for a literary career, and a revisit after some forty years aroused in him a sense of renewed poetic passion.

In early March 1870 Hardy, at that time a promising young architect, left Dorchester before dawn for westernmost St Juliot on the remote coast of Cornwall. His intention was to survey the dilapidated old church for restoration. Here he met and fell in love with Emma Lavinia Gifford, his future wife, who would change his life decisively. She was the daughter of a Plymouth solicitor and sister-in-law of the rector of St Juliot. Over his several visits to Cornwall to superintend the restoration of the church, Emma encouraged Hardy to pursue his literary talents rather than his career in architecture. She helped him practically, too, 'by making copies of his manuscripts for publishers, doing research and suggesting alterations' (Lewis and Lewis, 2003, 11). Just as the West Country had brought Wordsworth a new self-awareness as a poet with the help of his sister Dorothy, Hardy became more confident in his literary talent with the support of his new-found lover, Emma.

It was more than forty years later, however, that Hardy came fully to appreciate what had happened at St Juliot, following the shock of Emma's death in November 1912. Long estranged, Hardy had been unaware that she was ill. Overtaken by remorse and grief, by the 'yawning blankness / Of the perspective' ('The Going', 20–1), and now 'faltering forward' ('The Voice', 13), Hardy needed to look beyond the failure of their later life. To do so he made the journey back to Cornwall in March 1913, to attempt a recovery of their first affections by revisiting the places associated with their courtship.

This westward pilgrimage of March 1913 marked the most significant moment in Hardy's poetic career – an outpouring of the elegiac lyrics that comprise his 'Poems of 1912–13' that continued over the next fifteen years when Hardy would write more than 500 poems. Above all the return to Cornwall in 1913 made Hardy realise the significance of his first western journey in 1870 for his literary and personal life. For Hardy, as formerly for Wordsworth in 1795–98 and, later, in 1841, heading westward was part of a poetic process of regaining mental bearings, in which the topographical and geographical features of the landscape, weathers and climate had important roles to play.

Hardy's West Country is associated with, even dominated by, the presence of the sea that surrounds it. His poem 'The Place on the Map' visualises a remembered scene on the Cornish coast as represented by the lines and colours of a map:

> I look upon the map that hangs by me –
> Its shires and towns and rivers lined in varnished artistry –
> And I mark a jutting height
> Coloured purple, with a margin of blue sea.
>
> ('The Place on the Map', 1–4)

As the poet gazes on the hanging map, the 'charted coast' (23) recreates his romantic days with Emma albeit in the mocking guise of 'pantomime' (24), crossed by the awareness of their 'unforeboded troublous case' (10).[2] The poem shows how Hardy literally mapped the intersecting paths and tragic turns of human drama, across the vast sweep of Egdon Heath or, wider still, on the full extent of Wessex. In 'The Place on the Map' we see him trying to make sense of his own life from 'the map that hangs', aware now that the 'day of latter summer, hot and dry' (5) it brings to mind was so oppressively 'blazing' (13) and 'ruddy' (16) that it seemed to have 'lost the art of raining' (14) and 'even the waves seemed drying' (6).

'The Riddle' offers a similarly double vision of the woman 'Stretching eyes west / Over the sea' (1–2), who now in her grave 'eyes east' (10), towards 'Hills of blank brow / Where no waves plough' (13–14). In this two-stanza poem, Hardy's mental map contrasts the west (past) and the east (present), where the east–west direction is indicated by the woman's gaze, as it is in 'I Found Her Out There'. Here, the Cornish coast is configured more dynamically:

> I found her out there
> On a slope few see,
> That falls westwardly
> To the salt-edged air,
> Where the ocean breaks
> On the purple strand,
> And the hurricane shakes
> The solid land.
>
> ('I Found Her Out There', 1–8)

In this poem, too, Hardy maps out the life of Emma, in which the 'west-wardly' (past) is compared with the east (present). There and then in the west, in Cornwall, where the Atlantic smites and the hurricane shakes the heights, Emma was wild and radiant; here, now, in the east, in Dorset, she is confined in 'a noiseless nest' (11), motionless and colourless, with no sea beating near. On the Cornish coast, Emma is a figure of romance who 'often would gaze / At Dundagel's famed head' (21–2), and 'would sigh at the tale / Of sunk Lyonnesse' (25–6), or 'listen at whiles / With a thought-bound brow / To the murmuring miles' of the ocean (29–31). As the western seascape brings thoughts of a scene from Arthurian legend that has now 'sunk', the poet's memories and affections kindle through association with those legends, although the beloved woman has now also sunk irretrievably '[i]n her loamy cell' (14). Salt-edged, purple, haunted, famed, murmuring, swelling, and sobbing, the western sea is an elemental power like the 'hurricane', 'blind gales', and the dazzling sun. It compelled Emma's gazing and longing for the legendary past, and will draw her 'shade' to 'creep underground' back to her old haunts, towards 'the sound / Of that western sea' (35–6).

The sea and Emma's figure are inseparable in the memories of these 1912–13 poems – connecting images of breaking waves with the intimate detail of a tress or curl of her hair, in 'I Found Her Out There' and also in the following lines from 'Beeny Cliff':

> O the opal and the sapphire of that wandering western sea,
> And the woman riding high above with bright hair flapping free –
> The woman whom I loved so, and who loyally loved me.
>
> ('Beeny Cliff', 1–3)

The lines are full of alliterative motion, passion and an expansive sense of freedom, with the sea, the sun, and the wind (see Figure 26). The place and the figure of the woman lend each other vitality, radiance, and possibility. Even after death, he imagines, her phantom, liberated from her body, still rides there as the ghost-girl-rider of 'The Phantom Horsewoman', and draws him there 'by the hand' in 'The West-of-Wessex Girl'. Tracking through 'olden haunts' ('After a Journey', 9), Hardy's visionary map of the West Country is not static but kinetic; as he confesses in 'A Dream or No' the West Country has 'some strange necromancy' (2) – as it had for Keats – that draws him there powerfully, making him 'fancy / That much of [his] life claims the spot as its key' (3–4).

The poem 'When I Set Out for Lyonnesse', commemorating Hardy's first visit to Cornwall in 1870, was published in his fourth collection, *Satires of Circumstance* (1914) in which the 'Poems of 1912–13' were also published. It is given a date, 1870, but was probably written around the same time as the other elegies – at least, it could be argued that the significance of what is recorded in the poem was not fully realised until he set out once again for Lyonnesse in the aftermath of Emma's death. In the poem, the West Country is again represented as a magical land radiant with that legendary

Figure 26   Beeny Cliff, close to St Juliot.

place-name, Lyonnesse, and the 'rare and fathomless' (16) prospect of 'What would bechance' (7). When Edward Thomas asked Hardy in March 1915 for permission to extract some of his poems in an anthology, Hardy named 'When I Set Out for Lyonnesse' as one that would illustrate his own 'idiosyncrasy' as a poet.[3] In the poem we find many characteristics of Hardy's poetry: a remote westerly landscape romanticised by legend and human associations, a sense of fate or magic reality, and a travelling figure as unaware of his destiny as the starlight that twinkles on his 'lonesomeness'. Human drama is often developed on the road in Hardy's poetry and novels. In seeking to understand his own life Hardy maps its westerly vector, as if he had been irresistibly drawn to the West by some magnetic power. More consciously than Wordsworth, Hardy saw that his life, both personal and professional, was directed towards the West that had first been opened to him by Emma ('She Opened the Door').

Edward Thomas's 'western purpose'

In March 1913, in the same spring when Hardy set off on the westerly journey to revisit his old romance, Edward Thomas began pedalling westward on a cycling tour to the Quantock Hills. His 'western purpose' (*In Pursuit of Spring*, 15) was to encounter the landscape of poetry, the landscape enriched above all by Wordsworth and Coleridge's *Lyrical Ballads* (1798).

As he advanced slowly from London, he meditated upon various poets and writers associated with the places and landscapes he passed, including George Meredith, W. H. Hudson, George Herbert, Philip Sidney, William Barnes, and Thomas Hardy. His destination was the Quantocks – Coleridge's Nether Stowey and 'Kilve's delightful shore', celebrated in Wordsworth's 'Anecdote for Fathers'. Thomas recalls this literary pilgrimage in his imaginative travelogue, *In Pursuit of Spring* (1914), and, having read the book, Robert Frost encouraged Thomas to write poetry, advising him 'to write it in verse form in exactly the same cadence'.[4] So it was that Thomas became a poet in December 1914, at the age of 36, and he would continue to write verse until January 1917, just before embarking for France as a second lieutenant in the Royal Artillery.

It is generally understood that the First World War and Robert Frost's influence impelled Thomas into poetry, that they liberated him from literary drudgery of one kind or another and enabled him to channel his depressive tendency creatively.[5] But if Frost and, ironically, the war were poetic salvations *ab extra*, Thomas's westward search for spring stirred from within. As the title and the first chapter of *In Pursuit of Spring* suggest, his journey was driven by a strong sense of purpose and it was carefully planned for route and timing: he would arrive at the Quantocks with the spring as if the cycle's spinning wheels and the turning of the year were subtly synchronised (*In Pursuit of Spring*, 29). In his narrative Thomas is intermittently accompanied by another cyclist, a 'liberator of the chaffinch and collector of weather-vanes' (*In Pursuit of Spring*, 52) who might well be taken as an alter-ego, who, like Thomas at that time, has consumed himself with 'hack-writing'. Thomas calls him 'the Other Man' with capital letters. This apparently fictional figure reveals Thomas's intention of doing away with his past self – he is not seen again after Thomas's arrival at Kilve: '"There *is* no weather-cock," said the Other Man, laughing a little more freely and disappearing for the last time' (*In Pursuit of Spring*, 282). And on the final page of the book, Thomas announces: 'I had found Winter's grave; I had found Spring, and I was confident that I could ride home again and find Spring all along the road' (*In Pursuit of Spring*, 301). These words can be read as a declaration of his new-found confidence as a poet: as for Wordsworth in 1795–98, a westward journey marked the end of one phase of Thomas's life, dogged by personal and literary struggles, and the beginning of a new phase in his creative life.

The sense of a creative transformation in Thomas is suggested in the following passage from *In Pursuit of Spring* where he recalls the experience of rapid movement:

> Motion was extraordinarily easy that afternoon, and I had no doubts that I did well to bicycle instead of walking. ... I was a great deal nearer to being a disembodied sprit than I can often be. ... I fed through the senses

directly, but very temperately, through the eyes chiefly, and was happier than is explicable or seems reasonable. This pleasure of my disembodied spirit (so to call it) was an inhuman and diffused one, such as may be attained by whatever dregs of this our life survive after death. ... In a different mood I might have been encouraged to believe the experience a foretaste of a sort of imprisonment in the viewless winds ... (*In Pursuit of Spring*, 210)

Here elation, 'the pleasure of my disembodied spirit', approximates to a Shelleyan/Romantic ecstasy or joy but is swiftly shadowed by the foretaste of whatever may survive death, as Claudio has it in *Measure for Measure*, 'To be imprisoned in the viewless winds / And blown with restless violence round about / The pendent world' (Act 3, Scene 1). Three pages later, Thomas – a creature if not yet a prisoner of the winds – begins to feel 'some confidence in the Spring' (*In Pursuit of Spring*, 213):

The air was perfumed with something like willow-plait which I did not identify. The wind was light, but blew from behind me, and was strong enough to strip the dead ivy leaves from an ash tree, but not to stop the tortoiseshell butterfly sauntering against it. (*In Pursuit of Spring*, 250)

The wind is strong enough to dislodge the dead leaves of winter yet gentle enough to permit a butterfly, a token of spring, to stir a correspondent sense of renewal. It is at this point that Thomas's goal, the Quantock Hills, come into view for the first time from the summit of Glastonbury Tor:

The hill projects from the earth like a ship a mile long, whose stern is buried in the town, its prow uplifted westward towards Bridgwater; and the road took me up as on a slanting deck, until I saw Glastonbury entire below me, all red-tiled except the ruins and the towers of St. John and St. Benedict. (*In Pursuit of Spring*, 254)

The swell of the land is likened to a ship whose prow is pointed westward and seaward. Land and sea are inseparable in Thomas's evocation of the west: the Quantock ridge is elongated above 'that wood / Which slopes down to the Sea', as it is described in Coleridge's 'The Ancient Mariner' (547–8), and Thomas describes the scene as if touched by a gentle westerly light with the hills now seen 'fading down to the sea' (*In Pursuit of Spring*, 262). For Thomas the West is a series of such headlands extending into the ocean – a series that eventually arrives at Hardy's Beeny Cliff and, further west, Tintagel:

Westward, for men of this island, lies the sea; westward are the great hills. In a mere map the west of Britain is fascinating. The great features of that map, ... are the great promontories of Caernarvon, of Pembroke, of Gower and of Cornwall, jutting out into the western sea, like the features of a grim large face, such a face as is carved on a ship's prow. These protruding features, even on a small-scale map, thrill the mind with a sense of purpose and spirit. They yearn, they peer out ever to the sea, as if using eyes and nostrils to savour the utmost scent of it, as if themselves calling back to the call of the waves. (*South Country*, 6–7)

In touch with the region's maritime spirit and the salt savour of ocean air, Thomas is, like Hardy, aware of the West Country as great craggy features on a map. For Thomas, the land is likened to a yearning face whose eyes and nostrils are open, alert, and imbued with the purpose and spirit of a man intent upon the elemental call of the waves and what lies beyond. His description is not static but characterised by a sense of advance, a sense of energetic and responsive intent, as if communing with and led on by 'something evermore about to be'.

For Thomas the 'feeling of advance' accompanied every mile of his route to the Quantock Hills (*In Pursuit of Spring*, 27). Sometimes feeling himself like a god gliding through his own huge domain, sometimes he is more modest and eco-centric: 'the earth was the rooks', heaven was the larks', and I rode easily on along the good level road somewhere between the two' (*In Pursuit of Spring*, 209–10). Thus Thomas enjoyed advancing as a kind of medium between the sky and the land toward the sea, over the wind-swept hills in the West Country. And in so doing he pursued his new horizons:

> Often and often it came back again
> To mind, the day I passed the horizon ridge
> To a new country, the path I had to find
> By half-gaps that were stiles once in the hedge,
> The pack of scarlet clouds running across
> The harvest evening that seemed endless then
> And after, and the inn where all were kind,
> All were strangers.
>
> ('Over the Hills', 1–8)

The 'horizon ridge' in this poem is not necessarily among the western hills, although the sentiment of the poem is eloquently in touch with what Thomas describes in *The South Country* as 'the westward-going hills, where the sun has fallen, [that] draw the heart away and fill us with a desire to go on and on for ever, that same way' (*South Country*, 7).[6] It is as if, led by the evening scarlet clouds, finding his way in pathless terrain, he passes over the hills into a new realm, which is what Wordsworth, stepping westward, once felt.

'Stepping Westward' is about life's archetypal journey towards the setting sun that is both inspiring and final, led by a *'heavenly* destiny'. To this Wordsworthian intuition, Thomas adds a further cultural-historical insight:

> [O]ut towards them [westward-pointing promontories] continually have the conquered races of the world retreated ... Out from them conquerors in their turn have gone to found a legend like the Welsh Madoc, an empire like the men of Devon. The blood of conquered and conqueror is in our veins, and it flushes the cheek at the sight or thought of the west. *(South Country, 7)*

Here Thomas advances downwards into deep layers of historical consciousness, the communal memory of Islanders driven to the remotest peripheries in a process of retreat, recovery, and renewal – the route westward, and inwards, that Thomas himself has pursued. That last phrase, 'it flushes the cheek at the sight or thought of the west', recalls the image of a woman described by Hardy who gazed at the western sea and sighed at the thought of sunk Lyonnesse, while 'the dipping blaze / Dyed her face fire-red' ('I Found Her Out There', 23–4). Going westward involved something beyond a personal, incidental need for all three of these islanders – Wordsworth, Hardy, and Thomas. They all felt some inevitability – call it destiny, or a leading onwards – in their westerly yearning, as if to step westward was to come more fully into being: a far-flung, fire-red reincarnation.

Notes

1. Mary Moorman interprets the opening lines of *The Prelude* as celebrating Wordsworth's feeling of release in August or September 1795 after he left London to begin a new life with Dorothy in Racedown (Moorman, 1957, 272–5). The Norton edition of *The Prelude: 1799, 1805, 1850* assigns the passage to Wordsworth's travel to Grasmere in December 1799 (28).
2. When 'The Place on the Map' was first published in September 1913, it was subtitled 'A Poor Schoolmaster's Story', so the poem may be a fiction about a schoolmaster too poor to marry his sweetheart as J. O. Bailey suggests, but he also suggests the possibility that it treats an episode of Hardy's courtship of Emma when she told him about her father's vehement objection to their marriage (Bailey, 1970, 280–1).
3. See *The Collected Letters of Thomas Hardy*, ed. Richard Little Purdy and Michael Millgate (7 vols, Oxford: Oxford University Press, 1978–87), v. 87.
4. Letter from Frost to Harold Roy Brennan, 1926, quoted in Thomas, *Annotated Collected Poems*, ed. Longley, 15.
5. Edna Longley, who sees more rich and complicated influential factors in Thomas's poetry, does not find any particular significance in Thomas's westerly journey, March 1913, though she counts *In Pursuit of Spring* among the greatest prose works by Thomas. R. George Thomas devotes more space to the journey: '[*In Pursuit of Spring*] shows that at a desperate time in his family relationships, and in his determination to allay the mysterious voices that came into his head, [Thomas] was developing a new purpose in his writing. ... Certainly the Edward Thomas whom

Frost met and influenced so decisively, late in 1913, was already well along the road to the discovery of his gift as a writer' (R.G. Thomas, 1985, 222).

6. Edna Longley quotes a passage from Thomas's essay, *Beautiful Wales*, as a possible link with the poem, but she emphasises that the landscape described here is not necessarily 'Welsh'. Thomas, *Annotated Collected Poems*, ed. Longley, 179.

Bibliography

Bailey, James Osler, *The Poetry of Thomas Hardy: a Handbook and Commentary* (Chapel Hill: University of North Carolina Press, 1970).

Curtis, Jared (ed.), *The Fenwick Notes of William Wordsworth* (London: Bristol Classical Press, 1993).

Hardy, Thomas, *The Collected Letters of Thomas Hardy*, ed. Richard Little Purdy and Michael Millgate (7 vols, Oxford: Clarendon Press, 1978–87).

—— *The Complete Poems*, ed. James Gibson (London: Palgrave Macmillan, 2001).

Lewis, Heulyn and Ginny Lewis, *In the Footsteps of Thomas & Emma Hardy: a Brief History of their Time in North Cornwall* (The North Cornwall Coast & Country Service, 2003).

Moorman, Mary, *William Wordsworth: the Early Years, 1770–1803* (Oxford: Oxford University Press, 1957).

Shakespeare, William, *Measure for Measure*, ed. N.W. Bawcutt, The Oxford Shakespeare (Oxford: Oxford University Press, 1991).

Thomas, Edward, *The South Country* (London: J.M. Dent, 1909); with a Preface by R. George Thomas (London: Everyman, 1993).

—— *In Pursuit of Spring* (London: Thomas Nelson and Sons, 1914).

—— *The Annotated Collected Poems*, ed. Edna Longley (Tarset, Northumberland: Bloodaxe Books, 2008).

Thomas, R. George, *Edward Thomas: a Portrait* (Oxford: Clarendon Press, 1985).

Wordsworth, Mary, *The Letters of Mary Wordsworth 1800–1855*, ed. Mary E. Burton (Oxford: Clarendon Press, 1958).

Wordsworth, William, *The Prelude: 1799, 1805, 1850*, ed. Jonathan Wordsworth, M.H. Abrams, and Stephen Gill (New York: Norton, 1979).

—— *Poems, in Two Volumes, and Other Poems, 1800–1807*, ed. Jared Curtis, The Cornell Wordsworth Series (Ithaca: Cornell University Press, 1990).

Wordsworth, William and S.T. Coleridge, *Lyrical Ballads*, ed. R.L. Brett and A.R. Jones (2nd edn, London: Routledge, 1991).

Wordsworth, William and Dorothy Wordsworth, *The Letters of William and Dorothy Wordsworth*, ed. E. de Selincourt, 2nd edn, *The Early Years, 1787–1805*, rev. C.L. Shaver (Oxford: Clarendon Press, 1967).

Afterword

Tom Mayberry

The West of England, as this book memorably demonstrates, has long inspired creativity, debate and intense local pride. The pride has never been in doubt, and one version of a Somerset saying captures in a few words the West Country's habitual chauvinism. 'I was bore in Taunton Deane', it begins, before asking a question meant only partly in jest: 'Where should I be bore else?'

The rooted loyalties of West Country people were often passionately expressed, as in the 'defiant provincialism' of Joseph Cottle, or might sometimes take on a more darkly obsessive character. Such was the case with the Rev. John Skinner (1772–1839), the diarist and antiquarian of Camerton, near Bath. He became convinced that his own country parish was Camulodunum, the place where the father of Caractacus had lived, and where King Arthur had fought the traitor Mordred. Skinner ignored the advice of his mentor, Sir Richard Colt Hoare of Stourhead, who urged him to abandon unprovable theories and to stick to 'the authority of real facts'. Was it not Sir Richard's own grandfather, the aggrieved Skinner may have reflected, who built a great tower on the borders of Somerset and Wiltshire to mark the supposed place where King Alfred had raised his standard against the Danes? The antiquarian arguments have long been forgotten. But anyone who stands today at the top of Alfred's Tower, with the shires of Wessex stretching all around, will still find it easy to sympathise with the fervent localism of a man such as Skinner, for whom the West Country seemed almost the only world worth knowing.

The local pride of West Country people was matched by their fierce individualism and frequent defiance of authority. They flocked to Perkin Warbeck in 1497 when he raised a rebellion against Henry VII; and though the King was merciful after the rebellion failed, there was no such mercy two centuries later when the Protestant Duke of Monmouth led his yeoman army to defeat at the place Thomas Hardy would call 'sad Sedge-Moor'. The Bloody Assizes which followed the battle left the trees of Somerset and Dorset 'loaden almost as thick with quarters as with leaves'. Little wonder that West Country people developed such long memories, or that religious dissent flourished so readily.

However strongly marked some characteristics of the West Country might be, it was never a place to be narrowly defined. Whether experienced in the teeming streets of Bristol or within a 'quiet dell', it was everyone's and no one's, and many who discovered it were apt to see reflected in it a version of themselves, of their hopes and most deeply-held convictions. That was evidently William Hazlitt's experience when, after an absence of twenty years, he returned once more to the landscape of West Somerset. He was standing on a hill near Taunton, perhaps at Cothelstone or Wylls Neck, and looked over a prospect of hills and valleys that seemed at once to evoke a complete and coherent world. 'How was the map of my life spread out before me', he says, 'as the map of the country lay at my feet.'

Coleridge, of course, records many similar moments of recognition, not least in 'Fears in Solitude', his political meditation on the war with France written during his last Stowey months. At the end of the poem he describes his homeward walk along a Quantock sheep track and his sudden luminous encounter with the 'mighty majesty' of the coastal plain, and then, soon after, with the distant sight of his own 'lowly cottage'. Both Hazlitt and Coleridge would, perhaps, have been surprised to discover that on a Somerset hill not far away another person of a very different kind was apt to look out and be lost in contemplation. William Pitt spent important early years on his father's estate at Burton Pynsent, and there, with the elder Pitt's encouragement, would practise the oratorical skills that Coleridge so mistrusted in him. In 1783, the year in which he became Britain's youngest Prime Minister, Pitt remembered the landscape that reached north from Burton Pynsent over the Somerset levels, and concluded that even the celebrated grounds of his mother's family home at Stowe were not as beautiful.

The West Country, with a generous capaciousness, accommodated them all – the poets, antiquarians, dissenters and politicians who, with so many others, wrote and contended during those years in which English Romanticism was finding a voice. The essays this book contains recover for us part of a richly-textured history we hardly knew we had lost, and in doing so perform a great service.

Index